SOURCES OF INDIAN CIVILIZATION

BY THE SAME AUTHOR

Mahatma Gandhi : A Descriptive Bibliography
Jawaharlal Nehru : A Descriptive Bibliography
Vinoba and Bhoodan : A Descriptive Bibliography
A.I.C.C. Circulars : A Descriptive Bibliography
Indian National Congress : A Descriptive Bibliography
India's Struggle for Freedom (3 vols.)
Gyan-ki-khoj men (a travelogue in Hindi)
Santulan (a novel in Hindi) also published in Punjabi
Sidhi Path (a novel in Hindi)
Ghalna (Punjabi translation of *Sidhi Path*)
India's Struggle for Freedom
The Substance of Library Science
India Since the Advent of the British
Encyclopaedia of India's Struggle for Freedom
National Geographical Dictionary of India
National Biographical Dictionary of India
Encyclopaedia Indica (in Press)
Socialism in India (in Press)

SOURCES OF INDIAN CIVILIZATION

A BIBLIOGRAPHY
OF WORKS BY WORLD ORIENTALISTS
OTHER THAN INDIAN

Jagdish Saran Sharma

VIKAS PUBLISHING HOUSE PVT LTD
DELHI   BOMBAY   BANGALORE   KANPUR

VIKAS PUBLISHING HOUSE PVT LTD
5 Daryaganj, Ansari Road, Delhi 110006
5 Savoy Chambers, Wallace Street, Fort, Bombay 400001
10 First Main Road, Gandhi Nagar, Bangalore 560009
80 Canning Road, Kanpur 208004

COPYRIGHT © JAGDISH SARAN SHARMA, 1974

ISBN 0 7069 0316 1

PRINTED IN INDIA

At Michiko Printers, H.S. 14, Kailash Colony Market, New Delhi and published by Mrs Sharda Chawla, Vikas Publishing House Pvt Ltd, 5 Daryaganj, Ansari Road, Delhi 110006

वसुधैव कुटुम्बकम्

(the entire world is a family)

FOREWORD

It is indeed gratifying to note that Dr Jagdish Saran Sharma, Professor and Head of the Department of Library Science has prepared a bibliography of Indologists of foreign countries. It was indeed a stupendous task and I am glad that Dr Sharma took up this challenging work and with his characteristic determination and perseverance has been able to handle it with thoroughness. He has already prepared several bibliographies which have been acclaimed to be of immense utility for researchers and scholars.

He has included in this bibliography more than 3,500 entries relating to books written or translated by prominent Indologists of 15 countries in their respective languages. Entries have, of course, been duly annotated and all the essential bibliographical details added.

India is one of the ancient cradles of civilization and excavations of ancient mounds and ruins carried out extensively during the present century have taken back its history by three to four thousand years.

India is a country where the oldest book in the world, the *Rigved,* was written. The *Upanishads* appeared soon after and these are the storehouse of sublime thoughts. The *Bhagwat Gita* (the celestial song) propounds the philosophy of action. Latest

Foreword

research has shown that India had made a unique advance in pure and applied sciences—particularly mathematics, astronomy, medicine, chemistry, cosmology, biology, botany, etc. India had also made a rare contribution to the world folklore and fables. The *Panch Tantra* and *Hitopdesh* have been translated into a number of foreign languages.

India's culture and philosophy have had a marked impact on all countries which came into contact with her through commerce or through military operations. Small wonder then that great treatises in Sanskrit have been translated into Greek, Arabic, and many other languages.

The Renaissance movement in Europe gave an extraordinary fillip to the study of Indian thought and literature by European scholars.

During the last 150 years a number of foreign scholars have dedicated their lives in delving deep into Indian literature and some of them have produced monumental works on India's culture, thought, philosophy, religion, fine arts, linguistics, grammar, history, geography, architecture, polity, numismatics, archaeology, yoga, anthropology, dramatics, poetics, sculpture, etc. Some of them have even prepared encyclopaedias, bibliographies, catalogues and have conducted extensive surveys. Now information regarding all these has been put together in a classified form so that references on Indology may be available at one place.

I offer my sincere felicitations to Dr Sharma on this achievement and his fulfilling a long-standing need of the researchers and scholars. I am sure they will find a reference to this bibliography a rewarding experience and this will go a long way in enlightening their task of research in Indology.

Suraj Bhan
Vice-Chancellor
Panjab University
Chandigarh

INTRODUCTION

This study contains 3,573 books, written, translated, and edited by authors from 15 countries, in their respective national languages. The maximum number of books were written in the English language. The second and third largest number is in German and French. The rest belong to other major languages of the world, like Japanese, Chinese, Russian, etc.

Most of the entries are duly annotated and essential bibliographical details, that is, author, title, place of publication, publisher, year of publication, pages, volumes, etc. are furnished to assist research scholars in selecting their desired research material.

The work is divided into ten major divisions, based on the Dewey Decimal Scheme of Classification. In the cases of a few subjects such as Philosophy, Religion, Literature, and Indian History, necessary modifications have been made to suit the needs of scholars.

DIVISION I—000 : GENERAL WORKS

This division includes 113 entries concerning General Works: Bibliographies; Library Catalogues; Encyclopaedias; and Journ-

Introduction

alism. In the preparation of this work, the author has freely referred to these bibliographies and library catalogues of the British Museum, London, and the US Library of Congress, Washington D.C. For physical verification of more than 50 per cent of the titles, the author has mainly relied upon the holdings of the Panjab University Library, Chandigarh. For the literature on Modern India, he has used extensively his own descriptive bibliographies, that is, *Mahatma Gandhi; Jawaharlal Nehru*; and *India's Struggle for Freedom*. The books included in these bibliographies were already verified and physically checked by the author at the Library of Congress, Washington D.C., during the two years he worked there. He has also consulted the *Indian National Bibliography*, Calcutta; Sahitya Akademi's *National Bibliography of Indian Literature* (1901-1953); J. Michael Mahar's *India: a Critical Bibliography* and various other Indian and foreign trade and national bibliographies.

DIVISION II AND III—100 : PHILOSOPHY
200 : RELIGION

This division contains 438 entries on Philosophy and Religion and the books are arranged under the following subject-headings :
   (i) General Works; (ii) Vedism, Brahmanism and Upanishads; (iii) Hinduism; (iv) Philosophical Systems, Epics and Puranas; (v) Jainism; (vi) Buddhism; (vii) Christianity; (viii) Islam; (ix) Sikhism; (x) Tantraism; (xi) Theosophy; (xii) Vedanta; (xiii) Yoga; (xiv) Other Sects and Cults; (xv) Jews; (xvi) Zoroastrianism.

DIVISION IV—300 : SOCIAL SCIENCES

The material in this division has been entered under the following subject-headings and contains 512 entries:
   (i) Administration; (ii) Commerce and Industry; (iii) Communication; (iv) Communism; (v) Constitution and Constitutional

Introduction

History; (vi) Culture and Civilization; (vii) Customs and Manners; (viii) Economic Conditions; (ix) Education; (x) Folklore; (xi) Foreign Relations; (xii) Government and Politics; (xiii) Labour and Labour Classes; (xiv) Land and People; (xv) Land Reforms; (xvi) Laws; (xvii) Social Conditions; (xviii) Women, their Emancipation.

DIVISION V—400 : LINGUISTICS

This division contains 261 entries and has two sections. Under section one, books on Linguistics of general nature are arranged alphabetically while section two contains books on grammar and dictionaries of various Indian languages.

DIVISION VI and VII—500 and 600 : PURE AND APPLIED SCIENCES

Since this division contains only 64 entries, books on subjects like Anthropology, Botany, Geology, and Zoology are arranged alphabetically in one sequence.

DIVISION VIII—700 : FINE ARTS

This division contains 363 entries and books are arranged under the following subject headings:
    (i) General; (ii) Architecture; (iii) Dance; (iv) Handicrafts; (v) Iconography and Bronzes; (vi) Museology; (vii) Music; (viii) Numismatics; (ix) Paintings; (x) Photography; (xi) Theatre.

DIVISION IX—800 : LITERATURE

Contains 253 entries arranged under the following subject headings :
    (i) General Works; (ii) Classics and Epics; (iii) Essays and Letters; (iv) Fiction; (v) Poetry; (vi) Short Stories.

Introduction

DIVISION X—900 : HISTORY, GEOGRAPHY, DESCRIPTION AND TRAVEL, AND BIOGRAPHY

This is the largest division and contains 1,596 entries, which are arranged under the following subject headings:

(i) General Works; (ii) Ancient Period (from the remote past to A.D. 1206); (iii) Muslim Period (from A.D. 1206 to A.D. 1707); (iv) Advent of Portuguese, Dutch, British and French, etc. (from 16th century to A.D. 1857); (v) First Struggle for Freedom (1857); (vi) India under the British (1858-1947); (vii) Princes and their States; (viii) Marathas; (ix) Rajputs; (x) Sikhs; (xi) Nationalism, rise of; (xii) Second Struggle for Freedom; (xiii) India, Partition of; (xiv) Kashmir Issue; (xv) Independence and After (1947 to date); (xvi) Geography, Description and Travel; (xvii) Biography.

The account of the literature given above shows that there is no aspect of Indian life and thought on which the Orientalists did not write. However, it will be interesting to note that the British authors mainly wrote on Fine Arts, Archaeology, History, Government and Politics, Constitution, Literature and the National Movement, while the German and French authors mainly dealt with Philosophy, Religion, Grammar and Dictionaries. The American Orientalists, by having prepared and published more than 50 volumes of the Harvard Oriental Series, have shown keen interest in Indian classics. After India won her independence in 1947 and as the American influence grew in Indian affairs, they also contributed substantially to Biography, Government and Politics, Geography, Description and Travel. The work done by the American Orientalists is mainly descriptive and may not be considered of deep scholastic value as of the British, German, and French Orientalists. However, some of the American authors have done commendable survey work on political, social, and economic conditions of India.

For the benefit of those readers who might be interested in the location of the material included in this study, a list of the world's most prominent libraries is given below in the hope that these libraries might have in their holdings at least some books, if not all. However, from his personal knowledge of the Ameri-

Introduction

can and the British libraries, the author is quite confident that more than 85 per cent of these books are available in their collections.

1. FRANCE: (i) Bibliotheque due Centre Universitairs des Langues Orientales Vivanlas, Paris; (ii) Bibliotheque de l' Universite de Paris, Paris; (iii) Bibliotheque Nationale, Paris.

2. GERMAN DEMOCRATIC REPUBLIC, BERLIN: Deutsche Staatsbibliothek (Originally Preussische Staatsbibliothek, Berlin).

3. INDIA : (i) Aligarh Muslim University Library, Aligarh; (ii) Asiatic Society, Calcutta; (iii) Benaras Hindu University Library, Varanasi; (iv) Bombay University, Bombay; (v) Calcutta University Library, Calcutta; (vi) Khuda Baksh Library, Patna; (vii) Madras University Library, Madras; (viii) National Library of India, Calcutta; (ix) Panjab University Library, Chandigarh.

4. ITALY : National Centre of the Union Catalogue of Italian Libraries and Bibliographical Information, Rome.

5. JAPAN : (i) National Diet Library, Tokyo; (ii) Oriental Library, Bunkyo; (iii) University of Tokyo Library, Tokyo.

6. UK : (i) British Museum, London; (ii) India Office Library, London; (iii) London School of Economics and Political Science, London; (iv) University of Cambridge, Cambridge; (v) Royal Empire Society Library, London; (vi) University of London, London; (vii) University of Oxford, Oxford.

7. USA : (i) Columbia University Library, New York, (ii) Harvard University Library, Cambridge (Mass); (iii) Library of Congress, Washington D.C.; (iv) University of California Library, Berkeley; (v) University of Chicago Library, Illinois; (vi) The University of Michigan Library, Ann Arbor, Michigan; (vii) University of Pennsylvania, Philadelphia.

8. USSR : (i) All-Union State Library Foreign Literature, Moscow; (ii) "Patrice Lumumba" Peoples' Friendship University Library, Moscow; (iii) State V.I. Lenin Library of the USSR, Moscow.

In addition to the above libraries, the National Libraries and important university libraries of other countries may also be having some books on India in their respective holdings.

Introduction

The bibliographer has done his best to bring together, in a classified form, the books written by prominent Orientalists of the world on various aspects of Indian life and thought. However, if some lacunae are discovered by readers, the bibliographer would feel obliged to those who point them out, and would make good the omissions in a subsequent edition.

For the preparation of a work of this nature, information is collected from thousands of sources, and it is impossible adequately to thank by name all those who helped and encouraged the bibliographer to complete this work. He is indebted to his Vice-Chancellor, Padam Bhushan Suraj Bhan, who encouraged him to carry on his research work after office hours, and takes this opportunity to express his profound gratitude to him for writing the Foreword to this work. He also thanks Mr Bal Krishna, Secretary, Publication Bureau, Panjab University, Chandigarh, with whom he often discussed literary matters and whose valuable advice in this connection was readily available.

The bibliographer also thanks Mr D.R. Grover, who assisted him in reading proofs, Mr S.S. Pal for his secretarial assistance in typing the manuscript and Mr H.R. Chopra for his assistance in preparing the Index after their office hours.

JAGDISH S. SHARMA

CONTENTS

000	General Works	... ...	1
100	Philosophy, 200 Religion ...	...	16
300	Social Sciences	... ...	65
400	Linguistics	... ...	121
500	Pure Sciences, 600 Applied Sciences	...	146
700	Fine Arts	... ...	153
800	Literature	... ...	188
900	History	... ...	214
	INDEX	... ...	359

000 GENERAL WORKS

(i) Bibliographies and Catalogues

ALEXANDROWICZ, CHARLES HENRY. A bibliography of Indian Law. New York, Oxford University Press, 1958. ix, 69p. **1**
   Part A gives information about the general structure of Indian legal system and cites standard works, textbooks and important treatises of Indian Law.
   Part B lists the publications in an alphabetical order. Contains a directory of publishers of law books and journals and also an author index.

BACON, ELIZABETH E. Selected and annotated bibliography of sociology of India. New Haven, Human Relations Area Files, 1957. **2**
   An annotated bibliography of Indian art, history and religion.

BARNETT, L. D. *comp.* Punjabi printed books in the British Museum. London, British Museum, 1961. 121p. **3**

BARRIER, N. GERALD. The Sikhs and their literature: a guide to tracts, books and periodicals. 1849-1919, Foreword by Khushwant Singh. Delhi, Manohar Book Service, 1970. xii, 153p. **4**
   A brief bibliography of Sikh literature mainly published between 1849 and 1919.

BENDALL, CECIL. Catalogue of the Buddhist Sanskrit manuscripts in the university library. Cambridge. Cambridge University Library, 1883, xii, lvi, 225p. 5
——Catalogue of Sanskrit, Pali & Prakrit books in the British Museum acquired during the years 1876-92. London, Brit. Muse. Deptt. of Orient. Printed Books and Mss. 1893. vii, 624p. 6
BESTERMAN, THEODORE. A world bibliography of bibliographies. New York, The Scarecrow Press, 1955. 3 vols. 7
    Includes a list of bibliographies on India from p. 1993 to 2010.
Bibliografia Hispanica, ano. 1—. mayo/junio 1942—. Madrid, Instituto Nacional de Libro Espanol, 1942—. v. illus. Monthly. 8
    A good source for Spanish literature. Whenever any title is published, it finds a place in this bibliography.
Bibliografia Italiana. 1928—. Sotto gli auspici del Consigle nazionale delle riccrche. Bologne, N. Zanichelli, 1928—. v. 9
    A bibliography of current Italian literature published in Italy or abroad. Includes titles on India whenever they are published.
Bibliografia Maxicana. Obras editadas en Mexico, libros de autores mexicanos editados en el extranjero relativos a Mexico, Canje. v. 1., 1942—. Mexico, Depto. de Publicidad y Propaganda, 1944—. v. 10
    Includes books on India, whenever they are published.
Bibliotheque Nationale, Paris. Catalogue general des livres imprimes: Auteurs. Paris, Impr. Nat., 1900-1972. V. 11
    Includes a few titles on various aspects of Indian life and thought in French.
The Book Review Digest. V. 1-January 1906—. Minneapolis, The H. W. Wilson Co., 1906-1912; White Plains and New York City, The H.W. Wilson Co., 1913-72. 12
    Includes reviews of important books on India, published in USA from 1906 to-date.
BRITISH COUNCIL, New Delhi. British books on India: a selection written between the eighteenth century and the present day, showing something of the contribution made by British

scholars to Indian studies. New Delhi, 1961. 142p. **13**

BRITISH MUSEUM, London. General Catalogue of printed books. London, the British Museum, 1955-. Photo-lithographic edition to 1955. 263 vols. 1965-66. Ten-year supplement. 50 vols. 1956-65. **14**

> Includes some titles on India, published in the English language.

British National Bibliography: annual volume. London, Council of the British National Bibliography, 1950—. **15**

> Each volume includes a number of books published in the United Kingdom on India.

BURNELL, ARTHUR COKE. A classical index to the Sanskrit Mss. in the palace at Tanjore. Tanjore, Saraswati Mehal, 1880, xii, 239p. **16**

——A tentative list of books and some Mss. relating the history of the Portuguese in India proper. Manglore, Basel Mission pr., 1880. vi, 133p. **17**

CAMPBELL, FRANK. An index-catalogue of bibliographical works, chiefly in the English language relating to India, 1897. 99p. **18**

> One of the earliest bibliographies compiled on India in the 19th century.

CASE, MARGARET H. South Asian history, 1750-1950: a guide to periodicals, dissertations and newspapers. New Jersey, Princeton University Press, 1968. xiii, 561p. **19**

> This volume includes several types of source material important for the study of the history of the Indo-Pakistan subcontinent during the past two centuries.

Catalogue general de la librairie francaise, 1840-1925, Paris, Lorenz, 1867-1945. 34 v. **20**

> In its later volumes lists a few titles in French on India.

COMMONWEALTH RELATIONS OFFICE, London. Catalogue of European printed books in India Office Library. London G. K. Hall, 1964. 10 vols. **21**

CRANE, ROBERT I. The history of India: its study and interpretation. Washington, D.C., Service Centre for Teachers of History, 1958. 46p. **22**

> No. 17 of this series is a valuable bibliography on Indian historiography.

Sources of Indian Civilization

CRANFURD, Q. Researches concerning the laws, theology, learning, commerce, etc. of ancient and modern India, London, Printed by T. Cadell and W. Davis, 1817. 2 vols. **23**

"This work is intended as an epitome of what is authentically known, respecting the ancient condition of India, including all that is to be found in Greek and modern authors and also what has recently been obtained by modern research"—*Preface.*

CROOKS, WILLIAM. Rural and agricultural glossary for the North-West Provinces and Oudh. Calcutta, Superintendent, Government Printing, 1888. 285p. **24**

Cumulative book index: world list of books in English language. New York, H.W. Wilson Co. 1898—. **25**

Each volume includes books published on India in English language.

Das Schweizer buch; bibliographisches bulletin der Schweizarischen landesbibliothek, Bern. Lew Livre suisse. II Libro Svizzero. 1.—jahrg. Jan./Feb. 1901-. Bern, Verlag des Schweizerischen buchhandlervereins; etc. 1901—. v. **26**

Includes a few books on India.

DE BARY, W.J., ed. Approaches to the oriental classics: Asian literature and thought in general education. New York, Columbia University Press, 1959. xix, 262p. **27**

DE BARY, WILLIAM T. Sources of Indian tradition. New York, Columbia University Press, 1958. xxvii, 961p. **28**

A collection of translations, aims to provide background material on the culture, civilization and religious traditions of India from the remote past to the present day.

Der Schweizer Buchhandel; La librairie suisse; La libreria Svizzera. Jrg. 1, Hft. 1-., 15 Jan. 1943-., Off-izielles Organ. Bern., Verlag des Schweizerischen Buchhandlervereins, 1943. v. Monthly. **29**

Includes a few titles on India in Swiss.

Deutsches Bucherverzeichnis der Jahre, 1911-40, eine Zusammenstellung der im deutschen Buchhandel erschienenen Bucher, Zeitscherifen und Landkarten, mit einem Stich-und Schlagwortregister. Leipzig, Borsenverein der Deutschen Buchhandler, 1915-1943. **30**

Another source for German literature where books on India in German language are published, they find place in it.

Deutsche Nationale bibliographie, bearb. von der Deut-schen Bucherei, herausgegeben vom Borsenverein der deutschen buchhandeler, 1—. Jahrg., 1931-. Leipzig, Borsen, verein der deutschen buchhandler, 1931-. **31**

A useful source for German literature on India.

DIEHL, KATHARINE SMITH. Early Indian imprints. New York, London, The Scarecrow Press, 1964. 533p. **32**

Assisted by Hemendra Kumar Sircar, this useful bibliographical tool deals with early Indian imprints. The study is based on the William Carey Historical Library of Serampore College, located in the city of the same name north of Calcutta.

DUBESTER, HENRY J. Census and vital statistics of India and Pakistan, contained in official publications and famine documents: an annotated bibliography. Washington, Library of Congress, 1950. **33**

Contains 493 entries and an index.

ETHE, CARL HERMANN. Catalogue of oriental manuscripts, Persian, Arabic and Hindustani. Aberystythe, National Library of Wales. 1916. iv, 30p. **34**

——Catalogue of Persian manuscripts in the library of the India Office. Oxford. 1903. 2v. **35**

V. 2 revised and completed by Edwards.

——Catalogue of the Persian, Turkish, Hindustani and Pushtu manuscripts in the Bodleian Library. Begun by E. Sachau. Continued, completed and edited by Carl Hermann Ethe. Oxford Bodleian Library, 1889, 1930. xii, 1766p. **36**

——A descriptive catalogue of the Arabic and Persian manuscripts in Edinburgh University Library. By Mohammed Ashreful Hukk, H. Ethe, etc. Edinburgh, The University, 1925. viii, 454p. **37**

FARQUHAR, JOHN NICHOL. An outline of the religious literature in India. London, New York, Humphrey Milford, Oxford University Press, 1920. xxviii, 451p. **38**

A bibliographical study of religious literature in India.

FERNANDEZ, BRAZ A. Annual bibliography of Indian history and Indology. Bombay, Historical Society, 1933-1949. 5 vols. **39**

FURER-HAIMENDORF, ELIZABETH VON., *comp*. An anthropological bibliography of South Asia together with a directory of recent anthropological field work. Paris, Mouton & Co. 1958. 748p. **40**

    Useful source book of bibliographical data on the anthropology of South Asia.

GILDEMEISTER, JOHANN. Bibliothecae sanskaritae sive recensvs librovm sanskritorvm hvevrque typis vel lapide exscriptorvm cticici specimen. Concinnavit-Ioanmes Gildemeister. Bonnae ad Rhenvm (etc.) H.B. Koenig (etc.) 1847. xiii, 1920p. **41**

GUATEMALA (CITY). Biblioteca Nacional. Boletin. Director: Rafael Arevalo Martinez. Guatemala City. 1932—. **42**

    Lists a few titles in Spanish on India, whenever they are published.

Halbjahrsverzeichnis der Neuerscheinungen des deutschen Buchhandels mit Voranzeigen Verlagsund Presanderungen, Stich- und Schlagwortregister, 1797-1944. Leipzig, Borsenverein der Deutschen Buchhandler, 1798-1944. **43**

    A good source for German literature. Lists a few books on India in its later volumes.

HALL, FITZEDWARD. A contribution towards an index to the bibliography of the Indian philosophical systems. Calcutta, Baptist Mission Press, 1859. **44**

HANAYAMA, SHINSHO. Bibliography on Buddhism. Edited by the Commemoration Committee for Professor Shinsho Hanayama's sixty-first birthday. Tokyo, Hokusaido Press, 1961. xiii, 869p. **45**

    A comprehensive bibliography of materials on Buddhism published in European languages press up to 1928.

HOBBS, CECIL. Southeast Asia: an annotated bibliography of selected reference sources in Western languages. Rev. & enl. ed., Washington, Library of Congress, 1964. v, 180p. **46**

HUNTER Sir, WILLIAM WILSON. Bengal Ms records; a selected list of 14, 136 letters to the Board of Revenue, Calcutta, 1782-1807, with an historical dissertation and analytical index, by Sir William Wilson Hunter. London, W.H. Allen & Co., 1894. 4v. **47**

000 General Works

Index translationum indicaram: a cumulation of entries for India in "Index translationum". UNESCO, Paris, V. 2-11. Cumulation by D.L. Banerjee. Calcutta. National Library, 1963. 450p. **48**

    A cumulation of some 2800 translations published in India, 1847-58, and listed in Index translationum. Arranged by Indian languages and then alphabetically by author. Gives author of original title of translation, name of translator, place, publisher, date, pages, illustrations, price, and language and title of the original.

INGALLS, D.H.A. Materials for the study of navya nyaya logic, London, Geoffrey Cumberlege, O.U.P., 1951. **49**

IVONOW, WLADIMIR, *comp.* Catalogue of the Arabic manuscripts in the collection of the Royal Asiatic Society of Bengal. Calcutta, Royal Asiatic Society of Bengal, 1939. 694p. **50**

    An annotated catalogue of books which was originally published as work No. 250, under the programme of Bibliotheca Indica series.

Jahresverzeichris de deutschen Schriftums, 1945-46—. bearb und hrsg. von der Deutschen Bucherei und dem Borsenvenverein der. Deutschen Buchhandler zu Leipzig. Leipzig, Borsenvereins, 1948-v. **51**

    Includes books on India in German language, whenever they are published.

JOHNSON, JULIA EMILY, *comp.* Independence for India. New York, H.W. Wilson and Co., 1943. 292p. **52**

KEMP, STANLEY, *comp.* Union catalogue of the scientific periodicals in the principal libraries of Calcutta. Calcutta, Asiatic Society of Bengal, 1918. **53**

    It is a tentative mimeographed edition intended for limited circulation.

KERN INSTITUTE, Leyden. Annual bibliography of Indian archaeology. Leyden, E.J. Brill, 1926—. Annual. **54**

    A comprehensive bibliography of Indian archaeology.

KOTOVSKY, G.G. Bibliography of India. Moscow, Oriental Literature Publishing House, 1965. 607p. **55**

    First comprehensive bibliography of its kind published in USSR. It contains literature on India published in

Russia from 18th century up to 1964 in Russian and other languages.

LANDENDORF, JARICE M. Revolt in India 1857-58: an annotated bibliography of English language materials. Zug, Inter Documentation Co., 1966. v, 191p. **56**
(Bibliotheca Indica, No. 1).

La scheda comulative Italiana, direttae redatt da T.W. Huntington; indicatore bibliografico per autore, titolo, soggetto, delle nuove publicazioni italiane. Anno 1-5, 1932-36. Anacapri, Scheda cumulativa Italina, 1932-1937. 5v. **57**

    Includes a few books on India in Italian language.

LA TOUCHE, T.H.D., *comp.* Bibliography of Indian geology. Rev. and enl. Delhi, Manager of Publications, 1969. V. 1-2. illus. (To be complete in 10 vols.). **58**

    A useful source book for material in geology in India.

LEWIS, EVANS. Subject-catalogue of the library of the Royal Empire Society. London, Royal Empire Society, 1930-37. 4 vols. **59**

    A valuable bibliography containing references to books and other research materials available in the Library of the Royal Empire Society, London.

LINTON, HOWARD P., *ed.* Published annually, in the September issue of the Journal of Asian Studies this bibliography lists standard books and articles written on South Asia. **60**

LONG, JAMES. A descriptive catalogue of Bengali works, containing a classified list of fourteen hundred Bengali books and pamphlets, which were issued from the press, during the last sixty years, with occasional notices of the subjects, the price, and where printed. By J. Long. Calcutta, Printed by Sanders, Cones & Co., 1855. 3p. 1., 108p. **61**

MACDONELL, A. A. Vedic index of names and subjects. Delhi, Motilal Banarsidas, 1959. 544p. **62**

    A standard and reliable reference tool on Vedic antiquities giving complete information on social and political life of the Vedic Aryans, their manners and customs.

MAHAR, J. MICHAEL. India: a critical bibliography. Tucson, Arizona, The University of Arizona Press, 1966. 119p. **63**

    This useful bibliography contains 2022 annotated books

000 General Works

on history, politics, fine Arts, religion, philosophy, literature and other related subjects.

MANDELBAUM, DAVID G. A guide to books on India. In The American Political Science Review, vol. xlvi, no. 4, 1952. p. 1154-1166. **64**

A brief bibliography of important books on India.

——Materials on bibliography of the ethnology of India. California, the author, 1942. 220p. **65**

A useful reference tool, it contains books and articles on India published up to 1941.

MATTHEWS, WILLIAM. British autobiographies. Berkeley, University of California Press, 1955, xiv, 376p. **66**

An annotated bibliography of British autobiographies published or written before 1951. A useful reference book.

MONIER-WILLIAMS, Sir MONIER. Catalogue of the library of Sir M. Monier-Williams (Clerkenwell) Eng., Printed by Gilbert and Rivington, ld., 1891. 92p. **67**

Contains some books on India written by non-Indians.

MULLER, FRIEDRICH MAX. A history of ancient Sanskrit literature, so far as it illustrates the primitive religion of the Brahmans. Allahabad, B. D. Basu. Bhuvaneswari Ashrama, 1926. xiv, 326, 4p. **68**

First published in London by Williams and Novgate, 1859.

NEW YORK PUBLIC LIBRARY, New York. List of grammars, dictionaries etc. of the language of Asia, Oceania, Africa in the New York Public Library. New York, the Library, 1909. 201p. **69**

Out of the list of about 6,000 ɔ itries, this valuable bibliography contains some dictionaries of Indian languages.

Nordisk bok kalender. 1947—. Stockholm, Forlaget Biblioteks bocker, 1947—. v. **70**

Lists a few titles in Scandinavian languages on India.

OPPERT, GUSTAV SALOMON. Lists of Sanskrit manuscripts in private libraries of Southern India. Compiled, arranged and indexed by Gustav Oppert. Madras, Printed by E. Keys at the Government Press, 1880-85. 2v. **71**

PARRACK, DWAIN W. *comp.* Bibliography of rodent literature with emphasis on India. Calcutta, Johns Hopkins, 1967. 55p.

(Mimeographed). **72**

PATTERSON, MAUREEN, L.P. and R.B. INDEN. South Asia: an introductory bibliography, Chicago, University of Chicago Press, Syllabus Division, 1962. **73**
  A useful bibliography includes books, monographs, dissertations, and articles on the history and culture of South Asia including India.

PEDDIE, R.A. Subject index of books, published up to and including 1880. Third series A-Z. London, H. Pordes, 1962. xv, 945p. **74**
  Books on India published up to 1880, are given from pages 470 to 472.

POLEMAN, HORACE I., *comp*. Census of Indic manuscripts in the United States and Canada. Connecticut, American Oriental Society, 1938. 542p. (American Oriental Series, 12). **75**
  This valuable reference work includes 7,273 manuscripts in Sanskrit, Pali, Prakrit, the older and modern stages of the vernaculars, the various Dravidian languages and the languages of Burma, Siam, Ceylon and Tibet.

POTTER, KARL H., *ed*. Bibliography of Indian philosophies. Delhi, Motilal, for American Institute of Indian Studies, 1970. 811p. (Encyclopedia of Indian philosophies, xxx V. 1.) **76**

PRAGUE, UNIVERSITA KARLOVA, *Knihovna*. India, Burma, Indonesia. Vyberovy Seznam literary, Seat Miroslov Kaftan, Praha, 1956. 15p. **77**

PRINGLE, ARTHUR T., *comp*. Catalogue of books and serial articles relating to language, compiled by A. T. Pringle. Calcutta, 1899. iii, 760, 30p. folio. **78**

Reference catalogue of current literature. London, J. Whitaker, 1874—. 2v. **79**
  Title changed to British books in prints from 1965 onwards. Includes some books on India written by non-Indians.

RENOU, LOUIS. Bibliographie Vedique. Paris, Adrien-Maisonneuve, 1931. 160p. **80**
  This useful bibliography of Indian religion, history and literature includes about 6,500 works in various European languages.

000 General Works

Renou, Louis. Literature Sanskrit. Paris, Maisonneuve, 1945. 160 p. (Glossaires de L'Hindouisme, Fascicule V). **81**

Rice, Benjamin Lewis. Catalogue of Sanskrit manuscripts in Mysore and Coorg. Compiled for Government by Lewis Rice. Bangalore, Mysore Government Press, 1884. 1, 2, 2, 327p. **82**

Royal Empire Society. London. Library. Subject catalogue of the library of the Royal Empire Society, formerly Royal Colonial Institute, by Evans Lewis. London, The Society, 1930-1937. 4 vols. **83**

    Lists literature on various aspects of Indian life and thought.

Solvyns, Francois Balthazar. A catalogue of 350 coloured etchings; descriptive of the manners, customs, character, dress and religious ceremonies of the Hindoos. By Balt. Soloyns. Calcutta, Morror Press, 1799. 4, 1, 28p. **84**

Spencer, Dorothy, M. Indian fiction in English, an annotated bibliography. Philadelphia, University of Pennsylvania Press, 1960. 98p. **85**

    A useful book for those scholars who intend to undertake research on Indian fiction in English language.

Sprenger, Aloys. A catalogue of the Arabic, Persian, and Hindustany manuscripts, of the libraries of the King of Oudh, comp. under the orders of the Government of India by A. Sprenger. vol. 1, containing Persian and Hindustany poetry. Calcutta, Printed by J. Thomas, 1854. vii, 645, (2) p. **86**

——Report of the researches into the Muhammadan libraries of Lucknow. By Aloys Sprenger, published by authority. Calcutta, Office of the Superintendent of government printing. 1896. 1, 1, 32p. (Selections from the records of Government of India. Foreign department No. cccxxxiv Foreign department serial No. 82). **87**

    1st-3rd quarterly report, June 6th, 1848—,March 13th, 1849, with descriptions of works in the Topkhana and Farh Bukhsh Libraries.

Stewart, Charles. A descriptive catalogue of the oriental library of the late Tippoo Sultan of Mysore. To which are prefixed., Memoirs of Hyder Aly Khan and his son Tippoo Sultan.

Cambridge 1809. **88**

STUCKI, CURTIS W. American Doctoral Dissertations on Asia, 1933-1962. Ithaca, South Asia Program, Dept. of Far Eastern Studies, Cornell University, 1963. **89**

    Includes dissertations on subjects related to India.

Subject guide to books in print: an index to the publishers' trade list annual. New York, Bowker, 1957—. **90**

    Includes books on India written by non-Indians.

SUTTON, S.C. A guide to the India Office library. London, H.M. Stationery Office, 1952. iv-62p. **91**

    A descriptive catalogue of the India Office Library.

Svensk bokfortecking, 1913-. Stockholm, Svenska Bokhandlareforeningen, 1913-. **92**

    A useful bibliography for the Swedish literature on India.

TAKAKUSU, ZYUNZIUS. Daizokyo Somokuroku or general index to Daizokyo. Tokyo, Daizo Syuppen K.K., 1930. 487p. **93**

    It is a complete collection of the Buddhist scriptures.

TEMPLE, *Sir* RICHARD, 1ST *hart.* Journals kept in Hyderabad. Kashmir, Sikkim, and Nepal. By Sir Richard Temple. Ed. with introductions, by his son, R.C. Temple. London, W.A. Allen & Co., 1887. 2v. col. front., maps. **94**

UNESCO, SOUTH ASIA SCIENCE COOPERATION OFFICE, New Delhi. Bibliography of scientific publications of South Asia (India. Burma, Ceylon). New Delhi, UNESCO, 1949-64. **95**

    Classified by Colon scheme of classification, it is quite comprehensive and covers the period from 1949 to 1964.

Union Catalogue of Asian publications. London, Mansell, 1965-1971. 4 vols. **96**

    Includes books written on India by Indian and non-Indian authors.

United States Catalog; 4th edition; books in print. January 1, 1928, edited by Mary Burnham. New York, The H.W. Wilson Co., 1928. 3164p. **97**

——(Supplements). Cumulative book index, a world list of books in the English language, 1928-32, edited by Mary Burnham. New York, The H.W. Wilson Co., 1933-. **98**

    Practically all the volumes from 1928 to-date include

000 General Works

books on India.

U.S. DEPT. OF STATE, Library Division, India: a general reading list. Washington, D.C., 1950. 41p. (Bibliographic list-BL-32) **99**

UNITED STATES INFORMATION SERVICE, New Delhi. Books on India from the United States, exhibited by the USIS, New Delhi, n.d. ii, 27p. Supplement: issued in November 1971. 8p. **100**

Includes annotated lists of books published in America on India on subjects like Indian Art and Literature, Philosophy and Religion, Geography, Travel, Sociology, etc.

UNITED STATES, LIBRARY OF CONGRESS, Washington. Catalog of books represented by Library of Congress printed cards, N.Y., Pageant Books, 1942-1972. **101**

Includes comprehensive collection of books on India written both by Indian and non-Indians.

US LIBRARY OF CONGRESS, ORIENTALIA DIVISION. Southern Asia accessions list. V. 1—Washington, Jan. 1952-. **102**

Includes alphabetical list of books on India.

WILSON, HORACE HAYMAN. A glossary of judicial and revenue terms and of useful words occurring in official documents relating to the administration of the Government of British India, from the Arabic, Persian, Hindustani, Sanskrit, Hindi, Bengali, Uriya, Marathi, Guzarathi, Telugu, Karnataka, Tamil, Malyalam and other languages, *comp.* and *pub.* under the authority of the Honorable court of directors of the East India Co., By H.H. Wilson. London, W.H. Allen & Co., 1855. 1, 1, xxiv (4) 728p. **103**

———A glossary of judicial and revenue terms and of useful words occurring in official documents relating to the administration of the government of British India, from the Arabic, Persian, Hindustani, Sanskrit, Hindi, Bengali, Uriya, Marathi, Guzarathi, Telugu, Karnataka, Tamil, Malyalam and other languages. Originally compiled and published under the authority of the Honorable court of directors of the East India Co., By H.H. Wilson (case noted enl. ed.) ed. by A. C. Ganguli and N.D. Basu. Calcutta, Eastern Law House, 1940. 1, 2, xliv, 905p. **104**

WILSON, PATRICK. Government and politics of India and Pakis-

tan, 1885-1955. Berkeley, South Asia Studies, Institute of East Asiatic Studies, University of California, 1956. iii, 41p. **105**
   Contains material in Western languages. It is useful reference tool.
WILSON, PATRICK. South Asia: a selected bibliography on India, Pakistan, Ceylon. New York, American Institute of Pacific Relations, 1957. Rev. ed. iii, 41p. **106**
   A useful annotated bibliography.
—— A survey of bibliographies on Southern Asia. Berkeley, California, The Institute of International Studies, University of California, 1959. 365-376p. **107**
   This well-selected bibliography contains basic reference works on Southern Asia. Originally it was printed in The Journal of Asian Studies, Vol. XVIII, No. 3, 1959.
ZAUNMULLER, W. Bibliographisches Handbuch der sprachworterbucher. Anton Hiersemann, Stuttgart, 1958. xvi, 495p. **108**
   An index, it contains about 5,600 dictionaries of more than 500 languages, published between 1460 and 1958.

(ii) Encyclopaedias

BALFOUR, EDWARDS, ed. Encyclopaedia of India. Madras, Scottish and Adelphia Presses, 1871. 5 vols. **109**
   One of the earliest encyclopaedias compiled about India. Information is outdated.
BRILL, E.J. Encyclopaedia of Islam; tr. in Urdu by Deptt. of Urdu Encyclopaedia of Islam, Panjab University; new ed. Lahore, University, 1954. **110**

(iii) Journalism

BARNS, MARGARITA. The Indian press: a history of the growth of public opinion in India. London, George Allen & Unwin, 1940. xv, 491p. **111**
SKRINE, FRANCIS HENRY BENNETT. An Indian journalist: being

the life, letters and correspondence of Dr Sambhu C. Mookerjee, late editor of "Reis and Rayyet" Calcutta. By F.H. Skrine, ICS, Calcutta. Thacker Spink & Co., 1895. xxvii, 1 l., 477, (1)p. front (port.).   **112**

WOLSELEY, ROLAND E., *ed*. Journalism in modern India. Bombay, Asia Publishing House, 1953.   **113**

    Contains essays dealing with the role played by the press in India today by men actively engaged in journalism.

100 PHILOSOPHY
200 RELIGION

(i) General Works

ALEXANDER, F.J. In the hours of meditation. Almora, Advaita Ashram, 1951. iv, 111p. **114**
    A scholarly work, reflects the author's inner life imbued with Indian spirit and ideals. The author spent several years at the Ashram.

ARNOLD, Sir EDWIN. The light of Asia. N.Y., Hurts & Co., 1884. i, 1, 13-133p. **115**

BARTH, MARIE ETIENNE AUGUSTE. Bulletin des religions de l'
———Inde, par A. Barth. Paris, E. Leroux, 1885. 67p. (F). **116**

———Les religions de l' Inde, par A. Barth. Extrait de l' Encyclopedie des sciences religienses. Paris, G. Fischbacher, 1879. 2p. 1. 175, (1)p. (F) **117**

BARTH, AUGUSTE. Religions of India. Translated by J. Wood. Varanasi, Chowkhamba, 1963. xxiv, 309p. **118**
    Originally published in 1921, this scholarly survey of India's religions remains a standard work.

BEAMES, JOHN. Outlines of Indian philosophy, with a map showing the distribution of Indian languages, Calcutta, Wyman Bros., 1867. 60p. **119**

100 Philosophy   200 Religion

BENDALL, CECIL. The Megha-Sutra (The text with an English translation and notes). 1880. **120**

BESANT, ANNIE (WOOD). Four great religions. London, Theosophical Publishing Society, 1906. iv, 200p. **121**

    A collection of lectures on Hinduism, Zoroastrianism, Buddhism and Christianity, delivered at the twenty-first anniversary of the Theosophical Society at Adyar, Madras.

BLAVATSKY, HELENA PETROVNA. Synthesis of science, religion and philosophy. London, Theosophical Publishing Co., 1888. 2 vols. **122**

BOSCH, F.D.K. The golden germ: introduction to Indian symbolism. The Hague, Mouton, 1960. **123**

    An appraisal of the form and religious-philosophical significance of symbols appearing in Buddhist and Jain decorative art.

BRIGGS, GEORGE WESTON. The power of non-violence. Madison, N. J., 1953. 13p. (Drew University Studies, no. 7). **124**

BRUNTON, PAUL. Indian philosophy and modern culture. London, Rider & Co., 1939. 92p. **125**

    Traces the close parallels between the findings of the best modern thinkers of the West and the findings of India's early sages.

——Message from Arunachala. New York, E.P. Dutton & Co., 1935. 222p. **126**

BURNOUF, EUGENE. Bhagawatapurana. Paris, 1840. **127**

COUSINS, JAMES HENRY. A study in synthesis. Madras, Ganesh & Co., 1934. x, 495p. **128**

    An exposition of the unity and community of life and its forms.

CROOKE, WILLIAM. Popular religion and folk-lore of Northern India. Westminster, Archibald Constable, 1896. 2 vols. **129**

DE BARY, WILLIAM THEODORE, *ed.* Sources of Indian tradition. Compiled by William Theodore De Bary and others. New York, Columbia University Press, 1958. xxvii, 961p. (Records of civilization: sources and studies, 56. Introduction to oriental civilizations). **130**

DIEHL, CARL GUSTAV. Instrument and purpose; studies on rites and rituals in South India. Lund, CWK Gleerup, 1956. 394p. **131**

EIDLITZ, WALTHER. Der Glaube und die heiligen schriften der Inder. Olten, Walter-Verlag, 1957, 307p. illus. **132**

—— Unknown India: a pilgrimage into a forgotten world. London, Rider & Co., 1952. 192p. **133**

> An account of the author's spiritual quest in India.

ELLIS, FRANCIS WHYTE. The 'sacred' Kurral of Tiruvalluvar-Nayanar. With introduction, grammar, translation, notes in which are reprinted Fr. C.J. Beschi's and F.W. Ellis' versions, lexicon and concordance. By G.U. Pope. London, W.H. Allen & Co., 1886. vi, xxviii, 328, 30p. **134**

FALCKENBERG, RICHARD FRIEDRICH OTTO. History of modern philosophy, from Nicolas of Cusa to the present time. Tr. with the author's sanction by A.C. Armstrong Jr. Calcutta, Progressive Publishers, 1953. xvi, 653p. **135**

FARQUHAR, JOHN NICHOL. Modern religious movements in India. New York, Macmillan Co. 1915. 471p. **136**

> A collection of the Hartford Lawson lectures on the religions of the world.

—— An outline of the religious literature of India. London, Oxford University Press, 1920, 2nd ed. xxviii, 451p. (Religious quest of India). **137**

> A useful work on the subject covering the period from earliest times to the early 18th century.

FAUSBOLL, MICHAEL VIGGO. Fire forstudier till en fremstilling af den indiske mytholigie after Mahabharata, af V. Fausboll, Kjobenhavn Trykt hos Nielsen & Lydiche, 1897. vii, 92p. **138**

FINEGAN, JACK. The archaeology of world religions. Princeton, 1952. 599p. **139**

> The early history of the Eastern religions as known through discovered remains.

FORLONG, JAMES GEORGE ROCHE. Faiths of man; a cyclopaedia of religions, by Major General J.G.R. Forlong. Published by his executors. London, B. Quaritch, 1906. 3 vol. front. (ports., facsim v. 3). **140**

—— Rivers of life, or, sources and streams of the faiths of man in all lands; showing the evolution of faiths from the rude symbolism to the latest spiritual developments. By Major-General J.G.R. Forlong. With maps, illustrations, and separate chart of faith streams. London (Edinburgh, Printed by Turnbull and Spears), 1883. 2v. front (V. 2). Illus., plates (1 fold) fold. maps. fold tables. Folded plate in portfolio. **141**

FORLONG, JAMES GEORGE ROCHE. Short studies in the science of comparative religions, embracing all the religions of Asia; by Major-General J.G.R. Forlong. London, B. Quoritch, 1897. xxviii, 662p. 11. illus. fold maps. **142**

FRAZER, ROBERT WATSON. Indian thought: past and present. London, T. Fisher Unwin, 1915. ii, 339p. **143**

    A history of Indian thought as has influenced the aspirations, religious beliefs and social life of all thinking and orthodox Hindus.

GARBE, RICHARD. "Nyaya". In Hastings Encyclopaedia of Religion and Ethics. Vol. ix. **144**

——The Sankhya philosophy. Translated by R.D. Vedekar from German. Leipzig, H. Haessel, 1917. viii, 347p. **145**

GLASENAPP, HELMUTH VON, ed. Indische Geisteswelt; eine Auswahl von Texten in deutscher Ubersetzung. Baden-Baden, Holle Verlag, 1958-59. 2 vol. (Geist des Morgenlandes). **146**

GOBLET D'ALVIELLA, EUGENE FELICIAN ALBERT, COMTE. The contemporary evolution of religious thought in England, America and India by Count Goblet d'Alviella. Translated by J. Moden. London and Edinburgh, Williams & Norgate, 1885. xv, 344p. **147**

——Lectures on the origin and growth of the conception of God as illustrated by anthropology and history. By Goblet d'Alviella. London and Edinburgh, Williams and Norgate, 1892. xvi, 296p. (The Hibbert lectures, 1891). "Translated by the Rev. P.H. Wicksteed". **148**

——The true and false pacifism, by Count Goblet d'Alviella. London, T.F. Unwin, Ltd., 1917. xv, 85p. **149**

GONDA, JAN. De Indische; godsdiensten; de Vedische godsdienst, het Hindoeisme, het Boeddhisme. Den Haag, Servire, 1955. 147p. **150**

GRUNWEDEL, ALBERT. Alt-Kutscha; archaologische und religiousges chichtliche forschumgen an tempera-gemal den aus Buddhistischen hohlen der ersten acht Jahrhunderte nach christi geburt, von professor dr. Albert Grunwedel. Berlin O. Elsner vertagsgesell-schaft m.b.h., 1920. 3, 1. 8, 118, (6) p. incl. illus. (part mounted; incl. maps, plans). 2pl. on 1 l. double plates. and atlas of col. plates (part double). **151**

At head of title: Veroffeutlichung der Preussischen Turfan-expedntionen mit unter stutzung des Bassler-Institus. "No. 037 der in 400 stucken hergestellten auflage."

GRUNWEDEL, ALBERT. Buddhistche Kunst in Indien, von Albert Grundwedel mit 102 abbildungen. Berlin, W. Spemann. 1900. xv, 213, (1) p. illus. (Handbucher der Koniglichen museen zu Berlin (bd. 43); At head of title: Museum fur volkerkunde. "Litterature"; p. (viii)—xii. "Chronologische tabelle". p. (xiii)—xv. **152**

GUBERNATIS, ANGELODE, *conte*. Storia dei viaggiatori itiliani velle Indie orientali, compilata da Angelo de Gubernatis. Con estratti d'alcune relazioni di viaggio a stampa ed alcuni document: inediti Publicato in occasione del congresso geografico di Parigi Livorno, F. Vigo. 1875. viii, 400p. (I) **153**

GUENON, RENE. Introduction to the study of the Hindu doctrines. Translated by Marco Pallis. London, Luzac & Co., 1945. 351p. **154**

HASTINGS, JAMES, *ed*. Encyclopedia of religion and ethics. New York, Scribners', 1908-26. 13 vols. **155**

Includes several articles on various facets of Hinduism and related religious matters.

HAVELL, ERNEST B. Banares, the sacred city. London, Blackie & Son, 1905. xiii, 226p. **156**

A popular book of Hindu temples, shrines and religious practices.

HEBER, REGINALD, BP. OF CALCUTTA. Heber's Indian journal, a selection with an introduction by P.R. Krishnaswami. London (etc.), H. Milford, Oxford University Press, 1923. xiv, 221p. incl. front. (Half title: An Eastern Library, no. 111). **157**

HOPKINS, EDWARD WASHBURN. Ethics of India, by E. Washburn Hopkins. New Haven, Yale University Press, (etc. etc.). 1924. xiv, 265p. **158**

A faithful exposition of the subject.

HOPKINS, EDWARD WASHBURN. The history of religions, by E. Washburn Hopkins. New York, The Macmillan Company, 1918. 2, 1, 6, (4), 624p. **159**

——The religion of India, by Edward Washburn Hopkins. Boston and London, Ginn and Company, 1898. xiii, (2) 612p. map. (Half title: Handbook on the history of religions, ed. by M. Jastraw, vol. 1). **160**

INGALLS, DANIEL H.H. *ed.* Harvard oriental series—Vol. 1-. Cambridge, Harvard University Press, 1891-. **161**

    Formerly edited by Charles R. Lanman, the series contains scholarly translations of important Indian religious books.

INGE, W.R. AND OTHERS, *eds.* Radhakrishnan: comparative studies in philosophy presented in honour of his sixtieth birthday. Ed. by W.R. Inge; L.P. Jacks; M. Hiriyanna; E.A. Burtt and P.T. Raju. London, George Allen & Unwin, 1950. 408p. **162**

    A collection of 21 essays in contemporary philosophy.

JAST, LOUIS STANLEY. Reincarnation and *Karma*: a spiritual philosophy applied to the world today. New York, Bernard Ackerman, Inc., 1944. 190p. **163**

    An appraisal of the reincarnation philosophy.

JOAD, CYRIL EDWIN MITCHINSON, 1891-1953. Counter attack from the East: the philosophy of Radhakrishnan. London, George Allen & Unwin, 1933. 269p. **164**

JONES, MARCE E. Gandhi lives. Mckay, 1948. 184p. **165**

    A tribute to the influence of Gandhi's spirit in a turbulent world.

KELLOGG, SAMUEL HENRY. A handbook of comparative religion, by Rev. S.H. Kellogg. Philadelphia, The Westminster Press, 1899. viii, 179p. **166**

    On cover: Westminster handbooks.

KENNEDY, JAMES. The fifteenth report of the Benaras Auxillary. Drawn up by J.K., etc. London, Missionary Society, 1856. **167**

KERN, JOHAN HENDRIK CASPAR. The Saddharama-pundarika. Translated by H. Kern. Oxford, Clarendon Press, 1884. xxxix, 454p. (Sacred books of the East, v. 21). **168**

KONOW, STEN. The religions of India. Translated from the Dutch by Sten Konow. Copenhagen, G.E.C. God Publisher, 1949. 214p. (D). **169**

LACEY, ROBERT LEE. The holy land of the Hindus, with seven letters on religious problems. London, Robert Scott, 1913. xi, 246p. **170**

LASSEN, CHRISTIAN, ed. Gymnosophista; sive, indicae philosophiae documenta. Collegit, edidit, enarravit Christianus Lassen. Vol. 1, fasc. 1., Isvarachishnae Sankhyacaricam tenens. Bonnae ad Rhenum, prostat apud Eduardum Wehes, 1832. 2p. 1 (iii) xiv, 63p. **171**

LEVI, SYLVAIN. Eastern humanism. An address, etc. London, Dacca Printed, 1925. 9p. (Dacca University Bulletin No. 4). **172**

——Materiaux pour l' etude du systeme vijnaptimatra. Historique du systeme Vijnaptimatra, d' apres D. Shimaj, par M. Paul Demieville-Traduction de la "Fang yi ming yi tsi" traduit en collaboration avec Edouard Chavannes, etc. Paris, 1932. 206p. **173**

LILLY, WILLIAM SAMUEL. Many mansions, being studies in ancient religions and modern thought, by William Lilly. London, Chapman & Hall, Ltd., 1907. xi, 260p. **174**

LIN YUTANG, ed. The wisdom of India. London, Michael Joseph, 1948. 527p. **175**

    First published in a limited edition in 1944, it is a collection of essays on subjects like: Buddhism, Indian piety, hymns from Rigveda, the Upanishads, the Bhagavadgita, the Yoga etc.

LYALL, Sir ALFRED COMYN. Asiatic studies, religious and social, by Sir Alfred C. Lyall. 1st (-2d) series. London, J. Murray, 1899. 2v. **176**

MACDONELL, ARTHUR ANTHONY. Vedic mythology by A.A. Macdonell. Strassburg, K.J. Trubner, 1897, 1, 1, 189p. **177**

MACINTOSH, DOUGLAS CLYDE. The pilgrimage of faith in the world of modern thought. Calcutta, Calcutta University, 1931. 299p. **178**

    Collection of Stephanos Nirmalendu lectures at the Calcutta University.

100 Philosophy   200 Religion

MACKENZIE, DONALD ALEXANDER. India myth and legend. London, the Gresham Publishing Co., n.d. 463p. **179**
    Contains illustrations in colour by Warwick Coble and numerous monochrome plates.

MACNICOL, NICOL. India in the dark wood. London, Edinburgh House Press, 1930. 224p. **180**
    "A survey of the contemporary religious situation in India."

——The living religions of the Indian people. London, Student Christian Movement Press, 1934. 323p. **181**
    A collection of Wilde lectures, Oxford, 1932-34.

MARTIN, E. OSBORN. The gods of India: a brief description of their history, character and worship. London & Toronto, J.M. Dent & Sons, 1914. xviii, 330p. **182**

MITCHELL, JOHN MURRAY. The great religions of India, by the Rev. J. Murray Mitchell. With prefatory note by the Very Rev. James Mitchell, D.D. With portrait and map. Edinburgh and London. Oliphant, Anderson & Farrier, 1905. 287p. front (port.) fold. map. **183**
    A collection of Duff Missionary lectures.

——Two old faiths: essays on the religions of the Hindus and the Mohammedans, by J. Murray Mitchell and Sir William Muir. New York, Chantauggua Press, 1891. 152p. **184**

MONIER-WILLIAMS, Sir MONIER. Indian wisdom, or, examples of the religious, philosophical, and ethical doctrines of the Hindus: with a brief history of the chief departments of Sanskrit literature and some account of the past and present condition of India, moral and intellectual. By Monier Williams. London, W. H. Allen & Co., 1875. xlviii, 542p. **185**

——Religious thought and life in India. An account of the religions of the Indian peoples, based on a life's study of their literature and on personal investigations in their own country. By Monier Williams. Part I. Vedism, Brahmanism, and Hinduism. 2d ed. London, J. Murray, 1885. xv, (1) 552p. **186**

MOORE, CHARLES A., ed. The Indian mind; essentials of Indian philosophy and culture. East-West Center, 1967. 458p. **187**

MUIR, JOHN. An examination of religions. Mirzapore, Orphan Press, R.C. Mather, 1852-54. 2v. **188**

Sources of Indian Civilization

MUIR, JOHN. Original Sanskrit texts on the origin and progress of the religion and institutions of India; collected, translated into English, and illustrated by notes. Chiefly for the use of students and others in India. By J. Muir. London and Edinburgh, Williams and Norgate etc. etc. 1858-. **189**

────Religious and moral sentiments metrically rendered from Sanskrit writers, with an introduction, and an appendix containing exact translations in prose. By. J. Muir. London and Edinburgh, Williams & Norgate, 1875. 128p. **190**

──── MUIRHEAD, J.N. AND S. RADHAKRISHNAN, *eds.* Contemporary Indian philosophy. London, Allen & Unwin, 1952. 2nd ed. 375p. **191**

A collection of essays by several outstanding contemporary Indian philosophers.

MULLER, FRIEDRICH MAX. Comparative mythology; an essay, by Professor Max Muller; ed. with additional notes and an introductory preface on solar mythology, by A. Sonythe Palmer. D.D. London, G. Routledge & Sons, (etc. etc.), 1909. xlvii; 184p. **192**

────Contributions to the science of mythology, by the Right Hon. Prof. F. Max Muller. London, New York & Bombay, Longmans, Green & Co., 1897. 2v. **193**

──── India: what can it teach us? A course of lectures delivered before the University of Cambridge by F. Max Muller. Text and foot-notes complete. With an introduction and notes by Prof Alexander Wilder, M.D. New York, Funk & Wagnalls, 1883. xviii, (19)-282p. **194**

Also published by Longmans, Green & Co., 1934.

────Indian philosophy. Calcutta, Susil Gupta, 1952. 4 vols. **195**

First published under the title "The six systems of Indian philosophy", in 1899. Contents: Vol. I. The six systems of Indian philosophy; Vol. II. Vedanta and purvamimamsa; Vol. III. Samkhya and Yoga; Vol. IV. Naya and Vaiseshika.

────Lectures on the origin and growth of religion as illustrated by the religions of India. Delivered in the chapel house-Westminster Abbey, in April, May and June. By F. Max Muller,

M.A. New York, C. Scribner's Sons, 1879. xvi, 382p. **196**
MULLER, FRIEDRICH MAX. Life and religion: an aftermath from the writings of the Right Hon'ble Prof. F. Max Muller, by his wife. New York, Doubleday, Page & Co., 1905. viii, 237p. **197**
────Natural religion; the Gifford lectures delivered before the University of Glasgow in 1888, by F. Max Muller. London & New York. Longmans, Green & Co., 1889. xix, 608p. **198**
────On missions; a lecture delivered in Westminster Abbey on Dec. 3, 1873, by F. Max Muller. With an introductory sermon by Arthur Penrhyn Stanley. London, Longmans, Green & Co., 1873, 2, 1, 64p. **199**
────Physical religion; the Gifford lectures delivered before the University of Glasgow in 1890. By F. Max Muller. London, and New York, Longmans, Green & Co., 1891. xii, 410p. **200**
────, ed. The sacred books of the East. Oxford University Press, 1879. 51 vol. **201**

A basic and monumental work, it includes the major religions and philosophical texts of scholarly and classical Indian tradition.

────The six systems of Indian philosophy. By the Rt. Hon. F. Max Muller. New York (etc.), Longmans, Green & Co., 1899. xxxi, 618p. **202**
────Selected essays on language, mythology and religion, by F. Max Muller. London, Longmans, Green & Co., 1881. 2v. **203**
────Theosophy; or, Psychological religion; the Gifford lectures delivered before the University of Glasgow in 1892, by F. Max Muller. London and New York, Longmans, Green & Co., 1893. xxiii, 585, 9p. **204**
Noss, JOHN B. Man's religions. New York, The Macmillan Co., 1949. xi, 812p. **205**

Includes "Suggestions for future reading".

PISCHEL, RICHAR. Vedische studien: von Richard Pischel und Karl F. Geldner. Stuttgart, W. Kohlha mmer, 1889-1901. 3v. in 1. **206**
PRATT JAMES BISSETT. Life and its faiths. London, Constable

& Co., 1916. 494p. **207**

RAFFALT, REINHARD. Drei Wege durch Indian; Berichte und Gedanken uber einen Erdteil. Nurnberg, Glock und Lutz, 1957. 335p. illus. **208**

RENOU LOUIS. Religions of ancient India. London, University of London, Athlone Press; distributed by Constable, 1953. viii, 139p. (Jordan lectures in comparative religion, 1). Distributed in USA by J. de Graff, New York, 1953. **209**

 A concise survey of Indian religions, with the exception of Buddhism.

REYNA, RUTH. Concept of Maya from the Vedas to the 20th century. Bombay, Asia Publishing House, 1962. xiv, 120p. **210**

—— Introduction to Indian philosophy: A simplified text. Bombay, New Delhi, Tata McGraw-Hill Publishing Co. Ltd., 1971, xvii, 257p. **211**

 As its title indicates, the book is designed to appeal to the intelligent student interested in Indian philosophy. In writing it, the author had in view the Western as well as the Indian student. It is a reliable text book of Indian philosophy.

RICHTER, JULIUS. A history of missions in India. Translated by Sydney H. Moore. Edinburgh and London, Oliphant Anderson & Ferrier, 1908. vii, 469p. **212**

RIEPE, DALE. The naturalistic tradition in Indian thought. University of Washington, 1961. 308p. **213**

ROOF, SIMONS LUCAS. Journeys on the razor-edged path. Illustrations by Frank Kramer. New York, Crowell, 1959. 204p. illus. **214**

SCHIEFNER, FRAUZ ANTON VON. Eine tibetische lebensbeschreibung cakjamuni's des begrunders des buddhathums, in auszuge dentsche mitgetheilt von Anton Schiefner. St. Petersburg, Gedruckt bei der Kaiser-Lichen akademie der eiddrndvh aften. 1849, ip. 1., 102p. 11 **215**

—— Uber pluralbeziechnungen in tibetischen, von A. Schiefner. St.-Petersburg, Eggers etc. ; cie. (etc.; etc.). 1877. 17p. (memoires de l'Academie imperiale des sciences de St. Petersburg, vii, ser. t. xxv, no. 1.) (G). **216**

SCHILPP, PAUL A., *ed.* The philosophy of Sarvepalli Radhakrishnan. Tudor. 1952. 833p. **217**
In this important volume, twenty-three world-renowned scholars, including nine Americans, have written a series of essays covering every aspect of Dr. Radhakrishnan's thought.

SCHLAGINTWEIT, EMIL. Handworterbuch der tibetischen sprache von H.A. Jaschke. *In* Akademie der wissenscheften, Munich. Philosophisch-Philologische und instorische classe. Sitzungsberichte. Munchen, 1871. bd. 1 (Jagrg. 1871) p. 702-706. **218**

——Indien in wort und bild. Eïre schilderung des indischen kaiserreiches, von Emil Schalgintweit. Leipzig. H. Schmidt & C. Gunther. 1880-81. 2v. frats., illus., plates, fold map. (G). **219**

SCHLEGEL, AUGUST WILHELMVON. Hitopadesas, id est Instituti'o Salutaris. Textum codd. Mss. collatis recensuerunt interpretationem latinam et annotationes criticas adjacerunt A.G. a schlegel et C. Lassen. 2 pt. Sansk. and Lat. Bonnae ad Rhenum. 1829-31. **220**

SCHROEDER, LEOPOLD VON. Herakles und Indr ; eine mythenvergleichende untersuchung, von L. Von Schroeder, Wien, In Kommission bei Alfred Holder. 1914. 2v. in 1. (Denkschriften der Kaisertichen akademie dr wisenschaften in Wien. Philosophisch historische Kiasse. 58. bd., 3-4, abh.) (G) **221**

SCHROEDER, LEOPOLD VON. Mysterium and minus in Rigveda, von Leopold Von Schroeder. Leipzig, H. Haessal Verlag. 1908. xp., 1 1., 490p. **222**

SCHWEITZER, ALBERT. Indian thought and its development. Translated by Mrs C.E.B. Russell. Boston, Beacon Press, 1957. xii, 272p. **223**
   First published by Henry Holt of New York in 1936 it is a critical appraisal of the Hindu view of life.

SHERRING, Rev. MATHEW ATMORE. The Hindoo pilgrims. By M.A. Sherring. London, Trubner & Co., 1878. vi., 1, 1., (9)-125, (1) p. "in verse". **224**

SINNETT, ALFRED PERCY. Collected fruits of occult teaching, A.P. Sinnett. London, T.F. Unwin Ltd., 1919. 307; (1) p. **225**

SINNETT, ALFRED PERCY. The growth of the soul; a sequel to "esoteric Buddhism", by A.P. Sinnett. London, New York, The Theosophical Publishing, 1896. 459p. **226**

—— The growth of the soul; a sequel to "esoteric Buddhism". 2nd (enl) ed. by A.P. Sinnett. London and Benares, The Theosophical Publishing Society, 1905. xv, 483, (1)p. col. front., digrs. **227**

——The occult world, by A.P. Sinnett. 3d ed. London, Trubner & Co. 1883, xiv p. 1, 1, 140p. **228**

SMITH, VINCENT ARTHUR. The Oxford student's history of India, by Vincent A. Smith. 6th ed., rev. and enl. 11 maps and 34 illustrations. Oxford, The Clarendon Press, London, New York (etc.) H. Milford. 1916. 384p. incl. front. illus. ports. maps. fold map. **229**

STEIN, LUDWIG. Philosophical currents of the present day. Tr. by Shishir Kumar Maitra. Calcutta, the University, 1918-19. 3 vols. (G) **230**

TAYLOR, EDMOND. Richer by Asia. Houghton. 1947. 432p. **231**
 Mr Taylor worked in India during the war, and found that as he penetrated more deeply into Indian ways of thought, he developed a new and richer understanding of his own philosophy.

THILBANT, GEORGE FREDERICK WILLIAM. The Sulvasutras. By Thilbant. Calcutta, printed by C.B. Lewis, Baptist Mission Press, 1875. 1p. 1., 49p. fold diagrs. **232**

TURNOUR, GEORGE. The Mahavansa. Part II, containing chapters xxxiv to c. Translated from the original Pali by L.C. Wijesinha. To which is prefixed the translation of the first part published 1837 by G. Turnour (revised by L.C. Wijesinha) Colombo, Govt. 2pt. **233**

WEBER, MAX. The religion of India; the sociology of Hinduism and Buddhism. Translated and edited by Hans H. Gerth and Don Martindate. Glencoe, Ill. Free Press, 1958. 392p. **234**

WHITEHEAD, HENRY. The village of gods of South India. London, Oxford University Press, 1921. 2nd rev. ed. 175p. plate (The religious life of India series, ed. by J.N. Farquhar and Nicol Macnicol). **235**

100 Philosophy   200 Religion

A Christian missionary's appraisal of the village gods of South India.

WILSON, HORACE, HAYMAN. Essays and lectures chiefly on the religion of the Hindus. By the late H.H. Wilson. Collected and ed. by Dr Reinhold Rost. London, Trubner & Co. 1812. 2v. **236**

WILSON, JOHN. An exposure of the Hindu religion, in reply to Mora Bhatta Dandekara: to which is prefixed a translation of the Bhatta's tract. By the Rev. John Wilson. Bombay, Printed at the American mission press and sold by the agent of the oriental Christian Spectator, 1832. viii (9) 159. **237**

YOUNGHUSBAND, FRANCIS EDWARD. The Glean. London, John Murray, 1923. xviii, 297p. **238**

It is a story of spiritual adventures of a sannyasi who is a follower of Glean.

—— A venture of faith; being a description of the world congress of faiths, held in London, 1936. London, M. Joseph, Ltd., 1937. 287p. front. ports. **239**

—— Vital religion; a brotherhood of faith (by) Sir Francis Younghusband. London, John Murray, 1940. ix, 101p. **240**

ZIMMER, HEINRICH R. Myths and symbols in Indian art and civilization. Edited by J. Champbell. New York, Pantheon Books, 1946, xviii, 248p. Harper and Row of the New York, published in 1962 a paperbound edition of this book. **241**

An attempt to interpret basic tenets of Hinduism, Buddhism and Jainism to Western readers.

—— Philosophies of India. Edited by J. Campbell. New York, Meridian, 1956. xiv, 687p. **242**

Paperbound, this book can be considered as an introduction to the subject. It is not a scholarly interpretation of the vast philosophies of India.

(ii) Vedism, Brahmanism, Upanishads

BENFEY, THEODOR. Vedas-Samaveda. 1848. 210p. **243**
—— Vedica und linguistica. London. 248p. **244**
BESENT, ANNIE (WOOD) The wisdom of the Upanishads. Mad-

ras, Theosophical Publishing House, 1925. vii, 106p. **245**
A collection of four lectures delivered at the 31st anniversary of the Theosophical Society, at Adyar, December 1906.

BLOOMFIELD, MAURICE, *tr*. Hymns of the Atharva-Veda, together with extracts from the ritual books and commentaries. Oxford, Clarendon Press, 1897. lxxiv, 716p. (Sacred books of the East v. 42). **246**
A monograph, summarises the basic philosophy enshrined in Atharva Veda.

——The religion of the Veda, the ancient religion of India (from Rig-Veda to Upanishads). New York, G.P. Putnams, 1908. xv, 390p. (American lectures on the history of religions, 7th series, 1906-1907). **247**
A useful study of the Vedas.

DEUSSEN, PAUL. The philosophy of the Upanishads. Translated by A.S. Geden. Edinburgh, T. & T. Clark, 1906. xiv, 429p. (The religion and philosophy of India series). **248**
A western system interpretation of the philosophy of the Upanishads.

——The system of the Vedanta. Authorized translation by Charles Johnson. Chicago, The Open Court Publishing Co., 1912. xiv, 513p. **249**
"According to Badarayana Brahma-Sutras and Sankara's commentary thereon... a compendium of the dogmatics of Brahmanism from the standpoint of Sankara".—*t.p.*

EDGERTON, FRANKLIN. The beginnings of Indian philosophy: selections from the Rig Veda, Atharva Veda, Upanishads, and Mahabharata. Harvard. 1965. 362p. **250**

EGGERLING, J., *tr*. The Satapatha-Brahmana. Oxford, Clarendon Press, 1882-1900. 5 vols. **251**
These books from volumes No. 12, 26, 51, 53 and 54 of the Sacred Books of the East and their text provides information about Vedic society, its customs, rituals etc.

GRIFFITH, R.T.H., *tr*. Hymns of the Rigveda. Benaras, E.J. Lazarus, 1920-26. 2 vols. **252**
It is considered to be the only complete translation of the Rigveda available in English.

100 Philosophy   200 Religion

GRIFFITH, R.T.H., *tr*. The texts of the White Yajur Veda. Translated with a popular commentary. Benaras, E.J. Lazarus, 1899. xx, 344p.   **253**

HEESTERMAN, JOHANNES C. The ancient Indian Royal Conservation. The Hague, Mouton, 1957. 244p.   **254**

    A well written description and interpretation of a major Vedic ceremony, the Rajasuya, based on a comparative study of several Brahmanas.

HOPKINS, EDWARD WASHBURN. Gods and saints of the Great Brahmana. (In Connecticut Academy of Arts & Sciences. Transaction New Haven, Conn., 1909. v. 15, p. (19)—69).   **255**

HUME, R.E., *tr*. The thirteen principal Upanishads. London, Oxford University Press, 1962. 2nd ed.   **256**

    Considered to be a scholarly translation of the Upanishads.

KEITH, ARTHUR B. The religion and philosophy of the Vedas and Upanishads. Cambridge, Harvard University Press, 1925. 2 vols. (The Harvard Oriental Series, 31 and 32).   **257**

    Vols. 31 and 32 form part of the Harvard Oriental Series, it is a detailed survey of the Vedic tradition.

——— Rigveda Brahmanas, the Aitareya and the Kausitaki Brahmanas. Cambridge, Harvard University Press, 1920. xii, 555p.   **258**

    Also published as vol. 25, of the Harvard Oriental Series, contains mystical interpretations of Vedic rituals.

KEITH, ARTHUR B., *tr*. The Veda of the Black Yajur School, entitled Taittiriya Sanhita. Cambridge, Harvard University Press, 1914. 2v.   **259**

    Also published as vols. 18 and 19 in the Harvard Oriental Series, it is a translation of the Yajur-Veda belonging to the "Black" type.

LEVI, SYLVAIN. La Doctrine du sacrifice dans les Brahmanas. 1898. 181p.   **260**

MACDONELL, ARTHUR A. Vedic mythology. Strassburg, Trubner, 1897. 174p.   **261**

    A scholarly work, it is considered a basic reference work on Vedic mythology.

MACDONELL, ARTHUR A. A Vedic reader for students. London, Oxford Clarendon Press, 1917. xxxi, 263p. **262**
    A selection of thirty hymns from the Rigveda presented in the original text with transliteration and translation.

—— tr. Hymns from the Rigveda. London, Oxford University Press, 1922. 98p. **263**
    A selection of forty hymns accompanied by a brief introduction and descriptive notes.

MACDONELL, ARTHUR AND KEITH, A.B. Vedic Index of names and subjects. Delhi, Motilal Banarasidass, 1958. 2 vols. **264**
    First published in 1912, by J. Murray of London, it is a reprint. Considered to be a standard reference work in the field of Vedic studies, especially useful for the Samhitas and Brahmanas.

MACNICOL, NICOL. Hindu scriptures: hymns from the Rigveda, five Upanishads, the Bhagavadgita. Foreword by Dr Rabindranath Tagore. London, J.M. Dent & Sons; New York, E.P. Dutton & Co. Inc., 1938. xxiv, 293p. **265**

MILBURN, R. GORDON. The religious mysticism of the Upanishads. London, Theosophical Publishing House, 1924. 1000p. **266**

MONIER-WILLIAMS, Sir MONIER. Brahmanism and Hinduism. London, J. Murray, 1891. 4th ed. xxvii, 603p. **267**
    A scholarly survey of the Hindu tradition, including the early Vedic period, based mainly on sacred texts.

MUIR, JOHN. On the principal deities of the Rigveda. (In Royal Society of Edinburgh. Transactions. Edinburgh, 1864. v. 23. p. 547-579) **268**

MULLER, FRIEDRICH MAX. Three lectures on Vedanta philosophy, delivered at the Royal Institution in March 1894. By F. Max Muller. London, and New York, Longmans, Green & Co., 1894. vii, 173p. **269**

——Upanishads. Oxford, Clarendon Press, 1926. 2 vols. **270**
    Contains scholarly translations of eleven of the most important Upanishads.

——The Vedas. Calcutta, Susil Gupta, 1956. **271**
    Written in the 19th century, it is an abridged edition of his books on the significance of the Vedas.

MULLER, FREDRICK MAX. *tr.* Vedic Hymns. Oxford, Clarendon Press, 1891-1972. **272**
    A scholarly translation of major portions of the most ancient of the Vedic Samhitas, the Rigveda.

OLDENBERG, H., *tr.* The Grihya-Sutras: Rules of domestic Vedic ceremonies. Oxford, Clarendon Press, 1886-92. 2 vols. **273**

OMAN, JOHN CAMPBELL. The Brahmans, Theists, and Muslims of India. London, T. Fisher Unwin, 1907. xv, 342p. **274**
    "Studies of Goddess worship in Bengal, Caste, Brahmanism and social reforms, with descriptive sketches of curious festivals, ceremonies and faquirs". *t.p.*

STEVENSON, Mrs SINCLAIR. The rites of the twice-born. Foreword by A. Macdonell. London, Oxford University Press, 1920. xxiv, 474p. **275**
    A study of Brahmanical ceremonies.

THIBAUT, GEORGE FREDERICK WILLIAM. The Vedantasutras with the commentary by Sankaracarya (pt. 3 with the commentary of Ramayana). Translated by G. Thibaut. 1890-1904. (The sacred books of the East, etc.) vol. 34, 38, 48. **276**

WHITNEY, W.D. AND C.R. LANMAN, *trs.* Atharva Veda Samhita. Cambridge, Harvard University Press, 1905. **277**
    A scholarly translation with a critical and exegetical commentary.

WILKINS, WILLIAM J. Hindu mythology: Vedic and Puranic. Calcutta, Thacker, Spink, 1882. x, 423p. **278**
    A good source book on myths and legends of Hinduism.

WILSON, H.H., *tr.* Rigveda Sanhita. Bangalore, H.H. Wilson, Bangalore Printing and Publishing Co., 1946. 2nd ed. **279**
    First published in 1850, it is a reprint of the author's original translation in English.

(iii) Hinduism

BARNETT, LIONEL DAVID. The heart of India. London, John Murray, 1908. 122p. **280**
    "Sketches on the history of Hindu religion and morals."

BARNETT, LIONEL DAVID. Hinduism. London, Archibald Constable & Co., 1906. vi, 66p. **281**
    A brief appraisal.

BERNARD, THEOS. Hindu philosophy, New York, Philosophical Library, 1947. 207p. **282**
    Gives the essence of seven classic systems of Hindu philosophy. Includes a detailed bibliography.

BROWN, BRIAN, ed. The wisdom of the Hindus; the wisdom of the Vedic hymns, the Brahmanas, the Upanishads, the Mahabharata and the Ramayana, the Bhagavad-Gita, the Vedanta and the Yoga philosophies; wisdom from the ancient and modern literature of India. New York, Brentano's, 1921. xxvi, 293p. **283**

CAMPBELL, JOSEPH. The masks of God: Oriental Mythology. New York, Viking Press, 1962. 564p. **284**
    Controversial interpretation of Hindu mythology which may not be accepted by many Indian scholars.

CHAPLIN, DOROTHEA. Matter, myth, and spirit or Celtic and Hindu links. New rev. ed. London, Rider & Co., 1935. xii, 13-224p. **285**

DANIELOU, ALAIN. Hindu polytheism. New York, Pantheon Books, 1962. **286**

DOWSON, JOHN. A classical dictionary of Hindu mythology and religion. London, Routledge and Kegan Paul, 1961. **287**
    A useful reference work, containing the names and characteristics of Hindu deities, mythical beings, and places mentioned in Sanskrit texts. The work suffers from many inaccuracies.

ELIOT, Sir CHARLES N.C. Hinduism and Buddhism: a historical sketch. New York, Barnes & Noble, 1954. 3 vols. **288**
    Originally published in 1921, this work is of the best introductions to Hinduism and Buddhism.

FARQUHAR, JOHN NICHOL. The crown of Hinduism. London, Oxford University Press, 1930. 469p. **289**
    First published in 1913, it is an attempt to explore the relationship between Hinduism and Christianity.

——Primer of Hinduism. London, Oxford University Press, 1912. 2nd ed. 222p. illus. **290**

A work for general reader, provides the main features of Hinduism from pre-historic to modern times.

GUENON, RENE. Introduction to the study of the Hindu doctrines. Tr. from the original French by Marco Pallis. London, Luzac & Co., 1945. 351p. (F.) **291**

HAIGH, HENRY. Leading ideas of Hinduism. Calcutta, Susil Gupta, 1959. 113p. **292**

First published in 1903, it is a reprint of the thirty-second Fernley lecture delivered in Manchester, 1902.

HARRISON, MAX HUNTER. Hindu monism and pluralism, as found in the Upanishads and in the philosophies dependent upon them. Madras, Oxford University Press, 1932. xiv, 324p. **293**

HOWELLS, GEORGE. The soul of India, London, James Clarke & Co., 1913. 623p. **294**

An introduction to the study of Hinduism, in its historical setting and development, and in its internal and historical relations to Christianity.

JACOBS, HANS. Western Psychotherapy and Hindu Sadhana. London, International Universities Press, 1961. 231p. **295**

Beautifully written, it is a comparative study of concepts and methods employed by Freud, Jung and the Hindu tradition of religious exercises.

KENNEDY, VANS. Researches into the nature and affinity of ancient and Hindu mythology, by Lieutenant Colonel Vans Kennedy. London, Printed for Longman, Rees, Orme, Brown, and Green. 1831. xx, 494p. **296**

"Translations from the Puranas, Upanishads, etc. p. 423-494".

MACKENZIE, JOHN. Hindu ethics: a historical and critical essay. London, Oxford University Press, 1922. xii, 267p. **297**

"A scientific investigation into the ethical side of Hindu teaching".

MACNICOL, NICOL, ed. Hindu scriptures. New York, Dutton, 1938. xxiv, 293p. (Everyman's library, ed. by Ernest Rhys). **298**

An anthology of translations by Western scholars including R. Griffith and M. Muller.

MONIER-WILLIAMS, Sir MONIER. Brahmanism and Hinduism; or, religious thought and life in India, as based on the Veda and other sacred books of the Hindus. By Sir Monier, Monier-Williams. 4td ed., enl. and impr. London, J. Murray, 1891. xxii (i) 603p. front. (port). **299**

———Hinduism, by Monier Williams. Published under the direction of the Committee of General Literature and Education appointed by the society for promoting Christian knowledge; New York, Pott., Young & Co., 1877. 1, 1. 238p. front. (fold. map.). **300**

    Reprinted by Susil Gupta, Calcutta, in 1951.

MORGAN, KENNETH W. The religion of the Hindus. New York, Ronald, 1953. 434p. **301**

    The first book in English setting forth the beliefs and practices of the Hindus written by devout Hindus and designed to give a sympathetic understanding of Hinduism. The contributors are seven noted Indian scholars.

O'MALLEY, LEWIS, S.S. Popular Hinduism, the religion of the masses. New York, Macmillan, 1935. viii, 246p. **302**

    An account of the deities, beliefs and rites considered by some scholars to be a distinct level of Hinduism.

POTTER, KARL H. Presuppositions of India's philosophies. Englewood, Cliffs, New Jersey, Prentice-Hall, 1963. **303**

    A comparative study of the basic principles of the Hindu, Buddhist and Jain schools of philosophy.

RENOU, LOUIS. Religions of ancient India, *tr.* by S.M. Fynn. London, the University, 1953. ix, 139p. School of Oriental and African Studies, London University. Jordon lectures in comparative religion, 1951. **304**

    An appraisal of Hinduism and Jainism.

RENOU, LOUIS, *ed.* Hinduism. New York, G. Braziller, 1961. **305**

    Contains an anthology of translations by various indologists of Sanskrit sources that convey the principal ideas and practices of Hinduism from Vedic to modern times.

RIEPE, DALE. The naturalistic tradition in Indian thought. Seattle, University of Washington Press, 1960. **306**

    A critical review of Indian philosophical writings from

100 Philosophy 200 Religion

500 B.C. to A.D. 500 concerning Hinduism, Jainism and Buddhism.

SCHOMERUS, HILKO WIARDO. Der Caiva Siddhanta; eine Mystik Indiens. Nach den tamulischen Quellen bearbeitet und dargestellt. Leipzig, 1912. xi, 444p. (G). **307**

SCOTT, ROLAND W. Social ethics in modern Hinduism. Calcutta, Y.M.C.A. Publishing House, 1953. viii, 243p. (Religious quest of Indian series). **308**

> Examines the nature and development of Hindu ethical thought from the early nineteenth century to the beginning of India's national independence.

SLATER, T.E. The higher Hinduism in relation to Christianity; certain aspects of Hindu thought from Christianity standpoint. Introduction by John Henry Barrows. London, Elliot Stock, 1903. viii, 291p. **309**

SLOVYNS, FRANCOIS BALTHAZAR. Les Hindous, per F. Balthazar Solvyns. Paris, L' auteur (etc.). 1808-12. 4v. 288 col. pl. (part. fold). Title vignette in colours. Half title page: Les Hindous on description de leurs moeurs, costumes et ceremonies. (F.). **310**

> French and English "The English text by Mmne. Solvyns. The preliminary discourse by G.B. Depping".

THOMAS, WENDELL MARSHALL. Hinduism invades America. New York, The Beacon Press, Inc., 1930. 300p. **311**

> An account of the serious impact on American life of Hindu philosophy and culture, especially in the form of organized religion.

UNDERHILL, MURIEL M. The Hindu religious year. London. Oxford University Press, 1921. 194p. (The religious life of India, ed. by J.N. Farquhar and Nicol Macnicol). **312**

> A study of festivals and religious customs connected with the Hindu calendrical cycle including information on religious fairs, auspicious and inauspicious seasons, and places of pilgrimage.

VOGEL, JEEN P. Indian serpent-lore or the Nagas in Hindu legend. London, A. Probsthain, 1926, xiv, 318p. 30 plates. **313**

> The leading snake stories from the Vedas, the Buddhist

birth-tales and early Greek travellers.

WEBER, MAX. The religion of India, the sociology of Hinduism and Buddhism, translated and edited by H.H. Gerth and D. Martindale. Glencoe, Ill., Free Press, 1958. 392p. **314**
    First published in 1921 in German it is one of the standard work on the sociology of Hinduism and Buddhism.

WILSON, HORACE N. Religious sects of the Hindus. Edited by E.R. Rost. Calcutta, Susil Gupta, 1958. 2nd ed. 221p. **315**
    An appraisal of various popular Hindu sects mainly of North India.

ZAEHNER, ROBERT CHARLES. Hinduism. London, Oxford University Press, 1962. 272p. **316**
    An appraisal of the Hindu religious beliefs with special reference to their utility in the present day India.

(iv) Philosophical Systems, Epics and Puranas

ARCHER, WILLIAM GEORGE. The loves of Krishna. London, G. Allen & Unwin, 1957. 127p. **317**
    An appraisal of the Bhagavata Purana and an estimate of the life and work of Lord Krishna, with special emphasis on his early life.

EDGERTON, FRANKLIN, *tr.* Bhagavad Gita. New York, Harper Torchbook, 1952. 2 vols. (Harvard Oriental series ed. by Walter Eugene Clark, 38 and 39). **318**
    First edition published by Harvard University Press in 1944 in two volumes. This one volume paperbound edition includes the preface and the Sanskrit text is omitted.

———The Mimamsa Nyaya Prakasa of Apadevi. New Haven, Yale University Press, 1929. iv, 308p. **319**
    A translation of an elementary Mimansa manual or text book written in the 17th century.

FAUSBOLL, MICHAEL VIGGO. Indian mythology according to the Mahabharata, in outline by V. Fausboll. London, Luzac & Co. (Copenhagen, printed by Nielsen & Lydiche) 1903. 4, 1 (vii)—xxxii, 206p. (Half title: Luzac's oriental religions series).
320

100 Philosophy   200 Religion

GEAR, JOSEPH. The adventures of Rama. Boston, Mass. Brown. 1954. 210p. **321**
   The story of the great Hindu epic with a chapter on the Ram Lila.

GRIFFITH, R.T.H., *tr.* The Ramayana of Valmiki. Benares, E.J. Lazarus, 1895. xv, 195p. **322**
   One of the best translations of the Ramayana ever done by a Westerner.

GRIFFITH, RALPH THOMAS HOTCHKIN, *ed.* & *tr.* Scenes from the Ramayana, etc., by Ralph T.H. Griffith. London, Trubner & Co., Benares, E.J. Lezarus & Co., etc. etc., 1968. xv, 196p. **323**

HALL, FITZEDWARD. A contribution towards an index to the bibliography of the Indian philosophical systems, by Fitzedward Hall. Pub. by order of the Govt. N.W.L. Calcutta, Printed by C.B. Lewis. Baptist Mission Press, 1859. 1, ii, 1. 1., 236p. **324**

HILL, W.D.P., *tr.* The Holy Lake of the acts of Rama. London, Oxford University Press, 1952. xxxvii, 538p. **325**
   An excellent translation of Ramacharita Manasa, originally written in Hindi in 16th century by Tulsidasa.

HOPKINS, EDWARD WASHBURN. Epic mythology by Washburn Hopkins. Staranburg. K.J. Trubner, 1915. 2p. 1 277p. (Grundriss der Indoarischen philologie und altertumskunde (Encyclopedia of Indo-Aryan research) begrindet von G. Buehler. III bd. 1 hft. B.). **326**
   A useful work, describes gods and heroes mentioned in the Ramayana and Mahabharata.

——The great epic of India; its character and origin, by E. Washburn Hopkins. New York, C. Scribner's Sons, 1901. xvip. 1 1., 485p. (Half title: Yale bicentennial publication). **327**

——The mutual relations of the four castes according to the Manavadharmacastram. Leipzig, Breikppt and Hartel, 1881. vi, 114 (1)p. **328**

INGALLS, DANIEL HENRY HOLMES. Materials for the study of Navya-Nyaya logic. Cambridge, Harvard University Press, 1951. viii, 182p. (Harvard oriental series, edited by Walter

Eugene Clark, 40). **329**

KEITH, ARTHUR B. Indian logic and atomism. Oxford, Clarendon Press, 1921. 291p. **330**
    A survey of the literature and basic concepts of two systems of Indian philosophy.

——The Karm Mimamsa. London, Oxford University Press, 1921. iv, 112p. (The heritage of India series). **331**
    A simple interpretation of Purana Mimamsa to Western readers.

——The Samkhya system: a history of Samkhya philosophy. Calcutta, YMCA Publishing House, 1949. 2nd ed. iii, 126p. (Heritage of India series). **332**
    First published in 1918, it is a brief historical survey of the oldest school of Hindu philosophy.

MULLER, F. MAX. The six systems of Indian philosophy. London, Longmans, Green, 1919. xxxii, 478p. **333**
    An evaluation of six systems of Indian philosophy.

PARGITER, FREDERICK EDEN. The Purana text of the dynasties of the Kali Age with introduction and notes. London H. Milford, 1913. xxxiv, 97p. **334**

SINGER, MILTON, *ed.* Krishna: myths, rites and attitudes. East-West Center, 1966. 277p. **335**

WILSON, H.H., *tr.* The Vishnu Purana. Calcutta, Punthi Pustak, 5 vols. 1961. **336**
    It is a reprint of the author's work first published in 5 vols. in London in 1840. The Vishnu Purana which is one of the most important eighteen Puranas, deals with the creation and destruction of universe, the genealogy of gods, and the legends associated with ancient rulers.

(v) Jainism

ABBOTT, JUSTIN EDWARDS, *tr.* Dasopant Digambar. Poona, Scottish Mission Industries Co., 1928. ix, 81p. **337**

BASHAM, ARTHUR LLEWELLYN. History and doctrines of the Ajivikas. A vanished Indian religion, etc. London, Luzac & Co., 1951. xxxii, 304p. viii pl. **338**

100 Philosophy   200 Religion

BLOOMFIELD MAURICE. Life and stories of the Jaina savior Parecvantha. Baltimore, Johns Hopkins. 1919. 254p.   **339**
   An academic edition which includes translations of several previously unpublished stories, from manuscript sources.

BUHLER, JOHANN GEORG. On the Indian sect of the Jains. Translated from the German and edited with an outline of Jaina mythology by Jas Burgess. London, Luzac & Co., 1903. iv, 79p.   **340**

FRANKLIN, WILLIAM. Researches on the tenets and doctrines of the Jeynes and Boodhists conjectures to be the Brahmanas of ancient India. In which is introduced a discussion on the worship of the serpent in various countries of the world. By Lieut. Col. William Franklin. London, Printed for the author, and sold by J. Rodwell, 1827. vi, (2) 213, (1) p. 1. 1. plates.   **341**

GLASENAPP, HELMUTH VON. The doctrine of Karma in Jain philosophy. Tr. from the original German by G. Barry Gifford. and rev. by the author. Bombay, Bai Vijibai Jivanlal Panolal Charity Fund, 1942. xxvi, 104p. (G.)   **342**

GUERINOT, A. La religion Djaina. Paris, Louvain (printed), 1926. viii, 351p. xxv pl. (F.)   **343**

JACOBI, H.G., tr. Gaina Sutras. Oxford, Clarendon Press, 1884-95. 2 vols.   **344**
   A translation of ancient Jain texts containing the fundamental tenets of Jain religious belief and practice. It also includes an account of the life and teaching of the historic Jain founder, Mahavira and his legendary predecessors.

SCHUBRING, WALTHER. Die Lehre der Jainas. nach den alten Quellen dargestellt. Berlin & Leipzig, 1935. 251p. (G.).   **345**
────── The doctrine of the Jainas, translated by W. Beurlen. Delhi, Motilal Banarsidas, 1962. 335p.   **346**
   A scholarly work in German based on the study of ancient Jain texts.

SMITH, VINCENT ARTHUR. The Jain stupa and other antiquities of Mathura, by Vincent A. Smith. Allahabad, Printed by F. Luker, Superintendent Govt. Press, 1901. 2p. 1., iip., 2 1., iii, 63p. cvii (i.e. 109) pl. incl. front. (map) plans. (Half title page: Archaeological survey of India. New imperial series, vol. xx. North Western provinces and Oudh, vol. v). **347**

STEVENSON, MRS SINCLAIR. The heart of Jainism. Introduction by G.P. Taylor. London, Humphrey Milford, Oxford, University Press, 1915. xxiv, 336p. **348**

THOMAS, EDWARD. Jainism, or the early faith of Asoka, with illustrations of the ancient religions of the East, from the pantheon of the Indian scythiens. To which is prefixed, a notice on Bactrian coins and Indian dates. By Edward Thomas. London, Trubner & Co., 1877. viii, (3)—23, (3)—82p. illus. pl. facsim. **349**

WILLIAMS, R. Jaina Yoga: a survey of the mediaeval Sravakacaras. London, Oxford University Press, 1963. xxx, 296p. **350**

A study of Jain treatises, dating from the 5th to the 13th centuries, concerning the proper way of life for Jain layman.

(vi) Buddhism

ALEXANDER, P. C. Buddhism in Kerala. Annamalainagar, the University of Kerala, 1949. viii, 206, xp. **351**

Thesis approved for D. Litt. by the Annamalai University.

BARTH, MARIE ETIENNE AUGUSTE. Bulletin des religions de l'Inde; Bouddhism, Jainisme, par A. Barth. Paris, E. Leroux, 1894. Cover title, 85p. **352**

BESWICK, ETHEL. Jataka tales. London, J. Murray, 1956. 114p. **353**

A collection of thirty-three tales of the Buddha's former births.

BURLINGAME, EUGENE WATSON. Buddhist parables. Translated from the original Pali. New Haven, Yale University Press, London, Humphrey Milford, Oxford University Press, 1922. xxix, 348p. **354**

BURNOUF, EUGENE. Legends of Indian Buddhism. Translated with introduction by Winifred Steplevs. London, John

Murray, 1911. 128p. **355**

BURTT, E.A., *ed.* The teachings of the compassionate Buddha. New York, New American Library, 1955. 247p. **356**
   The early discourses, the Dhammapada, and later basic writings especially compiled for this paperbound edition.

BU-STON RIN-CHEN-GRUH-PA. History of Buddhism. Tr. from the Tibetan by E. Obermiller. Heidel-berg, Harrassowitz, 1931-32. 2 vols. **357**
   A detailed history of Buddhism in India and Tibet.

CONZE, EDWARD. Buddhism: its essence and development, Oxford; Cassirer, 1951. Paperbound edition was published by Harper of New York in 1959. 212, 10p. **358**
   This book can serve a useful introduction to Buddhism for Western readers.

CONZE, EDWARD, *ed.* Buddhist texts. Edited by Edward Conze in collaboration with I. B. Horner. New York, Philosophical Library, 1954. 322p. **359**

———Buddhist thought in India. London, G. Allen and Unwin, 1962. 302p. **360**
   A summary of the origin and development of Buddhism in India.

COWELL, EDWARD B., *ed.* The Jataka or stories of the Buddha's former births. Cambridge, University Press, 1895-1913, 7 vols. **361**
   A collection of over five hundred brief tales of Buddha's former births, translated by several scholars.

DAHlKE, PAUL. Buddhism and its place in the mental life of mankind. London, Macmillan & Co., 1927. viii, 254p. **362**

DAVID-NEEL, ALEXANDRA. Buddhism: its doctrines and its methods. Translated from French into English by H.N.M. Hardy and Bernard Miall. London, John Lane the Bodley Head, 1939. 299p. **363**

DAVIDS, CAROLINE AUGUSTA (FOLLEY) RHYS. The birth of Indian psychology and its development in Buddhism. London, Luzac & Co. 1936. xii, 444p. **364**

———Buddhism: a study of the Buddhist norm. London, Williams and Norgate, 1912. 255p. **365**
   A study of the Buddhist concept of five-fold order.

DAVIDS, C.A.F. RHYS, *ed.* Outlines of Buddhism: a historical sketch. London, Methuen & Co., 1934. viii, 117p. **366**

DAVIDS, C.A.F. RHYS, *ed.* Sacred books of the Buddhists. Oxford, Oxford University Press, 1899. v. **367**
  A collection of translations by several scholars of the Buddhist text.

DAVIDS, THOMAS WILLIAMS RHYS. Buddhism. In: The message of the world's religions, etc. London, Society for promoting Christian knowledge, 1898, p. 23-40. **368**

—— Buddhism, its history and literature. N.Y., G.P. Putnams Sons, 1896. xiii, 230p. **369**
  Lectures delivered at Cornell University, Ithaca, New York, under the auspices of the American Committee for lectures on the history of religions.

DAVIDS, THOMAS WILLIAMS RHYS, *ed.* Pali text society translation series. London, Pali Text Society, 1909. London, University Press for the Pali Text Society, 1909. v. **370**
  A collection of translations by various scholars.

EBERSOLE, ROBERT. Black Pagoda. Florida, University of Florida Press, published with assistance from the Ford Foundation, 1957. 105p. **371**

EVOLA, GIULIO CESARE ANDREA. The doctrine of awakening, a study on the Buddhist ascetic. Translation from Italian by H.E. Musson. London, Luzac & Co., 1951. ix, 310p. (I.) **372**

FEER, LEON. Le Bouddhisme a Siam; une soiree chez le phraklang en 1863. Le dernier roi de Siam et ses projets de reforme religeuse. *In* Societe academique indochinoise, Paris, Memoires, Paris, 1879. v. 1, p. (146)—162. port. (F.) **373**

FOUCHER, ALFRED CHARLES. The beginnings of Buddhist art and other essays in Indian and Central-Asian archaeology; rev. by the author and tr. by L.A. Thomas and F.W. Thomas, with a preface by the latter. London, Humphrey Milford, Oxford University Press; Paris, Paul Genthnr, 1917. xvi, 316p. Plates are accompanied by guard-sheets with descriptive letterpress. **374**

——The life of the Buddha. Translated by S.B. Boas. Middletown, Wasleyan University Press, 1963. 272p. **375**
  An abridged edition of *La Vie du Bouddha* first published

in 1949.

FOUCHER, ALFRED CHARLES. On the iconography of the Buddha's nativity, *tr.* by H. Hargreaves. Delhi, Manager of Publications, 1946. ii, 27p. plates. (Memoirs: Archaeological Survey of India, 1946). Plates are accompanied by leaves with descriptive letterpress. **376**

GODDARD, DWIGHT, *ed.* A Buddhist Bible. New York, E.P. Dutton & Co., 1952. 667p. **377**

GRIMM, GEORGE. The doctrine of the Buddha. Berlin, Akademie Verlag, 1958. 2nd rev. ed. 536p. **378**

A detailed introduction to the development of Buddhist doctrine in India.

—— The religion of reason. Leipzig, Offizin W. Drugulin, 1926. xxiv, 536p. **379**

GRUNWEDEL, ALBERT. Mythologic des Buddhismus in Tibet und der Mongolei Fuhrer durch dielamaistische sammlung des fursten E. Uchtomskij. Von Albert Grunwedel. Mit Einem einleitenden vorwort des fursten E. Uchtomskiji und 188 abbildungen. Leipzig, F.A. Brockhans, 1900. xxxv, (1), 244p. front. (port.) illus. (G.). **380**

GUENTHER, HERBERT V. Philosophy and psychology in the Abhidharma. Lucknow, Buddha Vihara, 1957. xii, 404p. **381**

An exposition of psychological views contained in Abhidharma texts, presented in modern philosophical terms.

HACKMAN, HEINRICH FRIEDRICH. Buddhism as a religion, its historical developments and its present conditions. London, Probsthain & Co., 1910. xiii, 315p. (G.). **382**

Originally published in German. This English edition is revised and enlarged by the author.

HAMILTON, CLARENCE H., *ed.* Buddhism, a religion of infinite compassion. New York, Liberal Arts Press, 1952. **383**

A popular version of Buddhism and a collection of Buddhist teachings.

HANAYAMA, SHINSHO. Bibliography on Buddhism. Edited by the Commemoration Committee for Professor Shinsho Hanayama's sixty-first birthday. Tokyo, Hokuseido Press, 1961. **384**

A comprehensive bibliography of materials on Buddhism

published in European languages prior to 1928.

HARDY, ROBERT SPENCE. The legends and theories of the Buddhists, compared with history and science: with introductory notices of the life and system of Goutama Buddha. London & Edinburgh, Williams and Norgate, 1866. lvi, 244p.   **385**

────── tr. A manual of Buddhism in its modern development; translated from Sinhalese Mss. London, Partiridge and Oakey 1853. 3p. 1. (ix)—xvi, 533 (1)p.   **386**

HILLIARD, FREDERICK H. The Buddha, the Prophet, and the Christ. New York, Macmillan, 1956. 169p.   **387**

    From a series entitled "Ethical and Religious Classics of East and West".

HODGSON, BRAIN HOUGHTON. Illustrations of the literature and religion of the Buddhists. Serampore, 1841. 1p. 1. ill. p. 11, 220p. 2 fold. pl.   **388**

    Papers reprinted from the transactions and journal of the Asiatic Society of Bengal and London.

HUMPHREYS, CHRISTMAS. Buddhism. Harmondsworth, England, 1955. 169p.   **389**

    This Penguin paperbound edition is a general survey of the history, and teaching of Buddhism. Useful for general readers.

    Also published under the title Studies in the Middle way: being thoughts on Buddhism applied by Allen Co. 1959.

────── A popular dictionary of Buddhism. London, Arco Publications, 1962. 223p.   **390**

    A useful reference tool.

KEITH, ARTHUR B. Buddhist philosophy in India and Ceylon. Oxford, Clarendon, 1923. 339p.   **391**

    A scholarly interpretation of the Buddhist philosophy.

KERN, JOHAN HENDRIK CASPAR. Geschiedenis van het Buddhisme in Indie. 2 dln. Haarlem. 1882-84.   **392**

────── Manual of Indian Buddhism. 1896. 137p.   **393**

LEVI, SYLVAIN. Dictionarie encyclopedique bu Bouddhisme. Publie. sous la direction de S. Levi. et. J. Takakusu etc. 1929.   **394**

MALASEKERA, G.P., *ed*. Encyclopaedia of Buddhism. Colombo,

Government of Ceylon, 1961. 152p. **395**
    Contains relevant information on the origin and development of Buddhism throughout the world. It also gives information on the principles, rites and ceremonies of this great religion.

MONIER-WILLIAMS, Sir MONIER. Buddhism, in its connexion with Brahmanism and Hinduism, and in its contrast with Christianity, by Sir Monier Monier-Williams. London, J. Murray, 1889. xxx, (27), 563p. front. illus. plates, port., map. **396**

MORGAN, KENNETH W. The path of the Buddha. New York, Ronald, 1956. 432p. **397**
    Buddhism interpreted by Buddhists. A companion volume to The religion of the Hindus.

MULLER, FRIEDERICH MAX, *ed.* Buddhist texts from Japan. Oxford, Clarendon Press, 1881-84. 3v. facsims (part fold) fold. tab. **398**

——Lectures on the science of religion, with a paper on Buddhist nihilism and a translation of the Dhammapada or "Path of virtue". By Max Muller. New York, C. Scribner & Co., 1872. iv. 300p. **399**

——*tr.* The Dhammapada. Oxford, Clarendon Press, 1881. lv, 99p. **400**
    Forms volume 10 of the Sacred books of the east. This is a scholarly version of Buddhism.

OLDENBERG, HERMANN. Buddha: his life, his doctrine, his order. Tr. from the German by William Hoeg. Calcutta, Book Co., 1927. viii, 454p. (G.). **401**
    Sifts the legendary elements of Buddhist tradition and gives a reliable residium of facts concerning the Buddha's life.

PISCHEL, RICHARD. Lehen und lehre des Buddha, von Richard Pischel. 2 amfl., mit einer tafel. Leipzig, B.G. Trubner, 1910. vip. li., 126p. **402**

PRATT, JAMES B. Pilgrimage of Buddhism and a Buddhist pilgrimage. New York, Macmillan, 1928. xii, 758p. **403**
    A brief history of Buddhism.

ROSS, Sir EDWARD DENISON. Alphabetical list of the titles of works in the Chinese Buddhist Tripitaka, being an index to

Bunyiu Nanjio's catalogue and to the 1950 Kioto reprint of the Buddhist canon, prepared by E. Denison Ross. Calcutta, Superintendent Government Printing, India, 1910. 2p. 1, xcvii, (1). **404**

SAUNDERS, KENNETH. Epochs in Buddhist history. Chicago, the University Press, 1925. xlxi, 243p. **405**

SCHLAGINTWEIT, EMIL. Buddhism in Tibet illustrated by literary documents and objects of religious worship. With an account of the Buddhist systems preceding it in India by Emil Schlagintweit. With twenty tables of native print in the text. Leipzig F.A. Brockhaus. London, Trubner & Co., 1863. xxiv-p., 21. (3)—403, (1) p. illus. plates (part fold). facsims (part fold). **406**

——Le Bouddhisme an Tibet. Precede d'un resume des precedents systems bouddhiques dan l' Inde, par Emile de Schlagintweit', Tradvit de-l' anglais par L. de Millove Paris, E. Leroux. 1881. 2p. 1., xxxviiip., 1 1., 294p. xii, pl. (incl. facsims; part fold) (Annales du Musee Guimet. t. 3) (F.) **407**

SENART, EMILE CHARLES MARIE. Essai sur la legende du Buddha, son caactere et ses origines. par E. Senart. 2 ed., rev. et. suivie d'un index. Paris, E. Leroux, 1882. xxxv, 496p. (F). **408**

First published in the Journal Asiatique, 1873-1875.

SEWELL, ROBERT. Early Buddhist symbolism. London, Trubner & Co., 1886. cover title, 43p. illus. **409**

"From the 'Journal of the Royal Asiatic Society of Great Britain and Ireland', vol. xviii, pt. 3".

SINNETT, ALFRED PERCY. Estoeric Buddhism. Boston, Houghton, Mifflin & Co., 1884. 300p. Also published by Trubner & Co., London, in 1883. **410**

——Esoteric Buddhism, by A.P. Sinnett, 8th ed. annotated and enl. by the author. London, The Theosophical Publishing Society. Reprinted 1911. xxiii, 284p. **411**

SMITH, FREDERIC HAROLD. The Buddhist way of life: its philosophy and history. London, Hutchinson's University Library, 1951. 189p. **412**

SNELLGROVE, D.L. Buddhist Himalaya. New York, Philosophical Library, 1957. **413**

SNELLGROVE, D.L. The Havajra Tantra: a critical study, London, Oxford University Press, 1959. 2 vols. **414**
   A translation from Sanskrit and Tibetan of one of the most important texts of Tantric Buddhism.
STCHERBATSKY, TH. Buddhist logic. New York, Dover, 1962. **415**
   Originally published in 1932 in Leningrad by the Academy of Sciences of the USSR, it is a standard work on Buddhist logic of the Mahayana school of Dignaga.
——The central conception of Buddhism and the meaning of the word 'dharma'. London, Royal Asiatic Society, 1923. viii, 112p. **416**
THOMAS, EDWARD J. History of Buddhist thought. London, Kegan Paul, 1951. 2nd ed. xvi, 814p. **417**
   First published in 1933 it is a standard work of the history of Buddhist thought.
——The life of the Buddha as legend and history. New York, Barnes and Noble, 1952. 3rd rev. ed, xxi, 297p. **418**
   First published in 1927 by K. Paul, Trench, and Trubner of London, it is an appraisal of Buddha's life and thought.
THOMAS E.J., tr. The perfection of wisdom: the career of the predestined Buddhism. London, J. Murray, 1952. 316p. **419**
   A collection of translations from Sanskrit of Mahayana scriptures.
TURNER, SAMUEL. Ambassade au Thibet et an Boutan contenant des details tres curieux sur les moeurs, la religion, les productions et le commerce du Thibat, du Boutan et des Etats voisins, et une notice sur les evenemens quisy sont passes jusquien 1793. par M. Samuel Turner. traduit de langlais anec des notes, par j. Castera. Avec une collection de 15 planches, dessinees sur les liense, et gravees en taille-douce par Tardien laine. Paris, F. Buisson an ix (1800). 2v. and atlas (2p. 1, xv pl. incl. fold map, fold facsim). (F). **420**
TURNOUR GEORGE. The Mahavansa in Roman characters with the translation subjoined, and introductory essay on Pali Buddhistical literature, by the Hon. G. Turnour. Pali & English. Ceylon, 1837. v.1. **421**
WADDELL, LAURENCE AUSTINE. The Buddhism of Tibet, or

Lamaism with its mystic cults, symbolism and mythology and in its relation to Indian Buddhism. London, W.H. Allen & Co., limited, 1895, 2, 1, vii-xviii, 11, 598p. front. illus. plates (part fold). 2nd ed. published by W. Heffer & Sons, Cambridge (England), in 1934. **422**

―――The Buddhism of Tibet. Cambridge, Heffer, 1958. **423**

First published in 1895, it is an account of Lamaism which deals with the Tantric tradition with native forms of shamanism.

―――Lhasa and its mysteries, with a record of the expedition of 1903-1904. With 200 illustrations and maps. London, J. Murray, 1905. xxii, 580p. 11 col. front. plates, (part col.) ports (part fold.) plans, facsims. **424**

WARREN, H.C., tr. Buddhism in translations. Cambridge, (Mass.) Harvard University Press, 1953. **425**

First published as volume III in 1896, of the Harvard Oriental Series, it is a selected collection from the Pali texts.

WATTERS, THOMAS, tr. On Yuan Chwang's travels in India. London, Royal Asiatic Society, 1904-05. 2 vols. (Oriental Translation Fund: new series, 14 and 15). Vol. 2 contains two maps on xii itinerary by V.A. Smith. **426**

A useful account by a Chinese Buddhist pilgrim-scholar of Buddhism in India during the 17th century.

WOODWARD, F.L., tr. Some sayings of the Buddha. London, Oxford University Press, 1939. xii, 356p. **427**

This collection contains passages from the Vinaya Pitaka, the four great Nikayas and the short Nikayas.

(vii) Christianity

ANDREWS, CHARLES FREER. The renaissance in India: its missionary aspect. London, Church Missionary Society, 1912. xii, 310p. **428**

KENNEDY, JAMES. The doctrines of the Bible confirmed and illustrated by observation and experience. Mirzapore, Orphan School Press, 1876. xxiv, 221p. **429**

100 Philosophy 200 Religion

KENNEDY, JAMES. Christianity and the religions of India. Essays, etc. Mirzapore, 1874. **430**

LILLY, WILLIAM SAMUEL. Christianity and modern civilization, being some chapters in European history, with an introductory dialogue on the philosophy of history. London, Chapman & Hall, Ltd., 1903, xx, 374p. **431**

——The claims of Christianity. 2nd and cheaper edition. London, Chapman & Hall, Ltd., 1897. vi, (v)—xxxv, 258p. **432**

LONG JAMES. Handbook of Bengali missions, in connection with the Church of England. Together with an account of general educational efforts in north India. London, J.F. Shaw, 1848. vii. (1) 520p. front. (fold map) tables (1 fold). **433**

LUCAS, BERNARD. Christ for India. London, Macmillan & Co., 1910. xi, 448p. **434**

"A presentation of the Christian message to the religious thought of India". *t.p.*

MCKENZIE, JOHN. Two religions. Boston, Beacon Press, 1952. 9-143p. **435**

A comparative study of Christianity and Judaism.

MEDLYCOTT, A.E. India and the Apostle Thomas : an inquiry with a critical analysis of the Acta Thomae. London, David Nutt, 1905. xviii, 303p. **436**

MONIER-WILLIAMS, SIR MONIER. The Holy Bible and the sacred books of the East : four addresses; to which is added a fifth address on genana missions. London, Seeley & Co., 1887. vi, (7) 63p. **437**

PLATTNER FELIX A. Christian India. New York, Vanguard Press, 1957. **438**

A history of Roman Catholic missions in India.

SHERRING, Rev. MATHEW ATMORE. The history of Protestant missions in India from their commencement in 1706 to 1881. By the Rev. M.A. Sherring. New ed., carefully revised and brought down to-date, by the Rev. Edward Storrow. With four maps. London, The Religious Tract Society, 1884. xv, 463 (1)p. incl. tables. 4 fold. maps. (incl. front). **439**

SMITH, Rev. THOMAS D.D. *tr.* Modern missions and culture, by Warneck, G., translated by T. Smith. 1883. xxvii, 415p. **440**

SMITH, GEORGE. Short history of Christian missions from Abraham and Paul to Carey, Livingstone, and Duff, by George Smith. 9th thousand. 5th ed. rev. Edinburgh, T. & T. Clark, 1897. xiv, 252p. diagr. "Added title page: Handbooks for Bible classes and private students". **441**

TISSERANT, CARDINAL EUGENE. Eastern Christianity in India. Bombay Orient Longmans, 1957. **442**
    It is a revised version of a French work first published in 1941, regarding the history of the Syrian Christian Church in Malabar from earliest times to the present day.

YOUNGHUSBAND, Sir FRANCIS EDWARD. Mother world in travail for the Christ that is to be by Sir Francis Younghusband. London, Williams and Norgate, 1924. vii, 151p. **443**

(viii) Islam

BARTHOLD, VASILLI VLADIMIROVICH. Mussulman culture. *tr.* from the Russian by Shahid Suhrawardy. Foreword by Hassan Suhrawardy. Calcutta, the University, 1934. xxviii, 146p. (R) **444**

BESANT, ANNIE (WOOD). Beauties of Islam. Madras, Theosophical Publishing House, 1932. ii, 56p. **445**
    This lecture was first printed as Adyar popular lecture, no. 20 in 1912.

HERKLOTS, G.A., *tr.* Islam in India. London, Oxford University Press, 1921. rev. ed. xi, 374p. **446**
    It is a translation of Sharif Jafar's book in *Qanun-Islam* originally published in 1832. Includes Islamic manners and customs as practised in early 19th century India.

HOLLISTER, JOHN N. The Shia of India. London, Luzac, 1953. 440p. **447**
    An account of the history and contemporary role of Shiaism in India with particular reference to the Ismaili sect.

HOUTSMA, M. TH. AND OTHERS, *ed.* Encyclopedia of Islam: a dictionary of the geography, ethnography and biography of Muhammadan people. Leyden, Brill. 4 vols. and a supplement. **448**

IVANOV, VLADIMAR ALEKSICEVICH. A brief survey of the evolution of Ismailism. Leiden, E.J. Brill, 1952. 357p. **449**
   A useful introduction to the history and literature of the Ismaili sect from its origin to modern times.

LEITNER, GOTTLIEB WILLIAM. Muhammadanism. Being the report of an extempore address delivered at South Place Chapel, Finsbury, on Sunday afternoon, January 6, 1889. By G. W. Leitner. With appendices. working (Eng.). The Oriental Nobility Institute, 1889. 36p. **450**

MUIR, Sir WILLIAM. Annals of the early Caliphate, from original sources. London, Smith, Elder & Co., 1883. xix, 470p. fold. map **451**

——— The Caliphate: its rise, decline and fall from original sources. ed., rev. with maps. London. The Religious Tract Society, 1892, xv (1) 612p. fold. maps. **452**

———The life of Mohammad from original sources. A new and rev. ed. by T.H. Weir. Edinburgh, J. Grant, 1912. 2, 1., cxix, 556p. front., illus., plates, fold. maps, fold plans. **453**

———Mahomet and Islam; a sketch of the prophet's life from original sources and a brief outline of his religion. 3d ed. rev. London, Religious Tract Society, 1895. 256p. front., plates, maps. **454**

ROSS, Sir EDWARD DENISON. Islam. New York, J. Cape & H. Smith, 1931. 127p. **455**

WALTERS, HOWARD A. The Ahmadiya movement. Calcutta, YMCA, Association Press, 1918. **456**
   A study of a modern sect within Islam which was founded in Northern India in 1879.

WEIL, GUSTAV. A history of Islamic people. *tr.* from German by S. Khuda Buksh. Calcutta, the University, n.d. 178p. (G) **457**

   A descriptive account of Mohammad and the *Quran,* as also of the Caliphate.

(ix) Sikhism

ARCHER, JOHN CLARK. The Sikhs in relation to Hindus, Mos-

lems, Christians and Ahmadiyas. Princeton, Princeton University Press, 1946. xi, 351p. **458**
    A study in comparative religion, with special reference to Sikhism.

BARRIER, N. GERALD. The Sikhs and their literature. Delhi, Manohar Book Service, 1970. 153p. **459**
    A brief bibliography of the Sikh literature mainly written between 1849 and 1919.

EZEKIEL, I.A. Mystic meaning of "the word". Beas, Radhasoami, n.d. 16p. **460**

FIELD, DOROTHY. The religion of the Sikhs. London, John Murray, 1914. 114p. (Wisdom of the East series). **461**

FRIPP, PETER. Mystic philosophy of Sant Mat, as thought by the present spiritual master at the Radhasoami colony Beas, India. London, Spearman, 1964. 174p. front., illus. **462**

JOHNSON, JULLIAN P. Path of the Masters: the yoga of the audible life stream: a comprehensive statement of the teachings of the Great Masters of the East. abridged ed. Beas, Ahluwalia, n.d. xv+176p. front. **463**

MACAULIFFE, MAX A. Sikh religion: its gurus, sacred writings and authors. Oxford, Clarendon Press, 1909. 6 vols. **464**
    A monumental work on Sikhism. Contains a detailed account of the life and teachings of the Sikh Gurus, or religious leaders, accompanied by extensive translations of the writings now held to be sacred.

MACULIFFE, MAX A. AND OTHERS. Sikh religion: a symposium. Calcutta, Susil Gupta, 1958. **465**
    A collection of five essays written by well known scholars, between 1810 and 1925.

TRUMPP, EARNEST, tr. Adi Granth; or, The Holy scriptures of the Sikhs; tr. from the original Gurmukhi, with introductory essays by Earnest Trumpp. 2nd ed. Delhi, Munshi Ram Manoharlal, 1970. cxxxviii, 715p. **466**

WASON, KATHERINE. Living Master. Beas, Radhasoami Satsang, 1966. x, 316p. front. **467**

WINDRESS, KATHRYN. Prayer. Beas, Radhasoami Satsang, 1964. 88p. **468**

WOOD, FLORA E. In search of the way: a diary. Beas, Radhasoami Satsang, 1965. xvi, 154p. illus. **469**

(x) Tantrism

GUENTHER, HERBERT V. Yuganaddha: the Tantric view of life. Banaras, Chowkhamba Sanskrit Series, 1952. xiii, 195p. **470**
    This study is based upon an interpretation of the original sources.

WOODROFFE, Sir JOHN GEORGE (ARTHUR AVALON, *pseud*) Garlann of letters. Madras, Ganesh, 1955. 3rd ed. **471**
    Contains a collection of a few essays on the *Mantra-Shastra* or Tantrism.

―― Introduction to Tantra Sastra. Madras, Ganesh, 1956. 3rd ed. vii. 151p. **472**
    First published in 1913, it is a brief account of the principles and practices of the Tantric traditions, with special reference to Vedic tradition.

―― Serpent power. Madras, Ganesh, 1958. 6th ed. 183p. **473**
    A study of the principles and practices of Yoga from the point of Tantrism.

―― Shakti and Shakta. Madras, Ganesh, 1959. 5th rev. ed. xviii, 734p. 1st published in 1918. **474**
    A collection of essays on the doctrines and practices of Tantric cults. This book is mainly meant for a general reader.

―― The world as power. Madras, Ganesh, 1957. 2nd ed. 118p. **475**
    Includes the first five books of a series written to explain to a common reader the basic principles of Tantrism.

WOODROFFE, Sir, JOHN GEORGE. *ed.* Principles of Tantra by Shiva C.V. Bhattacharya. Madras, Ganesh, 1952. 2nd ed. xii, 1172p. **476**
    First published in two volumes in London by Luzac, in 1914-16, it is a detailed study of the principles and practices of the Tantric tradition.

(xi) Theosophy

ARUNDALE, GEORGE SYDNEY. Freedom and friendship: the call of Theosophy and Theosophical Society. Madras, Theosophical Publishing House, 1935. xxxiv, 502p. **477**
    An analysis of the philosophy of Theosophy.

BESANT, ANNIE (WOOD). The ancient wisdom: an outline of Theosophical teachings. London, Theosophical Publishing Society, 1899. xiv, 432, liv p. **478**
    A survey of the general principles of the ancient religions of the world.

—— Death and after. London, Theosophical Publishing Society, 1901. 80p. **479**
    Seeks to explain some of the great truths that render life easier to bear and death easier to face.

—— Immediate future and other lectures. London, and Madras. Theosophical Publishing Society, 1911. viii, 176p. **480**
    Lectures delivered in Queen's Hall, London, about religion.

—— The path of disciplineship. 2nd ed. London, Theosophical Publishing Society, 1899. 150p. **481**
    Four lectures delivered at the Theosophical Society, Adyar, Madras, in 1895.

—— Reincarnation. London, Theosophical Publishing Society, 1892. 83p. (Theosophical manuals, 2). **482**

—— The seven principles of man. London, Theosophical Publishing Society, 1892. 82p. (Theosophical manuals, 1). **483**

—— Theosophy in relation to human life. Banaras and London, Theosophical Publishing Society, 1905. iv, 123p. **484**
    Four lectures delivered at the 29th anniversary meeting of the Theosophical Society at Banaras, December, 1904.

—— Thought power, its control and culture. London, Theosophical Publishing House, 1920. vi, 145p. **485**

—— Vegetarianism in the light of Theosophy. Adyar, Theosophical Publishing House, 1913. 28p. (Adyar pamphlets, 27). **486**

BLAVATSKY, HELENA PETROVNA. The secret doctrine: the synthesis of science, religion and philosophy. London, Theosophi-

cal Publishing House, 1950. 6 vols. **487**
    First published in 1888, it is a monumental work.
BLAVATSKY, HELENA PETROVNA. The Theosophical Society and the occult hierarchy. London, Theosophical Publishing House, 1925. 6p. **488**
    Three lectures delivered at Kensington Town Hall, London, to fellows of the Theosophical Society in Oct. 1925.

(xii) Vedanta

BARNETT, LIONEL DAVID. Brahma-Knowledge. London, John Murray, 1907. 113p. **489**
    "An outline of the philosophy of the Vedanta as set forth by the Upanishads and by Sankara".
DEUSSEN, PAUL. Das system des Vedanta. Leipzig, 1893. xv, 535p. (G.). **490**
────── The system of the Vedanta. Translated from the French by C. Johnston. Chicago, Open Court, 1912. xiv, 513p. **491**
    "According to Badarayana's Brahma-Sutras and Sankara's commentary thereon...a compendium of the dogmatics of Brahmanism from the standpoint of Sankara". t.p.
──────The philosophy of Vedanta in its relation to the occidental metaphysics. Bombay, Educational Society, 1893. xiv, 429p. (The religion and philosophy of India series). **492**
GUENON, RENE. Introduction to the study of the Hindu doctrines. Tr. from the original French by Marco Pallis. London, Luzac and Co., 1945. 351p. **493**
    Title in French: *Introduction general a' e' etude des doctrines Hindous'*.
──────Man and his becoming, according to the Vedanta. Translated from the French by R.C. Nicholson. New York, Noonday, 1958. xix, 267p. **494**
    Originally published in 1925, it is an interpretation of the Vedanta metaphysics by a Westerner of Westerners.
HAUGHTON, Sir GRAVER CHAMPENY. The exposition of the

Vedanta philosophy by H.T. Celebrooke. Vindicated; being a refutation of certain published remarks by Colonel Vans Kennedy. By Sir Graver C. Haughton. London, (Printed by J.L. Cox & Sons), 1835. 2, 1., 16, 10p. **495**

ISHERWOOD, CHRISTOPHER, *ed.* Vedanta for modern man, ed. with an introduction by Christopher Isherwood. London, George Allen & Unwin, 1952. xv, 410p. **496**

    A collection of writings by diverse hands.

—— Vedanta for the Western world. London, George Allen & Unwin, 1948. vii, 452p. **497**

    A collection of writings from Sri Chaitanya, Swami Vivekananda, Swami Shivananda, Swami Prabhavananda, Aldous Huxley, Christopher Isherwood and others.

JENNINGS, JAMES GEORGE, *ed.* and *tr.* The Vedantic Buddhism of the Buddha. London, Geoffrey Cumberledge. Oxford University Press, 1948. cxvii, 679p. **498**

    A collection of historical texts translated from the original Pali and edited by the author.

MULLER, FRIEDRICH MAX. Vedanta philosophy. Calcutta, Susil Gupta & Co. 1950. iv, 109p. **499**

    First published in 1894, it is a collection of three lectures delivered at the Royal Institution.

THIBAUT, G., *tr.* The Vedanta-sutras. Oxford, Clarendon Press, 1890-1904. 3 vols. **500**

    Also printed as vols. 34, 38 and 48 in *Sacred Books of the East,* it is a translation of the *Vedanta-Sutras* or Brahma Sutras, with commentaries.

WOOD, ERNEST. Vedanta dictionary. London, Peter Owen, 1964. 225p. **501**

    An introduction to the Vedanta philosophy, specially meant for general readers.

(xiii) Yoga

BEHANAN, KOVOOR T. Yoga, a scientific evaluation. New York, Macmillan, 1937. xviii, 270p. **502**

    A scientific appraisal of the yoga.

BRUNTON, PAUL. The hidden teaching beyond yoga. London, Rider & Co., 1941. 357p. **503**

——A search in secret India. London, Rider & Co., 1935. 312p. **504**
> It is an account of the Indian yogis of today from first-hand investigation.

COSTER, GERALDINE. Yoga and Western psychology: a comparison. London, Oxford University Press, 1934. iv, 249p. **505**

DANIELOV, ALAIN (SHIVA SHARAN). Yoga: the method of reintegration. London, Christopher Johnson, 1951. vi, 164p. 2nd ed. **506**
> A brief analysis of the principles and practice of Yoga—being largely a compilation from both the basic scriptures of Yoga and the teachings of a number of its living exponents.

ELIADE, MIRCEA. Yoga: immortality and freedom. Translated from the French by W.R. Trask. New York, Pantheon, 1958. xxii, 592p. **507**
> An appraisal of the history, theory and practice of Yoga from earliest times to the present day.

JOHNSTON, D., *tr.* The Yoga Sutras of Patanjali. London, J.M. Watkins, 1952. **508**
> Originally published in 1912, it is a translation with a brief commentary.

WOOD, ERNEST. Great systems of yoga. New York, Philosophical Library, 1954. 168p. **509**
> A useful study of the philosophy and practice of yoga.

WOODS, J.H., *tr.* The yoga system of Patanjali. Cambridge, Harvard University Press, 1927. 2nd ed. **510**
> Originally published as vol. 17 of the Harvard Oriental Series, it is a scholarly translation of Patanjali's system of yoga.

YEATS-BROWN, FRANCIS CHARLES CLAYPON. Yoga explained. London, Victor Gollancz, 1938. 288p. **511**
> Illustrations by Sheila Dunn and photographs by Howard Cosler.

YESUDIAN, SELVARAJAN AND HAICH, ELIZABETH. Yoga uniting East and West. New York, Harper, 1956. 161p. **512**

This book undertakes to bring together two human paths which lead to God: the individual path of the East and the collective path of the West.

(xiv) Other Sects and Cults

ALLISON, W.L. The Sadhs. Calcutta, YMCA Publishing House, 1935. x, 129p. (The religious life of India series). **513**

ARBERRY, ARTHUR JOHN. An introduction to the history of Sufism. London, Longmans, Green & Co., 1942. xx, 840p. **514**
Traces the origin and development of Sufi studies in the West.

BASHAM, ARTHUR LLWELLYN. History and doctrines of the Ajivikas. London, Luzac & Co., 1951. xxviii, 394p. **515**
An account of a vanished Indian religion.

BONDURANT, JOAN V. Conquest of violence : The Gandhian philosophy of conflict. Princeton, Princeton University Press, 1958. xvi, 256p. **516**
An exposition of Mahatma Gandhi's ideas on peaceful means for the resolution of conflict.

BRIGGS, GEORGE W. Gorakhnath and Kanphata yogis. Calcutta, YMCA Publishing House, 1938. xiv, 380p. (The religious life of India series). **517**
An exposition of the philosophy of a medieval North Indian saint Gorakhnath and Kanphata yogis.

BROWN, W. NORMAN, *ed. & tr.* The *Saundaryalahari* or Flood of Beauty. Cambridge, Harvard University Press, 1958. **518**
Beautifully illustrated, it is a translation of a Sanskrit poem belonging to Tantric Shaktism.

FISCHER, LOUIS. Gandhi: His life and message for the world. New York, New American Library, 1954. 189p. (Signet Key books). **519**

HOLMES, JOHN HAYNES. My Gandhi. New York, Harper, 1953. 186p. illus. **520**
A deeply moving testimony to what Gandhi's life meant to one of America's great liberal clergymen.

HOYLAND, J.S., *tr.* Tukaram: an Indian peasant mystic. London,

Allenson, 1932. 86p. **521**

Faithful translation of the hymns and devotional songs of the Maharashtrian poet, Tukaram who lived from 1608 to 1649. Tukaram was a great saint of the *bhakti* movement and was a devotee of the god Vithoba.

ISHERWOOD, CHRISTOPHER, *ed.* Vedanta for the Western world. London, George Allen & Unwin, 1948. 452p. **522**

Essays from Vedanta and the West, the magazine of the American Vedanta Society, by various writers, including Christopher Isherwood Aldous Huxley and John van Druten. The Society was established in New York in 1898, and now has over 1,200 members.

KEAY, FRANK E. Kabir and his followers. London, Oxford University Press, 1931. x, 186p. (The religious life of India series). **523**

A study of the history, literature, beliefs, and practices of the Kabir Panthis. Kabir was a great saint and lived in India in the 15th century.

KEITH, ARTHUR BERRIEDALE. The religion and philosophy of the Veda and Upanishads. Cambridge (Mass.), Harvard University Press, London, Humphrey Milford, Oxford University Press, 1925. 2 vols. (The Harvard oriental series, 31 and 32). **524**

KENNEDY, MELVILLE. T. The Chaitanya Movement: A study of the Vaishnavism of Bengal. Calcutta, YMCA Press, 1925. x, 270p. **525**

KINGSBURY, FRANCIS AND G.E. PHILIPS, *trs,* Hymns of the Tamil Saivite saints. London, Oxford University Press, 1921. viii, 132p. **526**

Faithful translation of hymns composed in Tamil between the 7th and 10th centuries by the saints of Shaivite section in South India.

KONOW, STEN AND TUXEN PAUL, *trs.* The religions of India. Tr. from Dutch. Copenhagan G.E.C. God Publisher, 194. 214p. illus. **527**

LEONARD, G.S. A history of the Brahmo Samaj. Calcutta, Adi Brahmo Samaj Press, 1934. 2nd ed. **528**

An account of the origin and expansion of the Brahmo

Samaj founded by Raja Ram Mohan Roy. The book covers the period up to 1878.

MACNICOL NICOL. Indian theism from the Vedic to the Muhammedan period. Edited by J.N. Farquhar and H.D. Griswold. Bombay, Oxford University Press, 1915. xvi, 292p. **529**

MULLER, F. MAX. Ramakrishna: his life and sayings. Mayavati, Almora, Advaita Ashrama, 1951. xi, 200p. First Indian edition. First published in 1898 in London. **530**

Originally published in 1899 by C. Scribner's Sons, New York, it is a biographical study of Sri Ramakrishna's life and thought.

OMAN, JOHN CAMPBELL. The mystics, ascetics and saints of India. London, T. Fisher Unwin, 1903. xv, 291p. **531**

"A study of sadhuism, with an account of the yogis, sanyasis, bairagis and other strange Hindu sectarians"—*t.p.*

ORR, WILLIAM G. A sixteenth-century Indian mystic. London, Butterworth Press, 1947. 238p. **532**

A biographical study of the life and thought of Dadu, founder of the Dadu Panthis.

OSBORNE, ARTHUR, *ed.* Collected works of Rama Maharshi. London, Rider, 1959. **533**

A collection of the writings of Rama Maharshi—a great mystic of modern India.

—— Ramana Maharshi and the path of self-knowledge. London, Rider, 1954. 207p. **534**

A biographical study of Ramana Maharshi's life and thought.

PALMER, EDWARD HENRY, *comp.* Oriental mysticism. Introduction by A.J. Arberry. London, Luzac & Co., 1938. 2nd ed. xviii, 84p. **535**

"A treatise on the Sufistic and unitarian theosophy of Persians ".—*t.p.*

PAYNE, EARNEST A. The Saktas : an introductory and comparative study. Calcutta, YMCA, 1933. xiv, 153p. **536**

PEARSON, NATHANIEL. Sri Aurobindo and the soul quest of man: three steps to spiritual knowledge. London, George Allen & Unwin, 1952. 127p. **537**

"A study of chapters 1 to 12 of Aurobindo's *The Life*

Divine".—t.p.

PIET, JOHN H. A logical presentation of the Saive Siddhanta philosophy. Madras, Christian Literature Society for India, 1952. xii, 190p. **538**

SHEEAN, VINCENT. Lead kindly light. New York, Random House, 1949. vii, 374p. **539**

    An intensely personal record of the author's progress to a philosophy of life based on Gandhiji's teachings.

SUBHAN, JOHN A. Sufism: its saints and shrines. Lucknow, Lucknow Publishing House, 1936. xii, 412p. **540**

    "An introduction to the study of Sufism with special reference to India".—t.p.

THOOTHI, N.A. The Vaishnavas of Gujarat. London, Longmans, 1935. xvi, 489p. **541**

    A study of devotional theism in Gujarat.

TUCCI, GIUSEPPE. The Theory and practice of Mandala. Translated by A.H. Brodrick. London, Rider, 1959. ix, 146p. **542**

    A study of symbolism of mystical ritual designs used in Hinduism and Tibetan Buddhism.

WESTCOTT, GEORGE H. Kabir and the Kabir Panth, Calcutta, Susil Gupta, 1953. 2nd ed, viii, 145p. **543**

    First published in 1907, it is a biographical study of the life and thought of Kabir (1440-1518).

YOUNGHUSBAND, Sir FRANCIS EDWARD. Modern mystics. London, J. Murray, 1935. viii, 315 (1)p. **544**

(xv) Jews

FERGUSSON, JAMES. The temples of the Jews and the other buildings in the Harom area at Jerusalem. London, J. Murray 1878. xviii, 304p. front. illus. spl. **545**

KELLOGG, SAMUEL HENRY. The Jews: or Prediction and fulfilment: an argument for the times, by Samuel H. Kellogg. New York, A.D.F. Randolph & Co., 1883. xx, 279p. **546**

LORD, J. HENRY. The Jews in India and the Far East. Bombay, S.P.C.K., Book Depot, 1907. vii, 120, 17p. **547**

Sources of Indian Civilization

(xvi) Zoroastrianism

HAUG, MARTIN. Essays on the sacred language, writings and religion of the Parsis. 4th ed. Edited and enlarged by E.W. West Ph. D. to which is also added a biographical memoir of the late Dr Haug. By Professor E.P. Evans. London, K. Paul, Trench, Trubner & Co., Ltd., 1907. xlviii, 427p. (Half title: Trubner's oriental series 1). **548**
    1st, 2nd and 3rd editions were published in 1862, 1878 and 1884, respectively.

HERZFELD, ERNEST EMIL. Zoroaster and his world. Princeton. University Press, 1947. 2 vols. illus. **549**

JACKSON, A.V. WILLIAMS. Zoroastrian studies. New York, Columbia University Press, 1928. xxxiii, 325p. **550**
    One of the best introduction of Zoroastrianism which was brought to India in 8th century by refugees fleeing the Arab conquest of Persia. The followers of the religion are known in India as Parsis. Their approximate number is 130,000 and they mostly live in Bombay.

WILSON, JOHN. The Parsi religion: as contained in the Zand Avasta, and propounded and defended by the Zoroastrians of India and Persia, unfolded, refuted and contrasted with Christianity. Bombay, American Mission Press, 1843. 610p. fold pl. **551**

300 SOCIAL SCIENCES

(i) Administration

BALFOUR, ELIZABETH. History of Lord Lytton's Indian administration, 1876-1880. London, Longmans, 1899. viii, 551p.   **552**

BLUNT, EDWARD ARTHUR HENRY. The I.C.S.: the Indian Civil Service. London, Faber & Faber, 1937. xiii, 291p.   **553**
   An ex-member of the ICS describes the British administration and its impact on the Indian people.

———Social service in India. London, H.M. Stationery Office, 1938. xxiii, 447p. plate, plan etc.   **554**
   "An introduction to some social and economic problems of the Indian people, written by six contributors"—*t.p.* The contributors are: A.H. Blunt; C.G. Chenevix-Trench, R.G. Allen, John W.D. Mcgaw George Anderson, Frank Noyce and C.F. Strickland.

BRAIBANTI, RALPH, *ed.* Administration and economic development in India. Published for the Duke University Commonwealth Studies Center by the Duke University, 1963. 312p.   **555**

CHAILLEY-BERT, M. JOSEPH. The administrative problems of the British India. Tr. from French by Sir William Meyer. London, Macnillan & Co., 1910. xv, 590p.   **556**

GILCHRIST, ROBERT NIVEN. The separation of executive and judicial functions. Calcutta, the University, 1923. x, 240p. **557**
    A study in the evolution of the Indian magistracy.

HUNTER, Sir WILLIAM WILSON. Bombay, 1885 to 1890, a study in Indian administration. London, H. Frowde, Bombay, B.M. Malobari, 1892. vii, 504p. **558**

KEENE, HENRY GEORGE. Indian administration: letters to a member of parliament on the Indian problem and its possible solution. London. 1867. 550p. **559**

MACONOCHIE, EVAN. Life in the Indian civil service, 1889-1921. London, Chapman & Hall, 1926. x, 269p. **560**

O'MALLEY, LEWIS SYDNEY STEWART. The Indian civil service, 1601-1930. London, J. Murray, 1931. xiv, 310p. **561**
    An analysis of the British bureaucracy in India.

STOCQUELER, JOACHIM HAYWARD. The British officer: his position, duties, emoluments, and privileges, being a digest and compilation of the rules, regulations, warrants and memoranda, relating to the duties, promotion, pay, and allowances of the officers in Her Majesty's service and in that of the Hon. East India Company. With notices of the military colleges, hospitals, and establishments in Great Britain, and a variety of information regarding the regular regiments and local corps in both services, and the yeomanry, militia and other volunteer corps. By J.H. Stocqueler (*pseud.*). London, Smith, Elder & Co., 1851. **562**

STRACHEY, Sir JOHN. India, its administration and progress, 4th ed., rev. by Sir Thomas W. Holderness, K.C.S.I. London, Macmillan & Co., Ltd., 1911. xxiv, 567p. front.(fold. map). **563**

TAUB, RICHARD P. Bureaucrats under stress: administrators and administration in an Indian state. Berkeley, University of California, 1969. 235p. **564**

TUPP, ALFRED COTTERELL. The competitive civil service of India: 1856-1882. Bombay, 1882. 23p. **565**

——The Indian civil service and the competitive system, etc. London, 1876. 24p. **566**

See also Government and Politics.

Bhoodan *See* Land Reforms.
Caste System *See* Culture and Civilization.
Customs and Manners.
Social Conditions.

(ii) Commerce and Industry

ANSTEY, VERA. The trade of the Indian ocean. London, Longmans, Green & Co.; 1929. xvi, 251p. front. illus. maps. diagrs. (The University geographical series, ed. by Dudley Stamp). **567**

MANSFIELD, WILLIAM ROSE. *Baron Sandhurst*. Minute...on the introduction of Gold Currency into India. Bombay, Education Society's Press, 1864. iv, 61p. **568**

MARTIN, ROBERT MONTGOMERY. The past and present state of the tea trade of England and of the continents of Europe and America; and a comparison between the consumption, price of, and revenue derived from, tea, coffee, sugar, wine, tobacco, spirits, etc. London, Parbury, Allen & Co., 1832. xi, 22p. 1. l. tables (1 fold). **569**

——— The political, commercial and financial conditions of the Anglo-Eastern empire in 1832; an analysis of its home and foreign governments and a practical examination of the doctrines of free trade and colonization, with reference to the renewal or modification of the Hon. East India Company's charter. By the author of the past and present state of the tea trade of England. London, Parbury, Allen and Co., 1832. xi, 403p. **570**

MARTIN, ROBERT MONTGOMERY. The sugar question in relation to free trade and protection. By the author of the "History of the British Colonies". London, J.B. Nicholas & Son, 1848. 21p. **571**

THOMAS, HENRY SULLIVAN. A report on pearl fisheries and Chank fisheries, 1884. Madras, R. Hill, 1884. 79p. folio. **572**

——— Tank fishing in India. Second edition. Edited by W.S. Burke, etc. Calcutta, Thacker Spink & Co., 1927. xiv, 120p. pl. xvi. **573**

WEISSE, HILDEGARD. Indian, entwicklung seiner wirtschoft und Kultur. Untar Leiturg von Edgar Lehmann bearb. Leipzig, Verlag Enzyklopadie, 1958. 2, 16 col. maps. (in portfolio).
574

See also Economic Conditions.
Social Conditions.

(iii) Communications

CLARKE, GEOFFREY ROTHE. The post office of India and its story. London, John Lane the Bodley Head. New York, John Lane Co., 1931. xi, 244p. **575**
See also History—Descriptive and Travel.

(iv) Communism

ALLEN, CHARLES. A few words from the "Red" pamphlet. The author, 1858. 30p. **576**
FOX, RALPH WINSTON. Communism and a changing civilization. Allahabad & London, Kitabistan, 1939. xvi, 150p. **577**
    First published in London in 1935, it is a learned commentary on the subject.
KAUTSKY, JOHN H. Moscow and the Communist Party of India. New York, Wiley, 1956. 220p. **578**
    A scholarly analysis of the relations between Moscow and the Communist Party of India (CPI). A former research associate at the Centre for International Studies at the Massachusetts Institute of Technology, Dr Kautsky is now Asstt. Professor of Political Science at Washington University, St. Louis.
OVERSTREET, GENE D. AND MARSHALL WINDMILLER. Communism in India. Berkeley, University of California Press, 1959. x, 603p. **579**
    A detailed, well-documented account of the history, organization and activities of the Communist Party of India.

300 Social Sciences

SPRATT, PHILIP. Blowing up India. Calcutta, Prachi Prakashan, 1955. **580**
Contains reminiscences of a British emissary of the Comintern, who came to India to organize the Communist Party of India.

See also Economic Conditions.
Social Conditions.

(v) Constitution and Constitutional History

ALEXANDROWICZ, CHARLES H. Constitutional development in India. Bombay, Oxford University Press, 1957. viii, 255p. **581**
Appraisal of the constitutional government of the Republic of India.

ARCHBOLD, WILLIAM ARTHUR JOBSON. Outlines of Indian constitutional history: British period. London, P.S. King & Sons, 1926. 367p. **582**

AUBER, PETER. An analysis of the constitution of the East India Company, and of the laws passed by Parliament for the Govt. of their affairs...to which is prefixed a brief history of the company, etc. London, Kingsbury & Allen, 1826. xx (ix)-lxxii, 507p. fold map. **583**

COUPLAND, REGINALD. India: A re-statement. New York, Oxford University Press, 1945. viii, 311p. tables, maps. **584**
A concise version of the author's earlier work entitled *The Indian Problem*. Suggests a form of government which might suit India.

———The Indian problem. New York, Oxford University Press, 1944. 3 vols. Vol. 1, 2, Indian problem, 1933-1935; Vol. 2, Indian politics, 1936-1942; Vol. 3, Future of India. **585**
Originally published in three volumes in 1942, it is a detailed study of constitutional developments in India between 1909 and 1942. Also comments on the future form of government in India.

CURZON, GEORGE NATHANIEL. British Government in India, The story of the Viceroys and Government houses. London, Cassell & Co., 1925. 2 vols. **586**

A valuable source book on the constitutional history of India by a former Viceroy.

——Indian speeches of Lord Curzon. Comp. by S.C. Sinha. Calcutta, Sanyal & Co., 1902. 2 vols. **587**

    Comprises the speeches delivered during the second and third years of his viceroyalty.

—— Speeches by Lord Curzon of Kedleston, Viceroy and Governor-General of India. Calcutta, Thacker, Spink & Co., 1898-1904. 3 vols. **588**

    Contents: Vol. 1, 1898-1901; Vol. 2, 1900-1902; Vol. 3, 1902-1904, Vols. 2-3 published by Supdt. Printing, India.

GALLOWAY, Sir ARCHIBALD. Observations on the law and constitution and present government of India. 2nd ed., with additions. London, Parbury, Allen & Co., 1832. xvi, 512p. **589**

GILCHRIST, JOHN BORTHWICK. Parliamentary reform, on constitutional principles: or British loyalty against continental royalty. Glasgow, printed by W. Cang. 1815. 3p. 1, (v)—xii, 203, 13p. **590**

GWYER, MAURICE L. AND A. APPADORAI, *eds.* Speeches and documents on the Indian Constitution, 1921-47. London, Oxford University Press, 1957. 2 vols. **591**

    A collection of 380 items containing statutes, committee reports, party announcements, letters, and biographical notes on major political figures of the day.

ILBERT, COURTENAY PEREGRINE. The Government of India; being a digest of the statute law relating thereto, with historical introduction and explanatory matter. 3rd ed. London, Oxford University Press, 1915. xxxviii, 499p. **592**

—— The new constitution of India; being three Rhodes lectures by Sir Courtenay Ilbert and three by Rt. Hon. Lord Meston, delivered at University of London. University College Session, 1921-22. London, University of London Press Ltd., 1923. 212p. **593**

JENNINGS, IVOR. Some characteristics of the Indian constitution. Bombay, Geoffrey Cumberlege, Oxford University Press, 1953. vi, 86p. **594**

    Lectures given in the Madras University in 1952 under

Sir Alladi Krishnaswami Aiyer Shashti-abdapoorthi endowment.

KEITH, ARTHUR B. Speeches and documents on Indian policy, 1910-1921. London, Oxford University Press, 1922. 2 vols. **595**

MACAULAY, THOMAS B. Lord Macaulay's legislative minutes. London, Oxford University Press, 1946. viii, 312p. **596**

A collection of Lord Macaulay's speeches on education, press laws and related subjects.

See also Government and Politics.
India's Struggle for Freedom Laws.

(vi) Culture and Civilization

BARNETT, LIONEL DAVID. Antiquities of India; an account of the history and culture of ancient Hindustan. London, P.L. Warner, 1913. xvi, 306p. xxviii, pl. diagrs. **597**

BASHAM, A.L. The wonder that was India: a survey of the culture of the Indian sub-continent before the coming of the Muslims. London, Sidwick and Jackson, 1954. xxi, 568p. **598**

"This book has been written to interpret ancient Indian civilization...to the ordinary Western reader who has little knowledge of the subject, but some interest in it".—*Preface*. A faithful interpretation of Indian civilization.

BREIT, HARVEY, *ed*. Perspective of India. New York, Intercultural Publications, 1958. 69p. illus. **599**

CAMPBELL, ALEXANDER. The heart of India. New York, Knopf, 1958. 382p. illus. **600**

CHICAGO UNIVERSITY, *College*. Introduction to the civilization of India; Changing dimensions of Indian society and Culture. Chicago, Syllabus Division, University of Chicago Press, 1957. 472p. illus. **601**

——— Source reading on Indian civilization; 1959. Chicago, University of Chicago Press, Syllabus Division, 1959. 1 vol. illus. **602**

CHIODINI, LUIGI. India parens; riflessione, lingua, scritture dell' antica India. Milano, SEDIT, 1955. (I) **603**

COEDS, G.C. Les Etats Hindouism d' Indochine et d' Indonesie.

(The Indianized states of South Asia). Honolulu, East-West Center, 1968. p. (F). **604**

COUSINS, JAMES HENRY. The cultural unity of Asia. Madras, Theosophical Publishing House, 1922. vi, 133p. **605**

DAVIS, THOMAS WILLIAM RHYS. Buddhist India. 3rd Indian ed. Calcutta, S. Gupta, 1957. 108p. **606**

FRANKLIN, FREDRIK. Intervju med Indien. Stockholm, Triargelforlaget, 1955. 189p. illus. **607**

GARRATT, G.T. AND OTHERS. The legacy of India. Oxford, The Clarendon Press, 1937. xviii, 428p. front. illus. 23pl. **608**

GUENON, RENE. East and West. Tr. by William Massey. London, Luzac & Co., 1941. v. 257p. (F) **609**
A study in proper understanding of the spirit of the Eastern and Western civilization.

ISAACS, HAROLD ROBERT. Scratches on our minds; American images of China and India. New York, J. Day Co., 1958. 416p. illus. **610**

LEGER, FRANCOIS. Les influences occidentales dors la revolution de l'Orient: Inde, Malaisie, China, 1850-1950. Paris, Plon, 1955. 2 vol. (Civilisations d'hier et d' anjourdbul). **611**

MACDONELL, ARTHUR ANTHONY. India's past; a survey of her literature, religions, languages and antiquities. Oxford, The Clarendon Press, 1927. xii, 293p. front. illus. **612**

MASSON-OURSEL, PAUL. L'Inde antique et la civilization indienne, par P., Masson-Oursel, H. de William-Grabowska, Philipe Stern. Paris, A. Michel, 1951. 497p. illus. (L' Evolution de l'humanite systhese collective, 1, sect. 28). (F) **613**

MASSON-OURSEL, PAUL AND OTHERS. Ancient India and Indian civilization. London, K. Paul Trench, Trubner & Co., Ltd., 1934. xxiv, 435p. illus. xvi pl. (Half title: The history of civilization, ed. by C.K. Ogden. Prehistory and antiquity). **614**

RANAY, JEANNE. Ce que l'Inde m' a dit. Paris, Editions de Navarre, 1955. 80p. (F) **615**

———Un essai de plus juste comprehension de l'Inde. Aurillac, Editions du Centre, 1955. 35p. (F). **616**

RAWLINSON, HUGH G. India, a short cultural history, edited by C.G. Seligman. New York, Appleton Century, 1938. xiv, 452p. illus. maps. **617**

RAWLINSON, HUGH G. Indian historical studies. London, Longmans, Green & Co., 1913. vv, 229p. illus. maps. **618**
"Gives a glimpse of India in nearly every epoch of her history by taking a leading figure of the period and attempting an estimate of his achievements".

———Intercourse between India and the Western world from the earliest times to the fall of Rome. Cambridge University Press, 1916. vii, 196p. front, plate, maps. **619**

——— Makers of India. London, Oxford University Press, 1942. ii, 78p. (Living names series). **620**
Contents: Asoka, Harsha, Akbar, Sivaji, Ranjit Singh, Saiyed Ahmad Khan, Mahatma Gandhi.

RENOU LOUIS. The civilization of ancient India. Translated from the French by Philip Sprat. 2nd ed. Calcutta, Susil Gupta Private Ltd., 1959. 189p. **621**

——— La civilization de l' Inde Ancienne. Paris, 1950. 189p. (F). **622**

———Classical India by Louis Renou and Jean Filliozat assisted by Pierre Meile Anne-Marie Esnoul and Liliene Silburn. Calcutta, Susil Gupta Private Ltd., 1951. vol. illus. **623**

———AND OTHERS. L' Inde Classique. Manuel des etudes indiennes. Paris, 1947. 2 vols. (F). **624**

RISLEY, HERBERT HOPE. The people of India. Calcutta, Thacker, Spink & Co., 1908. xvi, 289 (1) clxxxix p. incl. maps. fold tables, diagrs. front., xxiv pl. fold map. **625**

RUBEN, WALTER. Einfubrung in dis Indien Kunde; ein Uberblick uber die historischa Entwicklung Indiens. Berlin, Deutscher Verlag der Wissenschaften, 1954. 390p. illus (G). **626**

SINGER, MILTON, B., ed. Introducing India in liberal education. Proceedings of a conference held at the University of Chicago, May 17, 18, 1957. Chicago, University of Chicago, 1957, xiii, 287p. **627**

SLATER GILBERT. The Dravidian element in Indian culture. London, E. Benn Ltd., 1924. 2p., 1., 3-192p. viipl. **628**

SMITH, C. ROSS. In search of India. New York, Chilton, 1960. 230p. **629**
An American during his visit to India tries to describe

the greatness of her culture and civilization.

SPENCER, CORNELA. Made in India: the story of India's people. New York, Knopf, 1946. 204p. **630**

    An account of India's contribution to world culture and civilization, as shown in the development of the art, religion, philosophy, music, dance, literature, and handicrafts of her people.

THOMAS, FREDERICK WILLIAM. The mutual influence of Muhammadans and Hindus being the "La Bas" prize essay for 1891. Cambridge, Deghton, Bell & Co., 1892. vii, 117p. **631**

TOD, JAMES. Annals and antiquities of Rajasthan, or the central and western Rajput states of India by Lieut. Col. James Tod. ed. with an introduction and notes by William Crooke. London, New York (etc.) H. Milford, Oxford University Press, 1920. 3v. fronts. plates, ports fold, map, tables (1 fold). **632**

WADDELL, LAURENCE AUSTINE. The makers of civilization in race and history, showing the rise of the Aryans or Sumerians, their organization and propagation of civilization, their extension of it to Egypt and Crete, personalities and achievements of their kings, historical origins of mythic gods and heroes with dates from the rise of civilization about 3380 B.C. reconstructed from Babylonian, Egyptian, Hittite, Indian and Gothic sources. With 35 plates, 168 text illustrations and maps. London, Luzac & Co., 1929. Lvi, 646p. 11. front. illus., plates, maps, (part fold) plans, fold. tables. **633**

WALLBANK, T. WALTER. India. New York, Holt, 1948. 114p. **634**

    A survey of the heritage and growth of Indian nationalism, for college students.

YOUNGHUSBAND, Sir FRANCIS EDWARD. Culture as the bond of empire, by Sir Francis Younghusband. *In* Royal Society of Literature of the United Kingdom, London. Essays by diverse hands, being the transactions. London, 1921. New (i.e. 3rd). v. lp. 125-154. **635**

ZINKIN, TAYA. India changes. New York, Oxford University Press, 1958. 238p. **636**

See also   Fine Arts.
              History (General).

History (Ancient).
Social Conditions.

(vii) Customs and Manners

ABBOTT, JOHN. The keys of power; a study of Indian ritual and belief. London, Methuen & Co., Ltd., 1932. xi, 500p. illus. diagrs. **637**

——The keys of power. London, Methuen & Co., 1932. xi, 560p. **638**

"A study of Indian ritual and belief," *t.p.* Records numerous Indian customs and shows how far the concept of a supernatural cosmic power dominates popular practice.

BENTLEY, JOHN. Essays relative to the habits, character and moral improvement of the Hindoos. 1823. 351p. **639**

BOUGLE, CELESTIN CHARLES ALFRED. Essais sur b Regime des Castes. 3rd ed. Paris, F. Alcan, 1935. viii, 278(2)p. (F). **640**

BROUGH, JOHN. The early Brahminical system of Gotra and Pravara. Cambridge, University Press, 1953. xvii, 227p. **641**

It is a translation of the "Gotra-Pravera-manjari" of "Purusottama pandita".

DALTON, E. T. Descriptive ethnology of Bengal. Calcutta, Office of the Superintendent of Government Printing, 1872. lp. 1., vip. 1 1., 327, (12)p. front., illus., 39pl. **642**

Printed for the Govt. of Bengal under the direction of the Council of the Asiatic Society of Bengal.

DEBARY, WM THEODORE, *ed.* Sources of Indian tradition. New York, Columbia, 1958. 2 v. **643**

DUBOIS, ABBE JEAN ANTOINE. Hindu manners, customs and ceremonies. Prefatory note by F. Max Muller. Tr. from the author's later French Ms., and ed. with notes, corrections, and biography, by Henry K. Beauchamp. Oxford, Clarendon Press, 1953. xxvi, 741p. First published in 1906. (F) **644**

FUCHS, STEPHEN. The Gond and Bhumia of Eastern Mandla. Bombay, Asia Publishing House, 1960. 584p. illus and maps. **645**

IBBETSON, D. Panjab castes; being a reprint of the chapters on "The Races, Castes and Tribes of the People", in the report of the census of the Panjab, published in 1883, by late Sir Denzil Ibbetson, Lahore, Superintendent, Government Printing, Punjab, 1916. 3p. l., viii, 338p. incl. tables. front. **646**

KEENE, Rev. HENRY GEORGE. Persian stories, illustrative of Indian manners and customs (translated from the original Persian by H.G.K., translated into Tamil by Jesudesen Pillay, etc. English and Tamil. Madras. 1840. **647**

KITTS, E.J. A compendium of the castes and tribes found in India, compiled from the 1881 census reports, etc. Bombay, Educational Society's Press, 1885. xi, 90p. **648**

LUDERS, H. Das Wurfelspiel irn alten Indien. Berlin, 1907. (G). **649**

MARRIOTT, MCKIM. Village India: studies in the little community. Chicago, University of Chicago, 1955. 269p. **650**
> Eight villages in seven different linguistic areas and five provinces of India are here illuminated by detailed analysis of caste, community, structure, personality, religion, world view, and the current forces of social change. The editor is with the Institute of East Asiatic Studies, at the University of California.

NESFIELD, JOHN COLLINSON. Brief view of the caste system of the North-Western Provinces and Oudh together with an examination of names and figures shown in the census report, 1882, being an attempt to classify on a functional basis all the main castes of the United Provinces and to explain their gradations of rank and the process of their formation. Allahabad, North-Western Province and Oudh government press, 1885. 1p. l., v. 132p. **651**

O'MALLEY, LEWIS SYDNEY STEWARD. Indian caste customs, Cambridge, the University Press, 1932. ix, 190p. **652**

PARGITER, FREDERICK EDEN. Ancient Indian historical tradition. London, Oxford University Press, 1922. vi (2), 368p. incl. geneal. tables. fold. map. **653**

RAWLINSON, HUGH GEORGE. Intercourse between India and the Western world from the earliest times to the fall of Rome. Cambridge, University Press, 1916. vi (2) 196p. front. plates.

fold map. **654**

ROSE, HORACE ARTHUR. A glossary of the tribes and castes of the Punjab and North-West Frontier Province based on the census report for the Punjab, 1892. Lahore, Printed by the Superintendent, Government Printing, Punjab, 1911-19. 3 vols. plates. **655**

SCHOEBEL, CHARLES. Inde Francaise. L'Histoire des origines et du development des caste de l' Inde. Paris, Societe Academique Indo-Chinoise, 1882. 2 pts. (F). **656**

SENART, EMILE CHARLES MARIE. Caste in India, the facts and the system, by Emile Senart, translated by Sir E. Denison Ross. C.I.E. London, Methuen & Co., Ltd., 1930. xxiii p. 1 l., 220p. **657**

—— Les castes dams l'Inde; les faits et la systeme. Paris, E. Leroux. 1896. 2p. l., xxii, 257p. 1 l. **658**

On cover: Annales du Musee Guimet. Bibliotheque de vulgarisation. (x). (F).

SLEEMAN, Sir WILLIAM HENRY. A report on the system of Megpunnaism or the murder of Indigent parents for their young children (who are sold as slaves) as it prevails in the Delhi territories, and the native states of Rajpootana, Ulwar and Bhurtpore, by Major W.H. Sleeman. Serampore, Serampore Press, 1839. iv, 121p. fold. tab. **659**

SOLVYNS, FRANCOIS BALTHAZAR. The costume of Indostan, elucidated by sixty coloured engravings; with descriptions in English and French, taken in the years 1798 and 1799, by Balt. Solvyns. London, E. Orme, 1804. 132p. 60 col. pl. (incl. front). **660**

STEELE, ARTHUR. Law and custom of Hindoo castes with the Dekhun Provinces subject to the Presidency of Bombay chiefly affecting civil suits. A new ed. London, W.H. Allen & Co., 1868. xix, 460p. **661**

THURSTON, EDGAR. Ethnographic notes in Southern India. Madras, Printed by Superintendent, Government Press, 1906. 1p. l., viii, 580p. front. xxxviii pl. **662**

—— Omens and superstitions of Southern India. London T.F. Unwin, 1912. 320p. incl. front. plates. **663**

TREVELYAN, Sir CHARLES EDWARD. A report upon the inland

customs and town duties of the Bengal Presidency. Calcutta, printed at the Baptist Mission Press, 1834. xx, 197, xxp, 21, 27p. incl. tables. **664**

WILSON, JOHN. History of the suppression of infanticide in Western India under the Government of Bombay: including notices of the provinces and tribes in which the practice has prevailed. 1855. 457p. **665**

────── *Indian caste*. Bombay. 1877. 2 vol.

See also Culture and Civilization
        Social Conditions.

(viii) Economic Conditions

ALLEN, JAMES STEWART. World monopoly and peace. Calcutta, Bookman, 1947. 299p. **666**
    This books deals with "monopoly capitalism in its present post-war phase, and with the manner in which the war has affected nations among the major capitalist powers, as well as between them and Soviet Union".

ANSTEY, VERA. The economic development of India. London, Longmans, Green, 1954. xii, 582p. front. illus. maps. **667**
    A synthetic view of the recent development, present position and main problems of Indian economic life.

ARNIM, WOLF VON. Die wirtschaftliche. Entwicklung der Indischen Union unter Berucksichtigung der deutsechen Beteiligungsmoglichkeiten. Kiel, 1955. 19p. (Kieler Vertrage, gehalten im Institut fur Welt-wirtscheft an der Universitat Kiel, n.f. 7). **668**

BROUGHTON, G.M. Labour in Indian industries. Bombay, Humphrey Milford, Oxford University Press, 1924. vii, 214p. **669**
    Thesis approved for D.Sc. by the London University.

BROWN, ENRILY CLARA, *ed*. Foreign area studies: India: a syllabus: contributors: Richard S. Newelle and others. Maps by Lowell R. Goodmen; foreword by Ward Morehouse. Iowa, University of Northern Iowa, 1970. 122p. **670**

BUCHANAN, DANIEL HOUSTON. The development of capitalistic enterprise in India. New York, The Macmillan Co., 1934.

497p. **671**

It is a publication of international research, Harvard University and Radcliff College.

CHACKO, GEORGE KUTTICKAL. India: toward an understanding; *a de nove* inquiry into the mind of India in search of an answer to the question: "Will India go Communist"? New York, Bookman Association, 1959. 212p. **672**

CHATTERTON, ALFRED. Industrial evolution of India. Madras, "Hindu" Office, 1912. viii, 369p. **673**

COAB, ANSLEY J. Population growth and economic development in low income countries; a case study of India's prospects, by Ansley J. Coab and Edgar M. Hoover. Princeton, N.J. Princeton University Press, 1958. xxi, 389p. **674**

COVER, JOHN HIGSON. The economy of India. Berkeley, Human Relations Area Files, South Asia Project, University of California, 1956. 2v. (xvi, 624p.) (Human Relations Area Files, inc. Subcontractors' monograph, HRAF-82). **675**

DEAN, VERA (MICHELES). New patterns of democracy in India. Cambridge, Masc., Harvard University Press, 1959. 223p. **676**

DE MOLA CORPORATION, *New York*. India, Pakistan, Ceylon, Burma. New York, Friendship Press, 1954. col. maps. **677**

ECKAUS, RICHARD S. Planning for growth. Boston, M.I.T., 1968. 208p. **678**

ETIENNE, GILBERT. L'Inde, economie et population. Prof. de Pierre Meile. Geneva, E. Droz, 1955. 169p. (Etudes d'historire economique politique et sociale, 16). **679**

FISHER, MARGARET WELPLEY. Indian approaches to a socialist society by Margaret W. Fisher and Joan V. Bondurant. Berkeley, Institute of International Studies, University of California, 1956. 105, xiii p. (Indian press digest. Monograph series, no. 2). **680**

FOREST, GEORGE WILLIAM. The Famine in India. London, H. Cox, 1897. iv, 40p. **681**

FRANCE. Centre national du commence exterieur. Memento commercial: Inde. Paris, 1957. 126p. (F) **682**

GALBRAITH, JOHN KENNETH. Affluent society. Bombay, Lalvani, 1970. 333p. **683**

—— Economic development. Boston, Mass., Harvard, 1962. 109p. **684**

GOLD, NORMAN LEON. Regional economic development and nuclear power in India. With an introduction by Harrison Brown. Washington, National Planning Association, 1957. xvi, 132p. (National Planning Association. Reports on the productive uses of nuclear energy). **685**

GRAD, ANDREW JONAH. Economic planning in India. Submitted by the International Secretariat of the I.P.R. as a document for the 9th Conference of the I.P.R. to be held in January 1945. New York, International Secretariat, Institute of Pacific Relations, 1945. 21p. (Secretariat paper no. 10). **686**

GREGG, RICHARD BARTLETT. Economics of Khaddar. Madras, S. Ganesan, 1928. 226p. **687**

A study of the *Khadi* movement sponsored by Mahatma Gandhi.

—— Gandhism versus socialism. New York, John Day Co., 1932. vi, 7-30p. **688**

Issued by John Day in its pamphlets series it is a comparative study of the subject.

—— A philosophy of Indian economic development. Ahmedabad, Navajivan Publishing House, 1958. 232p. **689**

HOSELITZ, BERT. F. Sociological aspects of economic growth. Bombay, Vakils, 1970. vi, 950p. **690**

HUNCK, JOSEF M. Indiens laulose Revolution; Moglichkeiten und Grenzen einer deutsch-indischen Zusammenarbeet. Mit einem vorwort von F.K. Heller. Dussddorf, Verlag Handelsblatt, 1957. 106p. **691**

HUNTER, Sir WILLIAM WILSON. The uncertainties of Indian finance. Calcutta (Printed at the "Englishman" Press), 1869. 22p. **692**

"For private circulation".

KEYNES, JOHN MAYNARD. Indian currency and finance. London, Macmillan & Co., 1913 viii, 263p. **693**

KUZNETS, SIMON SMITH. Economic growth: Brazil, India, Japan. Edited by Simon Kuznets, Wilburt E. Moore, and Joseph J. Spengler. Durham, N.C. Duke University Press, 1955. xi, 613p. **694**

This study grew out of a conference conducted by the Social Science Research Council. Contributors include, in addition to economists, demographers, and anthropologists and sociologists.

MALENBAUM, WILFRED. East and West in India's development. Washington, National Planning Association, 1959, 67p. (The Economics of competitive coexistence). **695**

MANN, HAROLD HART. Rainfall and famine: a study of rainfall in the Bombay Deccan, 1865-1938. Bombay, Published by M.B. Desai for the Indian Society of Agricultural Economics, 1955. 47p. (Publications of the Indian Society of Agricultural Economics, 16). **696**

MARTIN, ROBERT MONTGOMERY. Taxation of the British empire. London, E. Wilson, 1833. xxvi, (2), 264p. incl. tables. **697**

MARYLAND, UNIVERSITY. Bureau of Business and Economic Research. India in world affairs. College Park, 1957. 12p. (*Its* studies in business and economics, V. ii, no. 1.). **698**

MASON, EDWARD S. Promoting economic development: the United States and Southern Asia. Claremont College, 1955. 83p. **699**

>Dr Mason, Dean of the Graduate School of Public Administration at Harvard University, has long been interested in the economic growth of underdeveloped areas.

MORELAND, WILLIAM H. From Akbar to Aurangzeb. London, Macmillan, 1923. xiii, 364p. map. **700**

>Based mainly on the descriptions of European merchants and travellers, it is an account of the economic conditions in India in early 17th century.

——India at the death of Akbar: an economic study. London, Macmillan, 1920. xi, 328p. **701**

>A study of economic conditions under the Mughals in the early 17th century.

MORISON, THEODORE. The economic transition in India, London, John Murray, 1931. iv, 251p. **702**

>Contains the substance of a course of lectures delivered at the London School of Economics and Political Science, 1910.

OXFORD UNIVERSITY PRESS. Oxford economic atlas for India and Ceylon, prepared by the Cartographic Dept. of the Clarendon Press, Oxford. Economic information compiled by Intelligence Unit of the Economist. Geographical adviser, C.F.W.R.

Gullick. Bombay, Indian Branch, Oxford University Press, 1953. viii, 97, xxxvip. **703**

PHILIPOS, V.A. A study of land use planning techniques of the USA by an Indian planner; report to the United Nations. Trivandrum. Editorial Board, Travancore-Cochin Town and Country Planning Association, 1953. 39p. **704**

REDDAWAY, W. BRAIN. The development of the Indian economy. Homewood, Illion, Irwin, 1962. 216p. **705**

    An analysis of the economic conditions in India with special reference to the Third Five-year Plan.

REPETTO, ROBERT C. Time in India's development programmes. Boston, Mass., Harvard, 1971. 237p. **706**

RICKER, H. Beggar among the dead. London, Rider, 1960. 224p. **707**

    A vivid account of the economic condition of the people of India.

ROSEN, GEORGE. Industrial change in India: Industrial growth, capital requirements, and technological change, 1937-1955. Glencoe, the Free Press, 1958. **708**

    A survey of five major Indian Industries based on financial data from companies' balance-sheets.

ROSENSTEIN-RODAN, P.N. Capital formation and economic development. New York, Allen & Unwin, 1964, 164p. **709**

ROYLE, JOHN FORBES. Essay on the productive resources of India: London, W.H. Allen & Co., 1840. x, 45, (1)p. **710**

—— On the culture and commerce of cotton in India, and elsewhere; with an account of the experiments made by the Hon. East India Co., up to the present time. Appendix: Papers relating to the great industrial exhibition. London, Smith, Elder & Co., 1851. xvi, 607p. illus. 4pl. (1 fold) 2 diagr (1 fold). **711**

RUBEN, WALTER *ed.* Die okonomische und soziale Entwicklung Indiena. Berlin, Akademie-Verlag, 1959—. **712**

SCOTT, J.R. In famine land: observations and experiences in India during the great drought of 1899-1900. New York, Harper, 1904. xi, 206p. plat. map. **713**

SEIPP, ROBERT CONRAD. Economic growth and the organization of scientific research; a study of some of the planning problems associated with the development of the water resources of the Indian subcontinent. Chicago, Deptt. of Photoduplication, University of Chicago Library, 1956. Microfilm 6078 H.D. **714**

SLATER, GILBERT. Southern India: its political and economic problems. Foreword by Marquess of Willingdon. London, George Allen & Unwin, 1936. 383p. plate. **715**

SMITH, H.B. LEES. Studies in Indian economics. London, Constable & Co., 1909. viii, 125p. **716**
"A series of lectures delivered for the Government of Bombay"—*t.p.*

SPENCER, DANIEL L. India: mixed enterprise and Western business. The Hague, M. Nijhoff, 1959, xi, 252p. **717**
A study of the joint Indian and British venture during the post-1918 period, to industrialize India.

STISSER, REINHOLD. Problems of India's economic development. Kiel, Institut fur, Weltwirtschaft an der Universitat Kiel, 1958. v, 83p. (G). **718**

STRACHEY, Sir JOHN. The finances and public works of India from 1869 to 1881. By Sir John Strachey and Lt. Gen. Richard Strachey. London, K. Paul, Trench & Co., 1882. xx, 467 (1) p. incl. tab. **719**

TEMPLE, Sir RICHARD, *Ist, hart*. Progress of India, Japan and China in the country. Philadelphia, The Linscott Publishing Co., 1900. xxivp. 11, 496p. front. ports. **720**

THOMPSON (J. WALTER) COMPANY. The Indian market, 1959; a descriptive and statistical survey of a market of over 390 million people. New York, 1959. 40p. (*Its* World markets series). **721**

THORBURN, SEPTIMUS SMET. Problems of Indian poverty. London, The Fabian Society, 1902. 15, (1)p. **722**

THORNER, DANIEL. Investment in Empire: British railway and stream shipping enterprise in India, 1825-1840. Philadelphia, University of Pennsylvania Press, 1950. **723**
A study of the factors that attracted private British capital to India during the years 1825-1849.

TREVASKIS, HUGH K. The land of the Five Rivers. London, Oxford University Press, 1928. xx, 372p. **724**

Contains information on the economic history of the Punjab in the 19th century. The author was the director of land records in Punjab.

US LIBRARY OF CONGRESS. Legislative Reference Series. Economic development in India and Communist China, prepared by J. Clement Happ of the Legislative Reference Service. Washington, US Govt. Print, Off., 1956. v., 51p. (Staff study no. 6, Subcommittee on Technical Assistance Programme). **725**

WEISSE, HILDEGARD. Indien, Entwieldung, seiner Wirtschaft und Kultur. Unter Leitung von Edgar Lehmann, von Hildegard Weisse. Leipzig, Verlag Enzyklopadie, 1958. 16 col. maps. **726**

WOYTINSKY, W.S. India: the awakening giant. New York, Harper, 1957. 202p. **727**

Deals mainly with India's plans for industrialization and the revival of her villages.

ZINKIN, MAURICE. Development for Free Asia. New York, Oxford University Press, 1963. rev. ed. viii, 243p. **728**

A survey of the economic development in Asia with special reference to Free India.

See also Commerce and Industry.
Labour and Labour Classes.
Social Conditions.

(ix) Education

ADAM, WILLIAM. Reports on the State of education in Bengal, 1835 and 1838, ed. by Anathnath Basu. Calcutta, the University, 1941. lxvii, 578p. **729**

Contains "some account of the state of education in Bihar and a consideration of the means adopted to the improvement of extension of the public instruction in both provinces, i.e. Bengal and Bihar".—*t.p.*

BOMAN-BEHRAM, B.K. Educational controversies in India: the cultural conquest of India under British imperialism. Bombay, D.B. Taraporevala Sons & Co., 1943, xvii, 653p. **730**

A comparative account of the educational controversies

300 Social Sciences

in the days of East India Company.

BROCKWAY, K. NORA. A larger way for women; aspects of Christian education for girls in South India, 1712-1948. Madras, Geoffrey Cumberlege, Oxford University Press, 1949. xi, 189p. **731**

JAMES, H.R. Education and statesmanship in India : 1797 to 1910. London, Longmans Green & Co., 1911. viii, 143p. **732**

—— Problems of higher education in India. Calcutta, Longmans, Green & Co., 1936. viii, 87p. **733**

KEAY, FRANK E. A history of education in India and Pakistan. London, Oxford University Press, 1959. 3rd ed. xiii, 204p. **734**
Originally published in 1918, it is a history of education in India from the remote past to the recent times.

—— Indian education in ancient and later times: an inquiry into its origin, development and ideals. 2nd ed. Calcutta, Humphrey Milford, University Press, 1938. xiii, 204p. **735**
First published in 1918 under the title: Ancient Indian Education.

LEITNER, GOTTBIEB WILLIAM. History of indigenous education in the Punjab since annexation and in 1882, Calcutta, Printed by the Suprintendent of Government Printing, 1882. (544p.) plates. **736**

—— The theory and practice of education with special reference to education in India, Lahore, "Indian Public Opinion" Press (1870). cover-title, lp. l., 32p. **737**

LETHBRIDGE, Sir, ROPER. High education in India: a plea for the state college. London, W.H. Allen & Co., 1882. viii, 216p. **738**

MAYHEW, ARTHUR. The education of India. London, Faber and Gwyer, 1926. 306p. **739**
"A study of British educational policy in India, 1835-1920 and its bearing on national life and problems in India today".—*t.p.*

McCULLY, BRUCE T. English education and the origins of Indian nationalism. New York, Columbia University, 1940. 418p. **740**
A history of education in India in 19th century. The study is pro-British.

MONTESSORI, MARIA. Education for a new world. Madras, Kalakshetra, 1948. vi, 113p. **741**

> The purpose of the book is, in the words of the author, "to expound and defend the great powers of the child, and to help teachers to a new outlook which will charge this task from drudgery to joy, from repression to collaboration with nature."

PEARCE, FREDERICK GORDON. Plan for education. Bombay, Geoffrey Cumberlege, Oxford University Press. 1948. viii, 80p. **742**

> "A descriptive and critical commentary on post-war educational development in India, otherwise known as the Sargent plan." *t.p.*

PEARSON, W.W. Shantiniketan: the Bolpur School of Rabindranath Tagore. London, Macmillan & Co., 1917. xv, 111p. **743**

SINGER, MILTON, *ed*. Introducing India in liberal education. Chicago, University of Chicago Press, 1957. xii, 287p. **744**

THOMAS, FREDERICK WILLIAM. The history and prospects of British education in India; being the "Le Bas" prize essay for 1890. Cambridge, Deighton, Bell & Co., 1891. vi, 158p. **745**

TREVELYAN, Sir CHARLES EDWARD, *hart*. On the education of people of India. London, Longman, Orme, Brown, Green & Longmans, 1838. vii, 220p. **746**

USEEM, JOHN AND RUTH H. The Western-educated man in India: a study of his social roles and influence. New York, Dryden Press, 1955. **747**

> An interesting study of the changed ideas and attitudes of these Indians who studied in Britain, and the United States. The authors also describe how these educated persons influence the present day society in India.

ZELLNER, AUBREY A. Education in India: a survey of the Lower Ganges Valley in modern times. New York, Bookman Associates, 1951. xxvi, 272p. **748**

> Outlines the history of education in India, under various administrations; the problems created by creed and language; and plans for the future. The writer spent almost three years in India.

(x) Folklore

BODDING, PAUL OLAF, *ed.* Santal folk tales. Oslo, H. Ashehoug and Co., and Cambridge (Mass.), Harvard University Press, 1925-29. 3 vols. (Oslo Institute for Comparative Research in Human Culture, B. series. 2, 7 and 11). **749**
BOMPASS, CECIL HENRY, *tr.* Folklore of the Santal Parganas. Tr. by Cecil Henry Bompass. London, David Nutt, 1909. 483p. **750**
CROOKE, WILLIAM. Religion and folklore of Northern India. Oxford, Oxford University Press, 1926, 2p. 1., 471p. **751**
ENTHOVEN, REGINALD EDWARD. Folklore of Bombay. Oxford, Clarendon Press, 1924. 353p. **752**
See also Literature.
  . Food Supply *See* Agriculture.
      . Economic Conditions.

(xi) Foreign Relations

AITCHISON, Sir CHARLES UMPHERSTON. A collection of treaties relating to India and neighbouring countries. India, Miscellaneous official publications, 1862-65. 7 vols. **753**
ANDREW, Sir WILLIAM PATRIC. India and her neighbour with maps and appendix. London, W.H. Allen, 1878. xv, 413p. **754**
BELDEN, MARVA ROBINS. American foreign policy in relation to India, with special emphasis on the period 1947 to June 1951. Chicago, Library, Deptt. of Photographic Reproduction, University of Chicago, 1952. Microfilm 4412 E. **755**
BERKES, ROSS N. The diplomacy of India; Indian foreign policy in the United Nations, by Ross N. Berkes and Mohinder Singh S. Bedi. Stanford, California, Stanford University Press, 1958. 221p. **756**
BIRDWOOD, CHRISTOPHER BROMHEAD, *2nd Baron Birdwood*, 1899. A continent decides. London, Robert Hale, 1953. xx, 21-315p. **757**

Deals with Indo-Pakistan relations. "Introducing two

new members in the great and diverse family of the Commonwealth, and some of the problems which they offer for our understanding and solution." *t.p.*

BRECHER, MICHAEL. India's foreign policy, an interpretation. Prepared for the Lahore Conference of the Institute of Pacific Relations, February 1958. New York, International Secretariat, Institute of Pacific Relations, 1957. 31p. (Institute of Pacific Relations. Secretariat no. 1). **758**

BULGANIN, NIKOLAI ALEKSANDROVICH. Sejour de N. Boulganine et de N. Khrouchtchev en Inde. 18 November— 1 December et 7-14 December, 1955. Paris, 1955. 62p. (Collection "Studes sovietiques"). **759**

——Speeches during sojourn in India, Burma and Afghanistan, November-December, 1955 by N.A. Bulganin and N.S. Khrushchev. New Delhi, Representative of Tass in India, 1956. 208p. **760**

—— Visit of friendship to India, Burma and Afghanistan; speeches and official documents, November-December, 1955. Translated from the Russian. Moscow, Foreign Languages Publishing House, 1956. 327p. illus. group ports. **761**

BUSCH, BRITON COOPER. Britain, India and the Arabs, 1914-1921. Berkeley, California, University of California Press, 1971. 522p. **762**

CHANG, CHIA-SEN. China and Gandhian India by Carsun Chang. Edited by Kalidas Nag. Calcutta, Book Co., 1956. 318p. **763**

CHIPMAN, WARWICK. India's foreign policy. Toronto, Canadian Institute of International Affairs, 1954. 12p. (Behind the headlines, v. 14, no. 4). **764**

DA COSTA, ERIC PAUL WOOLLETT. India in the free world. New Delhi, 1953. 29p. (Eastern economic pamphlets, 17). **765**

FISHER, MARGARET WELPLEY. Indian views of Sino-Indian relations by Margaret W. Fisher and Joan V. Bondurant. Berkeley, Institute of International Studies, University of California, 1956. 168, xxixp. (Indian press digest. Monograph series no. 1). **766**

FOREST, Sir GEORGE WILLIAMS, *ed.* Selections from the letters, dispatches, and other state papers preserved in the foreign departments of the Government of India, 1772-1785, ed. by George W. Forrest. Calcutta, Printed by the Superintendent of Govt. Printing, India, 1890. 3v. facsims. **767**

FRIEDMAN, HARRY I. Consolidation of India since independence; a comparison and analysis of four Indian territorial problems —the Portuguese possessions, the French possessions, Hyderabad, and Kashmir. Ann Arbor, University Microfilms, 1957. (University Microfilm, Ann Arbor, Michigan, Publications no. 18, 230). Microfilm Ac-1. no. 18230. **768**

GUNTHER, HANS OTTO, *ed.* Indian und Deutschland; ein Sammalband. Mit einem Vorwant von Bundestagsprasident Eugen Gerstenmaisen. Frankfurt am Main, Europaische Verlagsanstalt, 1956. 237p. **769**

The Indian Cultural Delegation in China, 1955. Peking, Foreign Languages Press, 1955. 108p. illus. **770**

KAUTSKY, JOHN H. Moscow and the Communist Party of India. New York, John Wiley, 1956. xii, 220p. **771**

    A study of the policies of the CPI in India with special reference to the years from 1945 to 1954.

LEVI, WERNER. Free India in Asia. Minneapolis, University of Minnesota Press, 1952. viii, 161p. **772**

    Indicates the trend of Indian relations with other Asian nations as they have developed especially since 1947.

LEWIS, JOHN PRIOR. Quiet Crisis in India. New York, Macmillan, 1963. xiii, 350p. **773**

    A study of the implications of the foreign aid to India by the USA to assist her in the development plans.

MANDE, TIBOR. Conversations with Mr Nehru. London, Secker and Warburg, 1956. 144p. **774**

——Nehru: conversations on India and world affairs. American ed. New York, G. Braziller, 1956. 144p. **775**

MARTIN, ROBERT MONTGOMERY. British relations with the Chinese empire in 1832. Comparative statement of the English and American trade with India and Canton. London, Parbury, Allen & Co., 1832. viii, (9)—148p. **776**

MARYLAND UNIVERSITY. Bureau of Business and Economic Research. India in world affairs. College Park, 1957. 12p.

(*Its* studies in business and economics, V. 11, no. 1). 777

MELLER, PER. Indien och den asiatiska neutralisman. Stockholm, Kooparativa jourbundets bokforlog, 1955. 32p. 778

MOREHOUSE, WARD. American institutions and organizations interested in Asia; a reference directory. New York, Tapling Publishing Co., 1956. Annual. 779

PHIBLES, PHILIP M. Nehru's philosophy of international relations. Chicago, Library Dept. of Photographic Reproduction, University of Chicago, 1957. Microfilm 5460 D.S. 780

REY RIOS, ROBERTO. Diplomacia y derecho de guerra en la India antigua-Arequipa, Universided Nacional de Sen Augustin. 1949. 16p. 781

ROSINGER, LAWRENCE K. India and the United States; political and economic relations. New York, Macmillan, 1950. viii, 149p. 782

An account of political and economic relations between India and the United States during the post-Independence period.

SELIGMAN, EUSTACE. What the United States can do about India. New York, New York University, 1956. 56p. 783

A brief and readable survey of differences on the subject of foreign policy between the United States and India, condensed from a report in the bulletin of the Foreign Policy Association.

TALBOT, PHILLIPS. India and America; a study of their relations, by Phillips Talbot and S.L. Poplai. 1st ed. New York, published for the Council on Foreign Relations, by Harper, 1958. 200p. 784

TITO V. ASII, navsteva V Indii a Burme, Beograd, "Jugoslavija", 1955. 71p. illus. 785

WARD, BARBARA. India and the West. London, Hamish Hamilton, 1961. 295p. 1964 ed. published by Norton. 786

An analysis of India's efforts to enlist economic support from various Western countries.

WOHLERS, LESTER PAUL. The policy of India in relation to the tension between the Soviet Union and the United States, with special reference to the United Nations. Chicago, Library

Deptt. of Photographic Reproduction, University of Chicago, 1951. Microfilm 4390 DS. **787**
WOLF, CHARLES, JR. Foreign aid: theory and practice in Southern Asia. Princeton, University Press, 1960. xix, 442p. **788**
    A study of the American military and economic aid to Southern Asia with special reference to India.
YOUNGHUSBAND, Sir FRANCIS EDWARD. India and Tibet; a history of the relations which have subsisted between the two countries from the time of Warren Hastings to 1910; with a particular account of the mission to Lhasa of 1904. With maps and illustrations. London, J. Murray, 1910. xvi, 455p. front. plates, port. 2 fold. maps. **789**
———Our position in Tibet. Read November 2, 1910. Central Asia Society, 1910. Cover title. 15p. (Proceedings of the Central Asian Society) **790**

(xii) Government and Politics

BEARCE, GEORGE D. British attitudes towards India, 1784-1858. London, Oxford University Press, 1961. viii, 315p. **791**
    This valuable study describes the attitude of the British people towards India before 1857.
BELL, THOMAS EVANS. Public service in India. London, Trubner & Co., 1871. viii, 62p. **792**
BIRDWOOD, CHRISTOPHER BROMHEAD. India and Pakistan; a continent decides. New York, Praeger, 1954. 315p. group ports. maps. (Books that matter). **793**
BROWN, DONALD MACKENZIE. The white umbrella; Indian political thought from Manu to Gandhi. Foreword by C.P. Ramaswamy Aiyer. Berkeley and Los Angeles, University of California Press, 1953. xv, 205p. **794**
    Presents the landmarks of the Hindu political tradition.
CAMPBELL, Sir GEORGE. Modern India : a sketch of the system of civil Govt. London, John Murray, 1852. xii, 560p. **795**
CHAILLEY-BERT, M. JOSEPH. The administrative problems of British India. Tr. from French by Sir William Meyer. London, Macmillan & Co., 1910. xv, 590p. (F) **796**

This English version is not a literal translation of the French text.

DEAN, VERA MICHELES. New patterns of democracy in India. 2d ed. Boston, Harvard, 1969. 255p. **797**

DIGBY, WILLIAM. 'Prosperous', British India: a revelation from official records. London, T. Fisher Unwin, 1901. xlvii, 661p. **798**

Reveals through records the impoverished condition of British India.

FOX, RICHARD G. Kin, clan, Raja, and rule: State-hinterland relations in preindustrial India, Berkeley, University of California, 1971, 187p. **799**

GETTEL, RAYMOND GARFIELD. Political science. Calcutta, World Press, 1950. Rev. ed. viii, 504p. **800**

First published in New York in 1933, it is a commentary on political condition in India in 1930s.

GWYAN, JOHN TUDOR. Indian politics: a survey. Introduction by Lord Meston. London, Nisbet & Co., 1924. xii, 344p. **801**

A collection of letters written from India on Indian politics.

GWYER, Sir MAURICE LINFORD. Speeches and documents on the Indian constitution, 1921-47, selected by Sir Maurice Gwyer and A. Appadorai, with an introduction by A. Appadorai. Bombay. New York, Oxford University Press, 1957. 2 vols. (lxx, 802p.) tables. **802**

KOCHANEK, STANLEY A. The Congress Party of India, the dynamics of one party democracy. Princeton, Princeton University, 1968. 516p. **803**

LILLY, WILLIAM SAMUEL. India and its problems. London, Sands & Co., 1902. xx, 324p. fold. map. **804**

LINLITHGOW, VICTOR ALEXANDER JOHN HOPE, 2nd Marquis of. The transitional provisions of the Government of India Act, 1935. Being the presidential address of the president of the Holdsworth Club. Birmingham, Eng. Holdsworth Club of the University of Birmingham, 1945. 11p. **805**

MACDONALD, JAMES RAMSAY. The Government of India. London, Swarthmore Press, 1919. ix, 202p. **806**

MONTAGUE, EDWIN S. An Indian diary, ed. by Venetia Montague. London, William Heinemann, 1930. xv, 410p. **807**

"The former Secretary of State for India and the author of the 1919 Reforms here describes impressions of men and affairs in India during the time of his visit."

MOON, PENDEREL. Strangers in India. New York, Reynal & Hitchcock, 1945. 212p. **808**
    An account in dialogue form of the political problem the British government faced and solved during 1930.

MORLEY, Viscount JOHN. Indian speeches (1907-1909). London, Macmillan & Co., 1909. viii, 164p. **809**
    A collection of eight speeches on British rule in India.

MORRIS-JONES, WYNDRAETH H. Parliament in India. Philadelphia, University of Pennysylvania Press. 1957. xii, 417p. **810**
    An account of the composition, organization and procedures of India's state and central legislation with special reference to Lok Sabha and Rajya Sabha.

PALMER, NORMAN D. The Indian political system. 2nd ed. New York, Houghton, 1971. 325p. **811**

PARK, RICHARD L. AND IRENE TINKER, eds. Leadership and political institutions in India. Princeton, Princeton University Press, 1959. **812**
    This collection of articles deals with many political and social issues prevailing in India after 1947.

PHILIPS, CYRIL H., ed. A collection of essays by P. Hardy, W.H. Morris-Jones, F.G. Bailey and others on politics and society in India. **813**
    A useful work.

ROSEN, GEORGE. Democracy and economic change in India. Berkeley, University of California, 1967. 340p. **814**

RUDOLPH, LLOYD I. The modernity of tradition; political development in India. Chicago, University of Chicago, 1967. 306p. **815**

SCHUSTER, GEORGE ERNEST AND WINT, GUY. India and democracy. Introduction by George Schuster. London, Macmillan & Co., 1941. xvi, 444p. **816**
    The book is in two parts; Pt. 1 by Guy Wint; Pt. 2 by George Schuster.

SICHROVSKY, HARRY. Dschai Hind; Indien ohne schleier. Wient,

Globus Verlag, 1954. 319p. **817**

STOKES, ERIC. The English utilitarians and India. Oxford, Clarendon Press. xvi, 350p. **818**

THORNTON, EDWARD. India, its state and prospects. London, Parbury, Allen & Co., 1835. 1p.] (v) xx, 354p. **819**

TINKER, HUGH. The foundations of local Self-Government in India, Pakistan and Burma. London, Athlone, 1954. xxiv, 376p. **820**

> A history of the British administration in India, Pakistan and Burma from 1882 to 1947. It is a controversial book.

WEINER, MYRON. Party politics in India: the development of a multi-party system. Princeton, Princeton University Press, 1957. **821**

> A study of the origin, development and politics of various political parties in India.

——— The politics of scarcity: public pressure and political response in India. Chicago, University of Chicago Press, 1962. 251p. **822**

> An analysis of the pressure tactics of some political groups, which try to influence the political and economic development in India.

WILSON, PATRICK, ed. Government and politics of India and Pakistan, 1885-1955; a bibliography of works in Western languages. Berkeley, University of California, 1956. 357p. **823**

> An extremely detailed bibliography, including even unpublished theses and pamphlets.

WOOD, WILLIAM MARTIN. The spoilt child of Indian family: or Bengal's favoured position at the Financial Board (The preface signed: W.M.W., i.e. W.M. Wood) 1868. 21p. **824**

ZINKIN, TAYA. India changes. London, Oxford University Press, 1958. vii, 233p. **825**

> An appraisal of the political conditions in India after 1947.

——— Reporting India. London, Chatto and Windus, 1962. 223p. **826**

> A journalistic study of the major political, economic and social issues in the post-independence period in India.

See also Administration.
Constitution and Constitutional Reforms.

(xiii) Labour and Labour Classes

BROUGHTON, G.M. Labour in Indian industries. Bombay, Humphrey Milford, Oxford University Press, 1924. vii, 214p. **827**
Thesis approved for D.Sc. by the London University.

LAMBERT, RICHARD D. Workers, factories and social change in India. Princeton, Princeton University Press, 1963. xiii, 247p. **828**
A socio-economic study of the problems of labour and workers in factories in India.

LUDLOW, JOHN MALCOLM FORBES. Progress of the working class, 1832-1867, by J.M. Ludlow and Lloyd Jones. London, A Straham, 1867. 1p. 1., (v)—xv, 304p. **829**

See also Economic Conditions.

(xiv) Land and People

BADEN-POWELL, BADEN HENRY. The Indian village community examined with reference to the physical, ethnographic and historical conditions of the provinces; chiefly on the basis of the revenue settlement records and district manuals. London, New York (etc.), Longmans, Green & Co., 1896. xvi, 456p. fold. maps. diagrs. **830**

—— The origin and growth of village communities in India. London, S. Sonnensckein & Co., lim., New York, C. Scribner's Sons, 1899. vip., 1 l., 155p. (Social Science Series, no. 94). **831**

BALL, VALENTINE. Notes on the Kheriahs, an aboriginal race living in the hill tracts of Manbhum. 1885. 4p. **832**

BIDDULPH, JOHN. Tribes of the Hindoo Koosh. Cal., Supdt. Govt. Press, 1880. vi, 164, clxvip. **833**

BLOCH, J. Les Tsiganes. Paris, 1953. 118p. (F). **834**

BLOCK, MARTIN. Zigeuner, ihr leben und ihre seele, dargestellt auf grund eigener reisen und forschungen; mit 99 abbildungen auf 64 kunstdrucktafeln. Leipzig, Bibliographisches institute, a.g. (1936). 8p. 1., 219 (1)p. plates, port. (G). **835**

BOTHWELL, JEAN. Cobras, cows and courage. New York, Coward-Mccann, 1956. 96p. **836**

"A simple but comprehensive look at peasant life in North India, this is one of the year's best non-fiction works for young readers." E.W. Foell in the Christian Science Monitor.

—— The empty tower. New York, Morrow, 1948. 160p. **837**
With some last-minute help from the Maharaja, Premi and her friends stage a fair to raise money for a school bell. Miss Bothwell spent twelve years in India, and writes about it with affection and understanding.

—— Story of India. New York, Harcourt, Brace, 1952. 180p. **838**

The history of India and its people, written for American children.

—— The thirteenth stone. New York, Harcourt, Brace, 1946. 225p. **839**

A prize-winning story of Rajputana, described by one reviewer as conveying "the colour, the sounds, the very odours of India so that the reader closes the book richer for experiencing life in a distant land."

BURTON, RICHARD FRANCIS. Sindh, and the races that inhabit the valley of the Indus; with notices of the topography and history of the Province. London, W.H. Allen & Co., 1851. viii, 422p. front. (fold map). **840**

CHAUVELOT, ROBERT. Mysterious India: its Rajas, its Brahmans, its Fakirs, tr. by Eleanor Stimson Brooks. London, Werner Laurice, 1922, xx, 277p. (F). **841**

CORBETT, JAMES EDWARD. My India. Bombay, Geoffrey Cumberlege, Oxford University Press, 1952. viii, 190p. **842**

"Describes the ways of the Indian villagers and labourers who live near the edge of the jungle and whose lives are spent in poverty and unceasing work and who find their happiness in simple pleasures and a trusting, unquestioning faith."

CUMPSTON, I.M. Indians overseas in British territories, 1834-1854. London, Oxford University Press, 1952. 208p. **843**

DAVIS, KINGSLEY, ed. The population of India and Pakistan. Princeton, Princeton University, 1951. 263p. **844**
  A comprehensive study of the population of India and Pakistan, as well as a careful interpretation of the social and economic structure.

DOUGLAS, WILLIAM O. Strange lands and friendly people. New York, Harper. 1951. 336p. **845**
  "I fell in love with India. Partly for its Himalayas, whose grandeur is not of this earth. Partly for its mysticism, its spiritual strength. Partly because India of today is an ancient civilization rising from the mire of poverty, illiteracy, and feudalism by the heroic efforts of a few men and women."

DUBOIS, JEAN A. A description of the character, manners, and customs of the people of India; and of their institutions, religious and civil. Translated from the French manuscript. London, 1817. **846**

—— Description of the character, manners and customs of the people of India, etc. Calcutta, Society for the Resuscitation of Indian Literature, 1905. iii, 434, xvip. **847**

ELSMIE, GEORGE ROBERT. Thirty-five years in the Punjab, 1858-1893. Edinburgh, David Douglas, 1908. xvii, 386p. **848**

ELWIN, VERRIER. The Agaria. London, Oxford University Press, 1942. xxxv, 292p. 36pl. **849**

—— The Baiga. London, J. Murray (1939). 3, 1, xxxi(1), 550p. front. illus. **850**

—— Maria murder and suicide. 2nd ed. Bombay, Oxford University Press (1950). xxxi, 259p. illus. ports. map. **851**

—— The Muria and their Ghotul. Bombay, Oxford University Press, 1947. xxix, 730p. CL pl. **852**

FOREST, Sir GEORGE WILLIAM. Cities of India. Westminster. A Constable and Co., ltd., 1903. xvi, 356p. illus. map. **853**

FORESTER, GEORGE. Sketches of the mythology and customs of the Hindoos. London, 1785. 3, 1, 84p. Dedication signed: George Forester. **854**

FRASER, ANDREW HENDERSON LEITH. Among Indian Rajahs

and ryots. 3rd ed. London, Seely & Co., 1912. xvi, 376p. **855**
"A civil servant's recollections and impressions of 37 years of work and sport in the Central Provinces and Bengal."

GARTH, RIGHT HON. Sir RICHARD. A few plain truths about India. London, W. Thacker & Co., 1888. 52p. **856**

GILBERT, WILLIAM HARLEN., Jr. People of India. Washington, D.C. Smithsonian Institution. War Background Studies, 1944. 86p. 21pl. **857**

GRIERSON, Sir GEORGE ABRAHAM. Bihar peasant life, being a discursive catalogue of the surroundings of the people of that province, with many illustrations from photographs taken by the author. Prepared (in 1885) under orders of the Government of Bengal, 2d and rev. ed. Patna, Superintendent, Government printing, Bihar and Orissa, 1926. 3, 1, 4, 29, vi, 433, xvii, civp. Illus., plates, maps. **858**

HAIMENDORF, C.F. Himalayan barbary. Abelard-Schuman, 1956. 241p. **859**

 At the request of the Government of India, the author and his wife spent several months exploring the geography and tribal life of the Indo-Tibetan borderlands.

HEBER, REGINALD, bp. of Calcutta Narrative of a journey through the upper provinces of India, from Calcutta to Bombay, 1824-1825 (with notes upon Ceylon); an account of journey to Madras and the Southern Provinces, 1826; and letter written to India. New ed. London, J. Murray, 1873. 2v. (On cover: Murray's colonial and home library). **860**

HOLDICH, Sir THOMAS HUNGERFORD. India. New York, D. Appleton and Company, 1905. xii, 375p. illus. (maps) viii fold. maps. diagrs. **861**

HOOTON, ERNEST G. Up from the ape. New York, Macmillan, 1946. rev. ed. xxii, 786p. **862**

 Useful for a standard classification of South Asia's races in India.

HOPKINS, EDWARD WASHBURN. India old and new, with a memorial address. New York, G. Scribner's Sons, (etc. etc.), 1901. **863**

HUNTER, Sir WILLIAM WILSON. Annals of rural Bengal. 7th ed.

London. Smith, Elder and Co., 1897. xivp. 1 l., 475p. **864**
HUNTER, Sir WILLIAM WILSON. A brief history of the Indian peoples. 23rd ed. Oxford, Clarendon Press, 1903. 260p. front. (fold map). **865**
—— The imperial gazetteer of India. 2d ed. London, Trubner & Co., 1885-87. 14v. fold maps. vol. 14 index. **866**
—— India, by Sir William W. Hunter and *modern Persia,* ed. by George M. Dutcher. (Ed. de Luxe). Philadelphia, J.D. Moris and Co (1906). xvii, 421p. front. plates (1 col.) port. maps. (Half title: The history of nations. (vol. v) **867**
—— Orissa. London, Smith, Elder & Co., 1872. 2v. fronts. (1 col). plates, fold, map. plan. **868**
—— A statistical account of Assam. London, Trubner & Co., 1879. 2v. fronts. (fold maps). **869**
Imperial Gazetteer of India. New ed., pub. under the authority of His Majesty's Secretary of State for India in Council. Oxford, Clarendon Press, 1907-31. 26v. maps. **870**

1st ed., 9v., 1881., and 2d ed., 14v., 1885-87, ed. by Sir William Wilson Hunter. The present may be considered as a new book, rather than a new edition-Cf. general pref.

Editor for India; 1902-4, William Stevenson Meyer; 1905-9, Richard Burn. Editor in England: James Sutherland Cotton.

v. 1-4, Indian-Empire: v. 1, Descriptive; v. 2, Historical; v. 3, Economic; v. 4, Administrative; v. 5-24, Gazetteer; v. 25, General index; v. 26, Atlas. (Atlas, new rev. ed. 1931).

Includes historical, topographical, ethnical, agricultural, industrial, administrative, and medical aspects of the various districts of British India.

IRVINE, ANDREW ALEXANDER. Land of no regrets. London, Collins, 1938. 352p. **871**

An account of personal impressions about India during thirty-two years of service in the country.

KEENE, HENRY GEORGE. Keene's handbook for visitors to Agra. Re-written and brought up to date by E.A. Duncan. 7th ed. Calcutta, Thacker, Spink & Co.; London, W. Thacker & Co., 1909. 295p. **872**

KENNEDY, JEAN. Here is India. New York, Scribner, (1945),

1954. 154p. **873**
> A "purview of India," first published in 1945 and now brought up to date, with new photographs. The author was born in India, and returned to teach after graduating from college.

LAWRENCE, ROSAMOND (NAPIER). Indian embers. Oxford, George Ronald, 1949. 397p. **874**
> An account of daily life in India, as experienced by senior civil servant.

LEWIN, THOMAS HARBERT. Wild races of South-Eastern India. London, W.H. Allen & Co., 1870. viii, 352p. **875**

LUARD, C.E. Ethnographical survey of the Central India Agency. Lucknow, 1909. **876**

MACMUNN, GEORGE FLETCHER. The martial races of India. London, Sampson Law, Marston & Co. xiii, 368p. **877**
> "Tells in a simple manner the story of Rajput and Turk, of Afghan and Sikh, of Maharatta and Mogul."

MACRITCHIE, DAVID, *ed.* Accounts of the Gypsies of India. London, K. Paul, Trench & Co., 1886. viii, 1 l., 254p. front. col. l. **878**

MATHEWS, BASIL JOSEPH. London, Humphrey Milford, Oxford University Press, 1937. viii, 192p. **879**
> "An account of the trend of life in India, from intimate talks with men and women in every walk of life, and of many faiths and political attitudes."

MILLS, JAMES PHILIP. The Ao Nagas. London, Macmillan & Co., 1926. xviii, 500p. **880**

—— The Lhota Nagas. London, Macmillan & Co., 1922. xxxix, 255p. **881**

MONIER-WILLIAMS, Sir MONIER. Modern India and the Indians; being a series of impressions, notes, and essays, by Monier Williams. 3d ed., rev. and augm. by considerable additions. London, Trubner & Co., 1879. 4, l, k, 365p. front. (map) illus. **882**

MUIR, JOHN. Original Sanskrit texts on the origin and history of the people of India, their religion and institutions. Collected, translated, and illustrated by J. Muir. 2d ed., rewritten and greatly enlarged. London, Trubner & Co., 1868-73.

5v. **883**

NAIPAUL, V.S. Area of darkness. London, Andre Deutsch, 1964. 281p. **884**

    A critical account of India's social, political and economic conditions which the author wrote after his visit to various cities of India.

NEBOSKY-WOJKOWITZ, R. VON. Where the gods are mountains. Translated from German by Michael. Bullock. London, Weidenfield, 1956. 256p. **885**

    A pen picture of the religious beliefs of the people who reside near Himalayas. The author stayed with them for three years.

NICHOLS, BEVERLEY. Verdict on India. Bombay, Thacker & Co., 1945. 256p. **886**

    "An endeavour to trace the working of the Indian mind not only in politics but *inter alia*—in art, in literature, in music, in medicine, in journalism, in cinema, and in religion."

O'MALLEY, LEWIS SYDNEY STEWART. Modern India and the West: a study of the interaction of their civilizations. Foreword by Lord Meston. London, Oxford University Press, 1941. xii, 834p. (Published under the auspices of the Royal Institute of International Affairs.) **887**

    "Discusses on the nature, extent, and effects of the influence which Western civilization has had upon the life and thought of India since the beginning of the sixteenth century, and traces the influence which India has had upon the West."

OPPERT, GUSTAV SALOMON. On the original inhabitants of Bharatavarsa or India. Westminster, A Constable & Co., 1893. xv, 711p. **888**

PARTON, MARGARET. Leaf and the flame. London, Bodley Head, 1959. 277p. **889**

    A journalistic account of the social, political and economic conditions of the people of India.

RAND, CHRISTOPHER. A nostalgia for camels. Boston Little, Brown, 1957. 279p. **890**

    Brief and meaningful episodes in Asian life as observed

by a well-known free lance writer. Portraits of Tenzing and Vinoba Bhave are included.

RISLEY, Sir HERBERT. The people of India. Calcutta, Thacker, Spink, 1915. xxxii, 472p. maps. **891**
First published in 1908, it is an outstanding contribution to the study of races and culture in India. Includes 36 photographic plates with brief descriptions.

RISLEY, HERBERT HOPE. Tribes and castes of Bengal—Anthropometric data. Calcutta, Printed at Bengal Secretariat Press, 1891. 2 vols. tables. **892**

ROBERT, L. Nadars of Tamilnad; political culture of a community in change. Bombay, Oxford University Press, 1970. 314p. **893**

ROWNEY, HORATIO BICKERSTAFFE. The wild tribes of India. London. De la Rue & Co., 1882. xv, 224p. **894**

SAUTER, J.A. Among the Brahmins and Parihas. Tr. from the German by Bernard Miall. London, T. Fisher Unwin, 1924. 241p. **895**

SERBOIANU, C.J. POPP. Le Tsiganes. Paris, 1930. 397p. **896**

SHERRING, MATTHEW ATMORE. Hindu tribes and castes. Calcutta, Thacker, Spink & Co., 1872-81. 3v. plates, general. tab. **897**

—— Hindu tribes and castes. Calcutta, Thacker, Spink & Co., London, Trubner & Co., (etc.) 1872-81. 3v. plates, general. tab. vol. 1 has title: Hindu tribes and castes, as represented in Benaras. **898**

SLEEMAN, Sir WILLIAM HENRY. Rambles and recollections of an Indian official. Edited by V.A. Smith. London, Oxford University Press, 1915. Rev. ed. xxxix, 667p. **899**
Originally published in 1844, it is a collection of essays on the land and people of North and Central India in the early 19th century.

—— Report on Budhuk alias Bagree dacoits, and other gang robbers by hereditary profession, and on the measures adopted by the Government of India, for their suppression. Calcutta, J.C. Sherriff, 1849. 2, 1., iv, 433p. front. (fold. map). **900**

—— The thugs of Pansigars of India: comprising a history of

the rise and progress of that extraordinary fraternity of assassins; and a description of the system which it pursues and of the measures which have been adopted by the supreme government of India for their suppression. Compiled from original and authentic documents published by Captain W.H. Sleeman, Superintendent of Thug Police. Philadelphia, Carey & Hart, 1839. 2v. in. l. **901**

TAYLOR, ALICE. India. Illustrated by Rafaello Busoni. New York, Holiday House, 1957. 28p. illus. (Lands and people volumes). **902**

TAYLOR, MEADOWS. The confessions of a thug, edited by F. Yeats Brown. London, Eyre & Spottiswoode, 1938. 326p. fold. map. **903**

THOMAS, LOWALL JACKSON. India: land of the black pagoda. New York, Century Co., 1930. 350p. **904**

THORBURN, SEPTIMUS SMET. The Punjab in peace and war. Edinburgh and London, William Blackwood & Sons, 1904. vi, 364p. 6 fold. maps. (partly col.). **905**

TURNER, Sir RALPH LILLEY. The position of Romani in Indo-Aryan. London, 1927. 47p. (Gypsy Lore Society. Monograph no. 4). **906**

WADDELL, LAURENCE AUSTINE. Among the Himalayas, by Major L.A. Waddell. With numerous illustrations by A.D. McCormick the author and others, and from photographs, (2d ed.) Westminster, A. Constable & Co., Philadelphia, J.B. Lippincott Co., 1900. xvi, 452p. incl. front. illus. pl. port, maps, fold, map. **907**

WARNER, Sir WILLIAM LEE. The citizen of India. Revised edition. London, Macmillan & Co., 1907. xii, 246p. First edition published in 1897. **908**

WATSON, J. FORBES, ed. ⁋People of India. London, Indian Museum, 1868. 5 vols. **909**

An illustrated account of races and tribes of India.

WATTS, NEVILLE A. Half-clad tribals of Eastern India. Calcutta, Orient Longman, 1970. 154p. **910**

WILKIN, E.C. Dekho; the India that was. New Hampshire. Wake-Brook House, 1958. 286p. **911**

A pen-picture of the authoress's impression of India in

the form of a dialogue.

YAUKEY, GRACE (SYDENSTRICKER). Made in India: the story of India's people and of their gift to the world. New York, Alfred A. Knoff, xii, 203, ivp. **912**

See also Biography
        Culture and Civilization
        Social Conditions

(xv) Land Reforms

BADEN-POWELL, BADEN HENRY. The land system of British India; being a manual of the land tenures and of the systems of land revenue administration prevalent in the several provinces. With maps. Oxford, Clarendon Press, 1892. 3v. maps. (part fold). fold tab. **913**

    A valuable source book on the land-system of the British Government in India before 1892.

——A manual of the land revenue systems and land tenures of British India (Primarily intended as a textbook for the use of officers of the Forest Service). Calcutta, Office of the Superintendent of Government Printing, 1882. xii, 787p. illus. **914**

——A short account of the land revenue and its administration in British India; with a sketch of the land tenures. With map. Oxford, Clarendon Press, 1894. vi., 1 l., 260p. fold. map. 2nd rev. ed. was published in 1907. **915**

CAMPBELL, Sir GEORGE. Tenure of land in India. London, Cobden Club, 1870. vi, 429p. **916**

MOORE, F.J., AND FREYDIG, V. A. Land tenure legislation in Uttar Pradesh. Berkeley, University of California, 1955. 124p. **917**

NIGHTINGALE, FLORENCE. Florence Nightingale's Indian letters; a glimpse into the agitation for tenancy reform, Bengal, 1878-82. Ed. by Priyaranjan Sen. Calcutta, Mihir Kumar Sen, 1937. xix, 67p. **918**

READ, MARGARET. Indian peasant uprooted : a study of the human machine. Foreword by J.A. Whitley. London, Longmans, Green & Co., n.d. xiv, 256p. **919**

Deals with the social and economic conditions of the voiceless millions of Indian peasants.

TAYLOR, MEADOWS, *i.e.* PHILIP MEADOWS. A statement and remarks relating to the expenses of irrigation from wells in the Deccan Khandesh, etc. By Captain Meadows Taylor, Deputy Commissioner, Raichor Doab. Bombay, Printed for Government at the Bombay Education Society's Press, 1856, 1, 1., 15p. **920**

TENNYSON, HALLAM. India's waking saint : the story of Vinoba Bhave. New York, Doubleday, 1955. 224p. **921**

"An absorbing and humane account of life and forces stirring today in India's villages." Marguerite Brown in the *New York Times.* The author walked with Vinoba Bhave to a number of villages both as an observer and as an advocate of Bhoodan.

THORNER, DANIEL. The agrarian prospects in India. Delhi, Delhi University Press, 1956. 89p. **922**

A detailed study of the land reforms in India after 1947.

WOOD, WILLIAM MARTIN. Land in India: whose is it: Being a comparison of the principles at issue. London, Philip S. King, 1862. 23p. **923**

See also Economic Conditions

(xvi) Laws

BADAN-POWELL, BADEN HENRY. A manual of jurisprudence for forest officers. Being a treatise on the forest law, and those branches of the general civil and criminal law which are connected with forest administration; with a comparative notice of the chief continental laws. Calcutta, Printed by the Superintendent of Government Printing, India, 1882. xiii 1 1., 558p. **924**

BUHLER, GEORGE, *tr.* The laws of Manu. Oxford, Clarendon Press, 1886. cxxxviii, 620p. **925**

A faithful translation of the *Manu Smirti* or Dharma Shastra.

———*ed. & tr.* The sacred laws of the Aryans. Oxford, Clarendon

105

Press, 1879-82. 2 vols. **926**

A translation of the most important *Dharma Sutras* which were probably composed between the 6th and 2nd centuries B.C.

DOUGLAS, WILLIAM ORVILLE. From Marshall to Mukherjea; studies in American and Indian constitutional law. Calcutta, Eastern Law House, 1955. xxxiii, 361p. (Tagore law lectures, 1955). **927**

——We the judges; studies in American and Indian constitutional law from Marshall to Mukherjea. Garden City, N.Y. Doubleday, 1956. 480p. tables. **928**

Comparative studies in American and Indian constitutional law, from Marshall to Mukherjea, delivered as the Tagore Lectures at the University of Calcutta in July 1955.

GARTH, RIGHT HON. Sir RICHAR. Minute on the Bengal Rent Bill. Calcutta, "Hindoo Patriot" Press, 1883. 36p. **929**

GOLDSTUECKER, THEODORE. On the deficiencies in the present administration of Hindu law; being a paper read at the meeting of the East India Association on the 8th of June, 1870, by Th. Goldstuecker. London, Trubner & Co., 1871. 56p. **930**

Includes bibliographies.

ILBERT, Sir COURTENAY PEREGRINE. The Government of India; a brief historical survey of Parliamentary legislation relating to India. Oxford, Clarendon Press, 1922. viii, 144p. **931**

——The Government of India, being a digest of the statute law relating thereto; with historical introductions and explanatory matter. 3rd ed. Oxford, Clarendon Press; London & New York, H. Milford, 1915. xxxvi (1), 1 l., 499p. The 1st and 2nd editions were published in 1898 and 1907 respectively. **932**

——The Government of India, supplementary chapter (Indian Councils Act, 1909). Oxford, Clarendon Press; New York, H. Frowde (etc), 1910. 2, 1., p. (409)-454p. **933**

——The mechanics of law-making. New York, Columbia University Press, 1914. viii, 209p. (Half title : Columbia University lectures, 1913. **934**

JONES, Sir WILLIAM. An essay on the law of bailments. From the last London edition, with notes, and an appendix. Philadelphia, Hogan and Thompson, 1836. xi, 123, 126, (cxxvii)-cxxxivp. **935**

JONES, Sir WILLIAM. Three tracts. An inquiry into the legal mode of suppressing riots, with a constitutional plan of future defence. London, E. Wilson, 1819. iv, (5)-68p. **936**

JOLLY, JULIUS, ed. & tr. The minor law-books, translated by Julius. Part I. Narada. Brihaspati. Oxford, Clarendon Press, 1889. xxiv, 396p. (Added title page: The sacred books of the East. vol. xxxiii). **937**

—— Outlines of a history of the Hindu law of partition, inheritance, and adoption, as contained in the original Sanskrit treatises. Calcutta, Thacker, Spink and Co., London, W. Thacker and Co.; (etc., etc.), 1885. xi, 347p. (Tagore Law lectures, 1883). **938**

KENNEDY, VANS. Practical remarks on the proceedings of general courts martial. London, Printed by A. Strahan for J. & W.T. Clarke, 1825. xxii, 355p. **939**

—— A treatise on the principles and practice of military law. A rev. ed. Bombay, American Mission Press, 1847. vii, (v)—xix, 371p. **940**

LINLITHGOW, VICTOR ALEXANDER JOHN HOPE, *2nd marquis of*. The traditional provisions of the Government of India Act, 1935. Being the presidential address of the President of the Holdsworth Club. Birmingham, Eng. Holdsworth Club of the University of Birmingham, 1945. 11p. **941**

LYON, ISIDORE BERNADOTTE. Lyon's medical jurisprudence for India, with illustrative cases, by T.F. Owens. 9th ed. Edited and rev. Calcutta, Thacker, Spink & Co., (1933) London, W. Thacker & Co., 1935. xvi, 767p. illus. **942**

MARSHMAN, JOHN CLARK, *comp*. Guide to the civil law of the presidency of Fort William, containing all the unrepealed regulations, acts, constructions and circular orders of government, and select and summary reports of the sudder courts. 2d ed., cor. to the 30th June, 1848 (Serampore). Serampore Press, 1848. 2, 1., xlviii, 1026p. **943**

PERRY, Sir THOMAS ERSKINE. Cases illustrative of oriental life, and the application of English law to India, decided in H.M. Supreme Court at Bombay. London, S. Sweet, 1853. xv,

Sources of Indian Civilization

602p. **944**

RANKIN, GEORGE C. Background to Indian Law. Cambridge, Cambridge University Press, 1946. 223p. **945**

    An account of the development of law in India during the period of British rule.

ROUTLEDGE, JAMES. Chapters in the history of popular progress, chiefly in relation to the freedom of the press and trial by jury. 1660-1820. With an application to later years. London, Macmillan & Co., 1876. viii, (1), 631, (1)p. **946**

STRANGE, Sir THOMAS ANDREW LUMISDEN. Elements of Hindu law; referable to British judicature in India. London, Payne and Foss (etc.), 1825. 2v. **947**

    V. 2 has title: Responsa prodentum; or Opinions of pandits attached to the courts established throughout the interior of the territories dependent upon the government of Madras: with other original papers, as prepared and arranged for the preceding work.

——Hindu law; principally with reference to such portions of it as concern the administration of justice, in the Kings courts in India. 4th ed. With an introduction, by J.D. Mayne and a digest of reported cases on points of Hindu law and notes indicating changes made by statue law. Madras, J. Higginbotham; (etc. etc.) 1864. 1p. 1., iii, 384 (i.e. 388)p. **948**

    First published in two volumes, London, 1825 under title: *Elements of Hindu Law.*
    See also Constitution and Constitutional History
    Government and Politics
    Peasants and landlords
    See Labour and Labour Classes
    Land Reforms

Political Parties See Govt. & Politics
Population See Land & People

(xvii) Social Conditions

ANSTEY, RUTH. The sun casts a shadow. Illustrations by T. David Grice. London, Cargate Press, 1957. 132p. illus. **949**

300 Social Sciences

ARONSON, ALEXANDER. Europe looks at India: a study in cultural relations. Foreword by D.P. Mukherji. Bombay, Hind Kitabs, 1946. x, 200p. **950**
"An analysis of the cultural relations between Europe and India within the context of modern social history during the last hundred and fifty years."

BALLHATCHAT, KENNETH. Social policy and social change in Western India, 1817-1880. London, New York, Oxford University Press, 1957. vii, 335p. port. maps. London, oriental series, v. 5). **951**

BALNEAVES, ELIZABETH. Peacocks and pipelines; Baluchistan to Bihar. London. Lutterworth Press, 1958. 144p. illus. **952**

BARTHOLOMEW, CAROL. My heart has seventeen rooms. New York, Macmillan, 1959. 177p. **953**

BLUNT, EDWARD ARTHUR HENRY. The caste system of Northern India with special reference to the United Provinces of Agra and Oudh. Madras, Oxford University Press, 1931. viii, 374p. **954**
"A full and connected account of caste as a system, describing the factors which brought caste into existence, the evolution of the present system, the nature of the customs common to all castes, and the difference between caste and caste."

BOWLES, CYNTHIA. At home in India. Illustrated with photos. New York, Harcourt, Brace, 1956. 180p. illus. **955**

BRIGGS, GEORGE WESTON. The Chamars. Calcutta, Y.M.C.A. Association Press, 1920. 270p. (The religious life of India series). **956**
"Deals mostly with the Chamaras of the United Province (now Uttar Pradesh), but the Chamars and the leather workers of other parts of India as well have been noted."

BURKE, NORAH. Jungle child. With 32 photos by Aileen Burke. New York, W.W. Norton, 1956. 278p. illus. **957**

CANNON, PHILIP SPENCER. Citizen in India; its privileges and duties. Bombay, Oxford University Press, 1923. 199p. **958**
"A book prepared for the use of Indian Army Education Corps."

CHACKO, GEORGE KUTTICKAL. India: toward an understanding;

a de novo inquiry into the mind of India in search of an answer to the question: "Will India Go Communist" New York, Bookman Associates, 1959. 212p. **959**

COHN, BERNARD SAMUEL. India : the social anthropology of a civilization. New Jersey, Prentice-Hall, 1971. 164p. **960**

CORMACK, MARGARET. The Hindu woman. Foreword by Lois Barclay Marphy. New York, Bureau of publications. Teachers College, Columbia University, 1953. xiii, 207p. **961**

> Based on the interviews with ten Indian women students at Columbia University, it is an attempt to delineate pattern of "typical" role behaviour for Hindu women.

CORNELL, UNIVERSITY. Deptt. of Far Eastern Studies India Program. India, sociological background; an area handbook. Editor: Elizabeth E. Bacon. Associate Editor: Baidya Nath Verma. Contributors: Elizabeth E. Bacon and others. Ithaca, N.Y., Cornell University for the Human Relations Area Files, 1956-. Vols. maps. (Human Relations Area Files, Inc. Subcontractor's monograph, HRAF-44). **962**

CROOKE, WILLIAM. The tribes and castes of N.W.F.P. and Oudh, with plates. Calcutta, Office Supdt. Govt. Press, 1896. 4 vol. **963**

DIGBY, WILLIAM. The famine campaign in Southern India. London, Longmans & Co., 1878. 2 vol. **964**

DOURESSAMY, C. Vengkatta. Paris, France Editions nouvelles, 1956. 187p. (F). **965**

DUNBAR, JANET. Golden interlude: the Edens in India, 1836-1842. London, J. Murray, 1955. 289p. illus. Also published in U.S.A. by Hougton, Mifflin, Boston, in 1956. **966**

EDWARDES, STEPHEN MEREDYTH. Crime in India. London, Oxford University Press, 1924. viii, 169p. **967**

> A brief review of the more important offences included in the annual criminal returns; with chapters on prostitution and miscellaneous matters.

ELLIS, FRANCIS WHYTE. Replies to seventeen questions, proposed by the Government of Fort St. George, relative to mirasi right; with two appendices, elucidatory of the subject. Madras, Printed at the Government Gazettee Office, 1818. vii, 65p. **968**

ELWIN, VARRIER. The Agaria. Foreword Sarat Chandra Ray. Calcutta, Bombay, Himphrey Milford, Oxford University Press, 1942. xxv, 292p. **969**
    Crafts and myths of the Agaria people of the Central Provinces (Madhya Pradesh). Shows how the myths lie at the root of the social relations and the religious economic structure of Agaria society.

——The Baiga. Foreword by J.H. Hutton. London, John Murray, 1939. xxxi, 550p. **970**

——Bondo highlander, Bombay, Calcutta, Geofferey Cumberledge, Oxford University Press, 1950. xix, 290p. **971**
    A study of a certain section of the tribal life of Orissa.

——Maria murder and suicide. Foreword by W. V. Grigson. 2d ed. Calcutta, Geoffrey Cumberlege, Oxford University Press, 1950. xxxi, 256p. **972**
    "This book is a contribution to social anthropology rather than to the study of crime."

——The Muria and their ghotul. Bombay, Calcutta, Geoffrey Cumberlege, Oxford University Press, 1947. xxix, 730p. **973**
    "A study of the aboriginal tribe of the Bastar State, Central Provinces (Madhya Pradesh).

——Myths of middle India. Madras, Geoffrey Cumberlege, Oxford University Press, 1940. xvi, 532p. (Specimens of the oral literature of Middle India series). **974**

——A philosophy for NEFA. Shillong, North-East Frontier Agency, 1959. 296p. **975**
    A useful study by the author who served for several years as adviser for Tribal Affairs in the NEFA.

——The religion of an Indian Tribe. New York, Oxford University Press, 1955. xxiv, 597p. **976**
    A study of the Saora tribe of Orissa.

——Suicide among the aboriginals of Bastar State. Ranchi, Nirmal Chandra Sarkarat 'Man in India' Office, 1942. 26p. **977**
    (Reprinted from 'Man in India').

——Truth about India: Can we get it? Preface by Laurence Housman. London, George Allen & Unwin, 1932. 105p. **978**

EMERSON, GERTRUDE. Voiceless India. Introduction by Pearl S. Buck and Rabindranath Tagore. New York, John Day & Co., 1944. xii, 458p. **979**
    First published in 1930, this book records the day-to-day life of one little North Indian village.

ENTHOVEN, REGINALD EDWARD. The tribes and castes of Bombay, printed at the Government Central Press, 1920. 3 vols. **980**
    Issued under the orders of the Government of Bombay, it enquires into the origin, social configuration, customs and occupations of the numerous castes and tribes of Bombay. Topics are arranged alphabetically.

FICK, RICHARD. Die sociale Gliederung. Kiel, 1897. English edition was published under the title : "Social Organization in North East India in Buddha's time". Calcutta, 1920. xii, 233p. **981**

—— The social organization in North East India in Buddha's time. Tr. by Shishir Kumar Maitra. Calcutta, The Calcutta University, 1930. xvii, 365p. **982**

FISHER, MARGARET WELPLEY. Indian approaches to a socialist society by Margaret W. Fisher and Joan V. Bondurant. Berkeley, Institute of International Studies, University of California, 1956. 105, xiiip. illus. (Indian Press digest. Monograph series, no. 2). **983**

FRYKENBERG, ROBERT ERIC, ed. Land control and social structure in Indian history. University of Wisconsin, 1969. 256p. **984**

FURER-HAIMENDORF, CHRISTOPH VON. The aboriginal tribes of Hyderabad. Foreword by K. De B. Codrington. London, Macmillan & Co., 1943-48. 3 vols. **985**

—— The naked Nagar : head-hunters of Assam in peace and war. Indian ed. rev. and enl. Calcutta, Thacker, Spink & Co., 1946. xv, 216p. **986**
    First published in 1939 by Methuen & Co., London, it is a personal narrative of thirteen months spent in the hills of Assam.

GEORGE, T.J. The Briton in India. Madras, Associated Printers, 1935. xiv, 708p. **987**
    A study in racial relations.

GIDAL, SONIA. My village in India, by Sonia and Tim Gidal. New York, Pantheon, 1956. 75p. illus. (*Their* My village books). **988**

GILBERT, WILLIAM H., *Jr*. People in India. Washington, Smithsonian Institution, 1944. 86p. **989**
   A brief technical study of the peoples and sociology of India.

GREGG, RICHARD BARTLETT. Which way lies hope ? An examination of capitalism, communism, socialism and Gandhiji's programme. Ahmedabad, Navajivan Publishing House, 1952. 82p. **990**

GURDON, P.R.T. The Khasis. Introduction by Sir Charles Lyall. 2nd ed. London, Macmillan & Co., 1914. xxiv, 232p. **991**

HAGEN, LOUIS EDMUND. Au Indes, cet antre monde. Traduit de l'anglais par S. de La Baume. Paris, Hachette, 1948. 247p. (F). **992**

———Indian route march. London, The Pilot Press ltd., 1946. 192p. plates. **993**

HARTOG, MABEL HELENE (KISCH). India : new pattern. Foreword by Lord Hailey. London, Allen & Unwin, 1955. 158p. illus. **994**

HERRING, PENDLETON. Development of social science research in India. New Delhi, Indian Council of Social Science Research, 1970. 34p. **995**

HODGSON, BRAIN HOUGHTON. Essay the first; On the Kocch Bodo and Dhimal tribes, in three parts. Calcutta, Printed by J. Thomas, 1847. 2, 1., x-p., 1 l., ix(ii)—200 (4)p. 2pl. (1 fold). **996**

HOPKINS, E. WASHBURN. India, old and new; with a memorial address. New York, Charles Scribner's Sons; London, Edwin Arnold, 1901. x, 342p. **997**

HUTTON, J. H. Caste in India : its nature, function, and origins, 2nd ed. Bombay, Geoffrey Cumberlege, Oxford University Press, 1951. x, 315p. **998**
   First published in 1946.

HUTTON, JAMES. A popular account of the thugs and dacoits the hereditary garotters and gang-robbers of India, London,

W.H. Allen & Co., 1857. 173, (1)p. **999**

INGHAM, KENNETH. Reformers in India, 1793-1883; an account of the work of Christian missionaries on behalf of social reform. Cambridge, Eng. University Press, 1956. xi, 149p. fold. map. **1000**

KARIM, ABUL KHAIR NAZMUL. Changing society in India and Pakistan; a study in social change and social stratification. Dacca, (now in Bangladesh), Oxford University Press, 1956. 173p. **1001**

KENNEDY, JAMES. Life and work in Benares and Kumaon, 1839-1877. With an introductory note by Sir W. Muir, London, T. Fisher Unwin, 1884. xxiii, 392p. **1002**

KINCAID, CHARLES AUGUSTUS. Our Hindu friends. Bombay, Times of India Press, 1930. xii, 69p. **1003**
   Describes the ordinary practices and observances of the orthodox Hindu communities, with special reference to the Brahmans and Prabhus of the Deccan.

LANNOY, RICHARD. India : people and places. Introductory essay and notes. New York, Vanguard Press, 1955. 28, 185-200p. 188 illus. map. (Vanguard art books). **1004**

LEWIS, OSCAR. Group dynamics in a north Indian village, a study of factions, By Oscar Lewis, with the assistance of Harvant Singh Dhillon. New Delhi, Programme Evaluation Organization, Planning Commission, 1954. iii, 48p **1005**

——— Village life in northern India; studies in a Delhi village. With the assistance of Victor Barnouw, Urbana, University of Illinois Press, 1958. xiii, 384p. **1006**

LEWIS, REBA. Three faces has Bombay. Sketches by K.K. Hebbar. Bombay, Popular Book Depot, 1957. 234p. illus. **1007**

LILLY, WILLIAM SAMUEL. Renaissance types, New York, Longmans, Green & Co., 1901. xxiv, 400p. **1008**

MACMUNN, GEORGE FLETCHER. The living India; its romance and realities. London, G. Bell & Sons, 1934. xi, 318p. **1009**
   "A popular survey of Indian life and conditions."

MACLEOD, RODERICK DONALD. Impressions of an Indian civil servant. London, H.F. & Co. and G. Witherby, 1938. 234p. **1010**
   Based on the author's twenty-three years' experience in

India this book is a study of social conditions in India before independence.

MANDELBAUM, DAVID G. Society in India. V. 1. Continuity and change. V. 2. Change and Continuity. Berkeley, University of California, 1970. 2v. **1011**

MARRIOTT, MCKIM, *ed*. Village India; studies in the little community, papers by Allen R. Beals and others. Chicago, University of Chicago Press, 1955. xix, 269p. illus. map. (Comparative studies of centres and civilizations). **1012**

MAYO, KATHERINE. Mother India : with forty-one illustrations. New York, Harcourt, Brace & Company, 1927. xiv, 440p. **1013**

A highly controversial book on India's social conditions. About a dozen books and innumerable articles have already been written in reply to this book by Indians and non-Indians.

MELLOR, JOHN W. Developing rural India plan and practice. N.Y., Cornell, 1968. 411p. **1014**

MINNEY, RUBEIGH JAMES. India marches past. London, Jarrolds, 1933. 292p. **1015**

An account of the history and social conditions of India.

MORGAN, THOMAS BRUCE. Friends and fellow students. Photos by Bob Lerner. New York, Crowell, 1956. 175p. illus. **1016**

MUELLER, J.H. AND SCHUSSELER, K.F. Statistical reasoning in sociology. New Delhi, Oxford and International Book House, 1970. 446p. Reprint. **1017**

MURPHY, GARDNER. In the minds of men. New York, Basic Books, 1953. 306p. **1018**

A study of human behaviour and social tensions in India, conducted by American and Indian experts at the request of the Indian Government.

NELSON, WILLIAM STUART. Bases of world understanding : an enquiry into the means of resolving racial, religious, class, and national misapprehensions and conflicts. Calcutta, the University, 1949. viii, 82p. **1019**

A collection of lectures delivered at the Calcutta University.

NIEHOFF, ARTHUR. Caste, class, and family in an industrial

community in northern India. Ann Arbor, University Microfilms, 1958. (University Microfilms, Ann Arbor, Michigan, Publications no. 25, 151). Microfilm AC-1. no. 25, 151. **1020**

O'MALLEY, LEWIS SYDNEY STEWART. Modern India and the West; a study of the interaction of their civilizations. Foreword by Lord Meston. London, Oxford University Press, 1941. xii, 834p. Published under the auspices of the Royal Institution of International Affairs. **1021**

"Discusses on the nature, extent, and effects of the influence which Western civilization has had upon the life and thought of India since the beginning of the sixteenth century, and traces the influence which India has had upon the West."

PARTON, MARGARET. The leaf and the flame. New York, Knopf, 1959. 277p. **1022**

PERRY, Sir THOMAS ERSKINE. A bird's eye view of India, with extracts from a journal kept in the provinces, Nepal, etc. London, 1855. **1023**

RICE, STANLEY PITCAIRN. Hindu customs and their origins. Foreword by H.H. the Maharaja Gaekwar of Baroda. London, George Allen & Unwin, 1937. 219p. **1024**

RISLEY, Sir HERBERT HOPE. The people of India. 2d. ed., edited by W. Crooke. With 36 illustrations and an ethnological map of India. Calcutta and Simla, Thacker, Spink & Co.; London, W. Thacker and Co., 1915. xxxii, 472p. incl. fold. tables. diagrs. front. (part.) 36pl., maps (1 fold). **1025**

——— The tribes and castes of Bengal. Anthropometric data. Calcutta, Printed at the Bengal Secretariat Press, 1891. 2 v. tables. **1026**

RUBEN, WALTER. Die Lage der Sklaven in her altindischen Gesellschaft. Berlin, Akademie-Verlag. 1957. 111p. **1027**

———Die okonomische und soziole Entwickberg Indiens. Berlin, Akademie-Verlag, 1959. **1028**

RUSKIN, JOHN. Unto this last : a paraphrase by M.K. Gandhi. Tr. from the Gujarati by Valji Govindji Desai. Ahmedabad, Navajivan Publishing House, 1951. xii, 64p. **1029**

Mahatma Gandhi translated the work under the title

Sarvodaya, when he was in South Africa.

RUSSELL, ROBERT VAN AND HIRA LAL. The tribes and castes of the Central Provinces of India. London, Macmillan & Co., 1916. 4 vols. Published under the orders of the Central Province administration. **1030**

SENART, EMILE CHARLES MARIE. Caste in India, the facts and the system, translated by Sir Denison Ross. London, Methuen & Co. ltd. (1930). xxiiip. 1 1. 220p. **1031**

SENART, E. Les Castes dars l' Inde. Paris, 1896. (F). **1032**

STARK, HERBERT ALICK. Hostages to India; or the life-story of the Anglo-Indian race. Calcutta, H.A. Stark, 1936. 2nd ed. x, 143, ix p. **1033**

    Originally published in "The Anglo-Indian Citizen", in 1926.

TAYLOR, ALICE. India. New York, Holiday, 1957. 26p. **1034**

THARANE, ELIZEBETH. Fantastiske Indien. Kobenhavn, H. Hirschsprung, 1957. 174p. illus. **1035**

    Written for small children, and colourfully illustrated.

THAYER, PHILIP W., *ed*. Nationalism and progress in free Asia. John Hopkins, 1956. 394p. **1036**

    Papers by businessmen, technical experts, diplomats, and others who participated in a two-part conference held in Washington and Rangoon. Introduction by Chester Bowles.

TICHY, HERBERT. Zum heiligsten Berg der Welt; auf Landstrassen und Pilgorpfaden in Afghanistan, Indien und Tibet. Gebitwort von Sven Hedin. Wien, Buchgemeinschaft Donaulard, 1953. 199p. plates, fold, maps. **1037**

TRUMBULL, ROBERT. As I see India. New York, W. Sloane Associates, 1956. 256p. illus. Also published in London, by Cassell in 1957. **1038**

VALVANNE, BIRGITTE (GUDLAGER). Dagen danser i gronne silkesko; historier frs. Indien. Kobenhavn, Jespersen, og Pio, 1958. 190p. **1039**

VENSITTART, EDEN, *comp*. Gurkhas. Calcutta, Supdt. Government Printing, 1906. xii, 200, xiip. **1040**

    Compiled under the orders of Government of India.

WEBER, MAX. The religion of India; the sociology of Hinduism and Buddhism. Translated and edited by Hans. H. Gerth and Don Martindale. Glenoce, Ill., Free Press, 1958. 392p. **1041**

WILKIN, ELIZABETH CRAWFORD. Dekho. The India that was. Illustrated by H.J.P. Browne. Sanbornville, N.H. Wake-Brook House, 1958. 286p. illus. **1042**

WISER, WILLIAM H. AND CHARLOTTE V. Behind mud walls, 1930-1960. x, 180p. **1043**

    A vivid account by an American missionary couple of social, cultural and economic conditions of the people of a village in North India.

WOFFORD, CLARE AND HARIS Jr. India afire. New York, John Day, 1951. 343p. **1044**

    A hurriedly written account of India's economic, social and political conditions, after 1947.

WOOD, ERNEST. An Englishman defends mother India : a complete constructive reply to 'Mother India'. Madras, Ganesh & Co., 1929. viii, 458, ixp. **1045**

    A reply to the assertions made in Katherine Mayo's book.

WOODACOTT, JOHN EVANS. India on trial: a study of present conditions. London, Macmillan & Co., 1929. xv, 257p. **1046**

    Seeks to show how India has derived, inestimable benefits' from the British connection.

WYON, JOHN B. The Khanna study : population problems in the rural Punjab. Boston, Mass. Harvard, 1971. 437p. **1047**

YEATS-BROWN, FRANCIS CHARLES CLAYPON. The lives of a Bengal lancer. New York, Grosset and Dunlap, 1957. 299p. (Printed for A.B.P.) **1048**

  See also Culture and Civilization
               Economic Conditions
               Land and People

Tribes and Castes *See* Social Conditions

(xviii) Women, their Emancipation

BADER, CLARISSE. Women in ancient India: moral and literary

studies. Tr. from the French by Mary E.R. Martin. London, Kegan Paul, Trench, Trubner & Co., 1925. xviii, 338p. (F.). **1049**

    Originally published in French under the title : *La femme dans l' Inde antique*, in 1867. It was partly translated by Toru Dutt, and after her death, by Mary E.R. Martin.

BROCKWAY, K. NORA. A larger way for women; aspects of Christian education for girls in South India, 1712-1948. Madras, Geoffrey Cumberlege, Oxford University Press, 1949. xi, 189p. **1050**

CORMACK, MARGARET. The Hindu women. Foreword by Lois Barclay Murphy. New York, Bureau of publications, Teachers College, Columbia University, 1953. xiii, 207p. **1051**

COUSINS, MARGARET E. The awakening of Asian womanhood. Madras, Ganesh & Co., 1922. x, 160p. **1052**

——Indian womanhood today. Allahabad, Kitabistan, 1947. 205p. **1053**

    First published in 1941, it is an appraisal of womanhood in India.

COWAN, MINNA G. The education of the women of India. Edinburgh & London, Oliphant, Anderson & Ferrier, 1912. 256p. **1054**

HAUSWIRTH, FRIEDA. *Purdah* : the status of Indian women. London, Kegan Paul, Trench, Trubner & Co., 1932. x, 290p. **1055**

HORNER, L.B. Women under primitive Buddhism: lay women and almswomen. London, George Routledge & Sons, 1930. xxiv, 391p. **1056**

KELMAN, JANET HARVEY. Labour in India. London, George Allen & Unwin, 1923. 281p. **1057**

    "A study of the conditions of Indian women in modern industry" *t.p.* The study is based on the author's visit to India from December 1920 to March 1921.

NIVEDITA, Sister (MARGARET ELIZABETH NOBLE) The web of Indian life. Introduction by Rabindra Nath Tagore. Almore, Advaita Ashrama, 1950. xii, 324p. **1058**

    Pictures of the Indian woman in her role as mother and wife and feeder and sustainer of the national culture and tradition; also other aspects of Indian life and ideals and Indian thought and what it stands for.

REGE, Y.M. Whither woman? Bombay, Popular Book Depot, 1938. xii, 292p. **1059**
"A critical study of the social life and thought of western women." *t.p.*

ROTHFELD, OTTO. Woman of India. Bombay, D.B. Taraporevala Sons & Co., 1928. viii, 222p. **1060**
48 illustrations in colour by M.V. Dhruandhar.

STERN, ELIZABETH GERTRUDE (LEVIN). The woman in Gandhi's life. New York, Dodd, Mead & Co., 1953. 304p. **1061**

THOMAS, PAUL. Women and marriage in India. London, George Allen & Unwin, 1939. 22p. **1062**
"A study of some aspects of the institution of marriage in India".

URQUHART, MARGARET M. Women of Bengal: a study of the Hindu pardanasins of Calcutta. Calcutta, Association Press, 1925. viii, 165p. **1063**
The sketch is limited to the caste women of Calcutta, who came within the range of the author's experience during a residence of twenty-five years in Bengal. Judges the Bengali woman against more ancient standards.

See also Culture and Civilization
Social Conditions

400 LINGUISTICS

(i) Linguistics (General)

ALLEN, WILLIAM STANNARD. Phonetics in ancient India. London, Geoffrey-Cumberlege, Oxford University Press, 1953. x, 96p. **1064**

BLOCH, JULES. Les Inscriptions d' Asoka : traduites et commentees. Paris, Les Belles lettres, 1950. 216p. (F.) **1065**

CALDWELL, ROBERT. A comparative grammar of the Dravidian or South Indian family of languages. 3rd ed. rev. ed. by J.L. Wyatt, and T. Ramkrishna Pillai. London, Kegan Paul, Trench, Trubner & Co., 1913. xi, 640p. **1066**
> First published in 1875 it examines and compares the grammatical principles and forms of the various Dravidian languages and determines their primitive structure and distinctive character.

FLEET, J.F., *ed.* Inscriptions of the early Gupta Kings and their successors. Calcutta, Superintendent of Govt. Printing, 1888. vii, 194, 350p. 45 facsim. **1067**

GILCHRIST, JOHN BORTHWICK. The British Indian monitor, or, The antijargonist, Strangers, guide, Oriental linguist and various other words, compressed into a series of portable volumes, on the Hindoostanee language. By the author of Hindoostanee philology, etc. etc. Edinburgh, Printed by Walker & Greig, for Manners & Miller; (etc. etc.). 1806-. v. **1068**

GILCHRIST, JOHN BORTHWICK. The oriental linguist, an easy and familiar lintroduction to the popular language of Hindoostan; vulgarly, but improperly called the Moors : Comprising the rudiments of that tongue with an extensive vocabulary, English and Hindoostanee, and Hindoostanee and English. Accompanied with some plain and useful dialogues, tales, poems etc. to illustrate the construction and facilitate the acquisition of the language. To which is added for the accommodation of the army, the English and Hindoostanee part of the articles of war (from Col. William Scott's translation) with practical notes and observations. By the author of the English and Hindoostanee dictionary. Calcutta, Printed by Ferris and Greenway, 1798. 3, 1, xviii, 163p. **1069**

——Practical outlines, or, a sketch of Hindoostanee orthoepy in the Roman character. Calcutta. 24p. fold. tab. **1070**

GRIERSON, Sir GEORGE ABRAHAM. Hatim's tales; Kashmiri stories and songs recorded with the assistance of Pandit Govind Kaul, by Sir Aurel Stein, K.C. (I. E., and edited with a translation, linguistic analysis, vocabulary indexes etc. by Sir George A. Grierson, K.C.I.E. with a note on the folklore of the tales by W. Crooke, C.I.E. London, J. Murray, 1923. lxxxvi, 527p. front. (port.) (Indian texts series). **1071**

——Linguistic survey of India, Calcutta, Central Publication Branch, Government of India, 1903-1928. 11 vols. **1072**

> A monumental work, on the Indian languages. Vol. I, part 1, published in 1927, contains a summary of the entire work.

——A manual of the Kashmiri language comprising grammar, phrase-book and vocabularies. Oxford, The Clarendon Press, 1911. 2v. **1073**

——The Pisaca languages of north western India. London, Royal Asiatic Society, 1906. vii, 192p. front. (fold. map). (Asiatic Society monographs. vol. viii). **1074**

——Towali, an account of a Dardic language of the Swat Kohistan. Based on materials collected in Torwal by Sir Aurel Stein. With a note by Sir Aurel Stein on Torwal and its people

400 Linguistics

and a map. London, Royal Asiatic Society, 1929. vii, 216p. front. (map.). (Prize publication fund, vol. xi). **1075**

GUMPERZ, JOHN J. Hindi reader. Berkeley, University of California Press, 1960. **1076**
    An elementary book for beginners.

HALL, FITZEDWARD. Hindi reader. Hertford, S. Austin, 1870. xix, 184 (2)p. Preface signed F.H. **1077**

——Modern English. New York, Sonboner, Armstrong & Co., 1873. xv (l) 394p. **1078**

HODGSON, BRAIN HOUGHTON. Comparative vocabulary of the languages of the broken tribes of Nepal, 1959. **1079**

——Essays on the languages, literature, and religion of Nepal and Tibet. Together with further papers on the geography, ethnology, and commerce of those countries. London, Trubner & Co., 1874. 147, 124p. 3 fold. tab. **1080**

HULTZSCH, E., *ed*. Inscriptions of Asoka. London, 1925.(F). **1081**

KENNEDY, VANS. Researches into the origin and affinity of the principal languages of Asia and Europe. London, Longman, Rees, Orme, Brown, and Green, 1828. xiv, (2), 324p. plates (partly fold.). **1082**

KONOW, S.K. *ed*. Kharosthi inscriptions, with the exception of those of Asoka. Calcutta, Oxford Printed, 1929. cxxvii, 192p. xxxvi pl. **1083**

LAMBERT, HESTER MARJORIE. Introduction to the Devanagari script for students of Sanskrit and Hindi. Introduction by J.R. Firth. London, Oxford University Press, 1953. x, 87p. **1084**

——Introduction to the Devanagari script for students of Sanskrit, Hindi, Marathi, Gujarati and Bengali : Introduction by J.R. Firth. London, Oxford University Press, 1953. xiii, 231p. tables. **1085**

——Marathi language course. London, Oxford University Press, 1943. xiv, 301p. **1086**

LISKER, LEIGH. Introduction to spoken Telugu. New York, American Council of Learned Societies, 1963. **1087**

MONIER-WILLIAMS, Sir MONIER. Sanskrit manual; 2d ed., enl., with a vocabulary, English and Sanskrit, by A.E. Gough, B.A. London, W.H. Allen & Co., (1868). viii, 117 (i.e.

297)p. **1088**

MUIR, JOHN. Some account of the recent progress of Sanskrit studies. *In* Royal Society of Edinburgh. Transactions. Edinburgh, 1864. 253-283. **1089**

MULLER, FRIEDRICH MAX. Last essays. First series. Essays on language, folklore and other subjects. London, New York. (etc.) Longmans, Green & Co., 1901. vii, (l) 360p. **1090**

——Lectures on the science of language. 7th ed. London, Longmans, Green & Co., 1873. 2v. illus. **1091**

——Max Muller on spelling. Reprinted, by permission from the "Fortnightly Review" for April, 1876. London, F. Pitman (etc. etc.), 1878. 48p. **1092**

——The science of language, founded on lectures delivered at the Royal institution in 1861 and 1863. New York, C. Scribner's Sons, 1891. 2v. illus. **1093**

MYERS, ADOLPH. Basic and the teaching of English in India. Bombay, Times of India Press for the Orthological Institute, Cambridge, 1938. 375p. **1094**

Based on lectures delivered before teachers in various centres in India and Burma.

OPPERT, GUSTAV SALOMON. On the classification of languages, a contribution to comparative philology. Madras, Higginbotham & Co., London, Trubner & Co., 1879. vi, 1.l., 146p. diag. tables (part fold). **1095**

RICE, B. LEWIS. Epigraphia Carnatica. General Index published by M.H. Krishna. Bangalore, 1886-1906. 12 vols. **1096**

ROSS, Sir EDWARD DENISON. This English language, London. New York, (etc.), Longmans, Green & Co., (1939). xxx, 266p. **1097**

SCHLEGAL, AUGUST WILHELMVON. Reflexions sur l'etude des langues asiatiques, addresses a Sir James Mackintosh, suivies d'une lettre a M. Horace Hayman Wilson. Par A.W. de Schlegel. Bonn, E. Weber; (etc., ete.), 1832. xii, 205, (2)p. (F). **1098**

SHAKESPEARE, JOHN. An introduction to the Hindustani language. Comprising a grammar and a vocabulary, English and Hindustani; also short sentences and dialogues, short stories in Persian and Nagari character... and military words of command,

400 Linguistics

Nagari and English. London, W.H. Allen & Co., 1845. viii, 564p. **1099**

TREVELYAN, Sir CHARLES EDWARD, *hart*. The application of the Roman alphabet to all the Oriental languages, contained in a series of paper written by Messrs. Trevelyan, J. Prinsep, and Tytler. Rev. A. Duff, and Mr H.T. Prinsep and published in various Calcutta periodicals in the year 1834 (Serampore). The Serampore Press, 1834. 1, 1., 162p. map. **1100**

VINSON, J. Manuel de la Langue Tamoule. Paris, 1908. (F.). **1101**

WADDEL, LAURENCE AUSTINE. The Aryan origin of the alphabet, disclosing the Sumero-Phoenician parentage of our letter, ancient and modern. London, Luzac & Co., 1927. viii, 80p. illus. II fold. pl. **1102**

WHITNEY, WILLLAM DWIGHT. Elementary lessons in English for home and school user. (Part I). By W.D. Whitney and Mrs. N.L. Knox. Boston, Ginn and Heath, 1880. vi ll, 192p. **1103**

────A German reader in prose and verse, with notes and vocabulary. New York, H. Holt & Co., Boston, C. Schoenhof, (c. 1870). x, 523p. **1104**

────Language, and the study of language. Twelve lectures on the principles of linguistic science. New York, C. Scribner & Co., 1867. 3, 1., (v) xi, 489p. **1105**

──── The life and growth of language: an outline of linguistic science. New York, D. Appleton & Co., 1887. vii., 1 l, 326p. **1106**

────Max Muller and the science of language: a criticism. New York, D. Appleton & Co., 1892. 2, 1., 29p. **1107**

WILSON, HORACE HAYMAN. Essays analytical, critical and philological on subjects connected with Sanskrit literature. By the late H.H. Wilson. Collected and edited by Dr. Reinhold Rost. London, Trubner & Co., 1864-65. 3v. **1108**

WOOLNER, ALFRED C. Introduction to Prakrit. Lahore, Punjab University, 1917. xvi, 219p. **1109**

YATES, WILLIAM. Introduction to the Hindostani language. Calcutta, Printed at the Baptist Mission Press, and sold by W. Thacker & Co., (etc.), 1827, xiv, 1 l., 307p. **1110**

See also Grammar and Dictionaries

(ii) Grammar and Dictionaries

ANDERSON, DINES. Pali glossary, including the words of the Pali reader and of the Dhammapada. Copenhagen, Gyldendalske Boghandd, Nordisk Porlag, 1904-05. **1111**

ANDERSON, JAMES D. A manual of the Bengali language. Cambridge, Cambridge University Press, 1962. 178p. **1112**

——, comp. Short vocabulary of the Aka language. Shillong, Assam Secretariat Press, 1896. vi, 20p. **1113**

ANDRONOV, M.S. Russko-bengalskij slovar. Moscow, Moskovskij Institute Vostokove-denija, 1953. (R.). **1114**

ASCOLI, G.S. Lezioni di Fonologia Comparata del Sanscrito, del Graco e del Latino. Torino e Firenze, 1870. (L). **1115**

BADGER, GEORGE PERCY. An English Arabic lexicon, in which the equivalents for English words and idiomatic sentences are rendered into literary and colloquial Arabic. London, Kegan Paul & Co., 1881. xii, 1244p. **1116**

BAILEY, B. Dictionary of high and colloquial Malayalam and English. Kottayam, the Church Mission Press, 1846. viii, 852p. **1117**

1971 ed. was revised and edited by Vettam Mari.

BAILEY, FREDERIC G., ed. Teach yourself Urdu. London, English Universities Press, 1960. **1118**

BAILEY, THOMAS GRAHAM. Hindustani English vocabulary. London, Linguaphone Institute, 1930. 78p. **1119**

—— Hindustani Urdu dictionary. London, Linguaphone Institute, 1930. 79p. **1120**

——Pronunciation of Kashmiri; Kashmiri sounds, how to make them and how to transcribe them. London, Royal Asiatic Society, 1937. 70p. **1121**

BAILEY, T.G. AND E.P. NEWTON. Panjabi manual and grammar. Patiala, Panjabi University, 1961. **1122**

BALLANTYNE, JAMES ROBERT. A grammar of the Hindustani languages : followed by a series of grammatical exercises etc. London, Cox & Co., 1838. x, 78p. **1123**

——A grammar of the Maratta language, etc. Edinburgh, I. Hall, 1839. 52p. **1124**

——Hindustani selections in the Naskhi and Devanagari character. With a vocabulary of the words. London, C. Smith, 1840. 10, 39, 20p. **1125**

BEAMES, JOHN. A comparative grammar of the modern Aryan languages of India : Hindi, Punjabi, Sindhi, Gujarati, Marathi, Oriya and Bengali. London, Trubner & Co., 1872-79. 3 vols. **1126**

——Grammar of the Bengali language; literary and colloquial. Oxford, Clarendon Press series, 1891. 68p. **1127**

BELSORE, MALHAR B. An etymological Gujarati-English dictionary. Ahmedabad, C.M. Shah, 1940. **1128**

BENDALL, CECIL. Application and testimonial for the professionship of Sanskrit. Cambridge University Press, 1903. 2pt. **1129**

BENEFY, THEODOR. Chrestomathie aus Sanskrit Werken. Leipzig, F.A. Brockhaus, 1854. 374p. (G). **1130**

——A practical grammar of the Sanskrit language for the use of early students. London, Trubner & Co., 1863. vii, 228p. **1131**

——Sanskrit English dictionary with references to best editions of Sanskrit authors and etymologies and comparisons of cognate-words chiefly in Greek, Latin, Gothic and Anglo-Saxon. London, Longmans & Co., 1866. xi, 1145p. **1132**

BERGAIGNE, ABEL. Edudes sur le lexique du Rigveda. Paris, Imprimerie Nationale, 1884. viii, 245p. (F). **1133**

BESKROVN, VASILI MATVEERICH AND KRASNODEMBSKU, V.E. Urdu-Russkuu slovar. Ed. by A.P. Barannikova. Moskva, Izdatelstvo Akademu Nauk, U.S.S.R., 1951. 844p. (R). **1134**

BIRJULEY, S.V. etc. *comps.* Urdu-russkij slovar. Moscow, Soviet Encyclopedia Publishing House, 1964. 890p. (R). **1135**

BLIN, A. Dictionnaire, Francais-Tamoul et Tamoul-Francais. Paris, 1831, viii, 282p. (F). **1136**

BLOCH, JULES. The grammatical structure of Dravidian languages. Poona, Deccan College Postgraduate and Research Institute, 1954. vii, 100p. **1137**

BODDING, PAUL OLAF. Santal Dictionary. Oslo, Norwegian Academy of Science and Letters, 1929-36. 5 vols. (N) **1138**

BOHTLINGK, OTTO, Sanskrit-Worterbuch, in Kurzerer Fassung. St. Petersburg, Buchdruckerei der Kaiserlichen akademie der Wissenschaften, 1879-89. (G). **1139**

BOHTLINGK, OTTO AND ROTH, RUDOLPH. Sanskrit Worterbuch Herausgregeben von der Kaiserlichen Akademie der Wissenschaften. St. Petersburg. Buchdruckerei der Kaiserlichen Akademie der Wissenschaften, 1855-75. (G). **1140**

BOPP, FRANCISCO. Glossarium Sanscritum. Berolini, 1847. viii, 412p. (L). **1141**

BOYD, ANDREW, K.H. Guide to 14 Asiatic languages. London, Pilot Press, 1947. 262p. **1142**

BRICE, NATHANIEL. Romanized Hindustani and English dictionary designed for the use of school. Banaras, E. J. Lazarus Press, 1880. viii, 307p. **1143**

BRIGHT, WILLIAM. An outline of colloquial Kannada. Poona, Deccan College Post-graduate and Research Institute, 1958. viii, 75p. **1144**

BRIGHT, WILLIAM AND SAEED A. KHAN. The Urdu writing system. New York, American Council of Learned Societies, 1958. 48p. **1145**

BROOKS, WILLIAMS. Oriya-English dictionary designed for the use of European and native students and schools. Rev. and enl. Cuttack, Orissa Mission Press, 1908. 314p. **1146**

BROWN, CHARLES PHILIP. Dictionary, Telugu and English explaining the colloquial style used in business and the poetical dialect, with explanations, in English and in Telugu. Madras Christian Knowledge Society Press, xvi, 1303p. **1147**

BUCHER, J. Kannada-English school dictionary. Mangalore Basel Mission Press, 1899. ix, 456p. **1148**

BUCK, CARL DARLING. Dictionary of selected synonyms in the principal Indo-European languages; a contribution to the history of ideas. Chicago, University of Chicago Press, 1949. xiv, 1515p. **1149**

BUCKLAND, CHARLES EDWARD. Dictionary of Indian biography. London, Sonnenschein, 1906. 494p. **1150**

    Contains about 2600 concise biographies of persons—English, Indian or foreign—noteworthy in the history, service, literature, or science of India since 1750.

BULCKE, C. Angrezi-Hindi Kosh. Ranchi, Catholic Press, 1968. 891p. **1151**

    An English-Hindi dictionary compiled chiefly for Hindi

learners as also for Hindi speaking students learning English.

BURNELL, ARTHUR COKE. On the Aindra school of Sanskrit grammarians, their place in the Sanskirt and subordinate literatures. Mangalore, Basel Mission Press, 1875. viii, 120p. **1152**

BURNOUF, EMILE. Dictionaire classique Sanskrit Francais on sont coordonnes revises, et completes les travaux de Wilson, Bopp, Westergaard, Johson etc. et. contenant le devanagari sa transcription europeenne, l'interpretation les racineset de nambreaux rapproachments philologigues, par Emile Burnouf et L. Leupal Maisonneuve. Paris, 1896. viii, 781p. (F). **1153**

BURROW, T. The Sanskrit language. London, Faber and Faber, 1955. vii, 426p. **1154**

BURROW, T. AND EMENEAU, M.B. Dravidian etymological dictionary. London, Oxford University Press, 1961. xxix, 609p. **1155**

CAMPBELL, ALEXANDER DUNCAN. Dictionary of the Teloogoo language, commonly termed the Gentoo, peculiar to the Hindoos of the North Eastern Provinces of the Indian peninsula. Madras, Hindu Press, 1821. xii, 312p. **1156**

CAMPBELL, ALEXANDER. Santali-English and English-Santali dictionary. Ed. by R. M. Macphail. Pokhuria, Santal Mission Press, 1933. 906p. **1157**

CAPPELLER, CARL. Sanskrit-English dictionary. London, Luzac and Co., 1891. viii, 672p. **1158**

——Sanskrit-Worterbuch. Berlin, Walter de Gruyter, 1955. vii, 541p. (G) **1159**

CAREY, WILLIAM. Dictionary of the Bengali language in which the words are traced to their origin and their various meanings. Serampore, Mission Press, 1818-25. 2 vols. **1160**

CHAPMAN, FRANCIS ROBERT HENRY. Urdu reader for beginners together with a complete vocabulary of all the words occurring in the text. London, W. Thacker & Co., 1882p. 137p. **1161**

CHILDERS, ROBERT CAESAR. Compendious vocabulary of Sanskrit in Devanagari and Roman characters. London, Hall and Co., 1885. 912p. **1162**

——Dictionary of the Pali language. London, Trubner and Co.,

1875. xxii, 622p. **1163**

CHRISTIAN, JOHN. Behar proverbs: classified and arranged according to their subject matter and giving the subject of each proverb in English and the important words in Hindi. London, Trubner & Co., 1891. lix, 256p. **1164**

CLARK, E.W. Ao-Naga dictionary. Calcutta, printed at the Baptist Mission Press, 1911. 977p. **1165**

CONZE, EDWARD, *comp.* Materials for a dictionary of the Prajnaparamita literature. Tokyo, Suzuki Research Foundation, 1967. **1166**

CRAWFURD, JOHN. A grammar and dictionary of the Malaya language. With a preliminary dissertation. London, Smith Elder, 1852. 2 vols. **1167**

DABBS, JACK AUTREY. Short Bengali-English; English-Bengali dictionary. Texas, Department of Modern Languages, A. and M. College of Texas, 1962. xii, 173p. **1168**

EASTWICK, EDWARD BACKHOUSE. *tr.* A comparative grammar of the Sanskrit, Zend. and Slavonic languages by Franz Bopp. Translated by Edward Backhouse Eastwick. London, Madden & Malcolm,1845-50. 3 parts. xv, 1462p. **1169**

—— A concise grammar of the Hindustani language to which are added, selections for reading. London, J. Madden, 1847. 1p. 1., iii, (5)-88p. 11., (22), p. 21. **1170**

EDGERTON, FRANKLIN. Buddhist Hybrid Sanskrit grammar and dictionary V.1. Grammar. V.2 Dictionary. Delhi, Motilal Banarasidass, 1970. 2 v. 1st ed. was published by American Oriental Society in 1953. **1171**

EITEL, ERNEST, J. Handbook of Chinese Buddhism: being a Sanskrit-Chinese dictionary. With vocabularies of Buddhist terms in Pali, Singhalese, Siamese, Burmese, Tibetan, Mongolian and Japanese. London, Trubner, 1888. (C) **1172**

FALLON, S. W. Hindustani-English law and commercial dictionary. Banaras, E.J. Lazarus & Co., 1879. ii, 286p. **1173**

—— A new English-Hindustani dictionary with illustrations from English literature and colloquial English, tr. into Hindustani, by S.W. Fallon, Lahore, Rai Sahib M. Gulab Singh & Sons (1905 ?) 4p. 1., 703p. illus. **1174**

—— A new Hindustani-English dictionary with illustrations from

Hindustani literature and folk-lore, Benaras, printed at the Medical Hall Press, London, Trubner and Co., 1879. 3p. l. xxiv, p. 2.1, 1216, ivp. **1175**

FERGUSSON, J. Dictionary of the Hindustani language, in two parts. London, 1773. viii, 58, 112p. **1176**

FORBES, DUCAN. Dictionary, Hindustani and English; to which is added a reserved part English and Hindustani. London. W.H. Allen & Co., 1866. viii, 802, 318p. **1177**

GEIGER, W. Elementarbuch des Sanskrit unter Berucksichtigung der vedischen Sprache. Berlin, 1923. v, 170 p. (G). **1178**

GILCHRIST, JOHN BORTHWICK. Dialogues, English and Hindoostanee; for illustrating the grammatical principles of the Strangers' East Indian guide, and to promote the colloquial intercourse of Europeans on the most indispensable and familiar subjects, with the natives of India. To which has been added, a translation of the articles of war, with other objects of real importance and utility, including the Sukoontula natuk in the universal character. 4th ed. London, Printed for Kingsbury, Parbury & Allen, 1826. vii, 288p. xx, 104p. 11. fold. tab. **1179**

———A grammar of the Hindoostanee language, or, part third of volume first, of a system of Hindoostanee philology. Calcutta, 1796. 1p. 1., 336p. 11. 2 fold. diagr. **1180**

———The Hindee-Roman, orthoepigraphical ultimatum; or, A systematic, discriminative view of oriental and occidental visible sounds, on fixed and practical principles for speedily acquiring the most accurate pronunciation of many oriental languages; exemplified in one hundred popular anecdotes, tales, jests, maxims and proverbs, of the Hindoostanee story teller. 2d ed. London, printed for Kingsbury, Parbury & Allen, 1820. vi, clxvi, 88, 56, 42p. 11 fold. 1. **1181**

———Hindoostanee philology; comprising a dictionary, English and Hindoostanee; with a grammatical introduction. To which is prefixed a copper plate, exhibiting a comparative view of the Roman and oriental characters used in the Hindoostanee language. v. 1. London, Kingsbury, Parbury & Allen, 1825. 2p. 1., lxiv, 721p. port. **1182**

Reprinted from the edition of 1810.

GILCHRIST, JOHN BORTHWICK. The stranger's infallible East Indian guide, or Hindoostanee multum in parvo, as a grammatical compendium of the grand, popular and military language of all India. (Long, but improperly called the Moors or Moorish Jargon). 3rd ed., greatly enlarged and improved. London, Black, Kingsbury, Parsbury & Allen, 1820. 3p. 1, xxx, 431p. fold. tables. **1183**

GILMORE, MARY ELIZABETH. Esoteric dictionary: a key to the science of language. Definitions translated from the ancient Vedas by Santana Benedicione de Branconiers. Berkley, California, 1957. 341p. **1184**

GOLDSTRUCKER, T. Dictionary, Sanskrit and English, extended and improved from the 2nd ed. of the dictionary of H.H. Wilson with a supplement, serving as an English-Sanskrit vocabulary. Berlin, A. Asher & Co., 1856. iii, 480p. **1185**

——Panini: his place in Sanskrit literature. An investigation of some literary and chronological questions which may be settled by a study of his works. A separate impression of the preface to the facsimile of ms. no. 17 in the library of Her Majesty's home government for India, which contains a portion of the Manava-Kalpa-Sutra with the commentary of Kumarila-Swamin. London, N. Trubner & Co., (etc. etc.), 1861. xv, (1), 268p. **1186**

GRASSMANN, H. Worterbuch zum Rig-Veda. Leipzig, F.A. Bruckhaus, 1873. viii, 1775p.(G). **1187**

GRIERSON, Sir GEORGE ABRAHAM. A handbook to the Kayathi character. Calcutta, Thacker, Spink, and Co., 1881. 3p. 1., (c)—vi, 4p., xxx, 281p. **1188**

——An introduction to the Maithili language of North Bihar, containing a grammar, chrestomathy and vocabulary. Calcutta, J.N. Banerjee & Son, 1881-82. 2v. in 1 tables (1 fold).

"Part 2 has imprint: Calcutta, printed by J.W. Thomas, 1882."

"Extra number(s) to Journal Asiatic Society, Bengal, part 1 for 1880, 1882." **1189**

——Ishkashmi, Zebaki, and Yagghulami, an account of three Eranian dialects, London, Royal Asiatic Society, 1920. 4p. 1, 128p. tables (1 fold). **1190**

400 Linguistics

Prize publication fund, vol. v.

GRIERSON, SIR GEORGE ABRAHAM. Manual of the Kashmiri language, comprising grammar, phrase book and vocabularies. Oxford, Clarendon Press, 1911. 2 vols. **1191**

GRIGNARD, A. Oraon-English dictionary in the Roman character with numerous phrases illustrative of sense and idiom. Calcutta, Catholic Orphan Press, 1924. viii, 697p. **1192**

HALL, FITZEDWARD. On English adjectives in able, with special reference to reliable. London, Trubner & Co., 1877. vii (1) 238p. **1193**

HAUGHTON, GRAVES CHAMREY. Dictionary, Bengali and Sanskrit, explained in English and adapted for students of either language, to which is added an index, serving as a reversed dictionary. London, Allen & Co., 1833. xxxvi, 2851p. **1194**

——A short enquiry into the nature of language with a view to ascertain the original meanings of Sanskrit prepositions; elucidated by comparison with the Greek and Latin. London, printed for private circulation by J.L. Cox & Son, 1832. 2p. 1(3)-32p. **1195**

HERBERT, JEAN. Glossaire due Raja-Yoga et du Hatha-Yoga. Paris, Adrien Maisonneuve, 1944. 40p. (F) **1196**

HILLEBRANDT, ALFRED. Vedachrestomathie. Furden ersten gebrauch bei Vedavarlesungen hrsg. und mit einam glossar Verseheu. Berlin, Weidmaunsche Buchbandlung, 1885. vi, 130p. (G). **1197**

HODGSON, BRAIN HOUGHTON. Comparative vocabulary of the languages of the broken tribes of Nepal. (Calcutta ? 1859 ?). 262 (i.e. 270p.). **1198**

HUMPHREYS, C. Popular dictionary of Buddhism. London, Arco Publications, 1962. 223p. **1199**

HUNTER, ROBERT. The encyclopaedic dictionary. A new prolific and exhaustive work of reference to all the words in the English language. Ed. by Robert Hunter, assisted by S.J. Heutage, A.B. John, A. William...Prof. Chas. Morris, Philadelphia, Pa Syndicate Publishing Company, 1894. 4v. illus. pages continuously. American edition by Charles Morris and others of the Encyclopedic dictionary...by Robert Hunter (London 1879-89. 14v.). **1200**

HUNTER, Sir WILLIAM WILSON. A comparative dictionary of the languages of India and high Asia, with a dissertation. Based on the Hodgson lists, official records and mss. London, Trubner & Co., 1868. **1201**

—— A skeleton Santali grammar, based on the Rev. J. Phillips, 'Introduction to the Santal language', with additions from other missionaries, and from my own researches. (In his Annals of Rural Bengal. London. 1897. 462p). **1202**

HUTTON, JOHN H. Rudimentary grammar of the Sema Naga language, with vocabulary, Shillong, Assam Secretariat Press, 1916. 95p. **1203**

IRWIN, J.C.R. Lughat-e-Unani. Allahabad, Mission Press, 1887. 283p. **1204**

JACOB, G.A. Concordance to the principal Upanishads and Bhagavadgita. Bombay, Government of Bombay, 1891. **1205**

——Laukikayayanjalih: A handful of popular maxims current in Sanskrit literature. Bombay, Nirnayasagara Press, 1907. 2 vols. **1206**

JAESCHKE, HEINRICH AUGUST. Romanized Tibetan and English dictionary. Kyelang in British Lahour 1866. 158p. Lithographed. **1207**

—— A short practical grammar of the Tibetan language with special reference to the spoken dialects. Kyelang, 1865. **1208**

—— A Tibetan-English dictionary, with special reference to the prevailing dialects. To which is added an English-Tibetan vocabulary. London, Kegan Paul & Co., 1934. xxii, 671p. **1209**

——Tibetan grammar. Second edition prepared by Dr. H. Wenzel. 1833. viii, 104p. **1210**

"Traubner's collection of simplified grammars of the principal Asiatic and European languages, v. 7."

JOHNSON, FRANCIS. A dictionary, Persian, Arabic and English. Pub. under the patronage of the Honourable East India Company. London, W.H. Allen & Co., 1852. 2p. l., iv, 1420p. **1211**

JONES, Sir WILLIAM. A grammar of the Persian language. The 9th ed., with considerable additions and improvements, and some specimens of the finest Persian and Arabic hand-writing, for the exercise of the student, by the Rev. Samuel Lee. London, Printed by W. Nicol, for Parbury, Allen & Co., (etc.) 1828. 1p. 1., xxv, 283p. 6pl. (partly fold). **1212**

KELLNER, HERMANN CAMILLO. Savitri: Prakrtisches elementarbuch zur einfuhrung in die Sanskrits prache. Leipzig, F.A. Brockhany, 1888. xiv, 245p. (G) **1213**

KELLOGG, SAMUEL HENRY. A grammar of the Hindi language in which are treated the High Hindi, Braj, and the Eastern Hindi of the Ramayana of Tulsi Das, also the colloquial dialects of Rajputana, Kumaon, Avadh, Riwa, Bhojpur, Maghadha, Maithila, etc., with copious philological notes. 3rd ed. With notes on pronunciation by T. Grahame Bailey. London, K. Paul, Trench, Trubner and Co., Ltd., 1938. xxxiv, 584p tables (part fold). **1214**

"Bibliographical references in 'Note' p. (xxvi)".

KENNEDY, VANS. A dictionary of the Maratha language, in two parts; I. part containing Maratha and English, II. part containing English and Maratha. Bombay, Printed at the Courier Press, 1824. 2pts. in 1. v. **1215**

KIBIRKSHTIS, L.B. AND POMERANTSEV, L.M. Dasti Urdu-Rusi lughat. Moscow, Ghair Mulki aur Mulki Lughatun Ka Sarkari Ishaut-ghar, 1958. 612p. (R). **1216**

KIRKPATRICK, WILLIAM. Vocabulary, Persian, Arabic and English, containing such words as have been adopted from the two formes of those languages and incorporated into the Hindvi together with some hundreds of compound words formed from Russian or Arabic names and in universal use; being the seventh part of the new Hindvi grammar and dictionary. London, Joseph Cooper, 1785. viii, 190p. **1217**

KLIUEV, B.I. Russko-Urdu slover. Morkva, Sostavili Izd inostrannycln i nacional'nych slovarej, 1959. 1135p. (R) **1218**

LANGLES, LOUIS MATHIEU. Alphabet mantchou, redige d' apres le syllabaire et le dictionnaire universal de cette langue; part L. Langles. 3 ed., angm. d' unenotice Sur l' origine, l' historie, et les travaux litte faires des Mantchoux, actuellement maitres de la Chine. Paris, Imprimerie Imperiale, 18.7. xv(l) 208p. 2 fold, tab. (F). **1219**

LANMAN, CHARLES ROCKWELL. Sanskrit reader: text, vocabulary and notes. Cambridge, Harvard University Press, 1955. xx,

405p. **1220**

LAP, M.A. Petit vocabulaire Tamoul-Francais, contenant les mots tamouls de' un usage plus frequent, avec leurs francais les plus usites. Pondicherry, La Mission Cathoiique, 1886. 286p. (F). **1221**

LASERON, E. Dictionary of the Malayalam and English and the English and Malayalam language. Kottayam, 1856. 242p. **1222**

LASSEN, CHRISTIAN. Anthologia sanscritica glossario instrvcta. In vsvm Scholarvm edidit Christianvs Lassen. Denvo adornavit Ioannes Gildemeister. Ed. altera novis curis retractata. Bonnae ad Rhenvm, apvd A. Marcvm, 1868. xvi, 300p. 1 l. **1223**

LEBEDEFF, HERASIM. A grammar of the pure and mixed East Indian dialects, with dialogues affixed...arranged according to the Brahmenian system of the Shamscrit language. With a recitation of the assertions of Sir William Jones respecting the Shamscrit alphabet. London, Printed by J. Skirven, for, and sold by the author. (etc.). 2p. l (ix) - xxviii, viiip. 21, 85p. **1224**

LEITNER, GOTTBIEB WILLIAM. Introduction to a philosophical grammar of Arabic; being an attempt to discover a few simple principles in Arabic Grammar. Lahore, Printed at the "Indian Public Opinion" Press, 1871. Cover title, lp. l. 52p. **1225**

LEUMANN, EARNEST AND LEUMANN, JULIUS. Btymologisches worterbuch der Sanskrit-sprache. Leipzig, 1907. 112p. (G). **1226**

LITTON, DZEK. Russko-bengal'skij slovar. Moskva, Soviet enciklopedija, 1966. 759p. (R). **1227**

LI YEN. Deux lexigues Sanskrit-chinois. Fan Yu tsa mirg de Li Yen Fan yu Ts'ian tseu wen de Yi-Tsing. Paris, Librarlrie Orientaliste Paul Geuthner, 1929. 2 vols. (Sino Indica. Tome 2, 3), (F). **1228**

LONG, JAMES. Eastern proverbs and emblems illustrating old truths. London, Trubner & Co., 1881. xv, 280p. (Half title: Trubner's oriental series). **1229**

LORRAIN, JAMES HERBERT. Dictionary of the Abor-miri language with illustrative sentences and notes. Shillong, Eastern Bengal and Assam Secretariat Press, 1910. viii, 572p. **1230**

LORRAIN, JAMES HERBERT. Dictionary of the Lushai language. Calcutta, Royal Asiatic Society, 1940. xvi, 576p. **1231**

LORRAIN, REGINALD ARTHUR. Grammar and dictionary of the Lakher or Mara language. Gauhati, Govt. of Assam, Dept. of Historical and Antiquarian Studies, 1951. x, 372p. **1232**

MACDONELL, ARTHUR ANTHONY. A practical Sanskrit dictionary with transliteration, accentuation, and etymological analysis throughout. London, Oxford University Press, H. Milford, 1924. ix, (3) 382p. **1233**

—— A Sanskrit grammar for students. Third edition. London, Humphrey Milford, Oxford University Press, 1927. xviii. (2) 264p. **1234**

——A Vedic grammar for students, including a chapter on syntax and three appendixes: list of verbs, metre, accent. Oxford, The Clarendon Press, 1916. x, (2) 508p. 2nd ed. published by Harvard University Press, 1950. **1235**

MAINWARING, G.B. Dictionary of the Lepcha language. Rev. and completed by Albert Grunweded. Berlin, Unger, 1898. xx, 552p. **1236**

MAN, EDWARD HORACE. Dictionary of the Central Nicobarese language: English-Nicobarese and Nicobarese-English. London, W.H. Allen, 1889. cxiv, 243p. **1237**

MARSHMAN, JOSHUA. Elements of Chinese grammar, with a preliminary dissertation on the characters, and the colloquial medium of the Chinese, and an appendix containing the Tahyoh of Confusius with a translation. Serampore, printed at the Mission Press, 1814. 2p. 1., xvi, vii, 566, 56p. **1238**

MASTER, ALFRED. Introduction to Telugu grammar. London, Luzac, 1947. 31p. **1239**

MATHER, COTTON. Glossary, Hindustani and English, to the New Testament and psalms. London, Longman, Green, Longman and Roberts, 1861. x, 226p. **1240**

MENDIES, JOHN. Companion to Johnson's dictionary, Bengali and English peculiarly calculated for the use of European and native students. Calcutta, The Baptist Mission Press, 1874. xiv, 530p. **1241**

MENETRIER, E. Le vocabularie cambodgien daus ses rapports

evec la sancrit el le pali. Phnom-Penh, 1933. i, v. 168p. (F) **1242**
MOELLER, HERMANN. Vergleichendes indogermanisch-somitisches. Worterbuch, Gottingen, 1911. xxxvi, 316p. (G) **1243**
MOLESWORTH, J.T. Dictionary of Marathi and English. 2nd ed. Bombay, Govt. of Bombay, 1857. xxx, 921p. **1244**
MONIER-WILLIAMS, Sir MONIER. A dictionary, English and Sanskrit. London, W.H. Allen & Co., 1851. 4p. 1., xii, 859 (2) p. 2nd edition was published by Akhila Bharatiya Sanskrit Parishad in 1957. **1245**
——— An elementary grammar of the Sanskrit language, partly in the Roman character, arranged according to a new theory, in reference especially to the classical languages; with short extracts in easy prose. To which is added, a selection from the Institutes of Manu, with copious references to the grammar, and an English translation. London, W.H. Allen & Co., 1846. 2p. 1., ix, (4) 212, 48p. 1 1., (2) p. **1246**
——— An easy introduction to the study of Hindustani in which the English alphabet is adapted to the expression of Hindustani words, with a full syntax. Also, on the same plan, selections in Hindustani, with a vocabulary and dialogue, by Cotton Mather. London, Longman, Brown, Green, Longmans, xi (1) 1 1, 238p. **1247**
——— A practical grammar of the Sanskrit language arranged with reference to the classical languages of Europe, for the use of English students. 2d ed. Oxford, University Press, 1857, xxiv, 369, (1)p. fold tab. **1248**
——— A Sanskrit-English dictionary etymologically and philologically arranged with special reference to cognate Indo-European languages. New ed. greatly enl. and improved, with collaboration of Professor E. Lenmann. Professor C. Chappeller... and other scholars. Oxford, The Clarendon Press, 1899. xxxiv, (2) 1333p. Rev. edition was published in 1960. **1249**
MORRIS, RICHARD. Notes and queries on Pali lexicography. London, Unwin Brothers, 1884-87. 71p. **1250**
MULLER, FRIEDERICH MAX. Biographies of words, and the home of the Aryans. London, New York, Longmans, Green & Co., 1888. 3p. 1 (ix)-xxvii, 278p. **1251**
——— A Sanskrit grammar for beginners in Devanagari and

400 Linguistics

Roman letters throughout London. Longmans, Green & Co., 1886. xxiv, 307 (1) p. **1252**

NEEDHAM, JACK F. Outline grammar of the Singhpo language as spoken by the Singhpo Dowanniyas and others, residing in the neighbourhood of Sadiva, with illustrative sentences, phrase book and vocabulary. Shillong, Assam Secretariat Press, 1889. iv, 119p. **1253**

NEISSER, WALTER. Zum Worterbuch des Rgveda. Leipzig, Munchen, 1924. xiii, 205p. (G). **1254**

NEWTON, E.P. Panjabi grammar: with exercises and vocabulary. Ludhiana, The Mission Press, 1898. xiv, 533p. **1255**

PAGE, WALTER. An introduction to colloquial Bengali. Cambridge, W. Heffer, 1934. xi, 195p. **1256**
    A catalogue of records prepared by the Linguaphone Institute.

PEARSON, P. Beitrage zur indogermanischen Wortforschung. Upsal & Co., 1912. viii, 549p. (G). **1257**

PERCIVAL, PETER, *comp.* Tamil-English dictionary. Madras, Madras School Book and Literature Society, 1953. 442p. **1258**

——— Telugu-English dictionary, with the Telugu words printed in the Roman as well as in the Telugu character. Madras, Public Instruction Press, 1862. **1259**

PERRY, EDWARD D. Sanskrit primer. New York, Columbia University Press, 1936. xii, 230p. **1260**

PHILLIPS, H.L. Urdu military vocabulary with reading exercises. London, H. Milford, Oxford University Press, 1944. 89p. **1261**

PISCHEL, RICHARD. Grammatik der prakrit-sprachen, Strassburg, K.J. Trubner, 1900. 1p. 1., 429, (1) p. **1262**

PLATTS, JOHN THOMPSON. Dictionary of Urdu, classical Hindi and English. London, Oxford University Press, 1930. viii, 1259p. **1263**

PLATTS, JOHN T. Grammar of the Hindustani or Urdu language. London, Oxford University Press, 1920. xv, 339p. **1264**
    The author does not find difference between Hindustani or Urdu. The book is misleading.

POPE, G.U. First lessons in Tamil. Madras, American Mission Press, 1856. 308p. **1265**

PRICE, WILLIAM. Vocabulary; Khuree bolee and English of

Sources of Indian Civilization

the principal words occurring in the Prema Sagara of Lalluji 'Lal Kavi'. Calcutta, Hindoostanee Press, 1814. 241p. **1266**

PROENCA, ANTAO DE. Vocabulario Tamulico com a Significacam Portugueza. Na imprensa Tamulico da Provincia do Malabar, par Ignacio Aichamoni impresser della. Ambalacathem 30, de lulh' o. Kuala Lumpur; Department of Indian Studies, University of Malaya, 1966. 548p. (P). **1267**

PUXLEY, E.L. Vocabulary of the Santali language. London, W.M. Watts, 1868. vi, 139p. **1268**

RABINOVICH, I.S. AND SEREBRIAKOV, I.D. Pandjabsko-Russki slovar. Moscow, Gosudarstavennoe, Izdatelstvo Inostrannykh i. Natsionalaykh Slovarie, 1961. 1039p. (R). **1269**

RANKING, GEORGE SPIERS ALEXANDER. Urdu-English primer, for the use of colonial artillery. London, H.M. Stationery Office, 1899. 136p. **1270**

ROBERTS, T.T. Indian glossary, consisting of some thousand words and terms commonly used in the East-Indies. London, Murray and Highley, 1800. 120p. **1271**

ROBERTSON, ANDREW. Compilation of papers in Tamil language and glossary of words used chiefly in courts and cutcherries. Madras, 1839. i, 209p. **1272**

ROEPSTORFF, FREDRICK ADOLPH DE. Vocabulary of dialects spoken in the Nicobar and Andaman Isles, with a short account of the natives, their customs and habits and the previous attempts at colonisation. 2nd ed. Calcutta, Superintendent, Government Press, 1875. iii, 114p. **1273**

ROSEN, F. Radices sanscritae. Berolini, 1827. xx, 381p. (L).
1274

ROSS, Sir EDWARD DENISON. Dialogue in the eastern Turki dialect on subjects of interest to travellers, collected and edited by Sir E. Dension Ross, CIE, and Rachel O. Wingete. London, the Royal Asiatic Society, 1934. xxp. 2 l., 48p. **1275**

ROTTLER, J.P. Dictionary, Tamil and English language. Madras Society for Promoting Christian Knowledge, 1834-41. 4 pts.
1276

SALMONE, HABIB ANTHONY. An Arabic-English dictionary on a new system. London, Trubner & Co., 1890. 2v. tab. **1277**

SAVIDGE, FRED W. Grammar and dictionary of the Lakhar

language. Allahabad, Pioneer Press, 1908. iv, 210p. **1278**

SCHMIDT, RICHARD. Nachtrage zum Sanskrit-Worterbuch. Leipzig, Verlag, Von Otto Harrassowitz, 1928. viii, 398p. (G). **1279**

SCHULZE. F.V.P. Vocabulary of Kuvi-Kond language. Madras, 1913. 151p. **1280**

SHAKESPEAR, JOHN. A dictionary, Hindustani and English, and English and Hindustani, the latter being entirely new. 4th ed., greatly enl. London, P. Richardson, 1849. xiip., 2240. col. (2241)-2414p., 1 l. **1281**

——A grammar of the Hindustani language. 5th ed.; to which is added, A Short grammar of the Dakhni. London, Printed for the author, and sold by W.H. Allen & Co., 1846. xv, (1), 208p. 5pl. **1282**

——Muntakhbat-i-Hindi, or, Selections in Hindustani, with verbal translations or particular vocabularies, and grammatical analysis of some parts, for the use of students of that language. London, Printed for the author, by J. & H. Cox, and sold by W.H. Allen & Co., 1846, 1844. 2 v. in 1. Added title page in Hindustani. Vol. 1: 5th ed., 1846; v. 2: 4th ed., 1844. **1283**

SLEEMAN, Sir WILLIAM HENRY. Ramaseeana; or, A vocabulary of the peculiar language used by the thugs, with an introduction and appendix, descriptive of the system pursued by that fraternity and of the measures which have been adopted by the supreme government of India for its suppression. Calcutta, G.H. Huttman, Military Orphan Press, 1836. 1p. 1., v., 270 515p. fold. tab., diagrs (2 fold). **1284**

SOLONUTSEVA, N.E., *comp*. Russi-Hindi chattropayogi shabd kosh. Ed. by Kesari Narayan Shukla and Puran Somsundram. Moscow, Videshi tatha Rashtriya Bhashaon ke Shabda Koshon ka Rajkiya Prakashangrah, 1963. 143p. (R). **1285**

STACK, GEORGE. Dictionary. Sindhi and English. Bombay, 1855. vi, 437p. **1286**

STENZLER, ADOLF FRIEDRICH. Elementarbuch der Sanskritsprache (grammatik—texteworterbuch), von Adolf Friederich Stenzler, foregefuhrt von Richard Pischel. 9. aufl., ungearb. von. Karl. F. Geldner Giessen, A. Topel mann (vormals J. Ricker). 1915. viii, 120p. 1st, 2nd, and 3rd eds. published in

1868, 1875 and 1885, respectively. **1287**

STEWART, CHARLES. An introduction to the study of the Hindostany language as spoken in the Carnatic. 1808. **1288**

STSCHOUPAK, N. NITTI L AND RENOU, L. Dictionnaire Sanskrit-francais. Paris, Adrien Maisonneuve, 1931-32. iv, 897p. (F). **1289**

TAYLOR, JOSEPH. Dictionary Hindustani and English originally compiled for his own private use. Revised by William Hunter. Calcutta, Hindoostanee Press, 1808. 2 vols. **1290**

THOUMB, ALBERT. Haubuch des Sanskrit, eine einfubrung in das Sprachwisenschaft licha studium des altindischen. Heidelberg, Carl Winter, 1953. 2 vols. (G). **1291**

THOMPSON, JOSEPH T. Dictionary in Hindi and English. Banaras, Lazaras Press, 1895. Originally published in Calcutta in 1862. **1292**

——Dictionary in Oordoo and English, Serampore, 1838. 604p. **1293**

TISDALL, W. ST. CLAIR TOWERS. A simplified grammar and reading book of the Panjabi language. New York, F. Ungar, 1961. First edition was published in 1889. 189p. **1294**

——A simplified Gujarati-English dictionary. Ahmedabad, C.M. Shah, 1940. 3rd rev. ed. 179p. **1295**

TURNER, RALPH LILLEY. Comparative dictionary of the Indo-Aryan language. London, Oxford University Press, 1960-69. 2 vols. **1296**

TURNER, RALPH LILLEY AND D.R. TURNER. Comparative dictionary of the Indo-Aryan languages: Phonetic analysis. London, School of Oriental and African Studies, 1971. viii, 231p. **1297**

UHLENBICK, C.C. Kurzgefasstes etymologisches Worterbuch der altindischen Sprache. Amsterclan, Johannes Muller, 1889-99. xii, 367p. (G). **1298**

WADDELL, LAURENCE AUSTINE. A Sumer-Aryan dictionary; an etymological lexicon of the English and other Aryan languages ancient and modern and the Sumerian origin of Egyptians and its hieroglyphs. London, Luzac & Co., 1927-front. illus. **1299**

WALKER, G.D. Dictionary of modern spoken Monkhmer. London, Oxford University Press, 1962. **1300**

WATT, Sir GEORGE. Acacia catechu. Catechu or cutch, and kath. (Dictionary of economic products, v. l., A. 135-199) Review of the proceedings of the Government of India (Forest department) on the subject of the isolation of catechu and of kath from the wood *Acacia Catecchu*—by the editor. Calcutta, Office of the Superintendent, Government Printing, India. 1895. cover-title. 28p. **1301**

WESTERGAARD, NIELS LUDVING. Radices linguae sanscritae, ad deereta grammaticorum definivit atque copia exemplorum exquisititorum illustravit. N. L. Westergaard. Bonnae ad Rhenam impensis H.B. Konig, Havniae, typis fratrum verling, 1841. 2p. l., xiii, (1) p. 1 l, 379 (1) p. **1302**

—— Sanskrit laeselog med tilhorende ordsamling, af N.L. Westergaard. Kjobenhavn, C.A. Reitzel, 1846. 2p. l., 214 (2) p. **1303**

WHITNEY, WILLIAM DWIGHT. A brief German grammar, with reference to his larger grammar, New York, H. Holt & Co., (etc.), Boston, C. Schoenhof (1885). vii p. 21, 129p. **1304**

—— A compensions German and English dictionary with notation of correspondences and brief etymologies, by William Dwight Whitney assisted by Angust Hjalmar Edgren. New York, H. Holt & Co., (c. 1905). viii, 537 (4)1-362p. **1305**

—— The roots, verb-form, and primary derivatives of the Sanskrit grammar. Leipzig, Breit kopf and Hartel (etc.), 1885. viii, (1) 250p. **1306**

—— A sanskrit grammar, including both the classical languages, and the older dialects of Vedas and Brahmanas. Leipzig, Breitkopj and Hartel etc. (etc.) 1879. xxiv, 485, (1) p. **1307**

—— Sanskrit grammar. Boston, Harvard. (1875), 1950. 551 p. **1308**

A standard grammar which has been reprinted several times since the first edition in 1875. The author was professor of Sanskrit at Yale University.

—— Sanskrit grammar. Cambridge, Harvard University Press, 1950-xxiv, 485p. **1309**

WIDURUPDA, PIYATISSA, M.N.T. The English-Pali dictionary. Colombo, Colombo Apothecaries Co., 1949. **1310**

WILKINS, Sir CHARLES. A grammar of the Sanskrit language.

London, Printed for the author by W. Bulmer & Co., 1808. 2p. 1 (vii)-xx, 662p. v plates. **1311**

WILSON, HORACE HAYMAN. A dictionary in Sanskrit and English; *tr.* amended and enl. from an original compilation, prepared by learned natives for the college of Fort William. The 2d ed. greatly extended, and pub. under the sanction of the General Committee of Public Instruction, Bengal, Calcutta, Printed at the Education Press, 1832. 2p. 1 (vii)-x, 982p. **1312**

—— An introduction to the grammar of the Sanskrit languages for the use of early students. By H.H. Wilson, 2d. ed. London, Madden & Co., 1847. xv (1) 499p. **1313**

WILSON, J. Grammar and dictionary of Western Panjabi as spoken in the Shahpur district. Lahore, Punjab Government Press, 1899. 279p. **1314**

WITFIELD, W.W. Vocabulary of the Kui language. Calcutta, Kui-English Asiatic Society, 1929. xiv, 132p. (Bibliothece Indica series, 252). **1315**

WITTER, W.E. Outline grammar of the Lhota Naga Lushai language. Calcutta, Bengal Secretariat Press, 1897. 22p. **1316**

WOGIHARA, UNRAI. Sanskrit Chinese dictionary of Buddhist technical terms, based on the Mahavayutpatti. Tokyo, Sankibo, 1959. **1317**

WUST, W. Vergleichendes und etymologisches Worterbuch des All-Indoarischen. Heidelberg, Carl Winter, 1936. 3 pts. (G) **1318**

YATES, WILLIAM. A Bengali grammar, by the late Rev. W. Yates, D.D., reprinted with improvements from his introduction to the Bengali language. Edited by J. Wenger. Calcutta, printed at the Baptist Mission Press, 1864. iv, 150p. **1319**

—— A grammar of the Sansckrit language, on a new plan. Calcutta, Baptist Mission Press; London, Black, Parbury and Allen, 1820. vii, (v)-xxviii, 427, (1) p. **1320**

ZACHARIAE, THEODOR. Die Indischen Worterbucher. Strassburg, Trubner, 1897. 45p. **1321**

ZACHARIAS, TOBIAS. Anglo-Malayalam dictionary. Mangalore, Basel Mission Book and Tract Depository, 1933. 2nd ed. xiv, 1386p. **1322**

400 Linguistics

ZIEGLER, FRIEDRICH. English-Kanarese school dictionary. London, Kegan Paul, 1929. 6th rev. ed. **1323**
—— A practical key to the Kanarese language. Mangalore, Basel Mission Book and Tract Depository, 1935. 5th ed. **1324**
See also Linguistics (General)

500 PURE SCIENCES
600 APPLIED SCIENCES

Agriculture
Anthropology
Astronomy
Botany
Geology
Medicine
Zoology

AINSLIE, WHITELAW. Materia Indica, etc. London, Longman & Co., 1826. 2 vols. **1325**
———Materia Medica of Hindostan. Madras, Govt. Press, 1813. 301, xlviiip. **1326**
BALL, VALENTINE. The coalfield of India...entirely revised and largely re-written. Calcutta, Simpson, 1913. xliv, 147p. 20pl. (Memoirs of the Geological Survey of India, Vol. 41). **1327**
BEDDOME, RICHARD HENRY. A facsimile of R.H. Beddome's articles on Indian reptiles, 1862-70. By Malcolm Smith (The article appeared originally in The Madras Quarterly Journal of 'Medical Science' and 'The Madras Monthly Journal Medical Science'. London, 1940. Vol. 1. pt. 10. **1328**

BEDDOME, RICHARD HENRY. The ferns of British India. Madras, 1865-70. 545, vip. cccxlvpl. **1329**

———The fern of Southern India. Being description and plates of the ferns of Madras Presidency. Madras, Gantz Bros., 1863. vii, 88p. 271pl. **1330**

——— The flora sylvatica for Southern India. Madras, Gantz Bros (1869-73), 2 vols. **1331**

———Handbook to the ferns of British India, Ceylon and the Malaya Peninsula. with illus. Calcutta, London, Thacker & Co., 1883. xiv, 500p. **1332**

———Icones plantarum India orientalis; or plates and descriptions of new and rare plants, chiefly from Southern India and Ceylon. Madras, 1868-74. V. 1., 300pl. Ms. note. **1333**

BENTLEY, JOHN. Historical view of the Hindu astronomy from the earliest dawn of that science in India, down to the present time, etc. Calcutta Baptist Mission Press, 1823. xxvi, 228p. lxpl. **1334**

BIDIE, GEORGE. The timber trees of India, alphabetically arranged, etc. Madras, Gantz Bros., 1862. vii, 23p. **1335**

BIRDWOOD, Sir GEORGE C. MOLESWORTH. Catalogue of the vegetable productions of the Presidency of Bombay. Bombay, Education Society's Press, 1865. 45, 459p. **1336**

BLATTER, E. AND MILLARD, W.S. Some beautiful Indian trees. 2nd ed. rev. by W.T. Stearn. Bombay, Bombay National History Society, 1954. xiv, 165p. plates, maps, diagrs. **1337**

BRANDIS, Sir DIETRICH. The forest flora of North West & Central India. 1874. xxxi, 608p. **1338**

———Indian trees. Dehra Dun, Bishen Singh, Mahendra Pal Singh, 1971. 767p. Reprint. **1339**

——— Indian trees: an account of trees, shrubs, woody climbers, bamboos and palms, etc. 1907. 76p. **1340**

BROWN, DORRIS D. Agricultural development in India's districts. Cambridge, Mss., Harvard, 1971. 169p. **1341**

BUCHANAN, DANIEL H. The development of capitalist enterprise in India. New York, Macmillan, 1934. ix, 497p. **1342**

A valuable study of plantation agriculture as well as industrial activity in India in thirties.

BURNS, W., *ed.* Sons of the soil: studies of the Indian cultivator. Delhi, Manager of Publications, 1941. ix, 128p. **1343**
    Contains sketches about the life and living of Indian cultivators.

BYLN, GEORGE. Agricultural trends in India, 1891-1947: output, availability, and productivity. University of Pennsylvania, 1966. 370p. **1344**

COVENTRY, B.C. Wild flowers of Kashmir with descriptions and coloured illustrations, 1923-1930. 3vols. **1345**

DAY, FRANCIS. The fishes of India. London, Quaritch, 1878. 2 vol. xx, 278p. **1346**

—— The fishes of Malabar. London, Quaritch, 1865. xxxii, 293p. **1347**

ENDLE, SIDNEY. The Kacharis. Introduction by J.D. Anderson. London, Macmillan & Co., 1911. xix, 128p. **1348**
    An anthropological study of the Kacharis who differ in some material ways from their Hindu and Muslim neighbours.

ESDALLE, JAMES. Mesmerism in India, and its practical application in survey and medicine. American ed. Chicago, Printed by the Psychic Research Company, 1902. 165p. **1349**
    1st, 2nd and 3rd eds. published in 1846, 1847 and 1850, respectively.

EWART, JOSEPH, *comp.* The poisonous snakes of India. For the use of the officials and others residing in Indian Empire. 1878. viii, 64p. plates. **1350**
    Has 19 full page coloured plates and 2 monochrome plates.

FILLIOZAT, J. The classical doctrine of Indian medicine, its origin, and its Greek parallels; translated from the original in French by Dev Raj Chanana. First English edition was published in 1964. xxii, 298p. **1351**

—— La Doctrine Classique de la Medicine Indienne. Ses origines et ses paralleles grecs. Paris, 1949. vii, 230p. (F). **1352**

GABLE, JAMES SYKES. The Bambusea of British India. Calcutta, Printed at the Bengal Secretariat Press, 1896. 3p. 1., xviip., 1. 1., 133, 3.4p. 11. 119 pl. Added at the title page: Annals of the Royal Botanic Garden, Calcutta. vol. vii. **1353**

GABLE, JAMES SYKES. Flora of the presidency of Madras (B.J.J.S. Gamble. Published under the authority of the Secretary of State for India in Council). London, Adlard & Son, limited, 1936. 3 v. fold. map. Issued in 11 pt., 1915-36; paged continuously. **1354**
>The draft of the botanical portion of about the first 132 pages was prepared by Mr. S.T. Dunn. Vol. 3 by C.E.C. Fischer.

——Lists of the trees, shrubs and large climbers found in the Darjeeling district, Bengal. Calcutta, Printed at the Bengal Secretariat Press, 1878, 1p. 1., iv, 88, ii, xvip. **1355**

—— A manual of Indian timbers; an account of the growth, distribution and uses of the trees and shrubs of India and Ceylon with descriptions of their wood-structure. Reprint of 2d ed. With some additions and corrections. London, S. Low, Marton & Co., Ltd., 1922. xxvi, 868p. front., plates, fold map. **1356**

HOOKER, Sir JOSEPH DALTON. Botany. With illustrations 3d. ed.; rev. and cor. New York, D. Appleton & Company, 1882. x, 129p. illus. (Science primers No. viii). **1357**

—— A century of Indian orchids. Calcutta, printed at the Bengal Secretariat Press, (etc. etc.). 1895. 2p. 1., 68 11p. 101pl. (*In* annals of the Royal Botanic Garden, Calcutta. Vol. v (pt. i). **1358**

——Flora indica: being a systematic account of the plants of British India, together with observations on the structure and affinities of their natural orders and genera. By J.D. Hooker and Thomas Thomson. Vol. 1. Ranunculacea to Fumariaceac, with an introductory essay. London, W. Pamplin, 1855. xv(1) 280, 285p. 2 fold maps. No more published. **1359**

——The flora of British India. By J.D. Hooker. Assisted by various botanists. Published under the authority of the Secretary of State for India in Council. London, L. Reeve & Co., 1875-97. 7v. Issued in xxiv ports, 1872-97. **1360**

——Illustrations of Himalayan plants. Chiefly selected from drawings made for the late J.F. Cathcart esq. The description and analyses by J.D. Hooker. The plates executed by W.H. Fitch (London) Reoves, 1855). 3p. 1 (ix) - x, iv p., 1 1. 24 col. pl. **1361**

HOOKER, Sir JOSEPH DALTON. The rhododendrons of Sikkim-Himalaya : being an account, and botanical and geographical, of the rhododendrons recently discovered in the mountains of Eastern Himalaya from drawings and description made on the spot, during a government botanical mission to that country. Edited by Sir W.J. Hooker. 2nd ed. London, Reeve, Brenham and Reeve, 1849-51. 3 pt. in 1 v. **1362**

——A sketch of the flora of British India. Oxford, Clarendon Press, 1906. 60p. **1363**

"Bibliography" p. 59-60. Reprinted from the third edition of the 'Imperial Gazetteer'.

——The students flora of the British islands. London, Macmillan and Co., 1870. xxp. **1364**

ISAACS, MOZELLE. The commoner flowering plants of Western India. 1927. 344p. **1365**

JERDON, THOMAS CAVERHILL. The birds of India, being a natural history of all the birds known to inhabit continental India, etc. Calcutta. 1862-1864. 2v. "Vol. 2. in two parts, and the second part has a title page in which its is described as vol. 3. The pagination of the two pts. continuous." **1366**

——Catalogue of the birds of the Peninsula of India, arranged according to the modern system of classification. From the Madras Journal of Litrature and Science, no. 24, July-September 1839. Madras, 1839. 70p. **1367**

——Illustration of Indian orinthology, containing fifty figures of new, unifigured and interesting species of birds, chiefly from the south of India. Madras. 1847. Contains 50 figures. **1368**

——The mammals of India; a natural history of all the animals known to inhabit continental India. Roorkee, printed for the author by the Thomson College Press, 1867. 4p. l., xxi, 319, xvp. **1369**

KIPLING, JOHN LOCKWOOD. Beast and man in India; a popular sketch of Indian animals in their relations with the people, with illustrations. London & New York. Macmillan & Co., 1891. xii, 401, (1)p. **1370**

KNIGHT, Sir HENRY. Food administration in India. 1939-47. Stanford, 1954. 323p. **1371**

A description of the development of food administration

in India from nothing to a complete system capable of dealing with real emergency.

KURZ, SULPIZ. Preliminary report on the forest and other vegetation of Pegu. Calcutta, printed by C.B. Lewis, Baptist Mission Press, 1875. 3p. 1., 97, cxxxviii, 95, xxivp. 11., 34p. illus., plates (1 col.) 2 fold. maps. **1372**

LA TOUCHE, T.H.D. Bibliography of Indian geology and physical geography. Calcutta, Supdt., Govt. Printing Press, 1961. **1373**

"This retrospective bibliography is arranged first by authors alphabetically, and under each author the arrangement is chronological. At the beginning there is a list of abbreviated titles."

MOREHOUSE, WARD, ed. Science and the human condition in India and Pakistan. New York, Rockefeller University, 1968. 230p. **1374**

MOREHOUSE, W. Science in India. Bombay, Popular, 1970. 154p. **1375**

MORELAND, WILLIAM H. The agrarian system of modern India. Cambridge, W. Heffer, 1929. xvii, 296p. **1376**

An account of the revenue system of Muslim kings from the 12th to the 18th century.

ROYLE, JOHN FORBES. The fibrous plant of India, fitted for cordage, clothing and paper, with an account of the cultivation and preparation of flax, hemp, and their substitutes. London, Smith Elder & Co., (etc. etc.). 1855. xiv, 403, (1)p. illus. **1377**

—— Illustrations of the botany and other branches of the natural history of the Himalayan mountains and of the flora of Cashmere. London, W.H. Allen & Co., 1839. viii (8), (v)-xxxvi, xxix-xxxvi, xxxvii-lxxviii (2) 472p. Atlas (3p. 1 front.) 100 pl. **1378**

—— On the production of isinglass along the coasts of India, with a notice of its fisheries. London, W.H. Allen & Co., 1842. viii, 94p. **1379**

THIBAUT, GEORGE FREDERICK WILLIAM. Indische. Astronomie, Astrologie, und Mathematik. Strassburg, K.J. Trubner, 1899. 1p. 1., 80 (2) (G). **1380**

THORNER, DANIEL and ALICE. Land and labour in India. Bombay, Asia Publishing House, 1962. ix, 227p. **1381**
> A collection of articles on such problems as agricultural production, credit, and development in India's rural economy.

UI, HAKUJU, *tr.* The Vaisesika philosophy according to the Dasapadartha-sastra. London, Oriental Translation Fund, 1917. xii, 265p. **1382**

WATT, Sir GEORGE. The commercial products of India, being an abridgement of "The dictionary of the economic products of India." Published under the authority of His Majesty's Secretary of State for India in Council. London, J. Murray, 1908. vii, 1189, (1). **1383**

──── The pests and blights of the tea plant (2nd ed.). by Sir George Watt and Harold H. Mann. Calcutta, Office of the Superintendent, Government Printing, India, 1903. 2p. 1., xv, 416 (2) 416c-429p. illus, xxiv pl. 1st ed. published in 1898. **1384**

──── The principles of tea pruning. By Sir George Watt and Harold H. Mann. Calcutta, Office of the Superintendent, Government Printing, India, 1903. 36p., illus. **1385**

WHEELER, JAMES TALBOYS. Handbook to the cotton cultivation in the Madras Presidency : exhibiting the principal contents of the various public records and other works connected with the subject in a condensed and classified form, in accordance with a resolution of the Government of India. London, Virtue Bros & Co., 1863. 7p. 1, 238, lxviiip. front. plates. map. **1386**

──── Madras versus America : a handbook to cotton cultivation, exhibiting contents of public records in a condensed form, in accordance with resolution of the Government of India. N.Y., Virtue and Yorson, 1866. 7p. 1., 238, lxviiip. incl. front. 4 pl. map. **1387**

ZIMMER, HEINRICH R. Hindu medicine. Baltimore, John Hopkins, 1948. 203p. **1388**
> This volume had its origin in a course of lectures given by Professor Zimmer in 1940, as Noguchi Lecturer at the Johns Hopkins Institute of the History of Medicine. It was revised and completed by one of his colleagues.

700 FINE ARTS

(i) General

ARCHER, W.G. India and modern art. London, Allen and Unwin, 1959. 143p. **1389**
   A study of paintings in India from the end of the nineteenth century to the present day.

────Indian miniatures. Greenwich, N.Y. Graphic Society, 1960. 16p. 100 plates. **1390**

AUBOYER, J. Arts et styles de l'Inde. Paris, 1951. 171p. xlviii plates. (F). **1391**

BIRDWOOD, GEORGE CHRISTOPHER MOLESWORTH. The industrial arts of India. London, Chapman & Hall, 1880. 2 vols. in one. **1392**
   Published for the Committee of Council on Education.

BLACKER, JAMES F. The A.B.C. of Indian art. London, Stanley Paul & Co. 1922. 302p. **1993**

BOWERS, FAUBION. The dance of India. New York, Columbia University Press, 1953. xiii, 175p. **1394**

────Theatre in the East : a survey of Asian dance and drama. New York, Toronto, Nelson, 1956. 374p. **1395**
   The first chapter is on India, since the author believes that "out of India and from Indian theatre forms them-

selves, an aesthetic basis applicable to all Asian dance and drama definitely emerges." The book covers fourteen countries.

BREWSTER, EARL HENRY & BREWSTER, ACHSAH. The art of E.H. Brewster and Achsah Brewster. Text by M.S. Randhawa. New Delhi, Dhoomi Mal Dharam Das, 1953. viii, 19 plates. **1396**

BURGESS, JAMES. The Journal of Indian Art. London, Periodical Publication, 1900. 8 vols. **1397**

CLEMENTS, E. Introduction to the study of Indian music. London, Longmans Green, 1913. 96p. **1398**

An appraisal and analysis of both the ancient and modern systems of Indian music.

COUSINS, MARGARET, E. The music of Orient and Occident; essays towards mutual understanding. Madras, B.G. Paul & Co., 1935. vi, 199p. **1399**

DANIELL, THOMAS. Oriental scenery. London, The Daniell, 1797. 2 vols. **1400**

DANIELOU, ALAIN. A catalogue of recorded classical and traditional Indian music. Paris, UNESCO, 1952. 233p. **1401**

——Northern Indian music. London, C. Johnson, 1949. 2 vols. **1402**

Deals with raga-poems with English translations and traditional ragas.

ELWIN, VERRIER. The art of the Northeast Frontier of India. Shillong, North-East Frontier Agency, 1959. **1403**

A descriptive account of the distinctive art traditions of tribal people residing in the sub-Himalayan region of Assam.

—— Myths of Middle India. Bombay, Oxford University Press, 1949. xvi, 532p. (Specimens of the oral literature of Middle India series). **1404**

A collection of myths of folklore of Central India.

—— The Tribal Art of Middle India. Bombay, Oxford University Press, 1951. 214p. **1405**

An illustrated account of the art and social life of the tribal peoples of Madhya Pradesh, Orissa and Bihar.

ETIINGHAUSEN, RICHARD. Paintings of the Sultans and Emperors of India in American collections. New Delhi, Lalit Kala Akademi, 1961. 5p. 15 colour plates. **1406**

GRAY, BASIL. Rajput painting. London, Faber & Faber, 1948. 24p. **1407**

GRUNWEDEL, ALBERT. Buddhist art in India. Tr. from the 'Handbuch' of Prof. Albert Grunwedel by Agnes C. Gibson. Rev. and enl. by Jas. Burgess. With 154 illus. London, B. Quartich, 1901. vii, (1), 228p. 11, illus. **1408**

HENDLEY, THOMAS HOLBEIN. Asian carpets: XVI and XVII century designs from the Jaipur palaces and from material supplied with the permission of H.H. the Maharaja of Jaipur and from other sources, with text by Colonel T.H. Handley. London, W. Griggs, 1905. 2p. 1., 20p. (i.3. 145) pl. (port double, mostly col.) map. **1409**

———— Damascening on steel or iron, as practised in India by Thomas Holbein Handley; with thirtytwo full page illustrations, containing one hundred and four designs, photo-chromolithographed by W. Griggs from water colour drawing by Murli, Nand Lal, Chaju Lal, Ram Gopal, Jiwan and other Indian artists. London, W. Griggs & Sons, Ltd., 1892. 16p. xxxi (9. i.e. 32) col. pl. **1410**

———— Ulwar and its art treasures. London, W. Griggs, 1888. 4p. 1. 25 illus. part col.) 61 col. pl. (2 double inch. port). 20 pol. (incl. 2 plans maps). Added 1-p engraved in gold and colour within ornamental border. **1411**

HORWITZ, EARNEST P. The Indian theatre : a brief survey of the Sanskrit drama. London, Blackie & Son, 1912. 215p. **1412**

KRAMRISCH, STELLA. The art of India: traditions of Indian sculpture, painting and architecture. London, Phaidon Press, 1954. 231p. **1413**

The author, who held the chair of history of Indian Art at the University of Calcutta for ten years, is now attached to the University of Pennsylvania, the chief centre of Indic studies in the United States.

KUEHNEL, ERNEST and GOETZ, HERMANN. Indian book painting; from Jahengir's album in the State Library in Berlin. London, Kegan Paul, 1926. vii, 75p. 42 colour plates. **1414**

LAWRENCE, GEORGE. Indian art; Mughal miniature. London,

Methuen, 1963. 11p.15 plates. (A pocket book from the Little Library of Art Series) **1415**

LEVI, SYLVAIN. Le Theatre Indien. Paris, E. Bouillon, 1890. 2 v. in 1. (F). **1416**

MARCEL-DUBOIS, C. Les Instruments de Musique de l'Inde Antique. Paris, 1941. (F). **1417**

MARSHALL, Sir JOHN H. The Buddhist Art of Gandhara. Cambridge, Cambridge University Press, 1960. xii, 117p. **1418**
> A well illustrated survey of a school of Buddhist art that flourished in the Indus Valley region early in the Christian era.

MODE, HEINZ. The woman in Indian art. New York, McGraw, 1970. 53p. pls. **1419**

MUNSTERBERG, HUGO. Art of India and Southeast Asia, Abrams, 1970. 263p. **1420**

NAWRATH, ALFRED. Eternal India: the land, the people, the master-pieces of architecture and sculpture of India, Pakistan, Burma and Ceylon. Crown. 1956. 150p. **1421**
> Photographs of the oldest and most beautiful monuments of Indian art—Amber, Banaras, Ellora, Madurai, and many others.

RAMBACH, PIERRE, AND DE GOLISH, VITOLD. The golden age of Indian art. Crowell. 1955. 109 plates. **1422**
> A beautiful photographic record of the period from the fifth to the eighth century A.D. when the Chalukya Dynasty ruled in Central India.

ROSENTHAL, ETHEL. The story of Indian music and its instruments: a study of the present and a record of the past. London, William Reeves, 1928. xxviii, 220p. **1423**

ROSS, Sir EDWARD DENISON. Eastern art and literature, with special reference to China, India, Arabia and Persia. London, E. Benn Ltd. (1928). 80p. **1424**

ROWLAND, BENJAMIN. Art in East and West: an introduction through comparisons. Cambridge, Mass. Harvard, 1954. 144p. **1425**
> Professor Rowland began teaching Oriental art at Harvard University in 1933, and in 1936 published The Wall Paintings of India, Central Asia, and Ceylon. Here he

700 Fine Arts

uses a completely new approach, pairing masterpieces of the art of East and West to reveal their striking similarities and their essential differences.

ROWNALD, BENJAMIN. Harvard outline and reading lists for Oriental art. Cambridge, Mass., Harvard, 1952. 64p. **1526**
Intended for use both by students in introductory courses and as a reference book for others interested in the subject.

——Early Indian and Indonesian Art. Newton, Mass. University Prints, 1938. 111 plates. **1427**
Contains representative works of Indian art and architecture.

RUBISSOW, HELEN. The art of Asia. New York, Philosophical Library, 1954. 237p. **1428**
An introduction to all Asian art forms, beginning with India.

SCHLEGEL, AUGUST WILHELM VON. A course of lectures on dramatic art and literature. Tr. by John Black. Rev. according to the last German ed., by the Rev. A.J.W. Morrison. London, H.G. Bohn, 1846. 1p. 1., (v)—vii, 535, (1)p. front. (port). **1429**

——Lectures on dramatic art and literature. Tr. by John Black. 2d. ed. rev. by Rev. A. J. W. Morrison, M.A. London, G. Bell & Sons, 1902. viii, 535p. front. (port.) (Half-title page: Bohn's standard library). **1430**

SMITH, VINCENT ARTHUR. A history of Fine Art in India and Ceylon. Bombay, D.B. Taraporewala, 1962. 219p. **1431**
First published in 1911, the present book is a revised edition by K. Khandalavala. It contains a detailed account of the main developments in Indian art and architecture in ancient and medieval times.

SOLOMON, WILLIAM EWART GLADSTONE. The charm of Indian art. London, T. Fisher Unwin, 1926. 142p. **1432**

——Essays on Mogul art. Bombay, Humphrey Milford, Oxford University Press, 1932. xxx, 96p. **1433**
First published in 'Islamic Culture' at interval from 1927 to 1932.

STATTERHEIM, WILLEM F. Indian influence in old-Balinese art.

Tr. from the Dutch by Claire Holt. London, India Society, 1935. xiii, 41p. (D). **1434**

    Plates are accompanied by guardsheets with descriptive letterpress.

STRANGWAYS, ARTHUR HENRY FOX. The music of Hindostan. Oxford, at the Clarendon Press, 1914. xii, 364p. **1435**

TAYLOR, MEADOWS, i.e. PHILIP MEADOWS. Sketches in the Deccan, by Captain Philip Meadows Taylor. Drawn on stone by Weld Taylor, Edward Morton and George Childs. London, C. Tilt, 1837. 2p. 1, 191 20 pl. (Incl. engr. t. p.). **1436**

UNESCO. India; paintings from Ajanta caves. Foreword by Jawaharlal Nehru. New York, Graphic Society, 1954. 10p. 32 colour plts. **1437**

    First of the UNESCO World Art Series devoted to the rare art masterpieces of Ajanta Frescoes dating from 2 B.C. to 18 A.D.

VOGEL, J.P. Catalogue of Bhuri Singh Museum at Chamba. Calcutta, the author, 1909. 90p. **1438**

    A catalogue of the objects in the museum. Divided into nine classes such as stone inscriptions, inscriptions on metal, documents on paper etc., the catalogue contains three appendices also one of which is on the Rajas of Chamba.

—— Catalogue of the archaeological museum at Mathura. Allahabad, Supdt. Govt. Press, 1910. x, 209p. 25 plates. **1439**

    A catalogue with detailed description of the exhibits in the museum based on their arrangement into three main divisions consisting of images, base-reliefs and architectural sculptures.

WELCH, STUART CARY. The art of Mughal India: paintings and precious objects. New York, Asia House Gallery, 1963. 179p. **1440**

    It is a catalogue of the exhibition held in the galleries of Asia House during the winter of 1964. The introduction and the notes by the author provide a valuable source material for researches.

WELLESZ, EMMY. Akbar's religious thought, reflected in Mogul painting. London, George Allen & Unwin, 1952. xi, 47p. **1441**

WILSON, ANNE C. A short account of the Hindu system of

music. Lahore, Gulab Singh & Sons; London, Simpkin, Marshall, Hamilton, Kent & Co., 1904. 48p. **1442**

WILSON, HORACE HAYMAN. Selected specimens of the theatre of the Hindus translated from the original Sanskrit by Horace Hayman Wilson. 3rd ed. London, Trubner & Co., 1871. 2 vol. **1443**

WINSTEDT, RICHARD OLOF *ed*. Indian art : essays by H.G. Rawlinson, K. de B. Codrington, J.V.S. Wilkinson, and John Irwin. London, Faber & Faber, 1947. 200p. **1444**

ZIMMER HEINRICH R. The Art of India, Asia. New York, Pantheon Books, 1955. 2 vols. **1445**

> Completed and edited by Joseph Campbell, Vol. 1, is devoted to Zimmer's views on myths and symbols in Indian art. A good source book on the Art of India.

———Myths and symbols in Indian art and civilization. New York, Pantheon, 1946. 248p. 70 plates. **1446**

> This book interprets for the Western mind the key motifs of India's legend, myth and folklore taken directly from the Sanskrit, and illustrated with seventy plates of Indian art.

(ii) Architecture

BATLEY, CLAUDE. Designs development of Indian architecture. Bombay, Taraporevala, 1954. 52 plates. **1447**

> "Illustrates 52 plates of Indian architecture re-drawn from the Archaeology Department Publications of Government of India."

BROWN, PERCY. Indian architecture. 3rd ed. Bombay, D.B. Taraporevala, 1956. 2 vols. **1448**

> A standard work on Indian architecture covering the Buddhist, Hindu and Muslim periods of Indian history.

———Indian architecture—Islamic period. Bombay, Taraporevala, 1956. 146p. 250 illus. **1449**

> A standard work on Indian architecture, covering the Islamic period.

BRUHL, O. Indian temples. London, O.U.P. 1937. 136p. **1450**

BURGESS, JAMES. The Buddhist stupas of Amravati, and Jaggayyapeta in the Krishna District, Madras Presidency. London, Trubner & Co., 1887. ix, 131p. vol. 6. **1451**
——Muhammadan architecture of Ahmedabad. London, William Coriggs & Sons, 1900-1905. 2 vols. **1452**
    Vol. I, A.D. 1412-1520; Vol. 2, Muslim and Hindu remains in the vicinity.
——The Muhammadan architecture of Ahmedabad. London, W. Grings, 1900-5. v. 24p. **1453**
——Notes on the Buddha rock-temples of Ajanta, their paintings and sculpture. Bombay, Survey of Western India, 1879. iv, 111p. xxx pl. **1454**
—— Photographs of architecture and scenery in Gujarat and Rajputana. Calcutta, Bourne and Shepherd. 1874. **1455**
—— Provisional lists of architectural and other remains in Western India including Bombay Sindh, Berar, Central Provinces and Hyderabad. Bombay, Government Press, 1875. 60p. **1456**
——The rock-temples of Elephanta or Gharapuri. Bombay, Thacker, Vining & Co., 1871. 40p. **1457**
BURGESS, J. and COUSENS, H. Architectural antiquities of Northern Gujarat, Calcutta, Archaeological Society of India, 1903, 118p. 114 plates. **1458**
CAMERON, R. Shadows from India, an architectural album. Bombay, Taraporevala, 1958. 212p. **1459**
CODRINGTON, KENNETH de BURGH. Ancient India, from the earliest times to the Guptas, with notes on the architecture and sculpture of the medieval period. London, Ernest Benn, 1926. xv, 65p. Prefactory essay on India's sculpture by William Rothenstein. **1460**
COLE, H.H. The architecture of ancient Delhi, especially buildings around Kutab Minar. London, Arnold Society, 1884. 10 plates. **1461**
COOMARASWAMY, A.K. Bibliography of Indian art. Boston, Museum of Fine Arts, 1925. 53p. **1462**
——Introduction to Indian Art. Adyar, Theosophical Publishing House, 1956. 123p. **1463**
COUSENS, HENRY. Architectural antiquities of Western India.

700 Fine Arts

London. Indian Society, 1926. 86p. 57 plates. **1464**

EVENSON, NORMA. Chandigarh. Berkeley. University of California, 1966. 116p. pls. **1465**

FABRI, CHARLES A. An introduction to Indian architecture. Bombay, New York, Asia Puplishing House, 1962. **1466**

FERGUSSON, JAMES. An historical inquiry into the three principles of beauty in art, more especially with reference to architecture. Part first. London, Longman Brown, Green, and Longmans, 1849. xvi, 536p. col. front. illus. v. pl. (1 fold) No more published. **1467**

—— Histoire de l' architecture cambodgienne d' apres M James Fergusson. Memoire transcnt de l' anglois, avec l' autorisation de l auteur et annote, par M., de croizier. (In Soaete academique Indo-Chinise, Paris. Memoires. Paris, 1879. v. 1; p. (85)-(106) (F). **1468**

——History of Indian architecture. London, John Murray, 1910. 2 vols. (Vol. I, 450 p., Vol. II, 520p.) **1469**

"Traces the history of Indian architecture of different styles from Buddhist period to Muslim period and its influence on other neighbouring countries."

——A history of architecture in all countries. New ed. Edited by R. Phene Spiers. With notes and additions by George Knehn. New York, Dodd, Mead and Company, 1907. 2 v. col. fronts. illus (incl. plans) plates. **1470**

—— History of Indian and Eastern architecture. Rev. and edited with additions; Indian architecture, by R. Phine Spiers. London, J. Murray, 1910. 2 v. illus. ports. maps, plan, diagrs. First published in 1876. **1471**

——History of the modern style of architecture being a sequel to the handbook of architecture. London, J. Murray, 1862. xvl, 538p. incl. front., illus. **1472**

——The illustrated handbook of architecture being a concise and popular account of the different styles of architecture prevailing in all ages and all countries. 2d ed. London, J. Murray, 1859. lviip. 1 l. 1004p. incl. front illus. Later revised, expanded and rearranged and published as a new work under the title: History of architecture in all countries, from the earliest times to the present day. **1473**

FERGUSSON, JAMES. Illustrations of various styles of Indian architecture. London. Science and Art Department of Committee of Council on Education, 1869. **1474**

——On the study of Indian architecture. London, John Murray, 1867. 364p. **1475**

"A lecture delivered at the meeting of Society of Arts, London, 19th December, 1866."

——The palaces of Nineveh and Persepolis restored; an essay on ancient Assyrian and Persian architecture. London, J. Murray, 1851. xvi, 368p. front. illus. plates (part fold). **1476**

——Picturesque illustrations of ancient architecture in Hindostan. London, J. Hogarth, 1848. 20. 1., (iii)—ivp. 1. 1., 68p. illus, xxiiip. 1. (incl. front) map. Added t.p. engr. dated 1852. **1477**

——The rock-cut temples of India, one hundred illustrations of architecture and natural history in western India photographed by Major Gill and described by James Fergusson. New ed. London, Cundau, Downes Company, 1864. xii, 100p. phot. **1478**

GILL, ROBERT. One hundred stereoscopic illustrations of architecture and natural history in Western India, described by James Fergusson. London, Cundell, 1864. 100 plates. **1479**

GOETZ, HERMAN. Art and architecture of Bikaner State. London, Bruno Cassirer, 1950. 125p. 95 plates. **1480**

"Describes in details various styles of architecture, i.e. Temples, Mausolea, Fortifications, Palaces, Tanks and private houses. Also traces the history of sculpture, painting and industrial art of Bikaner."

——India: five thousand years of Indian art. New York, Crown Publishers, 1959. 275p. **1481**

A well illustrated introductory, historical survey of Indian art, including architecture, painting, sculpture, and handicrafts, from the late stone to modern times.

GRIGGS, W. India: photographs and drawings of historical buildings. London, the author, 1896. 100 plates. **1482**

HARLE, J.C. Temple gateways in South India. Oxford, Bruno, 1963. 179p. **1483**

HAVELL, E.B. Ancient and medieval architecture of India: a study of Indo-Aryan civilization. London, John Murray, 1915. **1484**

"Traces the history and development of ancient Indian architecture and discusses its influence on the Indo-Aryan civilization."

HAVELL, E.B. Indian architecture, its psychology, structure, and history from the first Muhammadan invasion to present day. London, John Murray, 1929. 282p. **1485**

HOPE, T.C. Architecture at Ahmedabad. London, John Murray, 1866. 100p. 119 plates. **1486**

JOUVEAV-DUHRCUIL, G. Dravidian architecture. Madras, S.P.P.C.K. Press, Vepery, 1917. 57p. **1487**

KAYE, G.R. Guide to old observatories at Delhi, Jaipur, Ujjain, Banaras; Calcutta, Supdt. Govt. Press, 1920. 108p. illus. **1488**

KRAMRISCH, STELLA. Art of India, traditions of Indian sculpture, painting and architecture. London, Phaidon Press, 1954. 213p. **1489**

——— Hindu temple. Calcutta, University of Calcutta, 1946. 466p. 80 plates. **1490**

LITAWSKI, O.J. Glimpses of Indian architecture. London, Luzac, 1947. **1491**

LONGHURST, A.H. Pallava architecture, Calcutta, Archaeological Survey of India, 1924. (Memoir no. 40). 25p. 13 plates. **1492**

NELSON, I.W. Chinese and Indian architecture. London, Prentice Hall, 1963. 128p. **1493**

"Discusses similarities and differences of Chinese and Indian architecture."

ROWLAND, BENJAMIN. The art and architecture of India. Buddhist, Hindu and Jain. Harmonds, Worth. Penguin Books, 1953. 289p. **1494**

"This book is written for those who, understanding art as a universal means of human expression, wish to study one of the most significant and beautiful aspects of that expression in India." *Introduction.*

SIMPSON, WILLIAM. Origin and development in Indian and Eastern architecture, London, Royal Institute of British Architects, 1891. **1495**

SMITH, E.W. Mughal architecture of Fatehpur Sikri. Allahabad, Archaeological Survey of India, 1898. 3 vols. **1496**

SMITH, V.A. History of Fine Art in India and Ceylon. 3rd rev. ed. by Karl Khandalavala. Bombay, Taraporevala, 1961. 219p. **1497**

"Describes with illustrations the history of fine arts including architecture."

TAYLOR, MEADOWS, *i.e.* PHILIP MEADOWS. Architecture at Beejapoor, an ancient Mahomedan capital in the Bombay Presidency, photographed from drawings by Cap. P.D. Hart, B.E., A. Cumming, C.E. and native draftsmen; addition on the spot Lt. Colonel Biggs, and the late Major Loch with an historical and descriptive memoir by Captain Meadows Taylor and architectural notes by James Fergusson. Pub. for the committee of architectural antiquities of Western India under the patronage of Kurusondas Madhowdas. London, J. Murray, 1866. 3p. 1 (ix)—xii, 93 (1) p. front. illus., lxxvi pl. (photos incl. plans) 2 maps. **1498**

——Architecture in Dharwar and Mysore. Photographed by late Dr. Pigau. A.C.B. Neill and Colonel Biggs with an historical and descriptive memoir by Colonel Meadows Taylor and architectural notes by James Fergusson. Pub. for the committee of architectural antiquities of Western India under the patronage of Premchand Raichund. London, J. Murray, 1866. 3p. 1., (ix)—xii, 76p. front. illus. xcviii photos 93 pl. 2 maps. **1499**

TAYLORE, C. MEADOWS. Architecture of Dharwar and Mysore. London, Murray, 1886. 98 pls. **1500**

TOY, S. Strongholds of India. London, Heinemann, 1957. 133p. **1501**

ZANNAS, ELIKY. Khajuraho. The Hague. Mouton. 1960. 227p. 171 pls. **1502**

(iii) Dance

AMBROSS, KAY. Classical dances and costumes of India. London, Adam and Charles Black, 1950. 95p. 14pls. **1503**

The first book of its kind to appear in print. The author worked closely with Ram Gopal, and has illustrated the

text with many sketches and photographs of his dances.
BOWERS, FAUBION. The dance in India. New York, Columbia University Press, 1953. xiii, 175p. **1504**
This is the product of a year's intensive work in India, wherever there was dancing. For the past ten years Mr. Bowers has devoted most of his attention to the dance and drama in Asia, not only in order to interpret those art forms to the West, but also to use them as a key to greater understanding of the people of Asia and to closer relations between East and West. He is married to the Indian writer Santha Rama Rau.

COLLUM, VERA CHRISTINA CHUTE. The dance of Siva; life's unity and rhythm. London, Kegan, Paul, Trench, Trubner & Co., New York, E.P. Dutton & Co., 1927. 94p. **1505**

DE ZOETE, BERYL. The other mind : a study of dance in South India. London, Victor Gollancz, 1953. 256p. **1506**

—— The other mind; a study of dance in South India. London, Victor Gollancz, 1953. 256p. pls. **1507**

SPREEN, HILDEGARD L. Folk-dances of South India. Foreword by Marie Buck. 2nd ed. Bombay, Oxford University Press, 1948. xvi, 134p. 1st ed. Published in 1945. **1508**
A study of folk-dances in South India, written with the assistance of R. Romani.

—— The other mind. London, Gollancz. 1953. **1509**
A study of South Indian dance system.

(iv) Handicrafts

ANDREWS, F.H. One hundred carpet designs from various parts of India. London, W. Griggs, 1906. 125p. **1510**

BAKER, GEORGE PERCIVAL. Calico printing and printing in the East Indies in 17th and 18th century. London, Edward Arnold, 1921. xiii, 78p. **1511**

BALL, KATHERINE M. Decorative motives of oriental art. London, Bodley Head, 1927. 286p. **1512**

COOMARASWAMY, ANANDA KENTISH. Bibliographies of Indian art. Boston, Museum of Fine Arts, 1925. v, 54p. **1513**

COOMARASWAMY, ANANDA KENTISH. Catalogue of Indian collections in museum of fine arts. Boston, Museum of Fine Arts, 1923. 194p. **1514**
———History of Indian and Indonesian art. London, Edward Goldston, 1927. 295p. illus. **1515**
———Introduction to Indian art. Edited by Mulk Raj Anand. Adyar, Theosophical Publishing House, 1956. 123p. **1516**
ELWIN, VERRIER. Tribal art of middle India. Bombay, Oxford, 1951. 214p. **1517**
ERDMANN, KURT. Oriental carpets; an account of their history, translated from the German by Charles Grant Ellis. London, Zwemmer. 1961. 78p. illus. 189 pls. **1518**
FABI, C.L. History of Indian dress. Calcutta, Orient Longmans, 1960, vi, 106p. **1519**
GOETZ, HERMAN. India : 5,000 years of Indian art. New York, McGraw Hill, 1959. 275p. **1520**
HAACK, HERMANN. Oriental rugs: an illustrated guide; edited and translated by George and Corndia Wingfield Digby. London, Faber, 1960. 376p. illus. 44 pls. **1521**
HADAWAY, W.S. Cotton painting and printing in the Madras Presidency. Madras, Government Press, 1917. 93p. **1522**
HARRIS, HENRY T. Monograph on the carpet weaving industry of Southern India. Madras, Supdt. Government Press, 1908. **1523**
HARRIS, KATHLEAN MARY. Embroidery: a reader's guide published for the National Book League. Cambridge, Cambridge University Press, 1950. 20p. **1524**
HAVELL, ERNEST BINFIELD. Basis for artistic and industrial revival in India. Adyar, Theosophist Office, 1912. 197p. **1525**
———Handbook of Indian art. London, John Murray, 1927. xxi, 222p. **1526**
———Ideals of Indian art; South Indian bronze, sculpture etc. London, John Murray, 1911. 188p. **1527**
———Monograph on stone carving in Bengal. Calcutta, Bengal Secretariat Book Depot, 1906. 16p. 5 pls. **1528**
HAWLEY, WALTER AUGUSTUS. Oriental rugs; antique and modern. New York, John Lane, 1913. 320p. **1529**
HENDLEY, THOMAS HOLBEIN. Asian carpets; 16th and 17th

century designs from Jaipur palaces. London, W. Griggs, 1905. 20p. **1530**

HOPKINS, A.J. Musical instruments, historic, rare and unique. Edinburgh, A. and C. Black, 1921. 123p. **1531**
    An illustrative account of Indian sitar, vina and drums etc.

IRWIN, JOHN. Shawls: a study in Indo-European influences. London, H.M.S.O., 1955. 66p. illus. 54pls. (Victoria and Albert Museum monographs series, no. 9). **1532**

JOHNSTONE, D.C. Monograph on woollen manufactures of the Punjab. Lahore, Punjab Government Press, 1886. 25p. **1533**

KRAMRISCH, STELLA AND OTHERS. Arts and crafts of Travancore; crafts of metalworker, jewellery, ivory, etc. Travancore, Royal Indian Society and Government of Travancore, 1948. 193p. **1534**

LEWIS, ALBERT BUELL. Blackprints from India for textiles. Chicago, Field Museum of National History. 1924. **1535**

ROWLAND, BENJAMIN. Harvard outline and reading lists of oriental art. Cambridge, Harvard University Press, 1958. 74p. **1536**

STARR, RICHARD F.S. Indus valley painted potteries; a comprehensive study of the designs on the painted wares of the Harappa culture. N.J., Princeton University Press, 1941, xiii, 106p. **1537**

STEEL, F.A. Monograph on Silk industry in the Punjab. Lahore, Punjab Government Press, 1887. 38p. **1538**

WATSON, JOHN FORBES. Collection of specimens of illustrations of the textile manufactures of India. London, India Museum, 1873-80. 4 vols. **1539**

WATT, GEORGE. Indian art at Delhi, being the official catalogue of the Delhi exhibition, 1902-03. Calcutta, Supdt. Govt. Printing Press, 1904. 346p. **1540**

WHEELER, MONROE, *ed.* Textiles and ornaments of India. New York, Museum of Modern Art, 1956. 95p. **1541**

WINSTEDT, RICHARD OLOF, *ed.* Indian art: essays by H.G. Rawlinson and others. London, Faber, 1947. 200p. 16 pls. **1542**

ZIMMER, HEINRICH ROBERT. Art of Indian Asia; its mythology and transformation. Edited by Joseph Campbell. New York, Pantheon Books, 1955. 465p. **1543**

(v) Iconography

BARRETT, DOUGLAS. Early Chola bronzes. Bombay, Bhulabhai Memorial Institute, 1965. viii, 46p. 102 pls. **1544**

BASHAM, A.L. Metal sculpture and engraving. *In his* Wonder that was India. London, Sidgwick and Jackson, 1954. 373-376p. **1545**

BERNET, KEMPERS. The bronzes of Nalanda, and Hindu Javanese Art. Leiden, E.J. Brill, 1933. 88p. 33 pls. **1546**

CLARK, W.E. Two Lamaistic Pantheons. Cambridge, Mass., Harvard, 1937. 2 vols. (Harvard Yenching Institute Monograph series). **1547**

CODRINGTON, K. DE B. Plague with figures of a Yaksha and Yakshin gold repouse on a lac filling. London, Faber, 1950. **1548**

────Standing Buddha; bronze from Mohamands territory, N.W. Frontier Province: Gandhara, 3rd-4th centuries A.D. London, Faber, 1950. **1549**

COOMARASWAMY, A.K. Dance of Shiva. Bombay, Asia Publishing House, 1952. 196p. illus. **1550**

A collection of essays on Hindu view of art, Indian images, music, dance etc.

──── Elements of Buddhist iconography. Cambridge, Mass. Harvard, 1935. 96p. 15 plates. **1551**

A treatise on the Buddhist iconography.

────History of Indian and Indonesian art. London, Edward Goldston, 1927. 295p. 128 pls. **1552**

An excellent reference work on the history of Indian and Indonesian art.

FERGUSSON, J. Tree and serpent worship; or illustrations of mythology and art in India in the first and fourth centuries after Christ from the sculptures of the Buddhist topes at Sanchi and Amarvati. London, India Museum, 1868. xii, 247p. 99 plates. **1553**

FOUCHER, A. Etude Sur P. Iconographie Bouddhique de l' Inde. Paris, 1900. 2 vols. (F). **1554**

A treatise on the Gods and Goddesses of the Buddhist Pantheon.

FOUCHER, A. On the iconography of the Buddha's nativity. Delhi, Manager of Publications, 1934. 27p. 6 pls. (Memoirs Archaeological Survey, no. 46). **1555**

GETTY, ALICE. Ganesa : a monograph on the elephant-faced god. Oxford, Clarendon Press, 1936. xxiii. 103p. 40 plates. **1556**

A historical account of the origin of the iconography of Ganesa.

——The Gods of Northern Buddhism; their history, iconography and progressive evolution through the Northern Buddhist countries. 2nd ed. Oxford, Clarendon Press, 1928. iii, 220p. **1557**

An account of the iconography of the Tibetan, Chinese, Indo-Chinese, Japanese gods and goddesses of the Mahayana Pantheon.

GORDON, A.K. The iconography of Tibet Lamaism. New York, Columbia University Press, 1939. Tokyo, Charles E. Tuttle, 1959. xxi, 131p. illus. **1558**

GRUNWEDEL, A. Buddhist art in India; translaled from German by Gibson. London, Bernard Quaritch, 1901. vii, 228p. illus. **1559**

JOUVEAU-DUBREUIL, G. Iconography of Southern India. Translated from the French by A.C. Martin. Paris, Librarie Orientaliste Paul Geuthner, 1937. 135p. 78 pls. **1560**

An account of the Hindu iconography of South India.

MARSHALL, Sir JOHN. Bronze of figurine of dancing girl. London, Arthur Probsthain, 1931. 3 vols. **1561**

REEVES, RUTH. Cire perdue casting in India. New Delhi, Crafts Museum, 1962. 124p. 74 pls. **1562**

ROWLAND, J.B. Evolution of the Buddha image. New York, Asia Society, 1963. 146p. 68 pls. **1563**

A brief history of the evolution of the Buddha image through a series of illustrations of art objects of the Eastern world, India and Southeast Asia of various periods.

SMITH, V.A. History of Fine Arts in India and Ceylon. 3rd ed. revised by Karl Khandalavala. Bombay, Taraporevala, 1962. xxiii, 219p. **1564**

VOGEL, J.P. The goose in Indian literature and art. Leiden.

E.J. Brill, 1962. vi. 74p. 12 pls. **1965**
ZIMMER, HEINRICH. Art of Indian Asian; its mythology and transformation. New York, Pantheon Books, 1955. 2 vols. **1566**
  A standard work on the subject.

(vi) Museology

FOOTE, R.B. Catalogue of the prehistoric antiquities. Madras, Supdt. Govt. Press, 1901. xix, 131p. 35 pls. **1567**
——The Foote collection of Indian prehistoric and protohistoric antiquities. Madras, Supdt. Govt. Press, 1914-1916. 2 vols. **1568**
GOETZ, H. AND A. Maharaja Fateh Singh Museum, Baroda, Maharaja F.S. Museum Trust, 1961. xii, 11p. 7 pls. **1569**
GWYER, M. Central National Museum of Art, Archaeology and Anthropology. New Delhi, Manager, Government of India Press, 1946. 13p. (Report of the Gwyer Committee). **1570**
HENDLEY, T.H. Handbook to the Jeypore Museum. Calcutta, The Calcutta Centre Press, 1895. 126p. illus. **1571**
MARKHAM, S.M. AND HARGREAVES, H. Museums of India. London, Museums Association, 1936. 229p. **1572**
SIMON, E.S. Guide to the State Museum, Trivandrum. Trivandrum, Government Press, 1961. 92p. illus. **1573**
STEIN, AUREL AND ANDREWS, F.H. Catalogue of wall paintings from ancient shrines in Central Asia and Sistan recovered by Sir Aurel Stein and described by F.H. Andrews. Delhi, Manager of Publications, 1933. xiii, 201p. 6 pls. **1574**
——Descriptive catalogue of antiquities recovered by Sir Aurel Stein during his explorations in Central Asia, Kansu and Eastern Iran by F.H. Andrews. Delhi, Manager of Publications, 1935. x, 445p. **1575**
VOGEL, J.P. Catalogue of the Bhuri Singh Museum at Chamba Calcutta, Baptist Mission Press, 1909. 80p. 6 pls. **1576**

(vii) Music

BOATURIGHT, HOWARD. Handbook on staff notation for Indian music. Bombay, Bharatiya Vidya Bhawan, 1960. 560p. **1577**
    An interpretation of Indian music for use of Western musicians and listners.

CLEMENTS, ERNEST. Introduction to the study of Indian music. London, Longmans, Green & Co., 1913. xv, 104p. **1578**
    An attempt to reconcile modern Hindustani music with ancient musical theory and to propound an accurate and comprehensive method of treatment of the subject of Indian musical intonation.

COUSINS, MARGARET, E. The music of Orient and Occident; essays towards mutual understanding. Madras, B.G. Paul & Co., 1935. vi, 199p. **1579**
    A comparative study of the Indian and Western music.

DANIELOU, ALAIN. A catalogue of recorded classical and traditional Indian music. Paris, UNESCO, 1952. 233p. **1580**
    An appraisal of the theory and practice of Indian music.

——Introduction to the study of musical scales. London, Indian Society, 1943. 279p. **1581**
    Deals with universal laws which the notations in music present, and makes a rapid survey of their application to music in different traditions.

——Northern Indian music. London, C. Johnson, 1949 and 1954. 2 vols. **1582**
    Vol. I treats the theory and techniques of music in north India while Vol. II discusses the main *Ragas* and provides a discography of Indian music.

DANIELOU, ALAIN. Religious music of India. New York, Folkways Records, 1952. **1583**

DYE, WILLIAM. A primer of Hindustani music. Lucknow, Lucknow Publishing House, 1936. 68p. **1584**

GOVER, CHARLES E. The folk-songs of Southern India. Madras, South India Saiva Siddhanta Works Publishing Society, 1959. xxxviii, 300p. **1585**
    A study of the folk-songs of South India.

JONES, Sir WILLIAM. Veber die musik der Indier. Eine abhand-

Sources of Indian Civilization

lung des Sir Willam Jones. Aus dem englishen ubersetzt, miterlauterndem anmerkungen und zusatzen begleitet, von F.H.V. Dalberg. Nebsteinersammlung indischer und anderer volks-gesange, und 30 Kupfern. Erfurt, Beyer und Maring, 1802. 2p. 1, xvi, (4), 132, (2), 56p. front., xxix pl.   **1586**
   "The original of Sir William Jones' work, 'On the musical modes of the Hindus', was published in Asiatic researches, Calcutta, 1792. v. 3, p. 55-87."

JONES, WILLIAM AND OTHERS. Music of India. Calcutta, Anil Gupta, 1962. 114p.   **1587**
   An appraisal and estimate of Indian music.

KAUFMANN, WALTER. The Ragas of North India. Bloomington, Indiana University, 1968. 625p.   **1588**

LENTZ, DONALD A. Tones and intervals of Hindu classical music. Lincoln, University of Nebraska, 1961. 25p.   **1589**
   A comparative study of the Indian classical music and the Western music.

POPLEY, HERBERT. The music of India. Calcutta, Y.M.C.A. Publishing House, 1921. 2nd ed. 1950. xii, 184p.   **1590**
   A brief history of the theory and practice of Indian music.

ROSENTHAL, ETHEL. The story of Indian music and its instruments: a study of the present and a record of the past. London, William Reeves, 1933. xxviii, 220p.   **1591**
   Contains Sir William Jones' celebrated treatise on 'The musical modes of the Hindus' in full.

STOOKE, HERBERT JOHNSTON AND KHANDALAVALA, KARL. The Land Ragamala miniatures; a study in Indian painting and music. Oxford, Bruno Cassirer, 1953. 66p.   **1592**
   A critical study of Indian painting and music.

STRANGWAYS, A.H. FOX. The music of Hindustan. Oxford, Clarendon Press. 1914. 364p.   **1593**
   A short history of Indian music.

WHITE, EMMOUS E. Appreciating India's music: an introduction to the music of India with suggestions for its use in the churches of India. Madras, Christian Literature Society, n.d. 179p.   **1594**

WILLARD, N. AUGUSTUS. A treatise on the music of Hindoostan: comprising details of the ancient theory and modern practice.

Calcutta, Baptist Mission Press, 1834. 89p. **1595**
WILSON, ANNE CAMPBELL (MACLEOD). A short account of the Hindu system of music. Lahore, Gulab Singh & Sons, 1904. iii, 48p. **1596**
    An account and appraisal of the Hindu system of music.

(viii) Numismatics

ALLAN, JOHN. Catalogue of the coins in the Indian museum. Calcutta, including the Cabinet of the Asiatic Society of Bengal. Oxford, Indian Museum, 1928. 8, 390p. **1597**
——Catalogue of the coins of ancient India. London, British Museum, 1936. 167, 318p. **1598**
——Catalogue of the coins of the Gupta dynasties and of Sasarka, King of Gauda. London, British Museum, 1914. 135, 184p. **1599**
BROWN, C. J. Catalogue of coins in provincial museum, Lucknow. Oxford, Clarendon Press, 1920. 2 vols. **1600**
—— Catalogue of the coins of the Guptas, Maukharis, etc. in the provincial museum. Lucknow, Supdt. Govt. Press, 1920. 6, 45p. **1601**
——Coins of India. Calcutta. Bible Association Press, Y.M.C.A., 1922. 120p. (Heritage of India series). **1602**
CUNNINGHAM, A. Coins of ancient India from the earliest times to the 7th century, A.D. Varanasi, Indological Book House, 1963. 118p. **1603**
——Coins of medieval India from 7th century A.D. to the Muhammadan conquest. London, the author, 1894. **1604**
——Later Indo-Scythians. London, 1898. 4, 130p. **1605**
ELLIOT, Sir WALTER. Coins of Southern India. The International Numismata Orientalia. London, Trubner & Co., 1886. 11, 159p. **1606**
GARDNER, PERCY. Coins of the Greek and Scythic Kings of Bactria and India. London, British Museum, 1886, 76. 193p. **1607**
HENDERSON, J.R. Coins of Haider Ali and Tipu Sultan. Madras, Government Press, 1921. 10, 123p. **1608**

LANE-POOLE, STANLEY. Coins and medals: their place in history and art. London, Ellot Stock, 1894. 285p. **1609**
The role coins and medals play in writing history of a particular century or region is discussed in this book.
——Coins of the Mughal emperors of Hindustan in the British Museum. Edited by R.S. Poole. London, Order of Trustee, 1892. 152, 401p. **1610**
MARSHALL, Sir JOHN. Taxila, an illustrated account of coins. Cambridge, University of Cambridge, 1951. 751-794p. **1611**
PRINCEP, JAMES. Essays on Indian antiquities, historic, numismatic and palaeographic. Edited by Edward Themans. London, author, 1858. 2 vols. **1612**
RAPSON, E.J. Catalogue of the coins of the Andhra dynasty; the Western Ksatrapas; the Traikutaka dynasty and the Bodhi dynasty. London, British Museum, 1908. 208, 268p. 21pls. **1613**
——Indian coins. Strassburg, Karl J. Trubner, 1898. 46p. **1614**
RODGERS, CHAS J. Coin-collecting in North India. Allahabad, Pioneer Press, 1894. 148p. **1615**
RODGERS, CHAS J., *comp.* Coins of the Moghul emperors of India collected by Chas. J. Rodgers and purchased by the Punjab Government. Calcutta, Baptist Mission Press, 1893. 19, 275p. **1616**
SMITH, VINCENT A. Catalogue of the coins in the Indian Museum, Calcutta including the Cabinet of the Asiatic Society of Bengal. Oxford, Indian Museum, 1906. 18, 346p. **1617**
THOMAS, EDWARD. Ancient Indian weights. London, Trubner & Co., 1874. 82p. **1618**
THURSTON, EDGAR. History of the coinage of the territories of the East India Company in the Indian Peninsula. Madras, Madras Government, 1890. 123p. **1619**
VALENTINE, W.H. Copper coins of India. London, Spink and Sons, n.d. 266p. **1620**
WALSH, E.H.C. Punch-marked coins from Taxila. Memoirs of the Archaeological Survey of India. Delhi, Archaeological Survey of India, 1939. 4+164p. 48 pls. **1621**
WEBB, WILLIAM WILFRID. Currencies of Hindu States of Raj-

putana. London, Arc Con. and Co., 1898. 24, 135p. **1622**
WHITEHEAD, R.B. Catalogue of coins in the Punjab museum. Lahore, Punjab Government, 1914. 12, 218p. 20 pls. **1623**
WRIGHT, H. NELSON. Coinage and metrology of the Sultans of Delhi. Delhi, Manager of Publications, 1936. 20, 432p. **1624**
 It incorporates a catalogue of the coins in the author's cabinet museum.
WRIGHT, L.V.W. Colonial and Commonwealth coins—A practical guide to the series. London, George G. Harrap, 1959. 234p. **1625**

(ix) Painting

ARCHER, MILDRED. Indian painting from the British, 1770-1880. By Archer Mildred and Archer W.G. London, Oxford, 1955. 147p. 24 pls. **1626**
—— Patna painting. London, Royal India Society, 1948. 47p. 43 pls. **1627**
ARCHER, W.G. Bazar paintings of Calcutta; the style of Kalighat. London, H.M.S.O., 1953. 76p. illus. **1628**
 A monograph on Kalighat paintings.
—— Central Indian painting. London, Faber & Faber, 1958. 24p. 10 colour pls. **1629**
—— Garhwal painting. London, Faber and Faber, 1954. 24p. 10 colour pls. **1630**
—— India and modern art. London, Allen & Unwin, 1959. 143p. **1631**
 A valuable appraisal of modern art in India.
—— Indian miniatures. Greenwich, Conn., New York, Graphic Society, 1960. 16p. 100 pls. **1632**
 Vol. 9 of this work gives an account of Indian miniatures paintings from the early 20th century in the late eighteenth one. Includes one hundred plates which provide representative reproductions along with introductory notes.
—— Indian painting. London, Batsford, 1955. 22, xvp. 15 colour pls. **1633**
 "Presents a glimpse of the typical specimens of different

periods of Indian painting. Also describes its evolution, past glory and future promise."

ARCHER, W.G. Indian painting in Bundi and Kotah. London, H.M.S.O., 1959. V. 58p. 56 pls. **1634**

—— Indian painting in the Punjab hills. London, H.M.S.O., 1952. 98p. **1635**

—— Kangra painting. London, Faber and Faber, 1952. 24p. 10 colour pls. **1636**

A brief study of one of the most important schools of Indian painting.

—— Rajasthan paintings from Sri Gopi Krishan Kanoria collection. Calcutta, 1962. 30p. 5 pls. **1637**

ASHTON, LEIGH, ed. The art of India and Pakistan. London, Faber and Faber, 1950. xi, 219p. 152 pls. **1638**

An appraisal.

BARRETT, DOUGHLAS. Painting of the Deccan. 16th, 17th century. London, Faber and Faber, 1958. 24p. 10 colour pls. (Faber Gallery of Oriental Art series). **1639**

BROWN, PERCY. Indian painting. 3rd ed. Calcutta, Y.M.C.A. Publishing House, 1947. 132p. 20 illus. **1640**

One of the best short surveys of Indian painting.

—— Indian painting under the Mughals. A.D. 1550 to A.D. 1750. London, Oxford, 1924. 204p. 77 pls. **1641**

A useful study of the Mughal paintings.

CADRINGTON, K. DE B. The study of Indian art: being an informal talk given before the Tagore Society, London on March 9, 1944. London, the Society, 1944. 15p. **1642**

Summarizes some of the major cultural trends of the creative life of India.

CARUS, PAUL. Portfolio of Buddhist art; historical and modern. Chicago, Open Court Publishing Co., 1906. 8p. 31 pls. **1643**

COOMARASWAMY, A.K. Art and Swadeshi. Madras, Ganesh & Co., n.d. 193p. 18 pls. **1644**

A collection of his essays on Indian paintings.

—— Bibliographies of Indian art. Boston, Museum of Fine Arts, 1925. v, 54p. **1645**

A valuable bibliography of fine arts in India including painting.

700 Fine Arts

DICKINSON, ERIC AND KHANDALAVALA, KARL. Krishangarh painting. New Delhi, Lalit Kala Akademi, 1959. 51p. 16 pls. **1646**

ETTINGHAUSEN, RICHARD. Paintings of the Sultans and Emperors of India in American collections. New Delhi, Lalit Kala Akademi, 1961. 5p. 15 colour pls. **1647**

—— The art and architecture of Bikaner state. Oxford, Bruno Cassirer, 1950. 180p. illus. **1648**

GOETZ, HERMANN. India: five thousand years of Indian art. Bombay, Taraporevala, 1959. 275p. illus. (Art of the World series, no. 1). **1649**

    A detailed study of Indian Fine Arts.

GRAY, BASIL. Rajput painting. London, Faber and Faber, 1958. 24p. 10 colour pls. **1650**

GRIFFITHS, JOHN. The paintings in the Buddhist cave-temples of Ajanta, Khandesh, India. London, W. Griggs, 1896-97. 2 vols. 159 pls. **1651**

    This book is considered to be an authentic study of the Buddhist cave-temples.

HAJEK, TUBOR AND FORMAN, W.B. Indian miniatures of the Moghal school. Prague, Artia, 1960. 88p. 51 colour pls. **1652**

HARRINGHAM, *Lady* AND OTHERS. Ajanta Frescoes; being reproductions in colour and monochrome of Frescoes in some of the caves at Ajanta after copies taken in the year 1909-1911 by Lady Herringham and her assistants. London, Oxford, 1915. 2 vols. 42 pls. including 15 in colour. **1653**

HAVELL, E.B. The art heritage of India. Revised edition with notes by Pramod Chandra. Bombay, Taraporevala, 1964. 199p. 207 illus. 18 colour pls. **1654**

    The author's two books entitled: "Indian sculpture and painting" and "The ideals of Indian art" have been incorporated in this volume.

—— The ideals of Indian art. London, John Murray, 1911. xx, 188p. 32 pls. **1655**

    "A comprehensive analysis of Indian aesthetic ideals, emphasizing the importance of the influence of Indian thought to the evolution of Asiatic art."

—— Indian sculpture and painting, illustrated by typical masterpieces, with an explanation of their materials and ideals,

London, John Murray, 1928. xxiv, 288p. illus. **1656**
Summarizes the history of painting in India.

KRAMRISCH, STELLA. The art of India. London, Phaidon Press, 1954. 231p. 180 illus. with note. **1657**
A brief appraisal.

KUEHNEL, ERNEST. Moghul malerie mit wanzig miniaturen. Berlin, Verlog Gebr Mann, n.d. 64p. 20 colour pls. (G). **1658**
A collection of Mughal miniature paintings. Pages 1-10 give English translation by Dr. A.V. Kamath of the German text entitled : "Mughal Painting."

KUEHNEL, ERNEST AND GOETZ, HERMANN. Indian book painting from Jahangir's album in the State Library in Berlin. London, Kegan Paul, 1926. vii, 75p. 42 colour pls. **1659**
An important work describing Indian miniature painting with special reference to book illustrations of the Mughal school.

LAWRENCE, GEORGE. Indian art; Mughal miniatures. London, Methuen, 1963. llp. 15 pls. (A pocket book from the Little Library of Art series) **1660**
A short survey of miniature paintings done under the Mughal rulers: Akbar, Jehangir, Shahjahan and Aurangzeb.

——— Indian art; painting of the Himalayan slats. London, Methuen, 1963, 12p. 15 pls. **1661**

LEE, S.E. Rajput painting. New York, Asia House Gallery, 1961. 96p. 67 illus. including 15 in full colour. **1662**

LONDON, VICTORIA AND ALBERT MUSEUM. Indian art. London, H.M.S.O., 1952. iv, 28p. monochrome pls. **1663**
A selection of prominent schools of painting from all periods.

MARSHALL, JOHN AND OTHERS. The bagh caves in Gwalior state. London, India Society, 1927. viii, 78p. 26 pls. **1664**

RAWSON. P.S. Indian painting. New York, Universal books, 1961. 169p. illus. **1665**
A brief illustrated history of Indian painting from the remote past to the Rajput school of painting.

REIFF, ROBERT, ed. Indian miniatures: the Rajput painters. Rutland, Vermont, C.E. Tuttle, 1959. 32p. **1666**

700 Fine Arts

Contains twelve reproductions of miniature Rajput paintings done during the 17th to the 19th centuries.

ROERICH, NICHOLAS. Paintings with an introduction by A.S. Raman. New Delhi, Dhoomimal Dharamdas, 1947. iii, 14p. 14 pls. **1667**

ROWLAND, BENJAMIN. The Ajanta caves; early Buddhist paintings from India. New York, UNESCO, 1963. 24p. 28 pls. (A pocket book from the Mentor-4 UNESCO Art series.) **1668**

This brief study is meant to interpret the mythology of the morals of the Ajanta caves.

ROWLAND, BENJAMIN (JR.). Art in the East and West, an introduction through comparison. Cambridge, Harvard University, 1954. xiii, 144p. **1669**

SOLOMON, W.E.G. The charm of Indian art. London, T. Fisher Unwin, 1926. 142p. illus. **1670**

A collection of his essays on Indian art.

―― Essays on Mughal art. London, Oxford, 1932. xxx, 96p. 18 illus. **1671**

These essays deal with different phases of the Mughal painting.

STARR, RICHARD F.S. Indus valley painted pottery. N.J., Princeton, 1941. 105p. **1672**

Dr. Starr, who has directed a number of archaeological expeditions, is now in the Department of the State.

UNESCO. India: paintings from Ajanta caves. Foreword by Jawaharlal Nehru and introduction by Madanjit Singh. New York, Graphic Society, 1954. 10p. 32 colour pls. **1673**

The volume is first of the UNESCO World Art Series devoted to the rare art masterpieces of Ajanta Frescoes dating from 2 B.C. to 18 A.D.

WARNER ALFRED. Indian miniatures. New York, A.A. Wyn, 1950. 9p. 19 pls. **1674**

A brief study of Indian miniature painting.

WELCH, S.C. The art of the Mughal India; painting and precious objects. New York, Asia House, 1963. 179p. 88 plates. **1675**

WELLESZ, EMMY. Akbar's religious thought reflected in Mughal painting. London, Allen and Unwin, 1952. xii, 48p. 40 pls. **1676**

WILKINSON, J.V.S. Mughal paintings. London, Faber and Faber, 1948. 24p. 10 pls. **1677**

WINSTEDT, RICHARD, ed. Indian art. London, Faber & Faber, 1947. 200 p. 16 pls. **1678**
 It is a collection of essays by H.G. Rawlinson; K. de B. Codrington, J.V.S. Wilkinson and John Irwin.

ZIMMER, HEINRICH. The art of Indian Asia; its mythology and transformations. New York, Pantheon Books, 1955. 2 vols. Vol. I contains Text and xix, 465p. ; Vol. II contains xviii, 618 monochrome pls. (The Bilingan series). **1679**

(x) Photography

ARNOLD, THOMAS WALKER. Through India with a camera; a hundred photographic views of its famous cities and natural scenery. Bombay, D.B. Taraporevala Sons & Co., 1930. xxx, 100p. **1680**
 An album of photographs with an introduction by the author.

BIRDWOOD, GEORGE CHRISTOPHER MOLESWORTH. The arts of India as illustrated by the collection of H.R.H. the Prince of Wales. London, R. Clay Sons and Taylor, 1881. 98p. **1681**
 Contains a map of the Prince's tour and numerous illustrations.

LENNOY, RICHARD. India: people and places. New York, Vanguard, 1955. 199p. **1682**
 A book of superb photographs in both colour and black and white, with emphasis on the daily life of the Indian people.

NAWRATH, ERNEST ALFRED. The glories of Hindustan. London, Methuen & Co., 1935. xv. 242p. **1683**
 A photographic album of Indian scenes containing 240 photographs by descriptive letter press.

WHEELER, MONROE, ed. Textiles and ornaments of India: a selection of designs. New York, Museum of Modern Art, 1956. 93p. **1684**
 Photographs, with interpretative essays, from the magni-

ficent exhibits assembled by the Museum of Modern Art, New York, in 1955. It was seen by 303,000 visitors.

(xi) Sculpture

ARCHER, W.G. The vertical man: a study in primitive Indian sculpture. London, George Allen & Unwin, 1947. 122p. **1685**
BACHHOFER, LUDWIG. Early Indian sculpture. Paris. The Pegasus Press, 1929. 2 vols. Vol. I—137p.; Vol. II—161p. **1686**
  Plates are accompanied by guard-sheets with descriptive letters.
BARRETT, DOUGLAS. Guide to the Buddhist caves of Aurangabad. Bombay, Bhulabhai Memorial Institute, 1957. 23p. 21pls. **1687**
——Sculptures from Amaravati in the British Museum. London, British Museum, 1954. 75p. 48 pls. **1688**
BONER, ALIECE. Principles of composition in Hindu sculpture. cave temple period. Leiden, E.J. Brill, 1962. 260p. **1689**
BUCHTHAL, BUGO. Western aspects of Gandhara sculpture. London. G. Cumberledge, 1945. 28p. 56 pls. **1690**
BURGESS, J. Ancient monuments, temples and sculpture of India. London, the author, 1897-1911. 2 vols. **1691**
——Buddhist stupas of Amaravati and Jaggayapata. London, Trubner & Co., 1887. 131p. 66 pls. **1692**
BURNIER, RAYMOND. Hindu medieval sculpture. Paris, La Palme, 1950. 8p. 79 pls. **1693**
  Contains 79 original photographs. Plates are accompanied by descriptive letter press. The photographs mainly show details of sculpture in Khajuraho and Bhuvaneshvara temples.
CODRINGTON, KENNETH D. BRUGH. Introduction to the study of medieval Indian sculpture. London, E. Goldston, 1929. **1694**
COOMARASWAMY, ANANDA KENTISH. Elements of Buddhist iconography, Cambridge (Mass), Harvard University Press, 1935. 95p. 15 pls. **1695**
—— Introduction to Indian art, ed. by Mulk Raj Anand.

Adyar, Theosophical Publishing House, 1956. 123p. 84 pls.
1696

COOMARASWAMY, ANAND KENTISH. Vivakarma; examples of Indian architecture, sculpture, painting, handicraft. London, the author, 1912. 84 pls. **1697**

CRAVEN JR. Indian sculpture in the John and Mable Ringling Museum of Art. Gainesville, University of Florida Press, 1961. 28p. 17 pls. (University of Florida monographs, Humanities No. 6). **1698**

CUNNINGHAM, A. The Bhilsa Topes or Buddhist monuments of Central India. London, Smith Elder & Co., 1854. 368p. 33 pls. **1699**

DENECK, M.M. Indian sculpture. London, Spring Books, 1962. 34p. 261 pls. **1700**

EDEN, Hon. EMILY. Portraits of the princes and people of India, drawn on the stone by L. Dickinson. London, J. Dickinson & Son. 1844. 2p. 1., 24 numb, 1. 24 pls. **1701**

FERGUSSON, JAMES. The cave temples of India. By James Fergusson and James Burgen. Printed and published by order of Her Majesty's Secretary of State and C. London, W.H. Allen & Co., 1880. xx, 536p. front. illus. xcviii (i.e. 99) pls. (incl. plans) frid map. **1702**

———Illustration of the rock cut temples of India: selected from the best examples of the different series of caves at Ellora, Ajunta, Cuttack, Sabette, Kashi, and Mahovellipore. Drawn on stone by Mr. T.C. Diblin, from sketches made on the spot in the years 1838-9. London, J. Weab, 1845. xv, 63p. illus. 10 pls. (3 double) and atlas of xviii pl. **1703**

———The rock-cut temples of India; illustrated by seventy-four photographs taken on the spot by Major Gill. Described by James Fergusson. London, J. Murray, 1864. xxp. 1.1., 58 numb. 1. 1761-62p. 63-78 numbl. 74 photo. pls. **1704**

———Rude stone monuments in all countries; their age and uses. With two hundred and thirty-four illustrations. London, J. Murray, 1872. 1p. 1 (v)-xix, 559p. front. illus. fold map. diagrs. **1705**

———Tree and serpent worship or illustrations of mythology and art in India in the first and fourth centuries after Christ.

From the sculptures of the Buddhist topes at Sanchi and Amravati. Prepared under the authority of the Secretary of State for India in council. With introductory essays and descriptions of the plates by James Fergusson. London, India Museum, W.H. Allen and Co., publishers to the India Office, 1868. xii, 247 (1) p. front. illus. xcix pl. **1706**

FLEET, JOHN FAITHFULL, ed. Inscriptions of the early Gupta kings and their successors. Calcutta, Superintendent of Govt. Printing, 1888. vii, 194, 350p. 45 facsim. (Corous inscriptionum indicarum, v. 3). **1707**

FOUCHET, MAX PAL. The erotic sculpture of India. London, Allen & Unwin, 1959. 95p. **1708**
    A study of sculptures depicting sexual relations that appear in relief on various medieval Hindu temples, notably those at the site of Khajuraho.

FREDERIC, LOUIS. Indian temples and sculpture. London, Thames and Hudson, 1959. 464p. **1709**

GILL, ROBERT. The rock-cut temples of India. Illustrated by seventy-four photographs taken on the spot by Major Gill. Described by James Fergusson. London, 1864. xii p. 100 pls. **1710**

HAVELL, E.B. Handbook on Indian art. London, John Murray, 1920. 222p. 79 pls. **1711**

———Indian sculpture and painting. London, John Murray, 1908. 288p. 78 pls. **1712**

———Ideals of Indian art. London, John Murray, 1920. xx, 188p. illus. **1713**

HERRINGHAM, *Lady* AND OTHERS. Ajanta frescoes. London, Oxford University Press, 1915. 2 vols. **1714**

HULTZSCH, EUGEN. South-Indian inscriptions. Ed. and tr. by E. Hultzsch. Madras, Printed by the Superintendent, Govt. Press, 1890-1919. V. front., pls, facsims. (part fold). (Archaeological Survey of India. (Reports). New Imperial series, vols. ix, xxix, liiip. **1715**

JOUVEAV, DUBREUIL GABRIEL. Iconography of Southern India; tr. from French by A.C. Martin. London, Luzac, 1932. 136 p. 78 pls. **1716**

———Pallava antiquities. London, Probsthain, 1916. 76 p.

32 pls. **1717**
KRAMRISCH, STELLA. The art of India through the ages. London, Phaidon, 1952. 231p. **1718**
—— The Indian sculpture. Calcutta. Y.M.C.A. Publishing House, 1933. 240p. 56 pls. **1719**
—— Indian sculpture in Philadelphia museum of art. Philadelphia, University of Pennsylvania Press, 1960. 183p. 61 pls.
1720
LANGLES, LOUIS MATHIEU. Monuments anciens et modernes de l' Hindoustan, de' crits sous le double rapport archaeologigue et pithoresque, et precedes d' une notice geographique, d' une notice historique, et d' un discours sur la religion, la legislation et les moeurs des Hindous, par L. Langles. Ouvrage orne de cent quarante-auatre planches et de trois cartes geographiques dressees par M. Barbie-Dulocage. Paris, P. Didotl'aine, 1821. 2v. pls. (part col.) maps, plans, fold. tab. (F) **1721**
LEESON, FRANCIS. Kama shilpa: a study of Indian sculpture depicting love in action. Bombay, Taraporevala, 1962. 132p.
1722
MACKAY, E.J.M. Chanhu-Daro excavations. New York, American Oriental Society, 1943. 2 vols. **1723**
    Published for the American School of Indic and Iranian Studies and the Museum of Fine Arts, Boston. Professor Mackay excavated the Chanhu-Daro site in 1935-36.

MARSHALL, Sir JOHN H. A guide to Sanchi. Delhi, Manager of Publications, Government of India, 1955. **1724**
    An abridged version of Sir John Marshall's *Monuments of Sanchi* in 3 vols.

—— The monuments of ancient India; Cambridge history of India. Cambridge University, 1922. 615p. Vol. I was edited by E.L. Rapson. **1725**
—— Monuments of Sanchi. London, Probsthain, 1940. 3 vols.
1726
    An account of the sculpture and architecture of a major Buddhist religious center that flourished in Central India during the two centuries preceding the Christian era.

—— Taxila. Cambridge University Press, 1951. 3 vols. **1727**
    A well illustrated report of twenty-two years of archaeo-

700 Fine Arts

logical research at a site located in the Gandhara region.

MILWARD, MARGAERITE (EDGE). Artist in unknown India. Foreword by H.J. Fleure. London T. Werner Laurie, 1948. xiv, 274p. **1728**

    An account of journey in the tribal areas, and of the collection in sculpture of primitive and aboriginal tribes of India.

MONOD-BRUHI, ODETTE. Indian temples. Translated by R. Hawkins. London, Oxford University Press, 1955. xii, 31p. **1729**

    First published in 1937, it is a pictorial survey of temple structures and sculptures from earliest times to the present-day.

NAWRATH, ALFRED. Eternal India, the land of people, the master-pieces of architecture and sculpture of India, Pakistan, Burma and Ceylon. New York, Crown Publishers, 1956. 34p. 117 pls. **1730**

PAKISTAN, NATIONAL MUSEUM. Gandhara sculpture. Karachi, Department of Archaeology, 1956. 43p. **1731**

PIGGOT, STUART. Prehistoric India to 100 B.C. London, Penguin Books, 1962. 294p. **1732**

ROWLAND, BENJAMIN. The art and architecture of India. London, Penguin Books, 1953. 290p. 190 pls. **1733**

SMITH, V.A. History of Fine Arts in India and Ceylon. London, Oxford, 1930. xvip. 164 pls. **1734**

———The Jaina Stupa and antiquities of Mathura. Allahabad, Government Press, 1901. 63 pls. **1735**

TOLEDO MUSEUM OF ART. East Indian sculpture. Toledo, the Museum, 1940. 48p. **1736**

    An illustrated catalogue of an exhibition held at the Museum in 1940, assembled from American collections. A course in the art and culture of India was given in conjunction with the exhibit by the Museum and the University of Toledo.

WEINER, SHEILA L. From Gupta to Pala sculpture. Ascona, Artibus Asiac, 1962. 182p. 40 pls. **1737**

WINSTEDT, Sir RICHARD O, *ed.* Indian art. New York, Philosophical Library, 1948. 200p. 16 pls. **1738**

    A collection of four articles on Indian sculpture and

painting.

ZANNAS, ELIKY. Khajuraho. The Hague, Mouton, 1960. 227p. 171 pls. **1739**
    An illustrated account of the architecture of Khajuraho temples which were built between 954 and 1002.

ZIMMER, HEINRICH. The art of Indian Asia, its mythology and transformations. New York, Pantheon, 1955. 2 vols. **1740**

(xii) Theatre

BOWERS, FAUBION. Theatre in the East; a survey of Asian dance and drama : New York, Toronto, 1956. 374p. **1741**
    Based on the author's interviews with artists and specialists. This study describes the theatre in fourteen Asian countries including India.

BURTON, E.J. A students' guide to world theatre. London, Herbert, 1962. 207p. **1742**
    Chapter No. 6 traces the origin and development of Indian drama. Also deals with theory and practice of the stage craft.

FABRI, CHARLES A. A history of Indian dress. Calcutta, Orient Longmans, 1961. vi, 106p. **1743**
    A brief survey.

HORWITZ, E.P., *ed.* The Indian theatre. London, Blackie, 1912. **1744**
    A collection of articles on Indian theatre in different languages.

KEITH, A. BERRIEDALE. Sanskrit drama, its origin, development theory and practice. London, Oxford, 1959. 405p. **1745**
    A brief history of the origin and development of Sanskrit drama with special reference to the dramas of Bhasa, Kalidasa, Harsha, Bhavabhuti and Vishakhadatta.

LEVI, SYLVAIN. Le Theatre Indien. 1890. xv, 122p. (F) **1746**

SCHUYLES. Bibliography of the Sanskrit drama, with an introductory sketch of the dramatic literature of India. New York, Columbia University, 1906. xi, 105p. **1747**
    (Indo-Iranica Series, vol. 3).

700 Fine Arts

WELLS, H.W. Classical drama of Indian studies in the values for the literature and theatre of the world. Bombay, Asia Publishing House, 1963. 196p. **1748**
    "Deals with the aims of the Indian Drama and analyses the form and the style used to achieve them."

——, *ed.* Six plays. Bombay, Asia Publishing House, 1964. xxxi, 488p. **1749**
    A collection of prominent Sanskrit plays.

WILSON, HORACE HAYMAN, *tr.* Select specimens of the theatre of the Hindus, translated from the original Sanskrit. 2nd ed. London, Parbury, Allen & Co., 1835. 2 vols. **1750**

WILSON, H.H. AND OTHERS. Theatre of the Hindus. Calcutta, Susil Gupta, 1955. 224p. **1751**
    An account of the theory and practice of the theatre of the Hindus based on select specimens translated from the original Sanskrit. Also deals with the Indian stage craft in accordance with the Natyasastra of Bharata, dancing hall at Ramgarh and South Indian theatre.

800 LITERATURE

(i) General Works

ARNOLD, EDWIN. The light of Asia. New ed. London, John Lane the Bodley Head, New York, Dodd, Mead & Co., 1926. xxvii, 177p. Illustrations by Hamzeh Carr and Introduction by E. Denison Ross. **1752**

———, *tr*. Literature of India. New York, Colonial Press, 1902. 467p. **1753**
   A useful book on Indian literature.

ARONSON, ALEXANDER. Rabindranath through Western eyes. Allahabad, Kitabistan 1943. xv, 158p. **1754**

BALLANTYNE, JAMES ROBERT. The practical oriental interpreter; or hints on the art of translating readily from English into Hindustani and Persian. London, Madden & Co., 1843. 54p. **1755**

BANFEY, THEODORE. Handbuch der Sanskriat sprache. Leipzig, 1852. 54p. **1756**

COUSINS, JAMES HENRY. The renaissance in India. Madras, Ganesh & Co., 1918, x, 293p. **1757**
   A study of the new spirit of Indian literature and painting.

EASTWICK, EDWARD BACKHOUSE, *tr* The Bagh-o-Bahar, or, The garden and the spring by Amir Khusrau Dihlavi. Translated by Edward Backhouse Estwick, etc. London, Hertford, 1877. **1758**

EASTWICK, EDWARD BACKHOUSE. The Gulistan; or, Rose-Garden, of Sheikh Muslihud-Din Sadi of Shiraz. Translated by Edward Backhouse Eastwick, etc. (Trubner Oriental series). London and Edinburgh, Trubner and Co., 1880. **1759**

ELWIN, VERRIER. Myths of middle India. Madras, Geoffrey Cumberlege, Oxford University Press, 1949. xvi, 532p. (Specimens of the oral literature of middle India series). **1760**

Attempts to present samples and specimens of the oral literature of middle India—Madhya Pradesh, the Chhattisgarh, and Orissa States and Western Orissa.

FRAZER, ROBERT WATSON. The literary history of India. London T. Fisher Unwin, 1907. xv, 470p. **1761**

A useful work, it summarizes the literary history of India.

GEORGE, ROBERT ESMONDE GORDON (ROBERT SENCOURT, *pseud*) India in English literature. London, Simpkin, Marshall, Hamilton, Kent and Co., 1923. xi. 467p. **1762**

Studies how India has influenced the English mind since the days of the early adventures to the opening of the Canal in 1869.

GOLDSTUECKER, THEODORE. Literary remains of Professor Theodore Goldstuecker. London. W.H. Allen, 1879. 2 vols. **1763**

GOWEN, HERBERT HENRY. A history of Indian literature from Vedic times to the present day. New York and London, D. Appleton & Co., 1931. xvi, 593p. **1764**

GRIERSON, GEORGE ABRAHAM. The modern vernacular literature of Hindustan. Printed as a special number of the Journal of the Asiatic Society of Bengal, Part I, for 1888. Calcutta, Asiatic Society, 1889. xxx, 170p. 11., xxxvp. front. 2 fold. pl (facsims). **1765**

GRIFFITH, RALPH THOMAS HOTCHKIN, *ed. & tr.* Idylls from the Sanskrit. London, Smith, Elder and Co., 1866. 1, 151, 13p. **1766**

HAUGHTON, Sir GRAVER CHAMPNEY. A glossary, Bengali and English, to explain the Tota itihas, the Batris Singhasan, the history of Raja Krishna Chandra, the Purusha-Parikhya, the

Hitopadesha (Translated by Mrilyunjaya). London, printed by Cox and Baylis, 1825. lp. 1 (v) - xi (1) 124p. **1767**

HAY, STEPHEN N. Asian ideas of East and West: Tagore and his critics in Japan, China and India. Cambridge, Mass., Harvard University Press, 1970. 480p. **1768**

HORRWITZ, ERNEST P. A short history of Indian literature. Introduction by T.W. Rhys Davis. London, Fisher Unwin, 1907. xxxi, 188p. **1769**

> A history of old Indian literature for laymen.

INDEX TRANSLATIONUM INDICARAM: a cumulation of entries for India in "Index translationum", UNESCO, Paris, V. 2-11. Cumulation by D.L. Banerjee, Calcutta, National Library, 1963. 450p. **1770**

> A cumulation of some 2800 translations published in India, 1947-58, and listed in Index translationum. Arranged by Indian language and then alphabetically by author. Gives author of original title of translation, name of translator, place, publisher, date, pages, illustrations, price and language and title of the original.

KEAY, FRANK E. A history of Hindi literature. Calcutta, Y.M.C.A. Publishing House, 1960. 3rd ed. viii, 116p. **1771**

> A brief introductory survey of the Hindi literature.

KEITH, ARTHUR BERRIEDALE. Classical Sanskrit literature. Calcutta, Association Press (Y.M.C.A.), 1923. ii, 153p. (The heritage of India series). **1772**

——A history of Sanskrit literature. London, Oxford University Press, 1953. xxxvi, 575p. **1773**

> Probably the best history of Sanskrit literature ever written by a non-Indian.

KINCAID, CHARLES AUGUSTUS. The outlaws of Kathiawar and other studies. Bombay, The Times Press, 1905. x, 154p. Articles originally published in the *Times of India* and *East and West*. **1774**

> Contents: Outlaws of Kathiawar; A Gujarati novel (a review of *Karan Ghelo* by Nanda Shankar Tuljashankar). The Parsis and Hellenic Influence; The story of the Harpal Makawana; Envoi.

LESNY, VINCENT. Rabindranath Tagore: his personality and

800 Literature

work. Foreword by C.F. Andrews. Tr. by Guy McKeever Phillips. London, George Allen & Unwin, 1939. 288p. **1775**

LILLY, WILLIAM SAMUEL. Four English humourists of the nineteenth century. Lectures delivered at the Royal Institution of Great Britain in January and February, 1895. London, J. Murray, 1895. xxiii, 192p. **1776**

MACDONELL, ARTHUR ANTHONY. A history of Sanskrit literature. London, W. Heinemann. 1905, 2nd ed. vi, 472p. **1777**
   Considered to be one of the best works on the history of Sanskrit literature.

—— India's past; a survey of her literature, religions, languages and antiquities. Oxford, The Clarendon Press, 1927. xii, 293p. front., illus. (maps) plates, ports, facsims. **1778**

—— Vedic index of names and subjects, by Arthur Anthony Macdonell and Arthur Berriedale Keith. London, J. Murray, pub. for the Government of India. 1912. 2 vols. fold. map. (Indian texts series). **1779**

MONIER-WILLIAMS, Sir MONIER. Two addresses delivered before the International Congress of Orientalists at Berlin on September 14, 1881. London, W.H. Allen & Co., 1881. 15p. **1780**

MULLER, FRIEDRICH MAX. Chips from a German workshop. New York, Scribner, Armstrong & Co. 1871-76. 4 vols **1781**

—— A history of ancient Sanskrit literature so far as it illustrates the primitive religion of the Brahmans. 2nd ed. rev. London, Williams and Norgate, 1860. xix, 607 (1)p. **1782**
   Also published in India by Bhavnesari Ashram, Allahabad.

—— Oriental scholarship during the present century. *In* Smithsonian Institution. Annual Report. 1893. Washington, 1894. p. 681-700. **1783**

OATEN, EDWARD FARLEY. A sketch of Anglo-Indian literature. London, Kegan Paul, Trench, Trubner and Co., 1908. xiv, 215p. **1784**

RICE, EDWARD P. A history of Kanarese literature. Calcutta, Association (Y.M.C.A.) Press, 1921. iv, 28p. First published in 1915. **1785**
   A brief history of the Kanarese literature.

THOMPSON, EDWARD JOHN. Rabindranath Tagore; poet and dramatist. 2nd ed. rev. London, Oxford University Press, 1948.

xii, 330p. **1786**
>Ist edition was published in 1921, by the Associated Press, Calcutta.

WEBER, A. History of Indian literature. Varanasi, Chowkhamba series, 1961. 360p. **1787**
>A detailed study of Vedic and Buddhist literature.

WINTERNITZ MAURICE. Geschichte der indischen litteratur. Leipzig, C.F. Amelang, 1908-(22) 3 vols (G). **1788**

———A history of Indian literature. Translated from the original German by Mrs. S. Ketkar and Miss H. Kohn, and rev. by the author, Calcutta, the University, 1927- 33. 2 vols. n.p. **1789**
>First published in German in 1908-22, it is a classic on the history of ancient literature. Contents : Vol. I. Introduction, Veda, National epics, Puranas, Tantras; Vol. 2, Buddhist literature and Jaina literature.

———Some problems of Indian literature. Calcutta, the University, 1925. vi, 130p. **1790**
>It is a collection of the Calcutta University Readership lectures, 1923.

(ii) Classics and Epics

ARNOLD, EDWIN. Some phases in the life of Buddha taken from the *Light of Asia*. Arranged by Valerie Wyngate. London, Kegan Paul, Trench, Trubner & Co., 1950. xii, 78p. **1791**
>Incidental music by Hurbert Bata. Illustrations by Rupert Godfrey Lee. *Light of Asia dramatized*.

ARNOLD EDWIN AND OTHERS, *ed.* The literature of India: Renaissance. New York, Colonial Press, 1902. vii, 467p. **1792**
>This is Vol. 3 of the World's great classics, Oriental literature by Edwin Arnold, R.T.H. Griffths; Monier Monier-Williams etc.

BESWICK, ETHEL. Tales of Hindu gods and heroes. Bombay, Jaico, 1960. 287p. **1793**
>A collection of tales of gods, devas etc.

BROUGH, JOHN, *comp.* Selections from classical Sanskrit

800 Literature

literature. Translated with notes by John Brough. London, Luzac, 1952. viii, 157p. **1794**

BUITENEN, J.A.B. VAN. Tales of ancient India. New York, Bantam, 1961. **1795**

A collection of Indian tales drawn mainly from the Sanskrit works of Somadeva and Buddhaswamin.

CARPENTER, JAMES NELSON. The theology of Tulsi Das. Madras, Christian Literature Society for India, 1918. iv, 202p. (Thesis) **1796**

COWELL, E.B. AND THOMAS, F.W., *trs*. The Harsacarita of Bana. London, 1897. xiv, 284p. (Oriental translation fund New series. Sub-series 2. Vol. 8). **1797**

EDGERTON, FRANKLIN, *tr*. Panchatantra reconstructed. Text, critical apparatus, introduction, and translation, by Franklin Edgerton. London, Oxford University Press, 1924. 2 vols. (American Oriental series, 2-3). **1798**

Vol. I.—Text and critical apparatus;
Vol. II—Introduction and translation.
"An attempt to establish the lost original Sanskrit text of the most famous of Indian story-collection on the basis of the principal extant versions". *t.p.*

——Vikrama's adventures, or the thirty-two tales of the throne. Translated in four parallel recensions, Cambridge (Mass), Harvard University Press, 1926, cvi, 266p. (Harvard Oriental series, edited by Charles Rockwell Lanman, 26). **1799**

A collection of stories about King Vikrama, as told by the thirty-two statues that supported his throne". *t.p.*

FITZGERALD, EDWARD, *tr*. Rubaiyat of Omar Khayyam. Rendered into English verse by Edward Fitzgerald. 3rd ed. Calcutta, Susil Gupta (India) Ltd, 1943. xviii, 28, xxiii, 40p. **1800**

Contains Fitzgerald's two versions published in 1859 and 1868.

GEIGER, W., *tr*. Culavamsa: being the more recent part of the Mahavamsa. London, Pali Text Society, 1929-30. 2 vols. **1801**

——Mahavamsa. Colombo, Ceylon Govt. Information Department, 1950. 2nd impression was published with addendum by G.C. Mendis. lxiii, 323p. **1802**

A reissue of the edition of 1912.

GRAY, J.E.B. Indian tales and legends. London, Oxford, 1961. viii, 230p. **1803**
    A collection of tales and legends mainly selected from Sanskrit and Pali literature.

GRAY, LOUIS H., *tr.* Vasavadatta: a Sanskrit romance. Translated with an introduction and notes by Louis H. Gray. New York, Columbia University Press, 1913. xiii, 214p. (Columbia University Indo-Iranian series, edited by A.V. Williams Jackson, 8). **1804**

GRIERSON, Sir GEORGE ABRAHAM. Notes on Tulsi Das. Reprinted from the *Indian antiquary*, 1893. Allahabad, 1921. xvi, 158p. (with a portrait). **1805**

GRIFFITH, RALPH THOMAS HOTCHKIN. Idylls from the Sanskrit. Allahabad, Panini Office, 1912. xx, 137p. **1806**
    Contents: *Raghuvamsha; Mahabharata;* Fragments.

——Scenes from the Ramayan. Allahabad, S.N. Basu, 1924. x, 117p. **1807**

GURNER, C.W. Srngarasatakam: a century of passion. A rendering into English by C.W. Gurner. Calcutta & Simla, Thacker, Spink & Co., 1927. vi, 42p. **1808**

HARDING, H. JANE, *tr.* Sitar banavas or the exile of Sita. Translated from the elegant Bengali of the learned Pundit Iswarchundra Vidyasagara by H. Jane Harding. London, Henry J. Drane, n. d. 96p. **1809**

HERTEL, JOHANNES, *ed.* The Panchatantra text of Purnabhadna. Cambridge (Mass), Harvard University Press, 1912. 2 vols. **1810**
    Contents: Vol. I. Critical introduction and its variants; Vol. II. Its relation to texts of allied recensions as shown in parallel specimens.

HILL, W. DOUGLAS P., *tr.* The Holy Lake of the acts of Rama. Bombay, Calcutta, Delhi, Oxford University Press, 1952. xxxvii, 538p. Second impression was published in 1971. **1811**
    A translation of *Ramacarita-mansa* which was composed by Tulsi Das, towards the end of the sixteenth century, and for three hundred years, it has been the most popular scripture among the common people of North India. This translation is considered to be of high standard.

HOPKINS, F. WASHBURN. The great epic of India; its character

and origin. New York, Charles Scribner's Sons, 1902. xvii, 485p. **1812**
    An analysis of the *Mahabharata*.

IACOMB, FLORENCE, *tr.* Indian fables from the Sanskrit of the Hitopadesa. Translated and illustrated in colours from original designs by Florence Iacomb. London, Day and Son, n. d. 28 leaves. **1813**
    Chromo-lithographed by W.R. Tymms. Each leaf is vignetted.

JACOBI, H. Ausgewahlte Erzahlungen : Hindu tales: an English translation of *Ausgewahlte Erzahlungen* in Maharashtri, by John Jacob Meyer. London, Lusac & Co., 1909. x, 305p. **1814**

JOHNSON, FRANCIS. Anglo-Burmese Hitopadesa translated into Burmese from the Sanskrit by W.S. Semdy (together with an English version chiefly taken from Sir C. Wilkins and F. Johnson). Maulmain, Burman Press, 1889. **1815**

——The Gulistan (Rose-Garden) of Shaikh Sadi of Shiraj : a new edition with a vocabulary. London, Hertford (printed), 1863. vi, 170, 143p. **1816**

JOHNSON, FRANCIS, *tr.* Hitopadesa: the book of wholesome counsel: A translation from the original Sanskrit by Francis Johnson; rev. and in part re-written with an introduction by Lionel D. Barnett. London, Chapman & Hall, 1928. xix, 202p. (the treasure-house of Eastern story, edited by E. Denison Ross). **1817**

——Hitopadesa, or Salutary counsels of Vishnu Sarman in a series of connected fables interspersed with moral, prudential and political maxims, translated literally by F. Johnson. London, Hertford (printed). W.H. Allen, 1948. v, 121p. **1818**

——Hitopadesa. The Sanskrit text with a grammatical analysis (Sansk. & Eng.), alphabetically arranged. London, Hertford (printed), 1847. Second edition, London, Hertford (printed), 1864. **1819**

JOHNSTON, E.H., *ed.* Buddhacarita or Acts of the Buddha. Lahore, Punjab University, 1935-36. 2 vols. (Punjab University Oriental publications, 31-32). **1820**
    Contents : Vol. I. Sanskrit Text; Vol. II. English translation, introduction and notes.

JOHNSTONE, P. DE LACY, *tr.* Raghuvamsam: the Raghuvansa: the story of Raghu's line. London, J.M. Dent & Co., 1902. xlviii, 200p. **1821**

JONES, Sir WILLIAM, *tr.* Shakuntala or the fatal ring. Calcutta, Society for the resuscitation of Indian literature, 1901. xv, 215p. Reprinted from the original translation appearing in 1789.
1822

KINCAID, CHARLES AUGUSTUS. Tales from the Indian epics. Bombay and Madras, Oxford University Press, 1918. 130p.
1823

KINCAID, C.A., *tr.* Tales of King Vikrama. Bombay, Oxford University Press, 1921. viii, 155p. illus. Illustration by M.V. Dhurandhar. Translation is from the Marathi version of Sadashiv Chatre done in 1830. **1824**

KING, CHARLES, *tr.* Meghadutam : the cloud-messenger : an Indian love lyric. Translated from the original Sanskrit of Kalidasa. London, 1950. 58p. (Wisdom of the East series).
1825

KONOW, STEN, *ed.* Karpura-manjari. Critically edited in the original Prakrit, with a glossarial index, and an essay on the life and writings of the poet by Sten Konow, and translated into English with notes by Charles Rockwell Lanman. Cambridge (Mass), Harvard University Press, 1901. xxviii, 289p. (Harvard Oriental series, 4). **1826**

LILLIE, ARTHUR. Rama and Homer: an argument that in the Indian epics Homer found the theme of his two great poems. London, Kegan Paul, Trench, Trubner & Co., 1912. xiii, 284p.
1827

MATHERS, E. POWYS, *tr.* Rtusamhara : a circle of the seasons. Translated from various European sources by E. Powys Mathers. Walthom Saint Lawrence Berkshire, The Golden Cockered Press, 1929. 30p. **1828**

Issued in a limited number of 500 copies.

MORE, PAUL ELMER. A century of Indian epigrams. London & New York, Harper Brothers, 1899. iv, 124p. **1829**

Chiefly from the Sanskrit of Bhartrihari.

OMAN, JOHN CAMPBELL. Stories of the Ramayana and Mahabharata. London, George Bell & Sons, 1899. xii, 256p. (Great

Indian epics series) **1830**
>"Reproduces faithfully the main incidents and more striking features of the two epics and indicates the abiding influence of these works upon the habits and conceptions of the modern Hindu."

PETER, ISAIAH SUNDARUM. Beowulf and the Ramayana: a study in epic poetry. London, John Bale Sons & Danielsson, 1934. viii, 139p. **1831**
> A study in comparative literature, giving the roots of the Anglo-Saxon and Indian culture. Thesis approved for Ph. D. by the London University.

PISCHEL, RICHARD. Kalidasa's Sakuntala. Critically edited in the original Sanskrit and Prakrit of the Bengali recension. 1922. (Harvard Oriental series, vol. 16). **1832**

RICE, EDWARD PETER. The Mahabharata: analysis and index. Calcutta, Oxford University Press, 1934. xv, 112p. **1833**
> A book of reference indexing incidents, legends or doctrinal teachings in the great epic.

RICE, STANLEY, *tr.* Pancatantra: ancient Indian fables and stories. London, John Murray, 1924. 126p. (The wisdom of the East series). **1834**
> A selection from the *Panchtantra.*

ROOKE, G.H. *tr.* The Meghaduta of Kalidasa. Translated from the Sanskrit from Mallinatha's commentary, map and explanatory notes. London, Humphrey Milford, Oxford University Press, 1935. x, 82p. **1835**

RYDER, ARTHUR W., *tr.* Dasha Kumara Charita: the ten princes. Chicago, University of Chicago Press, 1927. **1836**
> A translation of Sanskrit tales of romance and adventure in India of the seventh century.

———, *tr.* Mrcchakatikam: the little clay cart: Mrcchakatika. Translated from the original Sanskrit and Prakrit into English prose and verse. Cambridge (Mass), Harvard University Press, 1905. xxix, 176p. (Harvard Oriental series, 9). **1837**
> This translation was produced on New York stage in 1953 with great success.

———The Panchatantra. Chicago, University of Chicago Press,

1962. xxix, 176p. **1838**
    A translation of the *Panchatantra* that presents lessons in statecraft and the art of human relations in an entertaining manner.

RYDER, ARTHUR WILLIAM, *tr*. Translations of Shakuntala and other works. London, J.M. Dent and Sons, n.d. xxv, 216p. (Everyman's library, ed. by Ernest Rhys). **1839**
    Contents: Shakuntala; Malavika and Agnimitra; Urvashi; Dynasty of Raghu; Birth of the War-God; Cloud-messenger; Seasons.

——Twenty-two goblins. Translated from the Sanskrit. London and Toronto, J.M. Dent and Sons; New York, E.P. Dutton and Co., 1927. x, 200p. Illustrations by Perham W. Nahl. **1840**

SEEGER, ELIZABETH. The five brothers. New York, John Day Co., 1948. xx, 300p. **1841**
    The story of the *Mahabharata* adapted from the English translation of Kishori Mohan Ganguli. Illustrated by Cyres Leroy Baldrige.

SYMONS, ARTHUR, *tr*. Mrcchakatikam: the toy cart. Rendered into English. Dublin and London, Maunsel & Co., 1919. viii, 114p. **1842**
    A play in five acts. Founded on the *Mrichchhakati*.

TAWNEY, C.H., *tr*. Uttararamacaritam: the English translation of Uttara Rama Charita. 3rd ed. by K.P. Vidyaratna. Calcutta, P.C. Das, 1924. 103p. (First published in 1871). **1843**

THILBANT, GEORGE FREDERICK WILLIAM. The Panchasiddhantika with translation and introduction by G. Thilbant and Sadakara Dvivedi. 1889. **1844**

THOMAS, FREDERICK WILLIAM. The Harsa-Carita of Bana, Translated by E.B. Cowell and F.W. Thomas. 1897. (Oriental Translation Fund, New series II). **1845**

WILSON, H.H., *tr*. Malatimadhavan: Malati and Madhava. Translated from the original Sanskrit. Calcutta, Society for the Resuscitation of Indian Literature, 1901. x, 133p. **1846**
    ——The Meghaduta, or Cloud messenger: a poem in the Sanskrit language. Translated into English verse with notes

800 Literature

and illustrations, edited by Lal Mohan Vidyaridhi. Calcutta, Sanskrit Press Depository, 1901. 93p. **1847**

WILSON, H.H. Mrcchakatikam: or the toy-cart. Translated from the original Sanskrit. Calcutta, Society for the Resuscitation of Indian Literature, 1901. xiv, 200p. **1848**

    Mudra-rakshasa or the signet of the minister. Translated from the original Sanskrit. Calcutta, Society for the Resuscitation of Indian Literature, 1901. xl, 137p. **1849**

WILSON, RICHARD, ed. The Indian story book. London, Macmillan & Co., 1914. 272p. illus. **1850**

    Contains tales from the *Ramayana*, the *Mahabharata* and other early sources.

WOOLNER, A.C., tr. Kundamala: the jasmine garland. Translated from Sanskrit into English. London, Oxford University Press, 1935. xiv, 50p. (Punjab University Oriental publications, 27). **1851**

YOHANNAN, JOHN D. A treasury of Asian literature. New York, Day, 1956. 487p. **1852**

    An anthology selected from the classics of Asia, including the *Panchatantra*, the *Bhagavad Gita*, and the *Gita-Govinda*.

(iii) Essays and Letters

ARONSON, ALEXANDER AND KRIPALANI, KRISHNA, R., eds. Rollands and Tagore. Calcutta, Visvabharati, 1945. viii, 104p. **1853**

    Comprises letters of Rolland to Tagore, and conversations between Rolland and Tagore.

COUSINS, JAMES HENRY. Work and worship: essays on culture and creative art. Madras, Ganesh & Co., 1922. viii, 159p. **1854**

EDEN, *Hon.* EMILY. Miss Eden's letters, *ed.* by her greatniece, Violet Dickinson. London, Macmillan & Co., limited, 1919. xv, 414p. front., parts. **1855**

    ————'Up the country'. Letters written to her sister from the Upper provinces of India, by the Hon. Emily Eden. New ed.

London, R. Bentlay, 1867. 2p. 1., 396p. **1856**
HODGSON, BRAIN HOUGHTON. Miscellaneous essays relating to Indian subjects. London, Trubner & Co., 1880. 2 vols. (Trubner's oriental series). Edited by Reinhold Rost. These essays are published from various sources. **1857**
KINCAID, CHARLES AUGUSTUS. Lakshmibai, Rani of Jhansi and other essays. London, the author, n.d. iv. 120p. (printed in India). **1858**
LILLY, WILLIAM SAMUEL. Essays and speeches. London, Chapman & Hall Ltd., 1897. xxvi, 265p. **1859**
ROST, REINHOLD, *ed*. Essays relating to Indian subjects. 1880. (Trubner's oriental series) 2 vols. **1860**

(iv) Fiction (Drama, Novels, Plays etc.)

ABBOTT, JAMES. The Thakoorine, a tale of Maandoo. London, J. Madden & Co., 1841. xxiv, 126p. **1861**
ALLARDYCE, ALEXANDER. Early court. A novel of provincial life. London, Edinburgh, 1894. 3 vols. **1862**
BARRET, GEORGE. Forty-three years: Jayant and Tara. Bombay, Thacker & Co., 1944. 335p. **1863**
    "George Barret is the composite pen-name of the two experienced writers." *Foreword*.
BESCHI, JOSEPH CONSTANTINE. Paramartta Kuru Katai : the adventures of the Gooroo Noodle. A tale in the Tamil language, translated by Benjamin Babington. Allahabad, Panini Office, 1915. xii, 111p. **1864**
BOTHWELL, JEAN. Little boat boy. New York, Harcourt, Brace, 1945. 252p. **1865**
    Hafiz, who lives on a mat-boat in Kashmir, is a real and delightful little boy, whose desire for schooling eventually brings prosperity to his whole family.
—— Little flute player. New York, Morrow, 1949. 159p.
1866
    Little Teka Ram, who entertained the cattle herders with his flute, finds a way to keep his family from starving, when famine strikes Northern India.

BOTHWELL, JEAN. River boy of Kashmir. New York, Morrow, 1946. 246p. **1867**
Continues the adventures of Hafiz (of little boat boy) after he enters the River School.

——Search for a golden bird. New York, Harcourt, Brace, 1956. 172p. **1868**
Jivan, grandson of the Prime Minister of Jaipur, with his cousin Dhuleep and a ruby-eyed golden bird are the central figures in this continuation of *The Thirteenth Stone*.

——Star of India. New York, Morrow, 1947. 224p. **1869**
Bittu and her father come down from the hills to recover the Star of India medal which has fallen into the hands of the wicked Rais of Kunwar.

—— Sword of a warrior. New York, Harcourt, Brace, 1951. 228p. **1870**
Miss Bothwell unravels with great skill the mystery which surrounds young Jai, apprentice to a famous Lucknow silversmith.

BROMFIELD, LOUIS. The rain came; a novel of modern India. 27th ed. London, Cassell & Co., 1941. vii, 578p. **1871**
First published in 1938, it is one of the earliest modern American novels about modern India. It is a story of the crises brought about by disaster in remote Indian state.

BUCK, PEARL SYDENSTRICKER. Come, my beloved. London, Methuen & Co., 1953. iv, 297p. **1872**
A novel of Indian life.

CLARK, T.W., *ed*. The novel in India: its birth and development. Berkeley, University of California, 1970. 239p. **1873**

COLLIER, RICHARD. Pay-off in Calcutta. London, Pilot Press, 1948. 224p. Published in U.S.A. under the title: *The Solitary Witness*. **1874**

COUSINS, JAMES HENRY. The bound of Uladh: two plays in verse. Madras, Kalakshetra, 1942. xii, 270p. **1875**
Contents: The King's wife, the hound of Uladh.

—— The King's wife. Madras, Ganesh & Co., 1919. 96p. **1876**
A drama based on Indian stories.

COX, PHILIP. The Rani of Jhansi. London, George Allen & Unwin, 1933. 119p. **1877**

A historical play in four acts.

CREEKMORE, RAYMOND. Ali's elephant. New York, London, Macmillan, 1949. 38p. **1878**

Ali was the only person who could handle the baby elephant his father had captured for the Maharaja. One day both of them proved their courage in a tiger hunt. A delightful picture-story for young children.

CRUMP, L. M., tr. The lady of the lotus; Rup Mati, Queen of Mandu: a strange tale of faithfulness. Translated with introduction and notes, together with twenty-six poems attributed to Queen Rup Mati, done into verse by L. M. Crump. London, Humphrey Milford, Oxford University Press, 1926. xi, 96p. **1879**

FORSTER, EDWARD MORGAN. A passage to India. New York, Harcourt, Brace & Co., 1924. 322p. **1880**

"A novel depicting a genuine picture of Indians and of the English in India."

GRACIAS, LOUIS. Eastern clay; fourteen stories. Calcutta, the author, 1948. xii, 145p. **1881**

GROWSE, F. S., tr. Ramayana of Tulsi Das; translated from the original. 7th rev. ed. Allahabad, Ram Narain Lal, n. d., xix, 534p. **1882**

HAMILTON, JOHN. In a Bengal backwater. Calcutta & Simla, Thacker, Spink & Co., 1920. iv, 296p. **1883**

"A novel depicting the internal economy of Bengali Hindu home life in the mofussil."

HESSE, HERMANN. Siddhartha. Translated by Hilda. Rosner. New York James Laughlin, 1950. vi, 153p. (New classics series). **1884**

HOLDEN, CHARLES LESLIE. Videhi: a novel of Indian life. London, Macmillan & Co., 1953. v, 401p. **1885**

KEITH, ARTHUR B. The Sanskrit drama in its origin, development, theory and practice. London, Geoffrey Cumberlege, Oxford University Press, 1924. x, 11, 405p. **1886**

A scholarly history of the origin, development, theory and practice of drama in India from the Vedic to the early Medieval times.

KIPLING, RUDYARD. Author's notes on the names of the Jungle

books. Garden City, N. Y., Doubleday, Doran & Co., 1937. 3p. 1., 3-10p. **1887**

KIPLING, RUDYARD. Ballads and barrackroom ballads, New York & London, Macmillan & Co., 1892. xvi, 207p. **1888**

—— His Majesty the King; Wee Willie Winkie. illust. by J.W. Kennedy. Boston, D. Estes & Co., 1899. 4 p. 1., 11-57p. incl. front. 3 pls. (The Young of heart series no. 13). **1889**

—— The jungle book. Calcutta, Macmillan & Co., 1943. vii, 192p. **1890**

—— Kim. New York, Doubleday. Page & Co., 1901. 3p. 1., 460p. front. 9 pls. **1891**

—— The light that failed. Authorized ed. New York, United States Book Company, 1890. 2p. 1., 3-186p. (Lovell's Westminster series, no. 25). **1892**

—— Plain tales from the hills. Authorized ed. New York, United States Book Company, 1889. vi, 7-287p. **1893**

MACFIC, J. M. The Ramayan of Tulsidas: or, the Bible of Northern India. Edinburg, T. & T. Clark, 1930. xxiv, 260p. **1894**

MASTERS, JOHN. Bhovani junction. London, Michael, Joseph, 367p. **1895**

—— Bugles and a tiger: a personal adventure. London, Michael Joseph, 1956. 344p. **1896**

—— Complete Indian angler. London, Country Life, 1938. xi, 115p. **1897**

—— Coromandel. London, Michael Joseph, 1955. 320p. **1898**

—— The deceivers. London, Michael Joseph, 1952. 288p. **1899**

A novel in Indian setting.

—— Fandango rock. London, Michael Joseph, 1959. 390p. **1900**

—— Far, far the mountain peak. London, Michael Joseph, 1957. 414p. **1901**

—— The lotus and the wind, London, Michael Joseph, 1953. 287p. **1902**

A novel in Indian setting.

—— Nightrunners of Bengal. London, Michael Joseph, 1960. 381p. **1903**

MASTERS, JOHN. Road past Mandalay: a personal narrative. London, Michael Joseph, 1961. 344p. illus. **1904**

—— To the Coral strand. London, Michael Joseph, 1962. 319p. **1905**

McLNNES, GRAHAM. Sushila. New York and London, Putnam, 1957. **1906**

A spirited novel based on the life of an Indian painter.

NARIMAN, G.K., *tr*. Priyadarsika: a Sanskrit drama, translated into English by G.K. Nariman, A.V. Williams Jackson and Charles J. Ogden. New York, Columbia University Press, 1923. 131p. **1907**

NORTHFIELD, GLAYS L., *ed*. The legends of Bengal. 2nd ed. Dacca and Calcutta, Bengal Library, 1930. 2 vols. pl. **1908**

PAYNE, PIERRE STEPHEN ROBERT. The emperor. London, William Heinemann, 1953. vii, 374p. **1909**

A novel of Indian life.

—— The great Mogul. London, William Heinemann, 1950. v, 344p. **1910**

A novel on the life of Emperor Shah Jehan.

REID, C. LESTOCK. Masque of mutiny. London, C. & J. Temple, 1947. 239p. **1911**

A historical novel based on the Indian mutiny of 1857.

RUBIN, DAVID, *tr*. The world of Premchand: selected stories. Bloomington, Indiana University Press, 1969. 215p. **1912**

RYDER, ARTHUR W., *tr*. Dasakumaracritam: the ten princes. Chicago, the University Press, 1927. xv, 240p. **1913**

—— Mrcchakatikam or the little clay cart: Translated from the original Sanskrit and Prakrit into English prose and verse. Cambridge, Mass., Harvard University Press, 1905. xxix, 176p. (Harvard Oriental series, no. 9). **1914**

This translation was produced on the New York stage in 1953 with great success.

SELIGMAN, HILDA MCDOWELL. When peacocks called. Foreword by Rabindranath Tagore. Bombay, Hind Kitabs, 1951. 278p. **1915**

A novel based on the times of King Asoka.

SINNETT, ALFRED PERCY. Karma, a novel. New ed. Chicago,

Rand, McNally & Company, 1886. 1p. 1., 2, (v.) viii, 285p. **1916**

TAYLOR, MEADOWS. The confessions of a thug. Edited by F. Yeats-Brown. London, Eyre and Spottiswoode, 1938. 326p. map. **1917**

——A noble queen : a romance of Indian history. London, 1878. 3 vols. **1918**

THOMPSON, EDWARD JOHN. Atonement: a play of modern India in four acts. London, Ernest Benn, 1924. 128p. (Contemporary British dramatists, 10). **1919**

——A farewell to India. London, Ernest Benn, 1931. 288p. **1920**

   A novel based on Indian life.

——An Indian day. London, Alfred A. Knopf, 1927. vi, 306p. **1921**

   A novel based on Indian life.

——Krishna Kumari. London, Ernest Benn, 1924. 89p. (Contemporary British dramatists, 10). **1922**

   A historical drama in four acts based on Rajput history.

—— The youngest disciple. London, Faber, 1938, 313p. **1923**

   A novel based on Buddhist tradition and canonical books.

THOMPSON, EDWARD JOHN, tr. Svarnalata: the brothers. Translated by Edward Thompson. London, India Society, 1931. 181p. **1924**

THOMPSON, EDWARD JOHN & THOMPSON. Theodosia. Three Eastern plays. London, George Allen & Unwin, 1927. vi, 128p. **1925**

   Contents: Eastern evening by Theodesia Thompson; two Indian plays by Edward Thompson. Contains also an essay on Suttee at the end.

WATERFIELD, WILLIAM, tr. The lay of Alha, a saga of Rajput chivalry as sung by minstrels of North India. London, Oxford University Press, 1923. 278p. **1926**

   Introduction and abstracts of the untranslated portions by Sir George Grierson.

WELLS, HENRY W. The classical drama of India. New York, Bombay, Asia Publishing House, 1963. 196p. **1927**

An appraisal of the classical drama in India. A careful work.

WELLS, HENRY W., *ed.* Six Sanskrit plays in English translation, New York, Bombay, Asia Publishing House, 1964. xxxi, 487p. illus. **1928**
    Contains representative selections from the works of Bhasa, Sudraka, Kalidasa, Bhavabuti, and Harsha. It is a useful introduction to Sanskrit plays.

WILSON, H.H., *tr.* Ratnavali or the Necklace. Translated from the original Sanskrit. Calcutta, Society for the Resuscitation of Indian Literature, 1901. x, 66p. **1929**

WOOLNER, A.C., *tr.* Thirteen Trivandrum plays attributed to Bhasa. Translated into English by A.C. Woolner and Lakshman Sarup. London, Published for Punjab University by Oxford University Press, 1930-1931. 2 vols, (Punjab University Oriental publications, 13). **1930**
    "This translation is of thirteen Sanskrit plays discovered in South India by the late Pandit Ganapati Sastri and edited by him in the Trivandrum Sanskrit series."

YOUNGHUSBAND, FRANCIS EDWARD. 'But in our lives'; a romance of the Indian frontier. London, John Murray, 1926. 317p. **1931**

(v) Poetry

ALLEN, STEPHEN, *ed.* Vidyapati. Renderings in English verse by Dinesh Chandra Datta, Calcutta, the editor, 1941. 64p. **1932**
    Contains translations of 59 poems.

ARCHER, WILLIAM GEORGE. The Blue Grove: the poetry of the Uraons. New York, Grove Press, 1953. **1933**
    A collection of poems written on the social customs of Uraons, a tribe of Central India.

ARNOLD, Sir EDWIN. Indian poetry and Indian idylls. N.Y., E.P. Dutton, 1915. viii, 270, 21, 282p. **1934**

BROUGHTON, THOMAS DUER. Selection from the popular poetry of the Hindoos. London, John Martin, 1814. 156p. **1935**

CHAPMAN, JOHN ALEXANDER. The Rampur anthology. Calcutta,

800 Literature

Humphrey Milford, Oxford University Press, 1934. xvi, 251p. **1936**
Collection of poems from Hafiz, Rumi, Hali, Omar Khayyam, Chittaranjan Das and the Sakta lyric poets of Bengal, and also poems of J.A. Chapman. Poems other than those of J.A. Chapman have been translated by different poets.

CHAPMAN, JOHN ALEXANDER. Lyrical poems. Calcutta, the author, 1927. viii, 168p. **1937**

——— Religious lyrics of Bengal. Calcutta, Book, 1926. iv, 92p. **1938**

ELENJIMITTAM, ANTHONY. The poet of Hindustan. Calcutta, Oriental Book Co., 1948. x, 119p. **1939**
Deals with the thoughts of Rabindranath Tagore.

GRIBBLE, R.T. *tr.* Mystic lyrics from the Indian middle ages. A free transcription by Paul Althaus; rendered into English (from German) by R.T. Gribble. Short biograpical notes on the different poets by Mr. Teikuhl at the end. London, George Allen & Unwin, 1928. 123p. **1940**

GRIFFITH, RALPH THOMAS HOTCHKIN, *ed. & tr.* Specimens of old Indian poetry. Translated from original Sanskrit into English verse. London, A. Hall, Virtue & Co. (etc.) 1852. xv, 128p. **1941**

•HERBER, REGINALD, bp. of Calcutta. The poetical works of Reginald Heber, late bishop of Calcutta. Philadelphia, Lea & Blanchard, 1841. 8p. 1 (v)—viiip, 1.1., (19)—309,(1)p. **1942**

HEINEMANN, S.O. Poems of Mewar. Calcutta, Printed at the Art Press, 1921. vi, 312p. Legends of Mewar in verse. **1943**

HOPE, LAURENCE. Songs from the garden of Kama. London, William Heinemann, 1909. viii, 113p. **1944**
Poems with Indian themes and setting.

HOPKINS, EDWARD WASHBURN. Legends of India. New Haven, Yale University Press, 1928. vii p. 11., 193p. **1945**
These legends are described in the form of poetry.

HOYLAND, JOHN S., *tr.* Village songs of Western India. Translated from Tukeram, London, Allenson & Co., 1934. 86p. **1946**
• "A collection of songs by Tukaram, the most famous of

Maratha poets, and one of the chief exponents of the *Bhakti* School."

INGALLS, DANIEL H.H., *tr*. Anthology of Sanskrit court poetry. Cambridge, Mass., Harvard University Press, 1965. 611p. **1947**

JESUDASAN, HEPHZIBAH, *tr*. The song of cuckoo and other poems. Trivandrum, the translator, 1950, x, 122p. **1948**
Appendix is on the life of Bharati.

KEENE, HENRY GEORGE. Peepul leaves. Poems written in India. London, W.H. Allen & Co., 1879. iv, 119p. **1949**

KEYT, GEORGE, *tr*. Shri Jayadevas' Gita Govinda : the loves of Krisna and Radha. Rendered from Sanskrit and illustrated by George Keyt. Bombay, Kutub Publishers, 1947. 103p. **1950**
A complete English version.

KUNHAN, C., *ed*. Anupasimhagunavatara. Edited with an English translation by C. Kunhan. Raja, Bikaner, Anup Sanskrit Library, 1942, vi, 104p. (Ganga oriental series, 1). **1951**
A poem in ten *Avataras* describing the various aspects of the character of Maharaja Anupa Simha of Bikaner. (1669-1690 A.D).

LYALL, Sir ALFRED. Poems, by Sir Alfred C. Lyall. Revised and slightly enlarged from verses written in India. 6th ed. London, G. Routledge & Sons, ltd., New York, E.P. Dutton & Co., 1907. vi, 150p. (Half title : The muses library). **1952**

LYALL, Sir ALFRED COMYN. Verses written in India. London, K. Paul, Trench & Co., 1889. vi, 138p. **1953**

MACNICOL, MARGARET, *ed*. Poems by Indian women. Selected and rendered by various translators. Calcutta, Association Press, 1923. iii, 99p. (The heritage of India series). **1954**

——Psalms of Maratha saints: one hundred and eight hymns. Translated from Marathi. Calcutta, Association Press, 1919. 95p: **1955**

MILFORD E.M., *tr*. Naksikamthar math: The field of the embroidered quilt : a tale of two Indian villages. Calcutta. Humphrey Milford, Oxford University Press, 1939. xii, 60p. **1956**

MONIER-WILLIAMS, Sir MONIER. Indian epic poetry; being the substance of lectures recently given at Oxford : with a full analysis of the Ramayana and of the leading story of the

Mahabharata by Monier Williams, London and Edinburgh, Williams and Norgate, 1863. viii, 133p. **1957**

MUIR, JOHN *tr.* Metrical translations from Sanskrit writers, with an introduction, prose versions, and parallel passages from classical authors. London, Trubner & Co., 1879. 4p. 1. (vii)-xliv, 376p. **1958**

NOBEL, JOHANNES. The foundation of Indian poetry and their historical development: general outlines. Calcutta, R.N. Seal, 1925. v. 193p. **1959**

QUACKENBOS, GEORGE PAYN, *ed*, & *tr*. The Sanskrit poems of Mayura. Edited with a translation and notes and an introduction together with the text and translation of Bana's Candisataka, New York, Columbia University Press, 1917. xxii, 362p. (Columbia University Indo-Iranian series, 9). **1960**

RUSSELL, CHARLES, *tr*. Sonnets, poems and translations, Calcutta, Thacker, Spink & Co., 1920. xxxiii, 70p. **1961**
    Contents : Translations from Lucratius, Catullus, Dante, Goethe, Schiller, and Heine; and from the Rigveda, Hitopadesha, Sutta-Nipata, Dhammapada, and other oriental texts, with eight introductory sonnets and a memoirs by John Alexander Chapman." *t.p.*

THOMPSON, EDWARD JOHN AND SPENCER, ARTHUR MARSHMAN, *trs*. Bengali religious lyrics: Sakta. Calcutta, Association Press, 1923. ii, 91p. (The heritage of India series). **1962**
    "The great bulk of the selections comprises the songs of Ramaprasad Seni."

TURUBULL, H.G. DALWAY, *ed*. Sarojini Naidu: select poems. Chosen and edited by H.G. Dalway. Calcutta, Oxford University Press, 1930. xii, 241p. **1963**

USBORNE, C.F. Punjabi lyrics and proverbs. Translated in verse and prose. Lahore, Civil and Military Gazette Press, 1905. vii, 65p. **1964**

WARNER, ARTHUR GEORGE AND WARNER, EDMUND *tr*. Shahnama, the Shahnama of Firdausi. London, Kegan Paul, Trench, Trubner & Co., 1905-1923. 8 vols. (Trubner's oriental series). **1965**

(vi) Short Stories

ANDERSON, J.D., *tr*. Indira and other stories. Calcutta, Modern Review Office, 1918. iv, 179p. Illustrations by Nandlal Bose. **1966**
    Contents: Indira; Radharani; the two rings; Doctor Macrus.

BABBITT, J.C. More Jataka tales. New York, Appleton-Century-Crofts (1922), 1940. 22p. **1967**
    A simple re-tellings of the Jataka stories, for young children.

BAIN, FRANCIS WILLIAM, *tr*. Ahipiditacandrika: an essence of the dusk. Translated from the original Sanskrit manuscript of an unknown author. London, Medici Society, 1914. xviii, 73p. (The Indian stories of F.W. Bain, Vol. 6). First published in 1906. **1968**

——, *tr*. Balataparaktasasini: a digit of the moon. Translated from the original manuscript. London, Medici Society, 1914. xx, 96p. (The Indian stories of F.W. Bain, Vol. 1). First published in 1898. **1969**

—— Bhavemanasalayajyotsna: an incarnation of the snow. Translated from the original manuscript. London, Medici Society, 1914. xxii, 70p. (The Indian stories of F.W. Bain, Vol. 7). First published in 1908. **1970**

—— Bhrngisasudhabhrtpusa: a syrup of the bees. Translated from the original manuscript. London, Medici Society, 1914. xix, 91p. (The Indian stories of F.W. Bain, Vol. 11). **1971**

—— Dosakarasaratusti: a mine of faults. Translated from the original manuscript. London, Medici Society, 1914. xviii, 94p. (The Indian stories of F.W. Bain, Vol. 8). **1972**

—— Phenopamamatrapriti: Bubbles of the foam. Translated from the original manuscript. London, Medici Society, 1914. xx, 103p. (The Indian stories of F.W. Bain, Vol. 10). **1973**

—— Puskareksnangata: a draught of the blue. Translated from the original manuscript. London, Medici Society, 1914. xvii, 70p. (The Indian stories of F.W. Bain, Vol. 5). **1974**

—— Ragodadhidugdhapusa: the living of Eve. Translated from the original manuscript, London, Medici Society, 1919. xvii,

106p. (The Indian stories of F.W. Bain, Vol. 12). First published in 1917. **1975**

BAIN, FRANCIS WILLIAM, *tr*. Smarabhasmanjivanitusti: the ashes of a god. Translated from the original manuscript. London, Medici Society, 1914. xxi, 100p. (The Indian stories of F.W. Bain, Vol. 9). **1976**
    First published in 1911.

——Svapnopamakanti: the substance of a dream. Translated from the original manuscript. London, Medici Society, 1920. xxiv, 150p. (The Indian stories of F.W. Bain, Vol. 13). **1977**

——Usriyasambhrtamrta: a heifer of the dawn. Translated from the original manuscript. London, Medici Society, 1914. xiv, 60p. (The Indian stories of F.W. Bain, Vol. 3). **1978**
    First published in 1904.

BRADLEY-BIRT, FRANCIS BRADLEY, Bengali fair tales. London, John Lane the Bodley Head; New York, John Lane Co., 1920. x, 209p. **1979**
    The tales are illustrated by Abanindranath Tagore.

CROOKE, WILLIAM. The talking thrush, and other tales from India. Collected by W. Crooke, and retold by W.H.D. Rouse, illustrated by W.H. Robinson. London, J.M. Dent & Sons, New York, E.P. Dutton & Co. Inc., 1938. xi, 217p. illus. **1980**
    First published in this edition, 1938.

EASTWICK, EDWARD BACKHOUSE, *tr*. Prem Sagar, or the Ocean of love by Chaturbhuja Misra. Literally translated into English, Edward Backhouse Eastwick. Hertford, London, 1851. **1981**

GEAR, JOSEPH. Fables of India. New York, Little, Brown, 1955. 176p. **1982**
    One of the most attractive children's books published in recent years, this collection is chosen from the *Panchatantra*, the *Hitopadesa* and the *Jatakas*.

GLEIG, *Rev*. GEORGE ROBERT. Tales of military life. Second series. By the author of 'The subaltern'. 2nd ed. Philadelphia, Key & Biddle, 1833. 267p. **1983**

KINCAID, CHARLES AUGUSTUS. The ancharita and other stories. Bombay, Oxford University Press, 1922. viii, 239p. **1984**
    A collection of stories based on Indian life.

KINCAID, CHARLES AUGUSTUS. Deccan nursery tales, of Fairy tales from the South. London, Macmillan & Co., 1914. 135p. Illustrated by M.V. Dhurandhar. **1985**
———The Indian heroes. London, Humphrey Milford, Oxford University Press, 1915. xi, 148p. **1986**
    A collection of stories drawing on the epics of India.
——— Shri Krishna of Dwaraka and other stories. Bombay, D.B. Taraporevala Sons & Co., 1920. viii, 96p. **1987**
    A collection of stories based on Indian mythology.
——— Tales from the Indian drama. Madras, Oxford University Press, 1923. vii, 96p. **1988**
    Contents : Sakuntala; Pururuvas and Urvasi; Malati and Madhava; The toy car; Rakshasa's signet ring; the cloud messenger.
———Tales of old Sind. Madras, Humphrey Milford, Oxford University Press, 1922, xii, 140p. illus. **1989**
——— The tale of the Tulsi and other studies. New and rev. ed. Bombay, D.B. Taraporevala Sons & Co., 1916. vi, 177p. **1990**
    Three legendary tales, historical and other sketches, proverbial philosophy of Western India.
KIPLING, RUDYARD. All the Mowgli stories. New York, Doubleday, (1936), 1954. 303p. **1991**
    An attractive edition of these familiar stories about a boy brought up by wolves in the Indian jungle.
———Departmental deities. Chicago, W.B. Conkey Company, 1950. 2p. 1; 3-207p. front (port). pls. **1992**
    "The incarnation of Krishna Mulvaney, and other stories. p. 59-207.
KNIGHT, MIRIAM S., tr. Stories of Bengalee life by Prabhat Kumar Mukherji. Translated by Miriam S. Knight and the author. Calcutta, Chuckervarthy, Chatterji & Co., 1912. viii, 256p. **1993**
    Selected from author's Bengali works, *Navakatha, Sadasi* and *Desi O bilati*. The first four stories translated by the author and remaining six by M.S. Knight.
LANGLES, LOUIS MATHIEU. Fables et Contes Indiens. traduits auec un discours preliminaire et des notes. 1790. (F). vii, 185p
1994

800 Literature

MACFARLANE, IRIS. Tales and legends from India. London, Chatto and Windus, 1965. 136p. **1995**
    A collection of ten tales and legends.

MILTON, DANIEL L. AND W. CLIFFORD, *eds.* A treasury of modern Asian stories. New York, New American Library, 1961. 237p. **1996**
    This paperbound edition contains stories written in English by Indian authors as well as modern stories translated from Bengali, Hindi, Marathi, Tamil and Urdu.

MONRO, W.D. Stories of Indian gods and heroes. London, George G. Harrap & Co., 224p. pls. 16 illus. by Evelyn Paul. **1997**

RANN, JOSEPHINE. Indian tales of love and beauty. Foreword by Annie Besant. Madras, Theosophist; Office, 1912. xvi, 191p. **1998**
    "A collection of humorous stories translated from the Persian of Shahryar Illahi...famous Birbal stories."

STEEL, FLORA ANNIE. A tale of Indian heroes. London, Hutchinson & Co., 1923. x, 11-256p. **1999**

SWYNNERTON, CHARLES, *comp.* Romantic tales from the Panjab Westminster, Archibald Constable, 1903. xlvi, 483p. illus. **2000**
    A collection of the village tales collected in the neighbourhood of Attock on the Upper Indus.

SYMINGTON, JOHN. In a Bengal jungle; stories of life on the tea gardens of Northern India. Chapel Hill, University of North Carolina Press, 1935. vi, 245p. illus. **2001**

TAWNEY, C.H., *tr.* Kathasaritsagara: the ocean of story. Being C.H. Tawney's translation. Edited with introduction and notes by N.M. Penzar. London, Chas J. Sawyar, 1925. 10 vols. **2002**
    Privately printed for subscribers only.

THOMPSON, SMITH and JONAS BALYS. The oral tales of India. Bloomington, Indiana University Press, 1958. xxvi, 448p. (Folklore series, no. 10). **2003**

WILLIAMS, ALFRED, *tr.* Tales from the Panchantantra. Translated from the Sanskrit. Oxford, Basil Blackwell, 1930. xvi, 207p. Illustrated by Peggy Whistler. Introductory note by A.A. Macdonell. **2004**

900 HISTORY

Description and Travel
Geography
Biography

(i) General

ABBOT, JOHN. Sind: a re-interpretation of the unhappy valley. London, Published for Bombay University Press, 1924. viii, 113p. maps. **2005**
    Parts appeared in *Calcutta Review* and *Pioneer*.

AL-BIRUNI. Alberuni's India. Translated by E.C. Sachau. London, Trubner, 1910. 2 vols. **2006**
    An original source book on the history of North India. It is a translation of Alberuni's *Tarikh-ul-Hind* written in the early 11th century.

AL-IDRISI. India and the neighbouring territories. Leiden, E.I. Brill, 1960. **2007**
    A useful source book of Indian history, it is a translation of the original work entitled *Nuzhar-ul-Mushtak*, a geography of the early 12th century.

ALLAN, JOHN, T.W. HAIG, H.H. DODWELL. The Cambridge

shorter history of India. Delhi, S. Chand & Co., 1958. xvi, 970p. **2008**
    A basic reference for the political history of India from earliest time to 1947.

ARBERRY, A.J. Asiatic Jones; the life and influence of Sir William Jones (1746-1794) pioneer of Indian studies. London, Published for the British Council by Longmans, Green & Co., Ltd. (1946). 39, (1) p. col. front. pls. facsim. **2009**

ARRIANUS, FLAVIUS. Arrian, History of Alexander and India. Cambridge, Harvard University Press, 1949. 2 vols. **2010**
    Translated by E. Iliff Robson, it is an account of Alexander the Great's invasion of India. Originally the account was written in the second century of the Christian era.

BALLHATCHET, KENNETH. Social policy and social change in Western India. London, Oxford University Press, 1957. **2011**
    An account of the British administration during the years 1817 to 1830. A valuable source book.

BASHAM, ARTHUR LLEWELLYN. The wonder that was India. London, Hawthorn Books, 1963. Also available in paperbound ed., 1959. Published by Grove Press, New York, xxi, 568p. **2012**
    Considered to be an excellent summary of India's cultural and social heritage.

BAYLEY, Sir EDWARD CLIVE. The history of India as told by its historians. The Local Muhammadan Dynasties. Gujarat. Partially based on translation by John Down. London, W.H. Allen, 1886. xx, 519p. **2013**

BEAMES, JOHN. Memoirs of the history of the races of the Northwestern provinces of India. Edited by J. Beames. 1869. **2014**

BECK, HORACE C. The beads from Taxila. Ed. by John Marshall. Delhi, Manager of Publications, 1941. v, 66p. (Memoirs: Archaeological Survey of India, 65). **2015**
    An examination of about 950 selected beads, dated from C. 700 B.C. to C. 500 A.D. exhumed during the excavations at the site of Taxila during the years 1912-1934.

BELL, THOMAS EVANS. The Bengal reversion, another 'Exceptional Case'. London, Trubner & Co., 1872. xxxix, 83p. **2016**
——The Mysore reversion 'An Exceptional Case'. London,

Trubner, 1865. viii, 225p. **2017**

BIARDEAN, MADELEINE, *tr.* India. New York, Viking Press, 1960. Translated from the French by F. Carter, it is a reliable appraisal of India's culture and civilization. **2018**

BIDDULPH, JOHN. The nineteenth and their times. London, John Murray, 1890. xxi, 330p. **2019**

BOULGER, DOMETRIUS, CHARLES. India in nineteenth century. London, H. Marshall & Sons. 1901. viii, 360p. **2020**

────── The story of India. London, H. Marshall & Sons, 1897. xx, 132p. **2021**

BROWN, C.J. The coins of India. Calcutta, Association Press, 1922. 120p. pls. index. (The heritage of India series). **2022**
    A valuable source book containing history of coinage in India from the remote past to 1857.

BROWN, CHARLES, PHILIPS. Cyclic tables of Hindu and Mahomedan chronology, regarding the history of the Telugu and Kannadi countries. Madras, S.P.C.K., 1850. iv, 66p. **2023**

BROWN, W. NORMAN. *ed.* India, Pakistan, Ceylon, Ithaca. N.Y., Cornell University Press, 1951. xii, 234p. **2024**
    "Restates the prehistory of India, describing the achievements in thought, literature, and the arts and characterizing the social structure, economic life and law."

BURNS, JAMES. A sketch of the history of Cutch from its first connexion with the British Govt. in India to conclusion of the treaty of 1849. 2 pt. 1829. 2 vols. **2025**

CAMPBELL, A. CLAUDE. Glimpses of Bengal. Calcutta, Campbell & Medland, 1907. 2 vols. Vol. 1, vii, 341p. **2026**
    "A comprehensive archaeological, biographical, and pictorial history of Bengal, Behar and Orissa."

CHIROL, VALENTINE. India. Introduction by H.A.L. Fisher. London, Ernest Benn, 1930. vii, 352p. **2027**
    First published in 1926, it is a general commentary on India's political and social conditions.

CRANE, ROBERT I. The history of India; its study and interpretation. Washington, Service Center for Teachers of History, 1958. 46p. (Service Center for Teachers of History, Publication no. 17). **2028**

CUMMING, JOHN GHOST, *ed.* Revealing India's past. Foreword

900 History

by Alfred Foucher. London, India Society, 1939. xx, 374p. **2029**

"A cooperative record of archaeological conservation and exploration in India and beyond, by twenty-two authorities. British Indian and continental."

DODWELL, HENRY H. *ed.* The Cambridge history of India. Cambridge, Cambridge University Press, 1922-53. 5 vols. Originally planned six volumes but vol no. 2 yet to be published. Professor A.L. Basham is reported to be working on it. Reprinted by S. Chand & Co., New Delhi. **2030**

By all standards this is considered to be a standard work concerning the history of India from the remote past to 1947. Each volume provides a comprehensive bibliography which makes it a valuable set. Contents: Vol. 1, Ancient India ed. by E.J. Rapson; Vol. 3, Turks and Afghans, ed. by Wolseley Haig; Vol. 4, Mughal period, planned by Wolseley Haig, ed. by Richard Burn; Vol. 5, British India. 1497-1858, ed. by H.H. Dodwell; Vol. 6, Indian empire, 1858-1918, ed. by H.H. Dodwell. Supplement. The Indus civilization, by Mortimer Whealer, 1953. xi, 98p. pls, maps.

ELLIOT, Sir HENRY MIERS. The history of India, as told by its own historians. Edited from the posthumous papers of Sir Henry Miers Elliot by J. Dowson. 8 vols. London, Hertford (printed), 1867-77. **2031**

——The history of India as told by its own historians. Forming a sequel to Sir Henry Miers Elliot's 'History of Muhammadan Empire of India' by Sir E.C. Baylen. London, W.H. Allen & Co., 1886. xx, 519p. **2032**

——Memoirs of the history, folk-lore and distribution of the races of the North Western Provinces of India; being an amplified edition of the original Supplemental Glossary of Indian Terms. Edited, revised and rearranged by J. Beames, etc. 2 vols. London, Hertford (printed), 1869. **2033**

ELLIOT, HENRY M., *ed.* A history of India as told by its own historians. London, Trubner, 1867-77. 8 vols. **2034**

Edited and continued by John Dowson, it was reprinted by Susil Gupta, Calcutta, in 31 volumes in 1952-59. This monumental compilation of translations by several historians, provides valuable source material on Indian history from the 9th to 19th century.

ELPHINSTONE, Hon. MOUNTSTUART. The history of India. London, J. Murray, 1841. 2 vols. **2035**

—— The history of India; the Hindu and Mohometan periods. With notes and additions by E.B. Cowell. 9th ed. London, J. Murray, 1911. xxxii, 767p. 3 maps. (2 folds). **2036**

EMERSON, GERTRUDE. The pageant of India's history. London, Longmans, Green & Co., 1948, Vol. I, xii, 408p. illus. maps. **2037**

GARRATT, GEOFFREY T., ed. The legacy of India. Introduction by Marquis of Zetland. London, Oxford University Press, 1937. Reprinted in 1962. xviii, 428p. **2038**

  A collection of writings from fifteen distinguished scholars both European and Indian. Indian writers are S.N. Das Gupta, R.P. Masani, S. Radhakrishnan, Abdul Qadir, and J.C. Ghosh.

GILDEMEISTER, JOHANN. Scriptorium orabum de rebus indicis loci et opuscula inedita. Ad codicum parisio-rium leidanorum gothanorum fidem recensuit et illustranit Ioannes Gildemeister. Fasciciculeis primus. Bonnae, H.B. Konig, 1838. 2p. 1., xiv p., 1l., 223, (83) p. **2039**

GOBLET D' ALVIELLA EUGENE FELICIAN ALBERT, comte. L'idee de Dieu d' apres l'a nthropologie et. l' historie; conferences faites en Angleterre sur l'instruction des administrateurs de la fondation. Hilbert. Bruxelles, C. Muquardt, 1892. xiv, 328p. **2040**

GORDON, D.H. The pre-historic background of Indian culture. Bombay, Bhulabhai Memorial Institute, 1958. **2041**

  An appraisal of Indian archaeology from the early stone age to the coming of the Iron Age.

HOLWELL, JOHN ZEPHANIAH. Evenemens histonques interessans-relatifs au provinces de Bengale & al' empire de l' Indostan. Only a joint la mythologie, la cosmogonie, les fetes le jennes des Gentous qui suivent le shastah une dissertation sm la metempsycose, dont on attribue foussement le dogme a Pythagou. ouverage composepar J.Z. Holwell Traduit de langlois 1-2 plie. Amsterdam, 1-2 plie, Amsterdam 2 plts. in iv fold pl. fold map. **2042**

HUNTER, Sir WILLIAM WILSON. A brief history of the Indian people. London, Trubner & Co., 1882. 2p. 1; 221p. front. (map). **2043**

——— India, by Sir William W. Hunter, and modern Persia, ed. by George M. Dutcher. (University ed.). New York, P.F. Coller & Son (1913), xvii, 421p. (i.e. 425) front. illus. (maps) pls. (1 col). 21 cm. (The history of nations; H.C. Wdge editor in chief, Vol. v). **2044**

JACKSON, A.V. WILLIAMS, *ed*. History of India. London, Grolier Society, 1906. 9 vols. **2045**

    Contents : Vol. 1, From the earliest times to the sixth century B.C. by Romesh Chunder Dutt; Vol. 2, From the sixth century B.C. to the Mohammadan conquest, including the invasion of Alexander the Great by Vincent A. Smith; Vol. 3, Medieval India from the Mohammadan conquest to the reign of Akbar the Great, by Stanley Lane-Poole; Vol. 4, From the reign of Akbar the Great to the fall of the Moghul empire, by Stanley Lane-Poole; Vol. 5. The Mohammedan period as described by its own historians, by Henry Miers Elliot; Vol. 6, From the first European settlement to the founding of the East India Company, by William Wilson Hunter; Vol. 7, The European struggle for Indian supremacy in the seventeenth century by William Wilson Hunter; Vol. 8, From the close of the seventeenth century to the present time, by Alfred Comyn. Lyall; Vol. 9, Historic account of India by foreign travellers, classic, oriental and occidental, by A.V. William Jackson. Connoisseur edition limited to 200 copies.

JOAD, CYRIL EDWIN MITCHINSON. The study of Indian civilization. London, Macmillan & Co., 1936. xii, 152p. **2046**

KEENE, HENRY GEORGE. History of India from the earliest times to the twentieth century, for the use of students and colleges. New and rev. ed. Edinburgh, J. Grant, 1915. 2 vols. maps. (2 fold). **2047**

LOW, CHARLES RATHBONE. History of the Indian Navy (1613-1863). London, R. Bentley and Son, 1877. 2 vols. **2048**

MAURICE, THOMAS. The history of Hindostan : its arts, and

its sciences, as connected with the history of the other great empires of Asia, during the most ancient periods of the world. With numerous illustrative engravings. By the author of Indian antiquities. London. Printed by W. Bulmer & Co., for the author (etc.) 1795-(99). 2 vols. plates. **2049**

MacCrindle, John Watson. Ancient India as described by Ptolemy. With Introduction. 1885. **2050**

——The invasion of India by Alexander the Great as described by Arrian, Q. Curtius. With an introduction. New edition. Westminster, A Constable & Co., 1896. xxxix, 432p. **2051**

Moreland, William Harrison. A short history of India by W.H. Moreland and Atul Chandra Chatterjee. 4th ed. London New York, Longmans Green, 1957. xii, 594p. maps. **2052**
> The present edition includes the story of the various forces which eventually led to the division of the Continent of India into two new countries.

Pargiter, Frederick E. Ancient historical tradition. London, Oxford University Press, 1922. viii, 368p. **2053**
> "Discusses the Indian historical tradition as obtained from the results of an examination of Puranic, Epic, Rigvedic and Vedic literature."

Payne, Christopher Harrison. Scenes and characters from Indian history as described in the works of some old masters. London, Oxford University Press, 1925. ix, 251p. **2054**
> Compiled and edited with historical and explanatory notes, it is based on the eyewitness accounts on India.

Philips, Cyril H., *ed.* Historians of India, Pakistan and Ceylon. London, Oxford University Press, 1961. **2055**
> The book provides a useful assessment of assumptions and points of view used in the writing of South Asian history from earliest times to the present.

Powell-Price, John Cadwgan. A history of India. London, New York, T. Nelson, 1955. xv. 679p. illus. ports. map. **2056**

Rawlinson, Hugh G. India : a short cultural history. New York, F.A. Praeger, 1952. xiv, 452p. **2057**
> A brief history of aesthetic and cultural achievements of India.

—— Indian historical studies. London, Longmans, Green &

900 History

Co., 1913. xv, 229p. illus. maps. **2058**
"Gives a glimpse of India in nearly any epoch of her history by taking a leading figure of the period and attempting an estimate of her achievements'.

RAWLINSON, HUGH G. Makers of India. London, Oxford University Press, 1942. ii, 78p. (Living names series). **2059**
Contents : Asoka, Harsha, Akbar, Shivaji, Ranjit Singh, Saiyed Ahmad Khan, Mahatma Gandhi.

RUBEN, WALTER. Einfuhrung in die Indien kunck; ein Uberblick ulur die historische Entwickberg Indiens. Berlin, Deutscher Verlag der Wissenschaften, 1954. 390p. illus. (G) **2060**

—— Indien gestern und heute. Berlin, Aufbau-Verlag, 1953. 126p. illus. **2061**

SELIMAN, ROGER RAYMOND. An outline atlas of Eastern history. London, E. Arnold, 1954. 68p. (p. 5-56 maps). **2062**

SEWELL, ROBERT. Indian chronolography; an extension of the "Indian Calendar" with working examples. London, G. Allen and Company, ltd., 1912. xii, 187. (1) p. incl. tables. **2063**

SHAFER, ROBERT. Ethnography of ancient India. Weisbaden, Otto Harrassowitz, 1954. **2064**

SIHOMBING, O.D.P. India, sedjorah dan Kebudaj. Bandung, W. Van Hoeve, 1953. 108p. illus. **2065**

SMITH, GEORGE. The conversion of India, from Pantaenus to the present time, A.D. 193-1893. With illustrations. New York, Chicago (etc.) Fleming H. Revell Company, 1894. 2p. 1., (vii)-xvi, (3), 258p. fold pls. **2066**

SMITH, VINCENT ARTHUR. The Oxford history of India. 3rd ed. Edited by Percival Spear. Pt. 1 rev. by Mortimer Wheeler and A.L. Basham; Pt. 2 rev. by J.B. Harrison, Pt. 3 rewritten by Percival Spear. Oxford, Clarendon Press, 1958. xiii, 898p. illus. ports. maps. **2067**

——The Oxford stndent's history of India. Oxford, Clarendon Press, 1908. 254p. 1 1., incl. front. illus. ports. 7 fold. maps. **2068**

SPEAR, PERCIVAL. India: A modern history. Ann Arbor, University of Michigan, 1961. x, 491p. **2069**
A brief survey of the history of India from earliest times to the present day.

STAMP, LAURENCE DUDLEY. Asia: a regional and economic geography. Revised ed. New York, E.P. Dutton & Co., Inc., (1936). xxi, 704p. incl. front. illus. (map) diagrs. **2070**

STEWART, CHARLES. The history of Bengal from the first Mohammedan invasion until the virtual conquest of that country by the English, A.D. 1757. 2nd ed. Calcutta, Bangabashi Office, 1910. iv, 596, xxxiip. **2071**

STOCKQUELER, JOACHIM HEYWARD. India: its history, climate, productions, and field sports; with notices of European life and manners, and of the various travelling routes. 8th thousand. London, G. Routledge and Co., 1854. viii, 207, (1)p. front., pls. **2072**

TAYLOR, MEADOWS. A student manual of the history of India from the earliest period to the present. 2nd ed. London, Longmans, Green & Co., 1871. xix (1) 884p. fold maps. col. plans. **2073**

TOWNSEND, MEREDITH WHITE. Asia and Europe, studies presenting the conclusions formed by the author in a long life devoted to the subject of the relations between Asia and Europe. New York, G.P., Putnam's Sons. London, A. Constable & Co., ltd., 1901. vii, 388p. **2074**

WABY, ADOLF. A peasant of India. London, Constable & Co., 1927. x, 556p. **2075**

———An account of history of India from pre-historic times to 1707.

WELPERT. STANLEY. India. New York, Prentice, 1965. 178p. **2076**

WHEELER, JAMES TALBOYS. A short history of India and of the frontier states of Afghanistan, Nepal and Burma. London, Macmillan & Co., 1884, xiv, 744p. **2077**

———The history of India from the earliest ages. London, N. Trubner & Co., 18 v. in fronts. maps. **2078**

YOUNGHUSBAND, Sir FRANCIS EDWARD. The coming country, a pre-vision by Sir Francis Younghusband. New York, E.P. Dutton & Co., 1929. x, 309p. **2079**

(ii) History—Ancient

BARNETT, LIONEL DAVID. Antiquities of India. London, Philip Lee Warner, 1913. 306p. **2080**

BENDALL, CECIL. A journey of literary and archaeological research in Nepal and Northern India, during the winter of 1884-5. Cambridge University Press, 1886. xii,100p. **2081**

BROWN, C.J. The coins of India. London, Oxford University Press, 1922. 120p. pls. index. (The heritage of India series). **2082**

    A valuable source book containing history of coinage in India from the remote past to 1857.

BROWN, J. COGGIN. Catalogue raisonne' of the prehistoric antiquities in the Indian Museum at Calcutta, Simla, Govt. Central Press, 1917. iii, 155p. (Archaeological Survey of India, ed. by John Marshall). **2083**

BURGESS, JAMES. Lists of the antiquarian remains in the Bombay Presidency, with appendix. Bombay, Miscell. Publications, no. 114, 1885. ix, 340p. **2084**

——Notes on the Amaravati Stupa. Madras, Archaeological Survey, 1882. 57p. xvii pl. **2085**

CHILDE, VERE GORDON. The Aryans; a study of Indo-European origins. London, K. Paul, Trench, Trubner & Co., ltd., 1926. xiiip. 2 1, (3)-221p. illus. viiipl. double map. (Half-title: The history of civilization (Prehistory and antiquity). **2086**

——New light on the most ancient East; The oriental prelude to European prehistory. London, K. Paul, Trench, Trubner & Co., ltd., 1934. xx, 326 (1)p. illus. (incl. map. plans) xxxii pls. **2087**

CRAWFORD, JOHN. History of the Indian archipelago. Edinburgh, Archibald Constable & Co., 1820., 3 vols. **2088**

CUMMING, Sir JOHN GHEST AND OTHERS. Revealing India's past; a cooperative record of archaeological conservation and exploration in India and beyond. London, The Indian Society, 1939. xx, 374p. front. illus. pls. ports. fold map. **2089**

DAVIDS, THOMAS W. RHYS. Buddhist India, Calcutta, Susil Gupta, 1951. 6th ed. xv, 322p. **2090**

    Originally published in 1903, it provides a brief introduction to the society, religion and literature of the Buddhist

Sources of Indian Civilization

period and the Mauryan Empire, C. 563-183 B.C.

DE GOLISH, VITOLD, AND OTHERS. Primitive India. New York, Dutton, 1954. 51p. and pls. **2091**

This book presents, through eighty fine photographs in colour and in black and white, and a short descriptive text, an account of four primitive Indian tribes: the Todas, the Gadabas, the Bondos, and the Kainis.

DREKMEIER, CHARLES. Kingship and community in early India. California, Stanford, 1962. 369p. **2092**

DURANT, WILL. The story of civilization: I, Our Oriental heritage. New York, Simon and Schuster, 1954. 1049p. **2093**

A history of civilization in the Near and Far East, including India, from the beginnings to the present day.

EGGERMONT, PIERRE HERMAN LEONARD. The chronology of the reign of Asoka Moriya; a comparison of the data of the Asoka inscriptions and the data of the tradition. Leiden, E.J. Brill, 1956. x, 222p. tab. **2094**

FAIRSERVIS, WALTER ASHLLN. The roots of ancient India; the archaeology of early Indian civilization: drawing by Jan Fairservis. New York, Macmillan, 1971. xxv, 482p. **2095**

FERGUSSON JAMES. Alexander the third, King of Scotland. London, A. Maclehose & Co., 1937. xiv, 199 (1) p. front. **2096**

FICK, RICHARD. The social organization of Northeast India in Buddha's time. Translated from the German by S.K. Mitra. Calcutta, University of Calcutta, 1930. xvii, 365p. **2097**

A standard work based on Pali texts.

FILLIOZAT, JEAN. Political history of India. Translations from the French by P. Spratt. Calcutta, Susil Gupta, 1957 viii, 199p. **2098**

A brief history of political events and personages from the remote past to the 7th century A.D.

FRANCKLIN, WILLIAM. Inquiry concerning the site of ancient Palibothra conjectured to lie within the limits of the modern district of Bhagalpur, according to researches made on the spot in 1811 and 1812. London, Black and Co., 1815-17. 2 vols. pls. (party fold). maps (partly fold). **2099**

GOBLET D' ALVIELLA, EUGENE FELICIEN ALBERT, *comte*. Ce que l' Inde a la Grece; des influences classiques dans la civilization de l' Inde, per le comte Goblet d' Alviella. Paris, E. Lerowx, 1897. vi, (3), 200p. illus. (F). **2100**

GHIRSHMAN, R. Recherches Archaeologiques et Historiques sur les Kouchars Le Caire, 1946. xiv, 232p. Liv pl. fold. (F). **2101**

KAEGI, ADOLF. Life in ancient India. Calcutta, Susil Gupta, 1950. **2102**

    Translated from the German by R. Arrowsmith, it gives a vivid account of the religious ideas prevailing in India in Vedic age.

KEENE, HENRY GEORGE. History of India from the earliest times to the end of the nineteeth century, for the use of students and colleges. New and rev. ed. Edinburgh, J. Grant, 1906. 2 vols. illus. 2 fold maps, tab. **2103**

    First edition printed in 1893.

LANGLES, LOUIS MATHIEU. Monuments anciens et modernes de l' Hindoustan, decrits sous le double rapport archaelogique (1) et. pittoresque; precedes dium discours sur la religion, la legislation et les moeurs des Hindous, d' une notice geographique, et d' une notice historique de l' Inde. Par L Langles. La gravoure dirigee par A. Boudeville. Paris, Chez A. Bouderville (etc.), 1817. 2 vols. in 1. 74 pl. (incl. plans) 2 maps. (F) **2104**

LASSEN, CHRISTIAN. Points in the history of the Greek and Indo-Scythian kings in Bactria, Cabul and India as illustrated by deciphering the ancient legends on their coins; tr. from the German of Professor Lassen. By T. (i.e. H) H. Edw. Roeer and the translation ed. by Henry Torrens. Calcutta, Bishop's College Press, 1840. 2p. 1; 185p. 4 pls. **2105**

LEEUW, J. E. VAN. LOHUIZEN DE. The 'Scythian' period; an approach to the history, art, epigraphy and palaeography of North India from the 1st century B.C. to the 3rd century A.D., etc. Leiden, E.J. Brill, 1949. x, 435p. xl p. **2106**

―― The 'Scythian period'. Leiden, E.J. Brill, 1949. **2107**

LEVI, SYLVAIN & OTHERS. Pre-Aryan and pre-Dravidian in India. By Sylvain Levi, Jean Przybiski and Jules Bloch. Translated from French by Prabodh Chandra Bagchi. Calcutta., the University, 1929. xxxv, 184p. (F). **2108**

MACCRINDLE, JOHN WATSON, ed. & tr. Ancient India as described by Megasthenes and Arrian. 2nd ed. Calcutta, Chuckervertty, Chatterjee & Co., 1926, xiv, 277p. maps. **2109**

"A translation of the fragments of the *Indika* of Megasthenes collected by Dr. Schwonbeck and the first part of the *Indika* of Arrian. Reprinted (with additions) from the *Indian Antiquary*, 1876-77."

MACCRINDLE, JOHN WATSON, *ed.* & *tr.* Ancient India as described in classical literature. Westminster, Archibald Constable & Co., 1901. xxi, 226p. **2110**

"The work is a collection of Greek, and Latin texts relating to India extracted from Herodotus, Strabo, Diodorus and others. *tr.* and copiously annotated."

MCCRINDLE, JOHN W. The invasion of India by Alexander the Great. Westminster, A. Constable, 1896. 2nd ed. **2111**

An account of Alexander's invasion of India. It contains an introduction, and translations from Arrian and the other classical authors.

———, *tr.* Topographia Christiana. London, Hakluyt Society, 1897. **2112**

A translation of an account by an Egyptian merchant who visited the Malabar Coast in the sixth century.

MACKAY, ERNEST, J.H. Excavations at Chanhu-Daro by the American School of Indic and Iranian studies and the Museum of Fine Arts, Boston: season 1935-36. (with 10 pls). (*In* Smithsonian institution. Annual report, 1937. Washington, 1938. p. 469-478. illus. (map). **2113**

"Reprinted from the Bulletin of the Museum of Fine Arts, Vol. 34, no. 205, Boston, October 1936."

——— Chanhu-Daro excavations. New Havan, American Oriental Society, 1943. xv, 338p. **2114**

A report of investigations conducted during 1935-36 at one of the major sites of the Indus Valley Civilization.

——— Further excavation at Mohenjo Daro; being an official account of archaeological excavations at Mohenjo-daro carried out by the Government of India between the years 1927 and 1931. Delhi, Manager of Publications, 1938. 2 vols. illus. cxlvi pl. **2115**

——— The Indus civilization. London, L. Dickson and Thompson, ltd., (1935). viii, (2), 202p. 2 l., (205)-210p. illus. **2116**

MANLEY, FRANK P. The Manley collection stone age tools. With topographical and other notes by Frank P. Manley. Delhi, Manager of Publications, 1942. vi, 90p. pls. (Memoirs: Archaeological Survey of India, 68). **2117**

MARSHALL, Sir JOHN HURBERT. A guide to Taxila. Cambridge, Cambridge University Press, 1961. viii, 124p. xxix pl. First published in 1918. **2118**

A popular account of the findings of twenty two years of archaeological research on the ancient site of Taxila.

———ed. Mohenjo Daro and the Indus civilization; being an official account of archaeological excavations at Mohenjodaro carried out by the Government of India between the years 1922 and 1927 ; with plan and map in colours and 164 plates in collotype. London, A. Probsthain, 1931. 3 vols. illus. clxiv pl. fold. maps. **2119**

An account of the archaeological excavation of Mohenjo-Daro carried out by the Government of India between 1922 and 1927.

MASSON-OURSEL, PAUL, WILLAM-GRABOWSKA, AND P. STERN. Ancient India and Indian civilization. London, Kegan Paul, Trench, Trubner, 1934. xxiv, 435p. (Indian records series) **2120**

A concise account of the aesthetic, intellectual and social aspects of ancient India.

MAURICE, THOMAS. A dissertation on the oriental trinities: extracted from the fourth and fifth volumes of Indian antiquities. Illustrated with engravings. London, Printed for the author, by C. and W. Galabin and sold by J. White, 1801. 2p. 1. (17). 460p. 1 1 fold. front. illus. 5 fold. pl. **2121**

———Indian antiquities: or, Dissertations, relative to the ancient geographical divisions, the pure system of primeval theology : grand code of civil laws, the original form of government, the widely extended commerce, and the various profound literature of Hindostan: compared throughout with the religion, laws, government, and literature of Persia, Egypt and Greece, the whole intended as introductory to the history of Hindustan, upon a comprehensive scale. London, the author,

1800-01. 7 vols. parts illus. plates (part fold.) fold map. **2122**

MAURICE, THOMAS. The modern history of Hindostan: comprehending that of the Greek empire of Bactria and other great Asiatic kingdoms, bordering on its Western frontier. Commencing at the period of the death of Alexander and intended to be brought down to the close of eighteenth century. London, for the author by W. Bulmer & Co., (etc.), 1802-3, 2 vols. fold. map. **2123**

NICKAM, N.A., *ed.* The edicts of Asoka. Chicago, University of Chicago, 1959. 69p. **2124**

OPPERT, GUSTAV SALOMON. On the original inhabitants of Bharata Versa or India. Westminster, A. Constable & Co., Leipzig, O. Harrassowitz, 1893. xv, 711p. **2125**

PARGITER, FREDERICK EDEN. Ancient Indian historical tradition. London, Humphrey Milford, Oxford University Press, 1922. xiii, 368p. **2126**

> "Discusses the Indian historical tradition as obtained from the results of an examination of Puranic, Epic, Rigvedic, and Vedic literature."

PIGGOTT, STUART. Prehistoric India, to 1000 B.C. London, Penguin Books, 1950. 293p. 8 pls. (Pelican books, No. 205).
2127

—— Some ancient cities of India. Bombay, Geoffrey Cumberlege, Oxford University Press, 1945. vi, 102p. **2128**

> "Gives a background of reliable knowledge concerning India's ancient cities and monuments."

POUSSIN, L. DE LA VALLE'E. Dynasties et Historire de l' Inde depuis Kanishka jusque' aux invasions musulmanes. Paris, E. de Boccard, 1935. 396p. fold. maps. **2129**

—— Indo-Europe'ens et Indo-Iraniens. Paris, E. de Boccard, 1924. 3p. 1., 345p. (F). **2130**

—— L' Inde aux Temps des Mauryas et des barbares, Grecs Scythes, Parthes et Yue-tchi. Paris, E. de Boccard, 1930. 376p. 2 1. fold. map. (F). **2131**

PRZYLUSKI, JEAN, *tr.* La Legende de l' Empereur Acoka dans les textes indiens et chinois, Paris. xv, 459p. (F). **2132**

RAPSON, EDWARD JAMES. Ancient India from the earliest times to the first century A.D. Cambridge. The University Press,

900 History

1914. viii, 199p. illus. **2133**
    It is the volume First of the *Cambridge History of India* and covers the period from earliest times to the middle of the first century, A.D. A good reference book.

RAWLINSON, HUGH GEORGE. India: a short cultural history. Edited by C.G. Seligman. New York, Appleton Century, 1938. xiv, 452p. illus. map. **2134**
    An outline, for the general reader, of the cultural history of the country from the time of the Indus valley civilization of 2500 B.C. to the present day. The British period is only lightly touched upon; the author's main concern is with the people themselves.

RENOU, LOUIS. The civilization of ancient India. Translated by P. Spratt from the French. Calcutta, Susil Gupta, 1959. **2135**
    A scholarly survey of India's cultural history from the remote past to the middle of the 7th century.

SACHAV, EDWARD C., *ed*. Alberuni's India. English edition with notes and indices by Edward C. Sachav. London, Kegan Paul, Trench, Trubner & Co., 1910. 2 vols. **2136**
    "An account of the religious, philosophy, literature, geography, chronology, astronomy, customs, laws and astrology of India about A.D. 1030."—*t.p.*

SAINT-HILAIRE, J. BARTHELOMY. Hiouen-Thsang in India. Translations from the French by Laura Enser. Calcutta, Susil Gupta, 1952. **2137**
    An account of Hiouen-Thsang's travels in India, during the 7th century.

SEWELL, ROBERT. A forgotten empire (Vijayanagar), a contribution to the history of India. London, S. Sonnenschein & Co., ltd., 1900. lp. l., xxii, 427p. front., pls. maps. plan. 2 facsim. 2nd ed. published in 1924. **2138**
    "Translation of the 'Chronica dos ries de Bisanga', written by Domingos Paes and Fernao Nunes about 1520 and 1535 respectively, with historical introduction."

——The historical inscriptions of southern India (collected till 1923) and outlines of political history. Published under orders of government, by the University of Madras; edited for the University by S. Krishna Swami Aiyangar, Madras, Printed at

Sources of Indian Civilization

the Diocesan Press, 1932, vi p. 4 1., 451, (1)p. incl. geneal. tab. fold map. (Half title page: Madras University historical series, no. v). **2139**

SEWELL, ROBERT. Lists of antiquarian remains in the presidency of Madras. Comp. under the orders of Government. Madras, Printed by E. Keys, at the Government Press, 1882. xii, 325, lxiip. (Archaeological Survey of Southern India. Reports. Old series, vol. 1). **2140**

    Archaeological Survey of Southern India. Reports. New series, vol. 2.

    Aachaeological Survey of India. Reports. New Imperial series, vol. vii.

    On cover: lists of antiquities, Madras, vol. 1.

—— Lists of inscriptions, and sketch of the dynasties of southern India. Compiled under the orders of government. Madras, Printed by E. Keys at the Government Press, 1884. xi, 297p. incl. tab. (Half title page: Archaeological Survey of Southern India. Reports: Old series, vol. II). **2141**

    Archaeological Survey of India. Reports. New Imperial series, vol. viii. On cover: Lists of antiquities, Madras, vol. II.

—— Report on the Amaravati tope, and excavations on its site in 1877. Printed by order of the Secretary of State for India in Council. London, Printed by G.E. Eyre and W. Spottiswoode, 1880. 69, (1)p. iv, pl. (part fold, incl. plans). **2142**

    "A report to the Government of Madras."

—— A sketch of the dynasties of southern India. Comp. under the orders of government. Madras, Printed by E. Keys, 1883. vi, 132p. **2143**

    "The contents of this volume are extracted from a larger work, vol. II of the Archaeological Survey Series of Southern India."—*Preface*

SLATER, GILBERT, The Dravidian element in the Indian culture. Foreword by H.J. Fleure. London, Ernest Beno, 1924. 192p. **2144**

    Dwells on the origin of Dravidian civilization and the extent of the Dravidian contribution to the totality of Indian culture.

900 History

SMITH, VINCENT A. Asoka, the Buddhist Emperor of India. Delhi, S. Chand & Co., 1957. rev. ed. 278p. **2145**
    First published in 1901, it is a standard account of the Mauryan ruler and his times.

SMITH, VINCENT ARTHUR. The early history of India from 600 B.C. to the Muhammadan conquest, including the invasion of Alexander the Great. 4th ed., rev. by S.M. Edwards. Oxford, The Clarendon Press, 1924. x, (2), 535, (1)p. front. pls. port. plans. maps. (part fold). geneal. tab. **2146**

—— General index to the reports of the Archaeological Survey of India, volumes I to XXIII, published under the superintendence of Major-General Sir A. Cunningham. With a glossary and general table of contents. Calcutta, printed by the Superintendent of Government printing, India, 1887. xviiip. 1.1, 216p. (Archaeological Survey of India. Reports. Old series. Index). **2147**

—— The Oxford history of India, from the earliest times to the end of 1911. 2nd ed., rev. and continued to 1928, by S.M. Edwards. Oxford, the Clarendon Press, 1928. 7p. 1., xxiv, 814p. front., illus. fold. map. **2148**

STEIN, Sir M.A., tr. Kalhana's Rajatarangini, a chronicle of the kings of Kashmir. Westminster, Archibald Constable & Co., 1900. 2 vols. **2149**

STEWART, CHARLES. The history of Bengal from the first Mohammadan invasion until the virtual conquest of that country by the English A.D. 1757. London, Broxbourne (printed), 1813. **2150**

TAKAKUSU, J., tr. A record of the Buddhist religion as practised in India and the Maley Archipelago. Oxford, Clarendon Press, 1896. **2151**
    An account by Chinese pilgrim I Tsing who travelled in the area from A.D. 671-695.

TARN, WILLIAM W. The Greeks in Bactria and India. Cambridge, Cambridge University Press, 1951. xxiii, 539p. maps. **2152**
    An account of Greek kingdoms in India from 206 B.C. to the first half of the second century B.C.

TOD, JAMES. Annals and antiquities of Rajasthan, Or the Central and Western Rajpoot states of India. Popular edition with a preface by Douglas Sladen. London, G. Routledge & Sons, limited, New York, E.P. Dutton & Co., (1914). 2 vols. fold. map. fold. tab. **2153**

    First published in 1829, this book is considered to be a classic and contains useful information about the culture and history of Rajasthan.

TORRENS, HENRY WHITELOCK. Points in the history of the Greek and Indo-Scythian kings in Bactria, Cabul and India as illustrated by decyphering the ancient legends on their coins. Translated by T.H.E. Rocer, Edited by H. Torrents. Calcutta, 1840. **2154**

TOWNSEND, MEREDITH WHITE. Asia and Europe, studies presenting the conclusions formed by the author in a long life devoted to the subject of the relations between Asia and Europe. 3rd ed. London, A. Constable & Co., ltd., 1905. xxiv, 404p. **2155**

WADDELL, LAURENCE AUSTINE. Discovery of the exact site of Asoka in classic capital of Pataliputra, the Palibothra of the Greeks and description of the superficial remains. Calcutta, The Bengal Secretariat Press, 1892. lp. 1 29p. iv pl. (incl. map. fold plan). **2156**

—— The Indo-Sumerian seals deciphered discovering Sumerians of Indus valley as Phoenicians, Barats, Goths and famous Vedic Aryans, 3100-2300 B.C. London, Luzac & Co., 195. xxiv, 146p. **2157**

—— Report on the excavations at Patliputra (Patna), the Palibothra of the Greeks. Calcutta, Bengal Secretariat Press, 1903. 2p. 1., 83p. iv pl. (incl. front. facsim) fold map. iv plans. **2158**

WATTERS, THOMAS. On Yuan Chwang's travels in India, 629-645 A.D. London, Royal Asiatic Society, 1904-05. 2 vols. 2 fold. maps. **2159**

WHEELER, JAMES TALBOYS. A short history of India and the frontier states of Afghanistan, Nepal and Burma. London; and New York, Macmillan & Co., 1894. xivp. 11, 744p. 13 maps (part fold). **2160**

WHEELER, Sir ROBERT ERIC MORTIMER. Early India and Pakistan: to Ashoka. New York, Praeger, 1959. 241p. illus. (Ancient peoples and places, vol. 12). **2161**

WHEELER, Sir ROBERT ERIC MORTIMER. Indus civilization. Cambridge University Press, 1953. xi, 98p. xxiv pl). **2162**
    It is the supplement to the *Cambridge History of India.*

WILSON, CHARLES ROBERT. List of inscriptions on tombs or monuments in Bengal, possessing historical or archaeological interest, 1896. xvi, 248p. folio. (Indian monumental inscriptions, v. 1). **2163**

(iii) History—Muslim Period

BADAUNI, ABDUL QADIR. Muntekhab-ut-Tawarikh. Calcutta, Royal Asiatic Society of Bengal, 1884-1925. 3 vols. Translated from original Persian: Vol. 1 by George S.A. Ranking; Vol. II by W.H. Lowe; Vol. III by Wolseley Haig. **2164**
    This valuable history provides an account of Akbar's reign.

BENDREY, V.S. A study of Muslim inscriptions. Bombay, Karnatak Publishing House, 1944, xi, 197p. **2165**
    "With special reference to the inscriptions published in the Epigraphis Indo-Moslemica, 1907. 1938, together with summaries of inscriptions chronologically arranged."—*t.p.*
    Tables of inscriptions recorded in the Epigraphia Indo-Moslemica, 1907-38 at the end.

——Tarikh-i-Ilahi: Poona, G.B. Nare, 1933. vii, 46p. **2166**
    "A Paper on the Ilahi Era, read at the First Bombay Historical Congress, 1933."

BEVERIDGE, ANNETTE S. Life and memoirs of Gulbadan Begam. London, Royal Asiatic Society, 1902. **2167**
    Gulbadan Begam was a daughter of the Mughal Emperor, Babur. She describes the life at the Mughal court in those days. Also relates the plight of her brother Humayun, son of Babur.

——Memoirs of Babur, emperor of India, first of the great Mughuls. London, Arthur L. Humphreys, 1909. xv, 254p. pl. map. **2168**

"An abridgement with an introduction, supplementary notes and some account of his successors, by F.G. Dalbot."—*t.p.* It is based on the translation into English by John Leyden & William Erskine, 1826.

BEVERIDGE, ANNETTE SUSANNAH, *tr.* The Babur-nama in English (Memoirs of Babur) translated from the original Turki text by Annette Susannah Beveridge. London, Luzac & Co., 1921. 2 vols. **2169**

BEVERIDGE, H., *tr.* Memoirs of Jahangir. London, Royal Asiatic Society, 1909-1914. **2170**

> A translation of the *Tuzuk-i Jahangiri* it is an account of Jahangir's personal life and his reign that began in 1605 and ended in 1627.

BINYON, LAURENCE. Akbar. London, Thomas Nelson and Sons, 1939. 165p. (Short biographies, 21). **2171**

BLAKISTON, J.F. The Jama Masjid at Badaun and other buildings in the United Provinces. Calcutta, Govt. of India Central Publication Branch, 1926. vii, 9. iip. pls. (Memoirs: Archaeological Survey of India, 19). **2172**

BLOCHMANN, H., *tr.* Ain-i-Akbari by Abul Fazl-i-Allami. Vol. I first published in 1873, translated from the original Persian by H. Blochmann; 2nd ed. rev. and ed. by D.C. Phillot. Vols. 2-3, translated by H.S. Jarrett, rev. corrected and further annotated by Jadunath Sarkar. Calcutta, Royal Asiatic Society, 1927-1949. 3 vols. **2173**

BRIGGS, J., *tr.* History of the rise of Muhammadan power in India. Calcutta, Susil Gupta, 1958. **2174**

> It is a translation of Firishta's history entitled: *Tarikh-i-Firishta* or *Gulshan-i-Ibrahimi.* The history was completed by Firishta in the early 17th century.

CALDECOTT, R.M. Life of Baber: Emperor of Hindustan. London, Darling, 1844. xxii, 339p. **2175**

CATROU, FRACOIS. History of the Mogul dynasty in India. Tr. from the French, accompanied with a detailed description of the court and harem, military strength, resources, polity, and character of the Mogul Government, at the epoch when the glory of the dynasty was in its zenith. Bhowanipur (Calcutta), Sreenath Benerjee, 1908. xx, 324p. (F). **2176**

900 History

A history of the Mughal dynasty from its foundation by Tamerlane in the year 1399, to the accession of Aurangzeb in the year 1657. The work was first published at the Hague in 1708. The first translation in English was published in London in 1826.

EDWARDS, STEPHEN M. Babur, diarist and despot. London, A.M. Philpot, 1926. 138p. pls. **2177**

Babur's life and work, an estimate.

EDWARDS, STEPHEN M. and H.L.O. GARRETT. Mughal rule in India. London, Oxford University Press, 1930. Reprinted by S. Chand & Co., New Delhi, 1956. viii, 374p. pls. **2178**

A standard work on the rise and fall of Mughal empire in India.

ELLIOT, Sir HENRY MIERS. Babar and Humayun. 2nd ed. by John Dawson. Calcutta, Susil Gupta, 1953. 168p. **2179**

——Bibliographical index to the historians of Muhammadan India. vol. 1. Calcutta and London, 1849. No more published. **2180**

ELLIOT, Sir HENRY MIERS and DOWSON, JOHN, *eds*. The history of India, as told by its own historians: the Muhammadan period; the posthumous papers of Sir H.M. Elliot. Edited by John Dowson. 2nd ed. Calcutta, Susil Gupta, 1958. 161p. (Studies in Indian history, pt. 6). **2181**

Contents: Subuktagin by Abul Fazal Al Baihaki, 1952, xii, 144p.; Autobiography of Timur, 1952, viii, 149p; Sher Shah by Abbas Khan, 1952, 157p.; Memoirs of Jahangir, 1952, viii, 256p; Akbar by Nijamuddin Ahmed, 1952, 2 vols; Aurangzeb by Khafi Khan, 1952, xvi, 172p.; Later Moghuls by Khafi Khan, 1952, xxii, 142p.; Ghaznivide Ghor and Slave dynasties or Tabakati Nasiri of Minhajus Siraj, 1953, vii, 155p.; Ghaznivide, Ghor and Slave dynasties of Uji; Nizami Asir, Baizavi and Juwairi, 1953, vii, 139p.; History of Ghazni, 1953, vi, 183p.; Firoz Shah, etc.

These volumes were originally published as part of Elliot and Dowson's *History of India as told by its own historians*, in 1867-1877.

ERSKINE, WILLIAM. A history of India under the two first sovereigns of the house of Taimur, Baber and Humayun. London, Longman, Brown, Green and Longmans, 1854. 2 vols. **2182**

FOSTER, WILLIAM. Early travels in India, 1583-1619. London, Humphrey Milford, Oxford University Press, 1921. xiv, 351p. **2183**

"Contains the narrative of seven Englishmen who travelled in Northern and Western India during the reign of Akbar and Jahangir."

—— The embassy of Sir Thomas Roe to the court of the Great Moghul, 1615-1619, as narrated in his journal and correspondence. Edited from contemporary records. London, The Hakluyt Society, 1909. 2 vols. **2184**

FRANCKLIN, W. The history of the reign of Shah Aulum, the present Emperor of Hindustan. Allahabad, Panini Office, 1934. vi, 259p. **2185**

"Contains the transaction of the court of Delhi, and neighbouring state, during a period of thirty-six years; interspersed with geographical and topographical observations on several of the principal cities of Hindustan"—*t.p.*

GIBB, H.A.R. *tr.* and *ed. Rehla of Ibn Battuta:* Travels in Asia and Africa, 1324-1354. Translated from Arabic, selected and edited by H.A.R. Gibb, with an introduction. London, George, Routledge & Sons, 1929. vii, 398p. (The Broadway travellers), edited by Sir Denisson Ross and Eileen Power). **2186**

GRENARD, FERNAND. Baber, first of the Moguls. tr. by Homer White and Richard Glaenzer. London, Butterworth, 1931. 253p. illus. **2187**

GUERREFIRO, FERNAO. Jahangir and the Jesuits. Tr. by C.H. Payne. London, George Routledge & Sons, 1930. xxv, 287p. **2188**

HARDY, P. Historians of medieval India: studies in Indo-Muslim historical writing. London, Luzac, 1960. v, 146p. **2189**

IBN BATUTA. Ibn Batuta's travels. Translated by H.A.R. Gibb. London, Hakluyt Society, 1929-62. vii, 398p. **2190**

An abridged translation of the *Kitab-ur-Rahlah*, which describes conditions of India in 14th century.

IBN HASAN. The Central structure of the Mughal Empire. London, Oxford University Press, 1936. x, 398p. **2191**

900 History

An account of the active part played by the Mughal emperors in the administration of the state and the efforts to achieve their ideals of kingship by means of an organized administrative machinery.

IRAN SOCIETY, Calcutta. Al-Biruni commemoration volume, A.H. 362-A.H. 1362. Calcutta, Iran Society, 1951. xxviii, 303p. **2192**

Contributed by leading Orientalists of England, U.S.A., Italy, the Netherlands, France, Iran and the Vatican to celebrate the millenary (Anno Hegirae) of Sheikh Abu Raihan Al-Biruni.

IRVINE, WILLIAM. The army of the Indian Moghuls. New Delhi, Eurasia Publishing House, 1962. vii, 324p. **2193**

First published in 1903 by Luzac, London, it is a standard work on the organization and administration of the Mughal army.

—— Later Mughals. Edited by Jadunath Sarkar. Calcutta, M.C. Sarkar, 1921-22. 2 vols. Vol. I, 1707-1720; Vol. II, 1719-1739. **2194**

A valuable study of the history of the later Mughals from 1707 to 1739.

IVANOV, VLADIMIR ALEKSIEEVICH. Ismaili tradition covering the rise of the Fatimids. Calcutta, Oxford University Press, 1942. xxii, 337p. (Islamic research association series, 10). **2195**

Attempts to collect, analyse and systematise the information contained in the genuine Ismaili literature concerning the history of the grand Shi'ite movement. Arabic text at the end.

KEENE, HENRY GEORGE. The fall of the Moghul empire; an historical essay, being a new edition of the Moghul empire from the death of Aurungzeb, with corrections and additions, a map, etc. London, W.H. Allen & Co., 1887. xvi, 299p. **2196**

——Hindustan under free lances, 1770-1820: sketches of military adventures in Hindustan during the period immediately preceding British occupation. London, Brown, 1907. xxxii, 238p. illus. maps. **2197**

——History of India from the earliest times to the present

day. London, Allen, 1893. 2 vols. **2198**
KEENE, HENRY GEORGE. Madhva Rao Sindhia, otherwise called Madhoji. Oxford Clarendon Press, 1891. 207p. (Rulers of India). **2199**
—— The Moghul empire; from the death of Aurangzeb to the overthrow of the Mahratta power. London, 1866. xv, 278p. **2200**
—— A sketch of the history of Hindustan, from the first Muslim conquest to the fall of the Mughol empire. London, W.H. Allen & Co., 1885. xxxv, 476p. **2201**
—— The Turks in India; critical chapters on the administration of that country by the Chugtai, Babar and his descendants. London, W.H. Allen & Co., 1879. 1., (v) - xvi, 255p. front. fold. map. **2202**
LAMB, HAROLD. Babur, the tiger, first of the Great Moguls. London, Hale, 1962. 224p. illus. **2203**
LANE-POOLE, STANLEY. Babur: Delhi, S. Chand & Co., 1962. 206p. **2204**

First published in 1899, by Oxford University Press, it is an account of Babur's life based mainly on Babur's memoirs.

LANE-POOLE, STANLEY, *ed.* Medieval India from contemporary sources. Bombay, K. & J. Cooper, 1920. 2nd ed. xviii, 499p. **2205**

A well-selected collection of brief extracts from Arabic and Persian chronicles and Eurpoean travellers' accounts from 1000 to 1764.

—— Medieval India under Mohammedan rule. Calcutta, Susil Gupta, 1951. xviii, 449p. **2206**

Originally published in 1903 is a useful introductory history about Muslim courts and Kings from 712 to 1764 (The history of the nations series).

LEYDEN, JOHN AND ERSKINE, WILLIAM, *trs.* Memoirs of Zehir-ud din Muhammed Babur, Emperor of Hindustan, written by himself in the Chaghatai Turki. Translated by John Leyden and William Erskine; annotated and revised by Lucas King. London, Milford. Oxford University Press, 1921. 2 vols. First published in 1826. **2207**

MACLAGAN, Sir, EDWARD D. The Jesuits and the Great Mogul. London, Burns, Oates and Washbourne, 1932. xxi, 433p. **2208**
    A critical study of the Jesuit missionaries and the Europeans at the Court of Jahangir in the early 17th century.

MANUCCI, NICCOLAO. The general history of the Mogol empire, from its foundation by Tamarlane, to the late Emperor Orangzeb. **2209**
    Extracted from the memoirs of N. Manouchi, by Father Francois Catrou. Calcutta, Bangabasi Office, 1907. xviii, 366p.

—— History of the Mogul dynasty in India, from its foundation by Tamerlane, in the year 1399, to the accession of Aurangzeb, in the year 1657. Translated from the French of Father Francois Catrou; founded on the memoirs of Signor Manouchi. Calcutta, Sreenath Banerjee 1908. xx, 324p. **2210**

—— A Pepys of Mogul India, 1653-1708. Translated by William Irvine. London, John Murray, 1613. xii, 310p. **2211**
    "An abridged edition of the *Storia do Mogor* of Niccolao Manucci," prepared by Margaret L. Irvine. The introduction comprises a note on N. Manucci, the man and author.

—— Storia do Mogor or Mogul India, 1653-1708. Translated with introduction and notes by William Irvine. London, John Murray, 1907-08. 4 vols. (The Indian texts series). **2212**

MAURICE, THOMAS. The fall of the Mogul, a tragedy, founded on an interesting portion of Indian history, and attempted partly on the Greek model. With other occasional poems. By the author of Indian Antiquities. London, printed for the author, by R. Taylor and Co., and sold by J. White, 1806 3p. l., xxi, (22)—153p. **2213**

MORELAND, WILLIAM HARRISON. From Akbar to Aurangzeb: a study in Indian economic history. London, Macmillan & Co., 1923. xiii, 364p. map. **2214**

—— India at the death of Akbar: an economic study. London, Macmillan & Co., 1920. xi, 328p. **2215**
    "Sketches the economic life of India at the opening of the

seventeenth century."

MORELAND, WILLIAM HARRISON, ed. Relations of Golconda in the early 17th century. London, Hakluyt Society, 1931. **2216**

    Describes the social and economic conditions of the Golconda Kingdom during the period from 1618 to 1622.

ORME, ROBERT. Historical fragments of the Mogul empire, of the Morattoes, and of the English concerns in Indostan; from the year M.D.C. LIX. Origin of the English establishment, and of the Company's trade, at Broach and Surat; and a general idea of the government and people of Indostan. To which is prefixed, an account of the life and writings of the author. London, printed for F. Wingrave, 1805. lp. l., lxvii, 472 (32)p. 2 port (incl. front). 3 fold. maps. **2217**

OSBORN, ROBERT DURIE. Islam under the Arabs. London, Longmans, Green & Co., 1876. xiip. 1l., 414p. **2218**

——— Islam under Khalifs of Baghdad. London, Seeley, Jackson & Halliday, 1878. xiiip. ii., 406p. **2219**

OWEN, SIDNEY J. The fall of the Mogul empire. Varanasi, Chowkhamba Sanskrit Series, 1960. xii, 271p. **2220**

    First published in 1912, it is a useful survey of factors affecting the decline of the Mughals during the period from 1657 to 1761.

POLIER, ANTOINE LOUIS HENRI. Shah Alam II and his court. Edited with an introduction, notes, and appendices by Pratul C. Gupta. Calcutta, S.C. Sarkar and Sons, 1947. viii, 116p. **2221**

    "A narrative of the transactions at the Court of Delhi from the year 1771 to the present time (1779)"—t.p. The author was a Swiss engineer in the service of the East India Company.

RANKING, GEORGE S.A., LOWE, W. AND HAIG, WOLSELEY. Muntakhabu-t-tawarikh. Translated from the original Persian.: Vol. I by George S.A. Ranking; Vol. II by W.H. Lowe: Vol. III—by Wolseley Haig. Calcutta, Royal Asiatic Society of Bengal, 1898-1925. 3 vols. **2222**

RENNELL, JAMES. Memoir of a map of Hindoostan; or, The Mogul empire; with an introduction, illustration of the geography and present division of that country and a map of the countries situated between the heads of the Indian rivers, and the Caspian Sea. To which is added an appendix containing an account of the Ganges and Burrampooter rivers. The 2nd ed. with very considerable additions and many corrections and a supplementary map, containing the geography of the countries contiguous to the head of the Indus. London, printed by W. Bulmer & Co. for the author, sold by G. Nicol (etc.) 1972. 2p. l., xviiip. 1 l., (xix). **2223**

RIDGWAY, R.T.I., *comp*. Pathans. Calcutta, Supdt. Government Printing, 1910. xi, 252p. (Handbooks for the Indian army). **2224**
Compiled under the orders of the Government of India.

ROSS, EDWARD DENISON. An index to the Arabic history of Gujarat, Zafar-ul-Walih bi Muzaffar wa atih, by Abdulla Muhammad Bin Omar al Makki, al-Asafi, Uluhkam. Being a list of persons and places connected with the history of the Muslims in India down to the beginning of the 17th century. London, J. Murray, for the Government of India, 1928. viii, 97p. **2225**

SCOTT, JONATHAN. Ferista's history of Dekkan, from the first Muhammedan conquests: (with) a continuation from other native writers (principally Mubarak Allah Iradat Khan, Wadhili) of the events in that part of India to the reduction of its last monarchs by the emperor Aulumgeer Aurungzebe; also the reigns of his successors to the present day; and the history of Bengal, from the accession of Aleverdee Khan to the year 1780 (chiefly from the Persian of Ghulam Husain Khan). In six parts. Translated by J. Scott Shrewsbury, 1794. 2 vols. **2226**

SMITH, VINCENT A. Akbar the Great Mogul, 1542-1605. Delhi, S. Chand & Co., 1958. xvi, 504p. **2227**
Originally published in 1919 by the Oxford University Press, it contains a detailed account of the Akbar's reign and covers the period from 1542 to 1604.

SPEAR, T.G. PERCIVAL. Twilight of the Mughuls. Cambridge, Cambridge University Press, 1951. x, 269p. **2228**
A study of the political and social conditions prevailing under the Mughal Empire between 1761 and 1857.

STEWART, CHARLES. The Tezkereh al Vakiah; or private memoirs of the Moghul Emperor Humayun. Translated by Charles Stewart, 1832. **2229**

THOMAS, EDWARD. The chronicles of the Pathan kings of Delhi, illustrated by coins, inscriptions and other antiquarian remains. London, Trubner & Co., 1871. xxivp. 11, 467p. front. (map) illus. vol. 1 pls. **2230**

———On the coins of the Pathan sultans of Hindustan. London, Printed by J. Wertheimer and Co., 1847. viii, 102, 5p. 11. 7 pl. fold tab. **2231**

THORBURN, PEPTIMUS. SMET. Bannu; or our Afghan frontier. London, Trubner & Co., 1876. xp. 11., 480p. front. (map). **2232**

THORNER, DANIEL. Feudalism in India. New Jersey, Princeton University Press, 1956. p. 133-150. **2233**

> On pages 133-150 of his book the author reviews the concept of feudalism as applied to the periods of Rajputs and the Muslim regimes.

WILLIAMS, L.F. RUSHBROOK. An empire builder of the sixteenth century. London, Longmans, Green & Co., 1918. xvi, 187p. illus. maps. Also published by S. Chand & Co., Delhi, in 1962. **2234**

> "A summary account of the political career of Zahir-ud-Din Muhammad, surnamed Babur, being the Allahabad University lectures for 1915-1916." -*t.p.*

(iv) Advent of Portuguese, Dutch, British and French

ALEXANDER, P.C. The Dutch in Malabar. Foreword by C.R. Reddy. Introduction by C.S. Srinivasachari. Annamalainagar, the University, 1946. xi, 217, (Annamalai University, historical series, 6). **2235**

ARBUTHNOT, Sir ALEXANDER JOHN. Lord Clive. The foundation of British rule in India. New York, Longman, 1899. v, xxi, ii, 318p. **2236**

AUBER, PETER. Rise and progress of the British power in India (with maps). London, W.H. Allen & Co., 1837. 2 vols. **2237**

BIDDULPH, JOHN. Dupleix. London, White, 1910. xvi, 186p. **2238**

BRUCE, JOHN. Annals of the Honourable East-India Company

from their establishment by the Charter of Queen Elizabeth, 1600 to the Union of London and English East India Companies, 1708. East India Company. 3 vols. **2239**

CAMBRIDGE, R.O., *comp*. An account of war in India between the English and French, on the coast of Caromandal, from the year, 1750-60. London, Jeffery, 1761. various pagination. **2240**

CAMPOS, J.J.A. History of the Portuguese in Bengal. Introduction by F.J. Monahan. Calcutta, Butterworth & Co., 1919. 283p. **2241**

CAREY, W.H., *comp*. The good old days of Honourable John Company. Calcutta, R. Cambray & Co., 1906-7. 2 vols. **2242**
"Curious reminiscences illustrating manners and customs of the British in India during the rule of the East India Company from 1600 to 1858, with brief notices of places and people of these times etc., compiled from newspapers and other publications."- *t.p.*

COMPTON, HERBERT, *comp*. Particular account of the European military account of the European military adventures of Hindostan from 1784 to 1803. London, Unwin, 1892. 419p. illus. **2243**

CORREIA-AFONSO, JOHN. Jesuit letters and Indian history; a study of the nature and development of the Jesuit letters from India (1542-1773) and of their value for Indian historiography. With a preface by George Schurhammer. Bombay, Indian Historical Research Institute, St. Xaviers' College, 1955. xxxix, 193p. maps. (Studies in Indian history of the Indian Historical Research Institute, no. 20). **2244**

DANVERS, FREDERICK, C. The Portuguese in India. London, W.H. Allen, 1894. 2 vols. **2245**
Probably the best account of the rise and fall of the Portuguese power in India during the 16th and early 17th century.

DODWELL, HENRY H. Dupleix and Clive. London, Methuen, 1920. **2246**
An analysis of the role played by Dupleix and Clive for supremacy of power, between 1742 and 1754.

FAWCETT, CHARLES, *ed*. The English factories in India, 1670-1684. Oxford, Clarendon Press, 1936-1955. 4 vols. **2247**

FERGUSSON, JAMES. An essay on a proposed new system of fortification with hints for its application to our national defences. London, J. Weole, 1849. 1p. 1., (v)—x. (2) 165p. 10p. (part fold). **2248**

FORREST, Sir GEORGE WILLIAM. The siege of Madras in 1746 and the action of La Bowdonnais. (*In* Royal Historical Society, London. Translations). London, 1908. 3rd ser., v. 2. (189-234).
2249

FOSTER, WILLIAM. The East India house; its history and associations. London, John Lane, the Bodley Head, 1924. xi, 250p.
2250

——England's quest of Eastern trade. London, A. & C. Black, 1933. **2251**

    An account of England's effort to establish trade with Asian lands, including India in the late 16th and early 17th century.

——The founding of Fort St. George, Madras. London, Eyre and Spottiswoode, 1902. xxiv, 43p. **2252**

    "Published by the order of His Majesty's Secretary of State for India in Council."

——John Company. London, John Lane, the Bodley Head, 1926. xi, 286p. **2253**

    Describes the internal affairs of the East India Company.

FOSTER, WILLIAM, *ed.* English factories in India, 1618-1669. Oxford, Clarendon Press, 1906-1927. 13 vols. **2254**

    A collection of letters, reports, and other documents written by the Company's servants in India.

FURBER, HOLDEN. John Company at work. Cambridge (Mass), Harvard, 1948. 407p. **2255**

    A study of European expansion in India in the late eighteenth century.

GRANT, Sir ROBERT. A sketch of the history of the East-India Company, from its first foundation to the passing of the Regulating Act of 1773; with a summary view of the changes which have taken place since that period in the internal administration of British India. London, Printed for Black, Parry and Co., (etc.), 1813. 13p., ii., 1iii, 397p. **2256**

HERPIN, E. Mahede la Boundonnais et la compagnie des Indes.

Saint-Brierg. Imprimerie, 1905. vii, 265p. **2257**

HILL, S.C. Three Frenchmen in Bengal or the commercial run of the French settlements in 1757. London, Longmans, 1903. x, 182p. **2258**

HOLWELL, JOHN ZEPHANIAH. Interesting historical events, relative to the provinces of Bengal, and the empire of Indostan. With a seasonable hint and persuasive to the honourable the court of directors of the East India Company, fasts and festivals of the Gentoo's followers of the Shastah. And a dissertation on the metampsychosis, commonly, though erroneously called the Pythagoreon doctrine. London, printed for T. Becket & PA De Hondt, 1766-71. 3pts. in 2 vols. 5 fold pl. 4 fold maps. **2259**

HUNTER, WILLIAM W. History of British India. London, Longmans, Green, 1899-1900. 2 vols. **2260**
    One of the best account of the activities of the East India Company in India.

HUTCHINSON, LESTER. European freebooters in Moghul India. Bombay, Asia Publishing House, 1964. 192p. **2261**

KAYE, Sir JOHN WILLIAM. The administration of the East India Company; a history of Indian progress. London, R. Bentlay, 1853. x, 712p. **2262**

KEENE, HENRY GEORGE. The great anarchy, or darkness before dawn. Sketches of military adventure in Hindustan during the period immediately preceding British occupation. With a preface by Sir Richard Temple Bart. London, W. Thacker & Co., 1901. xiv, 177p. **2263**

—— Hindustan under free lances, 1770-1820: sketches of military adventures in Hindustan during the period immediately preceding British occupation. London, Brown, 1907. xxxii, 238p. illus. **2264**

——A servant of "John Company": being the recollections of an Indian official. London, W. Thacker & Co., 1897. illus. **2265**

LAING, SAMUEL. India and China. England's mission in East. 2nd ed. London, 1863. **2266**

LAKE, EDWARD JOHN. Journals of the sieges of the Madras Army in the years 1817, 1818 and 1819. With observations on the system according to which such operations have usually been conducted in India, etc. London, Kingsbury, Parbury and Allen, 1825. 255p. **2267**

LOCKE, J.C. The first Englishman in India: letters and narratives of Sundry Elizabethans. London, Routledge, 1930. xvi, 229p. illus. maps. **2268**

LOHUIZEN, JAN VAN. The Dutch East India Company and Mysore. The Hague, N. Nijhoff, 1961. 205p. **2269**

    A study of Dutch activities in southern India during the 18th century including their struggle with the British and the native rulers of Mysore.

LOW, CHARLES RATHBONE. Great battles of the British navy from the earliest period down to the present time. London, G. Routledge & Sons, limited. New York, E.P. Dutton & Co., (1885) 3p. 1 (v)—xvi, 542p. front. pls. **2270**

LOW, URSULA. Fifty years with John Company. London, J. Murray, 1936. **2271**

    A biographical study of Sir John Low's life and work as soldier-administrator in India from 1805-58.

LYALL, Sir ALFRED COMYN. The rise and expansion of the British dominion in India. 4th ed. With a new chapter, bringing the history down to 1947. With maps. London, J. Murray, 1907. xviiip. 11., 388p. 5 fold. maps. **2272**

MALLESON, G.B. Dupleix. Oxford, Clarendon Press, 1890. 188p. (Rulers of India). **2273**

——— Dupleix and the struggle for India by the European nations. Oxford, Clarendon Press, 1899. 188p. (Rulers of India). **2274**

——— History of the French in India. London, W.H. Allen, 1893. 2nd ed. xi, 614p. **2275**

    Originally published in 1867, it is an account of the rise and fall of the French power in India.

MARTIN, ROBERT MONTGOMERY. British possessions in Europe, Africa, Asia, Australia connected with English by the India and Australia mail steam packet company. Prepared at the request of the committee by the author of the "History of the British Colonies". London, W.H. Allen & Co., 1847. 58p. front. (fold map) fold tab. **2276**

900 History

MARTIN, ROBERT MONTGOMERY. Colonial policy of the British empire. Part I, Government. London, 1837. lp. l., 87p. **2277**

——— History of Austral-Asia : comprising New South Wales, Van Dieman's Island, Swan River, South Australia, etc. 2nd ed. London, Whittaker & Co., 1839. vii, (1) 416p. front., fold maps. **2278**

———History of the British colonies. London, Cochrane & Co., 1834-35. 5 vols. fold. fronts. maps. (partly fold) fold. tab. **2279**

——— History of the British possessions in the Indian and Atlantic oceans; comprising Ceylon, Penang, Malacca, Singapore, the Falkland Islands, St. Helena, Ascension, Sierra Leone, the Gambia, Cape Coast Caste, etc., etc. London, Whittaker & Co., 1837. 11, 358p. front. fold maps. **2280**

———History of the colonies of the British empire. From the official records of the colonial office. London, W.H. Allen & Co., 1843. x, (3) 602, 304p. front. (fold map) illus., 3p. fold. tab. **2281**

——— History of the possessions of the Honourable East India Company. London, Whittaker & Co., 1837. 2 vols. front. fold. maps. **2282**

——— Statistics of the colonies of the British empire. From the official records of the colonial office. London, W.H. Allen & Co., 1839. v, (3) 602, 304p. front. (fold. map) illus. 3 pls. fold. tab. **2283**

MARTINEAU, ALFRED. Bussy in the Deccan. Preface by Nawab Ali Yavar Jung Bahadur. Translated by A. Commiade. Pondicherry, Society for the history of French India, 1941. viii, 306p. **2284**

"Being extracts from Bussy and French India."

MASON, PHILIP. The men who ruled India. By Philip Woodruff (pseud). London, Jonathan Cape, 1953. Vol. I, the founders. 402p. **2285**

An account of the men who founded British rule in India.

ORME, ROBERT. A history of the military transactions of the British nation in Indostan, from the year MDCCXLV. To which is prefixed a dissertation on the establishment made by Mahomedan conquerors in Indostan. London, printed for Wingrave, 1803. 2 vol. in 3 fold plts. folds. maps. plans.

(partly fold). **2286**

OSWELL, G.D. Sketches of rulers of India. Oxford, Clarendon, 1908. 228p. **2287**

    Contents : Governors General and Dupleix; Marquess Cornwallis, Wellesley, Hastings, Earl of Amherst, Lord William Bentick, Earl of Auckland and Viscount Harding.

PHILIPS, CYRIL, H. The East India Company, 1784-1834. Manchester, Manchester University Press, 1961. 2nd ed. vii, 374p. **2288**

    A study of the trade and commerce policies of the East India Company with special reference to the controversy that arose in 1784 whether or not the EIC should take steps to establish the British Empire in India by interfering in the affairs of the Kings and emperors.

RAWLINSON, HUGH GEORGE. British beginnings in Western India, 1579-1657: an account of the early days of the British of Surat. Oxford, at the Clarendon Press, 1920. v, 158p. **2289**

———Indian historical studies. London. Longmans, Green & Co. 1913. xv, 229p. **2290**

    "Gives a glimpse of India in nearly every epoch of her history by taking a leading figure of the period and attempting an estimate of his achievements."

———, ed. Narratives from Purchas, his pilgrims. Cambridge, Cambridge University Press, 1931. **2291**

    Describes a battle between British and Portuguese merchant ships and Sir Thomas Roe's visit to the court of Jahangir.

RENNELL, JAMES. The marches of the British armies in the Peninsula of India during the campaigns of 1790 and 1791. Explained by reference to a map. London, G. Nicol, 1792. 114p. **2292**

ROBERTS, PAUL ERNEST. History of British India under the Company and the Crown. 3rd ed. London, Oxford University Press, 1952. 716p. Completed by T.G.P. Spear. First published in 1921. **2293**

ROE, Sir THOMAS. The Embassy of Sir Thomas Roe to India. Edited by W. Foster. London, Oxford University Press, 1926.

900 History

lxxix, 532p. **2294**
Sir Thomas Roe, who stayed at Jahangir's court for three years, describes the court life. He was sent to India in 1615 by King James to negotiate a treaty with Jahangir to further the interest of English merchants.

SCOTT, JONATHAN. Observations on the Oriental Department of Hon. Company's East India College at Hertford. Hertford, St. Austin, 1806. 49p. **2295**

SEWELL, ROBERT. The analytical history of India, from the earliest times to the abolition of the honourable East India Company in 1858. London, W.H. Allen & Co., 1870. xxvi, 334p. **2296**

STEPHENS, H.M. Albuquerque. Oxford, Clarendon Press, 1892. 222p. fronts. maps. (Rulers of India). **2297**

SUTHERLAND, LUCY. S. The East India Company in 18th century politics. Oxford, Clarendon Press, 1952. xii, 430p. **2298**

THORNTON, EDWARD. A gazetteer of the territories under the government of the East India Co., and of the native states on the continent of India. Compiled by the authority of the Hon. Court of Directors, and chiefly from documents in their possession. Corrected to the latest period by the author. London, W.H. Allen & Co., 1857. 2p. 1., 1014p. 11., fold, map. **2299**

WHEELER, JAMES TALBOYS. Early records of British India: a history of English settlements in India, as told in the government record, the works of old travellers, and other contemporary documents, from the earliest period down to the rise of British power in India. London, Trubner and Company, 1878. xxxi, 391p. **2300**

——The history of Imperial assemblage at Delhi, held on the 1st January, 1877, to celebrate the assumption of the title of Empress of India by Her Majesty the Queen. Including historical sketches of India with portraits, pictures, maps, etc. London (1877). **2301**

WRIGHT, ARNOLD. Early English adventures in the East. London, Melrose, 1917. 331p. **2302**

(v) First Struggle For Freedom (1857)

ADYE, Sir JOHN MILLER. The defence of Cawnpore by the troops under the orders of Major General Charles A. Windham, C.B., in November 1857 (with a map). London, Longman & Co., 1858. 58p. **2303**

ANSON, O.H.S.O. With H.M. 9th Lancers during the Indian mutiny, edited by Harcourt S. Arson. London, Allen, 1896. viii, 280p. **2304**

BALL, CHARLES. History of the Indian mutiny: giving a detailed account of the sepoy insurrection in India; and a concise-history of the great military events which have tended to consolidate British Empire in Hindustan. London, Lion Printing Press, n.d. 2 vols. ports. **2305**

BELL, THOMAS EVANS. Holker's appeal: "The Office" or the Empire. Papers relating to his conduct during the Indian Mutiny. London, 1881. 97, 16, 4p. **2306**

———A letter to H.M. Durand Esq. (Commenting on certain statements in his works: "Central India in 1857," and "Life of Sir H.M. Durand). London, Chatto & Windus, 1884. viii, 64p. **2307**

BURNE, Sir O.J. Clyde and Strathnairn. Oxford, Clarendon Press, 1891. 194p. map. (Rulers of India series). **2308**

CAREY, W.H., comp. Mahomedan rebellion; its premonitory symptoms, the outbreak and suppression with an appendix. Roorkee, Directory Press, 1857. 261p. **2309**

CAVE-BROWNE, J. Punjab and Delhi in 1857. London, Blackwood, 1861. 2 vols. illus. **2310**

COLLIER, RICHARD. Great Indian mutiny: a dramatic account of the sepoy rebellion. New York, Dutton, 1964. 383p. illus. **2311**

———Sound of fury: an account of the Indian mutiny. London, Collins, 1963, 383p. illus. **2312**

COOPER, FREDERIC. Crisis in the Punjab, from the 10th of May (1857) until the fall of Delhi. London, Smith. 1858. xx. 254p. **2313**

DANGERFIELD, GEORGE. Bengal mutiny: the story of the sepoy rebellion, 1933. 286p. **2314**

DANVERS, ROBERT WILLIAMS. Letters from India and China,

900 History

during the years 1854-1858. London, Hazell, 1898. ix, 214p. **2315**

EDEN, C.H. India: historical and descriptive; with an account of the Sepoy mutiny in 1857-58: rev. and enlarged. London, Ward, 1876. 290p. illus. **2316**

EDWARDS, MICHAEL. Battles of the Indian mutiny. London, Batsford, 1963. 216p. illus. **2317**

——Personal adventures during the Indian rebellion in Rohilcund, and Oude. 4th ed. London, Smith, 1859. iv, 206p. **2318**

EMBREE, AINSLIE T. 1857 in India; Mutiny or war of independence? Boston, D.C. Heath, 1963. xii, 101p. (Problems in Asian civilizations). **2319**

    A collection of articles by various authors on Mutiny of 1857.

FITCHETT, W.H. The tale of the great mutiny. London, Smith, Elder & Co., 1902. vii, 384p. **2320**

FORBES-MITCHELL, WILLIAM. Reminiscences of the great mutiny, 1857-59. London, Mac., 1894. xii, 295p. map. **2321**

FOREST, Sir GEORGE WILLIAM. A history of the Indian mutiny. reviewed and illustrated from original documents. Edinburgh and London, W. Blackwood and Sons, 1904-12. 3 vols. fronts. pls. ports. fold maps. **2322**

—— Selections from the letters, despatches and other state papers preserved in the military department of the Government of India, 1857-58. Calcutta, Military Deptt., 1893. **2323**

GARRETT, H.L.O., ed. Trial of Muhammed Bahadur Shah: Ex-King of Delhi. Lahore, Punjab Government Record Office Publications, 1932. xiv, 282p. (Punjab Government Record Office Monograph, no. 14). **2324**

GILBERT, HENRY. Story of the Indian mutiny. London, Harrap, 1916. 350p. **2325**

GORDON-ALEXANDER, W. Recollections of a highland subaltern during the campaigns of the 93rd Highlanders in India, under Conl. Campbell Lord Clyde in 1857, 1858 and 1859. London, Arnold, 1898. xii, 360, 32p. illus. map. **2326**

GOVERNMENT OF INDIA. *North Western Frontier Province-Intelligence Department.* **2327**

Records of the Intelligence Department of the Government of the N.W.F.P. of India during the mutiny of 1857 : including correspondence, with the supreme government. Delhi, Caunpore, and other places, presented by and now arranged under the superintendence of Sir William Muir; edited by William Coldstram. Edinburgh, Clark, 1902. 2 vols.

GOWING, J. Soldier's experience; or a voice from the ranks : the cost of war in blood and treasure: a personal narrative of the Crimean campaign from the standpoint of the ranks of the Indian mutiny, and some of its atrocities, the Afghan campaigns of 1863, etc. Nothingham, the author, 1895. xv, 585p. **2328**

GRANT, Sir HOPE. Incidents in the Sepoy War, 1857-8; compiled from the private journal of the author; together with some explanatory chapters, by Henry Knollys, Edinburgh. Blackwood, 1873. xiv, 380p. **2329**

GRESTHED, H.H. Letters written during the siege of Delhi. London, Longmans, 1858. xxiii, 293p. **2330**

GRIFFITHS, CHARLES JOHN. A narrative of the siege of Delhi with an account of the mutiny of Ferozpore in 1857. Edited by Henry John Yonge. London, John Murray, 1910. xii, 960p. **2331**

GUBBINS, MARTIN RICHARD. An account of the mutinies in Oudh and of the sieze of the Lucknow residency. London, R. Bentley, 1858. xii, 464p. front. pls. fold. map. plans (part fold). **2332**

HARRIS, J. China Jim: being incidents and adventures in the life of an Indian mutiny veteran. London, Heinamann, 1912. xii, 218p. illus. **2333**

HAVELOCK, Sir HENRY. Memoirs : edited by J.C. Marshaman London, Longmans, 1860. x, 462p. **2334**

HILTON, RICHARD. The Indian mutiny : a centenary history. London, Hollis and Carter, 1957. 282p. illus. **2335**

History of the Delhi Massacre, its supposed origin by a lady. Liverpool, Tintling, n.d., 93p. **2336**

History of the Indian revolt and of the expeditions to Persia, China and Japan, 1856-58. London, Chambers, 1859. viii,

634p. illus. maps. plans. **2337**

HODSON, W.S.R. Twelve years of a soldier's life in India. London, Parker, 1859. xvi, 384p. **2338**

HOPE. A.P. Story of the Indian mutiny. London, Warne, 1896. 243p. illus. **2339**

INDIAN GOVERNMENT. Memorandum of the aid and services rendered by the Government of Indore to the British authorities during the mutiny of 1857-58. 129p. **2340**

INGLIS, Mrs. JULIA SELINA (THESIGER). Siege of Lucknow : a diary. London, Osgood, 1892. viii, 240p. **2341**

INNES, MCLEOD. Lucknow and Oude in the mutiny. London, Innes, 1893. xvi, 340p. illus. maps. **2342**

—— Sepoy revolt : a critical narrative. London, Innes, 1897. xviii, 303p. maps. **2343**

JACOB, Sir GEORGE LE GRAND. Western India before and during the mutinies : pictures drawn from life. London, H.S. King & Co., 1871. viii, 262p. **2344**

Appendix : The war with Baba Sahib (The Chief of Nurgoond) and the capture of that town by the English. A.D. 1858 (A Canarese epic translated by Mrs. Kies). p. 239-262.

JOCELYN, J.R.J. History of the Royal and Indian artillery in the mutiny of 1857. London, Murray, 1915. xxv, 520p. map. illus. **2345**

JONES, O.J. Recollections of a winter campaign in India in 1857-58; with drawings on stone from the author's designs. London, Saunders, 1859. xiv, 213p. **2346**

KAVANAGH, J.H. How I won the Victoria Cross. London, Word and Lock, 1860. x, 219p. Illus. **2347**

KAYE, Sir JOHN WILLIAM. A history of the Sepoy War in India, 1857-58. London, New York (etc), Longmans, Green & Co., 1896. 3 vols. V. 1, 9th ed. 1880; Vol. 2, 5th ed., 1888; Vol. 3, 4th ed. 1880. **2348**

—— Kaye's and Malleson's history of the Indian mutiny of 1857-58. Edited by Colonel Malleson. New impression. London, New York, Longmans, Green & Co., 1897-98. 6 vols. fold. maps. fold. plans. **2349**

KAYE, JOHN W. and G.B. MALLESON. History of the Indian

mutiny. London, Longmans, 1897-98. new ed. 6 vols. **2350**
A comprehensive history of First War of Indian independence.

KEENE, HENRY GEORGE. Fifty-seven. Some account of the administration of Indian districts, during the revolt of the Bengal Army. London, W.H. Allen & Co., 1883. xii, 145p. **2351**

KENNEDY, JAMES. The great Indian mutiny of 1857, its causes. features, and results. London, 1858. **2352**

KEYE, MARY MARGARET. Shadow of the moon. London, New York, Longmans, Green, 1957. 682p. **2353**
A novel on India's first war of Independence (1857).

LADENDORF, JANICE M. Revolt in India 1857-58 : an annotated bibliography of English language materials. Zug. Inter Documentation Co., 1966. v, 191p. (Bibliotheca Indica no. 1). **2354**

LEASOR, JAMES, Red Fort : an account of the siege of Delhi, in 1857. London, Laurie, 1956. 379p. illus. **2355**

LEWIN, J.H. Fly on the wheel, or how I helped to govern India. London, Constable, 1912. 318p. **2356**

LUDLOW, JOHN MALCOLM FORBES. British India, its races and its history, considered with reference to the mutinies of 1857 : a series of lectures. London, Cambridge, 1858. 2 vols. **2357**

—— The war in Oude. Cambridge, 1858. **2358**

LUNDGREN, EGRON. Relief of Lucknow and triumphant meeting of Havelock, Outram and Sir Colin Campbell: a plate; printed by Jones Barker. London, Hayward, 1862. A plate.

MACKEWZIE, A.R.D. Mutiny memories; being personal reminiscences of the great sepoy revolt of 1857. Allahabad, Pioneer Press, 1891. 211p. **2359**

MACMUNN, GEORGE FLETCHER. The Indian mutiny in perspective. London, G. Bell & Sons, 1931. xii, 276p. **2360**

MALLESON, J.B. History of the Indian mutiny, 1857-1858. Commencing from the close of the second volume of "Sir John Kaye's History of the Sepoy War." **2361**

—— Indian mutiny of 1857. 4th ed. London, Seeley, 1892. xiv, 421p. illus. **2362**

MARX, KARL. The first Indian war of independence, 1857-1859. Moscow, Foreign Languages Publishing House, 1960. 245p. **2363**

A collection of articles, Karl Marx originally had written in 1857-59, for the *New York Daily Tribune*.

MAUDE, J.C. Memories of the mutiny. London, Ramington, 1894. 2 vols. illus. **2364**
"With which is incorporated the *Personal narrative* of John Walter Sherer."

MECHAM, C.H. Sketches and incidents of the siege of Lucknow : from drawings made during the siege. London, Day, 1857. 27 paintings. **2365**

METCALFE C.J., *tr*. Two native narratives of the mutiny in Delhi. Westminster, Constable, 1898. 259p. illus. **2366**

MUIR, Sir WILLIAM. Records of the Intelligence department of the Government of North-West provinces of India during mutiny of 1857, including correspondence with the supreme government, Delhi, Cawnpore, and other places. Preserved by and now arranged under the superintendence of Sir William Muir...then in charge of the intelligence department. Edited by William Coldstream. Edinburgh, T. & T. Clark, 1902. 2 vols. **2367**

MUTER, ELIZABETH (MCMULLIN). My recollections of the Sepoy revolt (1857-58). London, John Long, 1911. 266p. **2368**
An account of the first war of independence. The authoress was the wife of one of the British officers who took part in the fight for Delhi in 1857.

NORTON, J.B. Rebellion in India; how to prevent another. London, Richardson, 1857. xii, 244p. **2369**

PALMER, J.A.B. Mutiny outbreak at Meerut in 1857. Cambridge, University Press, 1966. xi, 175p. map. **2370**

PEARSON, HESKETH. Hero of Delhi: a life of John Nicholson, saviour of India, and a history of his wars. London, Collins, 1939. 291p. pls. **2371**

PRICHARD, I. Mutinies in Rajputana; being a personal narrative of the mutiny at Nusseorabad; with subsequent residence of Jodhpur, and journey across the desert into Sind; together with an account of the outbreak at Neemuch and mutiny of the Jodhpur legion at Crinpoora and attack on Mount Aboo. London, Parker, 1860. vii, 311p. **2372**

RAIKES, CHARLES. Notes on the revolt in the North-Western

provinces (U.P.) of India. London, Longmans, 1858. viii, 195p. **2373**

REES, L.E.R. Personal narratives of the siege of Lucknow from its commencement to its relief by Sir Colin Campbell. London, Longman, 1858. xiii, 380p. **2374**

RICH, GREGORY. Mutiny in Sialkot; with a brief description of the cantonment from 1852 to 1857. Sialkot, Handa Printing Press, 1924. 80p. **2375**

ROBERTS, F.S. Forty-one years in India. London, Bentley, 1897. 2 vols. illus. **2376**

ROBERTS, FRED. Letters written during the Indian mutiny. London, Mac., 1924. xxii, 169p. illus. map. **2377**

RUGGLES, J. Recollections of a Lucknow veteran, 1845-1876. London, Longmans, 1906. xv, 185p. **2378**

RUSSELL, Sir, WILLIAM HOWARD. My Indian mutiny diary. Edited, with an essay on the mutiny and its consequences, by Michael Edwards. London, Cassell, 1957. 288p. illus. **2379**
   A pen picture of India during her first war of independence of 1857.

SEDGWICK, F.R. Indian mutiny of 1857: a sketch of the principal military events. London, Groom, 1919. 160p. **2380**

SHADWELL, LAWRENCE. Life of Colin Campbell, Lord Clyde. London, Blackwood, 1881. 2 vols. illus. **2381**

SHERER, JOHN WALTER. Daily life during the Indian Mutiny, etc. London, Swan Sonnenschein & Co., 1910. viii, 197p. **2382**
   First edition published in 1898.

—— Havelock's march on Cawnpore, 1857. A civilian's notes. (A new edition of "Daily life during the Indian mutiny"). London, Thomas Nelson & Sons, 1910. 366p. **2383**

—— Memories of the mutiny, with which is incorporated the personal narrative of J.W. Sherer, etc. 3rd ed. London & Sydney, Remington & Co., 1894. 2 vols. **2384**

SIEVEKING, I.J. Turning point in the Indian mutiny. London, Nutt, 1910. vii, 226p. **2385**

STEWART, C.C. Through Persia in disguise with reminiscences of the Indian mutiny; edited from his diaries by Basil Stewart. London, Routledge, 1911. xxiii, 438p. illus. maps. **2386**

THACKERAY, Sir EDWARD TALBOT, *comp.* Reminiscences of

the Indian mutiny, 1857-58 and Afghanistan, 1879. London, Smith, Elder & Co., 1916. 181p. **2387**

THACKERAY, Sir EDWARD TALBOT, *comp.* Two Indian campaigns in 1857-58. Chatham, Mackay and Co., 1896. vi, 130p. illus. map. **2388**

THOMSON, MOWBRAY. Story of Cawnpore. London, Bently, 1859. 262p. illus. **2389**

TREVELYAN, GEORGE. Cawnpore. London, Mac., 1894. vi, 280p. **2390**

TROTTER, L.J. Life of General Sir James Outram. Edinburgh, Blackwood, 1901. x, 320p. port. **2391**

VALBEZEN, E.D.C. English and India; translated by a diplomat. London, Allen, 1883. xv, 498p. **2392**

VEREY, GERALD LLOYD. The devil's wind; the story of the naval brigade at Lucknow, from the letters of Edmund Hope Verrey and other papers concerning the enterprise of the Ship's Company of H.M.S. Shannon in the campaign in India, 1857-58. 175p. illus. **2393**

VILBRART, EDWARD. Sepoy mutiny as seen by a subaltern, from Delhi to Lucknow, Smith, 1898. x, 308p. illus. map. **2394**

WILBERFORCE, R.G. Unrecorded chapter of the Indian mutiny; being the personal reminiscences of Reginald G. Wilberforce; compiled from a diary and letters written on the spot. 2nd ed. London, Murray, 1894. xviii, 234p. illus. **2395**

WOOD, Sir EVERLYN. Revolt in Hindustan, 1857-59. London, Methuen, 1908. xvi, 367p. illus. map. **2396**

YOUNG, KEITH. Delhi, 1857; the siege, assault and capture as given in the diary and correspondence of the late Colonel Keith Young, Judge-Advocate General, Bengal. Edited by Henry Wylie Norman and Mrs. Keith Young. London, and Edinburgh, W.R. Chambers, 1902. xxv, 371p. **2397**

(vi) British Period (1858 to 1947)

ADAMS, W.H.D. Episodes of Anglo-Indian history: a series of chapters from the annals of British India, showing the rise and progress of our Indian empire. London, Marlborough n.d. xi,

348p. **2398**

ADYE, Sir JOHN MILLER. Indian frontier policy; a historical sketch. With a map. London, Smith, Elder & Co., 1897. 61p. **2399**

AITCHISON, Sir CHARLES UMPHERSTON. Lord Lawrence and the reconstruction of India under the crown by Sir Charles Aitchison. Oxford, Clarendon Press, 1905. vi, 11., (9)-216p. (fold map). **2400**

ALDER, G.J. British India's Northern Frontier, 1865-95; a study in Imperial policy. London, Longmans, 1963. xiii, 392p. **2401**

ALLEN, JOHN AND *others*. Cambridge shorter history of India. By John Allen; T. Wolseley Haig and Henry Herbert Dodwell; Edited by H.H. Dodwell. New York, The Macmillan Co., 1934. xxi, 970p. **2402**

ANDERSON, G. AND SUBEDAR, M. Expansion of British India, 1818-58. London, Bell, 1918. xii, 196p. **2403**

ANDREW, Sir WILLIAM PATRIC. Indian railways, as connected with the power, and stability of the British Empire in the East. London, W.H. Allen, 1884. **2404**

ANDREWS, C.F. India and Britain: a moral challenge. London, Student Christian Movement, 1935. 189p. **2405**

——India and the Simon report. London, Allen & Unwin, 1930. 191p. **2406**

——True India: a plea for understanding. London, Allen & Unwin, 1939. 251p. **2407**

ARGYLL, G.D.C. India under Dalhousie and Canning. London, Longman, 1865. viii, 143p. **2408**

—— Afghan question, from 1841 to 1878. London, Straham, 1879. ix, 288p. **2409**

ARNOLD, EDWIN. The Marquess of Dalhousie's administration of British India. London, Saunders, Otley, 1862-65. 2 vols. **2410**

An account of Dalhousie's regime from 1848-1856, when major changes were brought, by the annexation of the Punjab and other native states.

ASPINALL, ARTHUR. Cornwallis in Bengal. Manchester, Manchester University Press, 1931. **2411**

Gives an account of Lord Cornwallis's regime as Governor-General of India from 1786-93. The book is important because during this period the East India Company had changed its goal from commerce to politics and government.

BARNS, MARGARITA. India today and tomorrow. London, Allen, 1937. 304p. illus. **2412**

BEARCE, G.D. British attitude towards India, 1784-1858. London, Oxford University Press, 1961. viii, 315p. **2213**

BELL, THOMAS EVANS. The empire in India: letters from Madras and other places. London, Trubner, 1864. vi, 412p. **2214**

——A letter to Sir J.D. Gordon (in reply to a memorandum by him upon the supposed loss of some of the Mysore State jewels). London, Chatto & Windus, 1882. viii, 66p. **2415**

——Memoir of General John Briggs of the Madras Army, etc. London, Chatto & Windus, 1885. viii, 285p. **2416**

——Retrospects and prospects of Indian policy. London, Trubner & Co., 1868. vi, 344p. **2417**

——The task of today. London, J. Watson, 1852. vi, 144p. **2418**

BESANT, ANNIE. India: a nation: a plea for Indian self-government. London, Jack, n.d. 94p. **2419**

—— India, bond or free?: a world problem. London, Putnam, 1926. 216p. **2420**

BEVERIDGE, HENRY. Comprehensive history of India, civil, military and social, from the first landing of the English, to the suppression of the sepoy revolt including an outline of the early history of Hindoostan. London, Blackie, n.d. 3 vols. illus. maps. **2421**

BEYNON, W.G.L. With Kelly to Chitral. London, Arnold, 1856. 160p. illus. map. **2422**

BIDIE, GEORGE. Cinchona culture in British India, etc. Madras, Higginbotham & Co., 1879. 24p. **2423**

BIRDWOOD, Lord CHRISTOPHER. India and Pakistan: a continent decides. New York, Praeger, 1954. 315p. **2424**

    Lord Birdwood served the British Army in India for many years.

BIRDWOOD, C.B. Continent experiments: a picture of the present and conjecture for the future with a few memories from the past; introduction by Earl of Halifax. London, Skeffington, 1945. 276p. **2425**

BIRDWOOD, Sir GEORGE C. MOLESWORTH. Handbook to the British Indian Section. 2nd ed. Paris, exposition universelle de, 1878 (India). vii, 162p. **2426**

BLUNT, W.S. India under Ripon: a private diary. London, Unwin, 1909. v, 343p. **2427**

BOLTON, GLORREY. Peasant and prince. London, Routledge, 1937. 295p. illus. **2428**

BOULGER, DEMETRIUS C. Lord William Bentinck. Oxford, Clarendon Press, 1897. **2429**

>An account of reforms, Lord Bentinck enforced during his tenure as Governor-General, 1828-35.

BRAILSFORD, H.N. Subject India. London, Gollancz, 1943. 223p. **2430**

BROWN, HILTON. Parry's of Madras : a story of British enterprise in India. Madras, Parry, 1954. 347p. illus. **2431**

BRUCE, Sir CHARLES. True temper of empire. London, Macmillan, 1912. vi, 211p. **2432**

BRUCE, R. Forward policy and its results. London, Longmans, 1900. 373p. illus. maps. **2433**

BRYCE, JAMES. Ancient Roman empire and the British empire in India; the diffusion of Roman and English law throughout the world. London, Oxford University Press, 1914. 138p. **2434**

BUCKLAND, C.E. Bengal under the Lieutenant-Governors. Calcutta, S.K. Lahiri & Co., 1901. 2 vols. **2435**

>"Being a narrative of the principal events and public measures during their periods of office, from 1854 to 1898."
>-t.p.

Butler, Sir Harcourt. India insistent. London, Heinemann, 1931. viii, 117p. **2436**

Cambridge history of India. Cambridge University Press, 1922. **2437**

>Contents:
>V. 1—Ancient India, edited by E.J. Rapson.
>V. 3—Turks and Afghans; edited by Sir Wolseley Haig.
>V. 4—Mughal period; edited by Sir Wolseley Haig.
>V. 5—British period, 1497-1858; edited by H.H. Dodwell.
>V. 6—Indian empire, 1858-1918; edited by H.H. Dodwell.

900 History

Reprinted by S. Chand & Company, Delhi.

CAMPBELL-JOHNSON, ALAN. Mission with Mountbatten. New York, Dutton, 1953. 383p. **2438**
An eye-witness account of the transfer of power from British to Indian hands, written by Lord Mountbatten's Press Attache.

CARTHILL, A.L. Cost dominion. Edinburgh, Blackwood, 1924. vi, 351p. **2439**

——Garden of Adonis. Edinburgh, Blackwood, 1927. 360p. **2440**

CHAILLEY, JOSEPH. Administrative problems of British India; tr. by Sir William Meyer. London, Macmillan, 1910. xv, 590p. **2441**

CHESNEY, G.M. India under experiment. London, Murray, 1918. xi, 192p. **2442**

CHIROL, Sir VALENTINE. India. London, Benn, 1926. vi, 352p. (Modern World: a survey of historical forces, vol. 5). **2443**

——Indian unrest. London, Macmillan, 1910. xvi, 371p. **2444**

COATMAN, JOHN. India: the road to self-government. London, Allen & Unwin, 1941. 146p. **2445**

COCKLE, J.D. Catalogue of books relating to the military history of India. Simla, U.S.I. of India, 1901. 101p. **2446**

COLQUHOUN, A.R. Russia against India: the struggle for Asia. London, Harper, 1900. vii, 246p. maps. **2447**

COLVIN, IVAN. Life of General Dyer. Edinburgh, Blackwood, 1929. x, 345p. **2448**

Coronation Durbar, 1911; being a reprint of articles and telegrams previously published in the Pioneer with 28 illustrations and a map. Allahabad, Pioneer Press, 1912. 251, Lxxiip. **2449**

COTTON, H.J.S. New India; or, India in transition. London, Paul, 1885, xii, 184p. **2450**

COTTON, SYDNEY. Nine years on the North West Frontier of India from 1854 to 1863. London, Bentley, 1868. xii, 352p. **2451**

COUPLAND, Sir REGINALD. Goal of British rule in India. London, Longmans, 1948. 22p. **2452**

CREAGH, Sir O'MOORE. Autobiography of General Sir O'Moore

Creagh. London, Hutchinson, n.d. 304p. **2453**

CREAGH, Sir O'MOORE. Indian studies. London, Hutchinson, n.d. 320p. **2454**

CURTIS, LIONEL. Letters to the people of India. London, Macmillan, 1917. 81p. **2455**

CURZON, G.N. *Marq. of Kedleston.* British government in India: the story of the Viceroys and Government houses. London, Cassell, 1925. 2 vols. illus. **2456**

———Leaves from a Viceroy's note-book and other papers. London, Macmillan, 1926. x, 414p. illus. **2457**

DARLING, Sir MALCOLM. Apprentice to power in India, 1904-1908. London, Hogarth, 1966. 256p. **2458**

DAVIES, C.C. Problems of North-West Frontier, 1890-1908, with a survey of policy since 1849. Cambridge, U.P., 1932. xii, 220p. **2459**

DEAN, V.M. New patterns of democracy in India. Bombay, Oxford University Press, 1959. viii, 226p. maps. **2460**

DIGBY, WILLIAM. India for Indians and for England. London, Talbros; 1885. xxxvii, 261p. **2461**

———Prosperous British India. London, T. Fisher Unwin, 1901. xlvii, 661p. **2462**

DILKS, DAVID. Curzon in India. London, Hart-Davis, 1970. 2 vols. **2463**

DIVER, MAUD. Royal India. New York, London, Appleton-Century-Crofts, 1942. 317p. **2464**

    A non-political description of fifteen Indian states, their romantic history and their rulers.

DODWELL, HENRY HERBERT. The Nabobs of Madras. London, Williams and Norgate, 1926. x, 263p. **2465**

    Describes social life of Englishmen in Madras during the 18th century.

———A sketch of the history of India, 1858-1918. London, Longmans, 1925. xi, 326p. **2466**

    An evaluation of political developments in India between 1858 and 1918.

DUFFERIN AND EVA, Marchioness of. Our Viceregal life in India; selection from My journal, 1884-88. London, Murray, 1890. 408p. **2467**

900 History

Dumbell, Percy. Loyal India; a survey of seventy years, 1858-1928. London, Constable, 1930. xxiv, 243p. **2468**

Durand, Sir Mortimer. Life of Field-Marshal Sir George White. London, Blackwood, 1915. 2 vols. **2469**

Durant, Will. Case for India. New York, Simon and Schuster, 1930. viii, 231p. **2470**

Edwardes, Michael. High noon of empire : India under Curzon. London, Eyre and Spottiswood, 1965. iv, 266p. **2471**

—— Battle of Plassey and the conquest of Bengal. London, Batsford, 1963. 167p. illus. **2472**

—— The necessary hall; John and Henry Lawrence and the Indian Empire. London, Cassell, 1958. xxi, 213p. illus. ports. **2473**

Elwin, Varrier. Truth about India: can we get it? London, Allen & Unwin, 1932. 8, 104p. **2474**

Finnemore, John. Delhi and the Durbar. London, Adam, 1912. vii, 88p. (Peeps at great cities). **2475**

Firminger, Walter Kelly, *ed.* The fifth report from the Select Committee of the House of Commons on the affairs of the East India Company, dated 28th July, 1812. Edited with notes and introduction. Calcutta, R. Cambrary & Co., 1917-18 **2476**

> First published in 1812, it is a standard authority of the time on land tenures and judicial and police systems of British India.

Fitze, Sir Kenneth. Twilight of the Maharajas. London, Murray, 1956. 180p. **2477**

Forrest, Sir George William. Selections from the State papers of the governors-general of India, edited by G.W. Forrest. Oxford, B.H. Blackwell; London, Constable & Co., ltd., 1910-26. 4 vols. fronts. (V. 1. 3 parts) fold. maps. (1 in packet). **2478**

Fortescue, John. Narrative of the visit to India of their Majesties King George and Queen Mary and of the coronation durbar held at Delhi 12th December, 1911. London, Macmillan, 1912. viii, 324p. **2479**

Francklin, W. The history of the reign of Shah Aulum, the present Emperor of Hindustan. Allahabad, Panini Office, 1934.

vi, 259p. **2480**

"Contains the transactions of the Court of Delhi, and the neighbouring states, during a period of thirty-six years; interspersed with geographical and topographical observations on several of the principal cities of Hindustan." -*t.p.* First published in 1798.

FRANZER, R.W. British India. 2nd ed. London, Unwin, 1898. xvi, 399p. illlus. **2481**

FRASER, LOVAT. India under Curzon and after. 3rd ed. London, William Heinemann, 19.2. xxiv, 496p. **2482**

FRAZER, ROBERT WATSON. British India. New York, G.P. Putnam's Sons, (etc.) 1897. lp. l., vii-xviii, 399p. front. illus. ports. maps. (1 fold). (The story of the nations). **2483**

FULLER, Sir BAMPFYLDE. Studies of Indian life and sentiment. London, Murray, 1910. xiii, 360p. **2484**

FULLER, J.F.C. India in revolt. London, Eyre and Spottiswood, 1931. 272p. **2485**

FURNEAUX, RUPORT. Massacre at Amritsar. London, Allen & Unwin, 1963. 183p. maps. **2486**

GILLIAT, EDWARD. Heroes of modern India; stirring records of the bravery, tact and resourcefulness of the founders of the Indian empire. London, Seelay, 1910. xiii, 336p. **2487**

GLADHILL, ALAN. The Republic of India : the development of its laws and constitution. London, Stevens & Sons, 1951. xii, 309p. **2488**

GRADDOCK, Sir REGINALD. Dilemma in India. London, Constable, 1929. xviii, 379p. **2589**

GRANT, JAMES. Illustrated history of India. London, Cassell, n.d. 2 vols. **2490**

GRIFFIN, Sir LEPEL HENRY. The rajas of the Punjab; being the history of the principal states in the Punjab and their political relations with the British government. 2nd ed. London, Trubner & Co., 1874. xiip., 11., 630p. **2491**

GRIFFITHS, PERCIVAL J. The British impact on India, London, Macdonald, 1952. 513p. **2492**

A pro-British appraisal of the British rule in India by an ex-member of the Indian Civil Service.

——British in India. London, Hale, 1946. 222p. **2493**

900 History

GRIFFITHS, PERCIVAL J. Modern India. London, Benn, 1957. xiv, 255p. maps. **2494**

GRINWOOD, Mrs. ETHAL FRANK St. CLAIR. My three years in Manipur and escape from recent mutiny. London, Bentley, 1891. xii, 321p. illus. **2495**

GROSER, H.G. Field-Marshal Lord Roberts: a biographical sketch. 3rd ed. London, Melrose, n.d. 152p. **2496**

HANNA, H.B. Can Russia invade India ? Westminster, Constable, 1895. xiv, 111p. **2497**

HARDINGE, CHARLES HARDINGE OF PENSHURST. My Indian years, 1910-1916. London, Murray, 1948. x, 150p. **2498**

——— Speeches by Lord Hardinge of Penshurst, Viceroy and Governor General of India. Calcutta, Govt. Press, 1914-16. 3 vols. **2499**

HARRISON, S.S. India : the most dangerous decades, Madras, Oxford University Press, 1960. x, 350p. **2500**

HENTY, G.A. With China in India, or, the beginnings of an empire. London, Blackie, n.d. 378p. **2501**

HILL, Sir C.H. India-stepmother. Edinburgh, Blackwood, 1929. xii, 333p. **2502**

HOGG, DOROTHY. India: a plea for understanding. Allahabad, Kitab Mahal, 1946. 142p. **2503**

HOLDICH, T.H. Indian borderland; 1880-1900. London, Methuen, 1901. xii, 402p. illus. **2504**

HOLMAN, DENNIS. Lady Louis: life of the Countess Mountbatten of Burma. London, Odhams Press, 1952. 191p. **2505**

HORNIMAN, B.G. Amritsar and our duty to India. London, Unwin, 1920. 196p. illus. **2506**

HUNTER, Sir WILLIAM WILSON. Earl of Mayo. Oxford, Clarendon Press, 1891. 206p. (Rulers of India series). **2507**

——— A history of British India. London, New York (etc.),. Longmans, Green & Co., 1899-1900. 2 vols. fold. maps. vol. 2 completed and edited by P.E. Roberts after the author's death. **2508**

——— The Indian empire: its peoples, history and products. New and rev. ed. (the third). London, Smith, Elder & Co., (1893). 852p. front. (fold map). **2509**

1st and 2nd edition published in 1882 and 1886 respectively.

HUNTER, Sir WILLIAM WILSON. The India of the queen, and other essays. With an introduction by Francis Henry Sknne. London, New York and Bombay, Longmans, Green & Co., 1903. xviii, 276p. 11 **2510**

—— The Indian Musalmans, are they bound in conscience to rebel against the queen? London, Trubner and Company, 1871. 3p. 1., (9). 215p. **2511**

—— The Marquess of Dalhousie and the final development of the company's rule. 7th thousand. Oxford, Clarendon Press, 1895. 3p. 1., (9)-228p. front. (port). facsim. fold map. (Half title : Rulers of India (vol. 22). **2512**

A biography.

HUTCHINSON, LESTER. The empire of the Nobobs : a short history of the British India. London, George Allen & Unwin, 1937. 277p. **2513**

A socialistic interpretation of the history of the British in India.

ILBERT, Sir COURTENAY PEREGRINE. The coronation durbar and its consequences; a second supplementary chapter to the Government of India. Oxford, The Clarendon Press, London and New York, H. Milford, 1913. 2, (455)-546p. **2514**

IMLAH, A.H. Lord Ellenborough: a biography of Edward Law; Earl of Ellenborough, Governor-General of India. Cambridge, Harvard-University Press, 1939. xii, 295p. **2515**

IMPERIAL GAZETTEER of INDIA. New ed. published under the authority of His Majesty's Secretary of State for India in Council. Oxford, Clarendon Press, 1907-31. 26 vols. maps. **2516**

1st edition, 9 v., 1881, and 2nd ed., 14v., 1885-87, ed. by Sir William Wilson Hunter. The present may be considerd as a new work rather than a new edition—cf. general pref.

Editor for India; 1902-4, William Stevenson Meyer; 1905-9, Richard Burn. Editor in England: James Sutherland Cotton.

V. 1-4, Indian Empire: v. 1, Descriptive; v. 2, Historical; v. 3, Economic; v. 4, Administrative; v. 5-24, Gazetteer; v. 25, General index; v. 26, Atlas. (Atlas, new rev. ed. 1931).

Includes historical, topographical, ethnical, agricultural, industrial, administrative, and medical aspects of the various districts of British India.

IRWIN, EDWARD F.L.W. Indian problems. London, G. Allen, 1932. (11)-376p. **2517**
    A collection of his speeches which Lord Irwin delivered as Viceroy of India from 1926-31.

KAYE, Sir J.W. History of the Sepoy war in India, 1857-1858. London, Allen, 1870-76. 3 vols. **2518**

——Lives of Indian officers : illustrative of the history of the civil and military service of India. London, Bogue, 1867. 3 vols. **2519**

KINCAID, DENNIS C. British social life in India, 1608-1937. London, Routledge, 1939. 312p. pls. Completed by David Farrar. **2520**
    An account of those Englishmen who served in India between 1608 and 1937.

KISCH, HERMANN M. A young Victorian in India. London, J. Cape, 1957. 242p. **2521**
    A collection of letters which describe the official life of the British officials in the late 19th century.

KNAPLUND, PAUL. British empire, 1815-1939. New York, Harper, 1941. xx, 850p. **2522**

KOCH, D.M.G. Sedjarah perdjuangan India. Djakarta, Pembangunan, 1951. 75p. **2523**

LACEY, PATRICK. Fascist India. London, Nicholson & Watson 1946. 150p. **2524**

LAWRENCE, Sir W.R. India we served. London, Cassell, 1926. xvi, 317p. **2525**

LAWSON, Sir CHARLES. Memories of Madras. London, Sonnenschein, 1905. xiii, 313p. **2526**

LAWSON, Sir CHARLES ALLEN. Narrative of the celebration of the jubilee of her Most Gracious Majesty Queen Victoria, Empress of India, in the Presidency of Madras. 2nd ed. London, Macmillan & Co., 1887. xxx, 358p. **2527**

——The private life of Warren Hastings. With 78 illustrations, etc. London, Swan Sonnenschein & Co., 1905. viii, 254p. **2528**

LEAR, EDWARD. Indian journal, 1873-1875, edited by Ray Murphy. London, Jarrolds, 1953. 240p. illus. **2529**

LEE-WARNER, WILLIAM, Native states of India. London, Macmillan, 1910. xxi, 425p. **2530**

LEWIS, MARTIN D., *ed.* The British in India; imperialism or trusteeship ? Boston, D.C. Heath, 1966. xiii, 114p. **2531**
> Intended for use as text book in colleges, this book analyses in detail whether or not the policies of the British Government were imperialist or for the good of the Indian people.

LINLITHGOW, J.A.L. HOPE, MARQUESS. Speeches and statements. New Delhi, Govt. of India, 1945. xxii, 467p. **2532**

LOTHIAN, Sir A.C. Kingdoms of yesterday. London, Murray, 1951. xii, 228p. illus. **2533**

LOW, CHARLES RATHBONE. The great battles of the British navy. London, New York, G. Routledge and Sons, 1872. xvi, 496p. col. front. col. pls. **2534**

LOW, D.A. Soundings in modern South Asian history. London, Weidenfeld and Nicolson, 1968. 391p. illus. **2535**

LUDLOW, JOHN MALCOLM FORBES. Thoughts on the policy of the crown towards India. London, J. Ridgway, 1927. 1p. 1., iv, vii, 330p. **2536**

LUMBY, E.W.R. Transfer of power in India, 1945-47. London, Allen & Unwin, 1954. 274p. maps. **2537**

LYALL, Sir ALFRED COMYN. The rise and expansion of the British dominion in India. 5th ed., cor. and enl. with maps. London, J. Murray, 1910. xviiip. 11., 397p. fold. maps. **2538**

───── The rise of the British dominion in India. London, J. Murray, 1893. xv. (1) 288p. 4 fold. maps. (Half title: University extension manuals, edited by Professor Knight). **2539**
> An evaluation of the British tradition from commerce to conquest.

───── Warren Hastings. London, New York, Macmillan & Co., ltd., 1902. vi, 235p. front. (port) double map. (Half-title : Englishmen of action). **2540**

MACFARLANE, CHARLES. History of British India; from the earliest English intercourse; with continuation to the termination of the late Afghan War. London, Routledge, 1881. 594p. **2541**

MALCOLIN, Sir JOHN. The political history of India. 1784 to 1823; edited by K.N. Panikkar. New Delhi, Associated Publishing House, 1970. 2 vols. **2542**

MARSHALL, P.J. Impeachment of Warren Hastings. London, Oxford University Press, 1965. xi, 217p. **2543**

——Problems of the empire : Britain and India, 1757-1813. London, Allen & Unwin, 1968. 239p. **2544**

MARTIN, ROBERT MONTGOMERY. The British colonial library, comprising a popular and authentic description of all the colonies of the British empire, their history—physical geography—geology—climate—animal, vegetable, and mineral kingdoms—government finance—military defence—commerce—shipping—monetary system—religion—population, white and coloured—education and the press—emigration, social state, etc. London, H.G. Bohn, 1844. 10 vols. front fold. maps. **2545**

——The progress and present state of British India. A manual for general use, based on official documents, furnished under the authority of Her Majesty's secretary of state for India. London, S. Lawson & Co., 1862. 3p. 1. (v)—xi, 308p. 2 fold. maps (incl. front) tab. (2 fold). **2546**

MASON, PHILIP. The men who ruled India, by Philip Woodruff (pseud). London, J. Cape, 1953-54. 2 vols. illus. ports. maps. **2547**

MERSEY, VISCOUNT. Viceroys and governors-general of India, 1757-1947. London, Murray, 1949. xi, 179p. illus. **2548**

MESTON, LORD. India and the empire. London, News, 1927. 27p. **2549**

METCALF, THOMAS R. Aftermath of revolt : India, 1857-1870. Princeton, Princeton University Press, 1964. xi, 352p. map. **2550**

MEYSEY, THOMPSON E.C. India today. London, Smith, 1913. 230p. map. **2551**

MILBURN, R.G. England and India. London, Allen & Unwin, 1918. 7, 126p. **2552**

MILLS, JAMES. History of British India. London, J. Madden, 1858. 10 vols. **2553**

> First published in 1817 it is an account of the efforts the Britishers made to establish their empire in India. It covers the period from 1805 to 1834.

MINNEY, RUBEIGH JAMES. Clive of India. Rev. and reset. London, Jarrolds, 1957. 264p. illus. **2554**

Sources of Indian Civilization

MINTO, G.J. ELLIOT—MURRAY-KYNYNMOND. India, Minto and Morley correspondence, edited by Mary Countess of Minto. London, Macmillan, 1935. viii, 447p. illus. map. **2555**

MODAK, CYRIL. What price freedom? Allahabad, Kitab Mahal, 1945. xx, 199p. **2556**

MOLESWORTH, G.N. Curfew on Olympus. Bombay, Asia, 1965. vii, 296p. **2557**

MONTAGU, E.S. Indian diary, edited by Venetia Montagu. London, Heinemann, 1930. xv, 410p. illus. **2558**

——On Indian affairs, Madras, Ganesh, 1917. xii, 438p. **2559**

MOON, PENDEREL. Divide and quit. London, Chatto & Windus, 1961. 302p. **2560**

——Strangers in India. London, Faber & Faber, 1945. 212p. **2561**

"Connects discussion of Indian problems with typical Indian incidents, illustrative of the way of life and the modes of thought and speech of the people."

——Warren Hastings and British India. New York, Collier, 1962. **2562**

An account of Warren Hastings efforts in establishing the British Empire in India during 1772 to 1785.

MORISON, THEODORE. Imperial rule in India : being an examination of the principles proper to the Government of dependencies. Westminster, Constable, 1899. 147p. **2563**

MORLEY, JOHN. Speeches on Indian affairs; 2nd rev. ed. Madras, Natesan, 1917. 239, 36, iv p. **2564**

MOSLEY, LEONARD. Last days of British Raj. London, Weidenfeld & Nicolson, 1961. 263p. photos. **2565**

MOULTON, EDWARD C. Lord Northbrook's Indian administration. Bombay, Asia, 1968. vi, 313p. **2566**

MOUNTBATTEN, LORD LOUIS. Speeches, 1947-48. New Delhi, Publication Division, 1949. vii, 217p. **2567**

——Time only to look forward: speeches. London, Kaye, 1949. vii, 276p. illus. **2568**

MUIR, RAMSAY, ed. The making of British India, 1756-1858. Described in a series of despatches, treatises, statutes and other documents, selected and edited with introductions and notes.

Manchester, at the University Press, London, Longmans, Green & Co., 1915. xiv, 398p. **2569**

MURRAY, HUGH. History of British India. London, Nelson, 1863. xvi, 731p. illus. **2570**

MUTER, Mrs. DUNBAR DOUGLAS. My recollections of the sepoy revolt, 1857-58. London, Longmans, 1911. 266p. illus. **2571**

NOLAN, E.H. History of the British empire in India and the East. London, Virtue, n.d. 8 vols. maps. illus. **2572**

O' DONNELL, C.J. Causes of present discontents in India, London, Unwin, 1908. 120p. **2573**

ODWYER, Sir MICHAEL. India as I knew it, 1885-1925. London, Constable, 1925. x, 453p. **2574**

OSBURN, ARTHUR. Must England lose India ; the nemesis of empire, London, Knopf, 1930. vii, 280p. **2575**

PHILIPS, CYRIL H. India. New York, Hutchinson's University Library, 1949. 176p. **2576**

> A brief account of political and economic conditions during the British period.

POLE, D.G. India in transition. London, Hogarth Press, 1932. xii, 395p. **2577**

PRINSEP, HENRY THOBY. History of the political and military transactions in India during the administration of Marquess of Hastings, 1813-1823. Enlarged from the narrative published in 1820. London, Kingsbury, Parbury, and Allen, 1825. 2 vol. front. (port.) pls. fold. maps. fold tab. **2578**

RAWLINSON, H.G. British achievements in India. London, Hodge, 1948. 248p. illus. **2579**

REED, STANLEY. The India I knew, 1897-1947. London, Odhams, 1952. 262p. **2580**

> Describes political, social and economic events which took place in India from 1897 to 1947.

REED, Sir STANLEY AND CADEL, P.R. India; the new phase. London, Allen, 1928. vii, 175p. **2581**

REES, J.D. Real India. London, Mathuen, 1908. xii, 352p. **2582**

REYNOLDS, REGINALD. White Sahibs in India. New York, John Day, 1937. xv, 247p. **2583**

> A sympathetic account of the nationalist movement in India; criticising some of the policies of the British rule.

RICHMOND, HERBERT W. The Navy in India, 1763-1783. London, E. Benn, 1931. **2584**

    An account of the British naval power in India from 1763-1783.

RIVETT-CARNAC, J.H. Many memories of life in India, at home, and abroad. Edinburgh, Blackwood, 1910. xx, 448p. **2585**

ROBERTS, FREDERICK S. Forty-one years in India. New York, Longmans, Green, 1914. 2 vols. **2586**

    An autobiography of a British Army Officer in India. Describes the organization of the British Army.

ROBERTS, PAUL ERNEST. History of British rule. London, Oxford University Press, 1952. 716p. First published in 1921. **2587**

    Completed by T.G.P. Spear, it is considered to be one of the best history of the British rule.

ROUTLEDGE, JAMES. English rule and native opinion in India. From notes taken 1870-74. London, Trubner & Co., 1878. ix, 338p. **2588**

RUSSEL, W.H. My diary in India in the year 1958-59. London, Routledge & Routledge, 1860. 2 vols. **2589**

RUSSELL, WILFRID. Indian summer. Bombay, Thacker, 1951. 250p. **2590**

    An account of the impressions of British merchants and their response to developing industries in India since 1857.

SEELEY, Sir J.R. Expansion of England. London, Macmillan, 1931. vi, 359p. **2591**

SETON, KAR, W.S. Marquess Cornwallis. Oxford, Clarendon, 1890. 202p. (Rulers of India). **2592**

SHARP, Sir HENRY. Good-bye India. London, Oxford University Press, 1946. viii, 244p. photos. **2593**

SHIPP, JOHN. Path of glory; being the memoirs of the extraordinary military career; edited by C.J. Stranks. London, Chatto and Windus. 1969. xiv, 247p. **2594**

SLEEMAN, Sir WILLIAM HENRY. Rambles and recollections of an Indian official. London, J. Hatchard & Son, 1844. 2 vols. col. fronts. col. pls. **2595**

SMITH, VINCENT ARTHUR. Indian constitutional reform viewed in the light of history. London, New York (etc.), H. Milford,

900 History

Oxford University Press, 1919. 118p. (mainly a criticism of the Report on Indian constitutional reforms, 1918). **2596**

SPEAR, PERCIVAL. The Nabobs. London, Oxford University Press, 1963. **2597**
    An account of social and cultural aspects of the British Empire during the 18th century.

——National harmony. London, Oxford University Press, 1946. 32p. **2598**

——Oxford history of modern India; 1740-1947. Oxford, Clarendon Press, 1965. x, 426p. **2599**

SPENDER, J.A. Changing East. London, Cassell, 1926. 286p. **2600**

——Indian scene. London, Methuen, 1912. x, 232p. **2601**

STEWART, Sir NORMAN. My service days; India, Afghanistan, Suakim and China. London, Bell, 1909. 402p. illus. **2602**

STOKES, E. English utilitarians and India. Oxford, Clarendon, 1959. xvi, 350p. **2603**

STRACHEY, Sir JOHN. India. London, Paul, 1888. xiv, 399p. **2604**

TAYLOR, PHILIP MEADOWS. Confessions of a Thug. Edited by C.W. Stewart. London, Oxford University Press, 1933. **2605**
    First published in 1839, it is a story of the suppression of Thugs in India. The author was one of the officials who was deputed to deal with the Thugs, a group of people who used to waylay people.

TAYLOR, WILLIAM. Thirty-eight years in India: from Juganath to Himalaya mountains. London, Allen, 1881. 2 vols. illus. **2606**

TEIXEIRA, LUIZ. Pequena cronica da India. Lisboa, Agencia Geral do Utramar. Dividao de Publicacoes e Biblioteca, 1954. 68p. **2607**

TEMPLE, RICHARD. Journals kept in Hyderabad, Kashmir, Sikkim and Nepal; edited with introduction by his son R.C. Temple. London, Allen, 1887. 2 vols. maps. illus. **2608**

——Men and events of my time in India. London, Murray, 1882. 526p. **2609**

THOMPSON, EDWARD & GARRATT, G.T. Rise and fulfilment of British rule in India. Allahabad, Central Book Depot, 1958.

xi, 601p. maps. **2610**
THORBURN, S.S. His Majesty's greatest subject. Westminster, Constable, 1897. 324p. **2611**
THORNTON, EDWARD. Chapters of the modern history of British India. London, W.H. Allen & Co., 1840. vii, 644p. **2612**
────── A gazetteer of the territories under the government of the viceroy of India. Rev. and edited by Sir Roper Lethbridge, and Arthur N. Woolaston. London, W.H. Allen & Co., 1886. 2p. 1 (vii)—viii, 1070p. **2613**
────── The history of the British empire in India. London, W.H. Allen & Co., 1841-45. 6 vols. fold maps. **2614**
TILBY, A.W. British India, 1600-1928. London, Constable, 1911. 286p. (English people overseas, vol. 2). **2615**
TRENCH, VICTOR, *pseud*. Lord Willingdon in India. Bombay, Samuel A. Ezekier, 1934. 333p. **2616**
TROTTER, L.J. History of India under Queen Victoria, from 1836 to 1880. London, Allen, 1886. 2 vols. **2617**
TUKER, Sir FRANCIS. While memory serves. London, Cassell, 1950. xiv, 663p. **2618**
TYSON, GEOFFREY. Danger in India; with an introduction by the Earl of Lytton. London, Murray, 1932. x, 133p. **2619**
VALBERZEN, E.D. English and India; translated by a diplomat. London, Allen, 1883. xv, 496p. **2620**
WALEY, S.D. Edwin Montagu; a memoir and an account of his visit to India. Bombay, Asia, 1964. ix, 343p. **2621**
WALLBANK, THOMAS W. A short history of India and Pakistan. New York, Mentor, 1958. **2622**

It is an abridged edition of the author's book *India in the New Era*. Is a useful title for a common reader.

WATT, Sir GEORGE. La ramie et ses analogues aux Indes anglaisea d'apris le D. George Watt Traduit de l'anglais DIG. Bigle de Cardo. Paris, A. Challomel, 1906. 3p. 1., 123p. (F). **2623**
WHEELER, JAMES TALBOYS. India under British rule, from the foundation of East India Co., London, Macmillan & Co., 1886. xvi, 312p. **2624**
WILBUR, MARGUERITE K. The East India Company and the British empire in the Far East. New York, R.R. Smith, 1945.
2625

Emphasises the role played by the East India Company in establishing the British Empire in India. It also surveys the political efforts of England in founding her Empire after 1857 when the administration of the Company was taken over by the Crown.

WILKS, MARK. Historical sketches of the South of India. Mysore, Government Branch Press, 1930-32. 2 vols. **2626**
"An attempt to trace the history of Mysore from the origin of the Hindoo government of that state, to the extinction of the Mohammedan dynasty in 1799." -*t.p.*

WILLIAMS, L.F.R. India in 1920 : a report. Calcutta, Supdt. Govt. Printing Press, 1921. xiv, 275p. **2627**

WILSON, CHARLES ROBERT. The early annals of the English in Bengal, being the Bengal public consultations for the first half of the eighteenth century, summarised, extracted and edited etc. London, W. Thacker & Co., 1895. **2628**

—— Old Fort William in Bengal; a selection of official documents dealing with its history. Edited by C.R. Wilson, 1906. 2 vols. **2629**

WINT, GUY. The British in Asia. New York, Institute of Pacific Relations, 1954. rev. ed. 224p. **2630**
A comparative study of the British and Russian efforts to establish their influence in Asia.

WOLPERT, STANLEY A. Morley and India, 1906-1910. Berkeley, University of California Press, 1967. x, 299p. **2631**

WOOD, Sir MARK. A review of the origin, progress and result of the late decisive war in Mysore. With notes and an appendix, comprising the whole of the secret state papers found in the cabinet of Tippoo Sultan. London, I. Cadell, Jun and W. Davies, 1800. 6p. 1., 63, 65, 68, 65, 276p. **2632**

WOOD, WILLIAM MARTIN. Things of India made plain; or a journalist's retrospect. London, Elliot Stock, 1884-89. pt. 1-3. **2633**

WOODRUFF, PHILIP. Men who ruled India. London, Cape, 1953-54. 2 vols. illus. **2634**

WOODYATT, NIGEL. Under ten Viceroys. London, Jenkins, 1922. 320p. illus. **2635**

YOUNGHUSBAND, Sir FRANCIS EDWARD. Dawn in India : British

purpose and Indian aspiration. New York, Frederick A. Stokes Co., 1931. xvi, 331p. **2636**

YOUNGHUSBAND, Sir FRANCIS EDWARD. India and Tibet: history of relations. London, Murray, 1910. xvi, 455p. illus. maps. **2637**

(vii) Princes and their States

BARTON, WILLIAM. The princes of India. Introduction by Viscount Halifax. London, Nisbet & Co., 1934. xvi, 327p. **2638**
"A comprehensive survey of the historical and constitutional position of the Indian princes."

DE MONTMORENCY, GEOFFREY FITZHERVEY. Indian states and their federation. Cambridge, the University Press, 1942. viii, 166p. **2639**

DERRETT, J. DUNCAN M. The Hoysolus, a medieval Indian family. Madras, Oxford University Press, 1957. xix, 257p. illus. tables. maps. **2640**

DIVER, MAUD. Royal India: a descriptive and historical study of India's fifteen principal states and their rulers. London, Hodder and Stoughton, 1942. xx, 278p. photos. **2641**

FERRET, *pseud*. Princes or puppets? Bombay, Thacker & Co., 1944. **2642**

FITZE, Sir KENNETH SAMUEL. Twilight of the maharajas. London, Murray, 1956. 189p. **2643**

GRIFFIN, Sir LEPEL HENRY. The rajas of the Punjab, being the history of the principal states in the Punjab and their political relations with the British Government. Lahore, printed by the Punjab Printing Company, ltd, 1870. 2p. l., viii, 17, 661, xvip. **2644**

HAHN, EMILY. The tiger house party; the last days of the maharajas. Line drawings by Ellen Raskin. 1st ed. Garden City, N.Y., Doubleday, 1959. 164p. illus. **2645**

LAWRENCE, ARNOLD WALTER. Captives of Tipu: survivors' narrative. London, Jonathan Cape, 1929. 243p. (The travellers' library series). **2646**

LEE-WARNER, WILLIAM. The native states of India. London, Macmillan, 1910. xxi, 425p. **2647**

First published in 1894 under the title : The protected Princes of India. A study of the relationship between rulers of the Princely states and the British Government.

LEE-WARNER, WILLIAM. Protected Princes of India. London, Macmillan, 1894. xix, 389p. **2648**

LOTHIAN, Sir ARTHUR CUNNINGHAM. Kingdoms of yesterday. Foreword by Compton Mackenzie. London, John Murray, 1951. xii, 228p. **2649**

"Contains the author's personal experience of Indian States and their vicissitudes during 1911-47."

LOW, Sir SIDNEY JAMES MARK. Indian states and ruling princes. London, Capes, 1930. 128p. **2650**

MACLEAN, JOHN. States in India. London, Macmillan, 1916. 145p. illus. **2651**

MAC MUNN, Sir GEORGE FLETCHER. Indian states and princes. London, Jarrolds, 1936. 287p. **2652**

Native States of India and their princes; with notices of some important zemindaris. Madras, Christian literature society, 1894. 96p. illus. **2653**

NICHOLSON, A.P. Scraps of paper : India's broken treaties, her princes and the problem. London, Benn, 1930. 355p. illus. maps. **2654**

SCOTT, J.B. Religion and short history of the Sikhs, 1469-1930. London, Mitre Press, 1930. 96p. **2655**

THOMPSON, EDWARD JOHN. Making of the Indian princes. London, Oxford University Press, 1943. xii, 304p. map. **2656**

"Describes events which shaped India's political framework during 1799-1819—between the death of Tipu Sultan and the elimination of the Peshwa."

THORNTON, THOMAS HENRY. General Sir Richarel Meade and the feudatory States of Central and Southern India; a record of forty-three years' service as soldier, political officer and administrator. London, New York (etc.). Longmans, Green & Co., 1898, xxvp. 11., 390p. 11. front. pls. ports. map. **2657**

WARNER, Sir WILLIAM LEE. The native states of India (Second edition of the 'The Protected Princes of India'). London, Macmillan & Co., 1910. xxi, 425p. **2658**

WARNER, Sir WILLIAM LEE. The protected princes of India. London, Macmillan & Co., 1894. xix, 389p.   **2659**

(viii) Marathas

BLACKER, VALENTINE. Memoir of the operations of the British army in India, during the Mahratta war of 1817, 1818 and 1819, xx, 482p.   **2660**

BROUGHTON, THOMAS D. Letters written in a Mahratta camp. London, A. Constable, 1892. 358p.   **2661**

    Describes the customs and manners of the Marathas during his stay in the camp of the Maratha leader Sindhia during 1809.

BURNS, JAMES. Narrative of a visit to the court of the Ameers of Sinde. 1827-28. Bombay Presidency, 1829. v, 166p.   **2662**

CRAWFORD, A.C. Our troubles in Poona and the Deccan. Westminster, Constable, 1897. xx, 253p.   **2663**

DUFF, JAMES GRANT. History of the Maharattas. Edited by S.M. Edwards. London, Oxford University Press, 1921. 3 vols.   **2664**

    Originally published in 1826, it is a complete history of the rise, progress and decline of the Marathas.

KEENE, HENRY GEORGE. Madhava Rao Sindhia and the Hindu reconquest of India. 4th thousand. Oxford, Clarendon Press, 1901. 207 (1) p. front. (fold. map). (Half title: Rulers of India edited by Sir W.W. Hunter).   **2665**

    The first edition was published in 1895.

KINCAID, CHARLES A. AND R.B. PARASNIS. A history of the Maratha people. London, Oxford University Press, 1931. 2nd ed. 3 vols. maps.   **2666**

    Contents: Vol. 1, From the earliest times to the death of Shivaji; Vol. 3, From the death of Shivaji to the death of Shahu; Vol. 3, From the death of Shahu to the end of the Chitpavan epic.

KINCAID, DENNIS. The grand rebel; an impression of Shivaji, founder of the Maratha empire. London, Collins, 1937. 329p.   **2667**

900 History

MACMILLAN, MICHAEL. In the days of Shivaji; from a wild Maratha battle; retold by Dorothy King. Bombay, Blackie, n.d. 128p. **2668**

MALCOHN, Sir JOHN. Memoir of central India, including Malwa, and adjoining provinces, with the history and copious illustrations, of the past and present condition of the country. 3rd. ed. London, Parbury, Allen Co., 1832. 2 vols. **2669**

MALLESON, LT. COL. G.R. Recreation of an Indian official, London, Longmans, 1872. xii, 467p. **2670**

ORME, ROBERT. Historical fragments of the Mogul empire, of the Marathas, and of the English concerns in Indoostan, from the year 1659; origin of the English establishment, people of Indostan. London, Wingrave, 1805. lxii, 472p. **2671**

OWEN, SIDNEY. India on the eve of the British conquest: an analytical history of India. 1627-1761, 2nd ed. Calcutta, Susil Gupta, 1954. iii, 204p. **2672**

TAYLOR. MEADOWS. Tata, a Maharatta tale. 4th ed. London, C.K. Paul & Co., 1881. 3p. 1 (v)-viii, 584p. front. **2673**

TEMPLE, Sir RICHARD, Ist hart. Personal traits of Mahratta Brahman princes. (In Royal historical society, London. Transactions. London, 1884. n.s. v. 1 p. 289-308). **2674**

TEMPLE, RICHARD AND OTHERS. Sivaji and the rise of the Mahrattas. Calcutta, Susil Gupta, 1953. 157p. illus. maps. **2675**
    Other authors are : M.G. Ranade, G.S. Sardesai, R.M. Betham, and James Douglas.

WELLESLEY, Sir ARTHUR. Notes relative to the late transactions in the Marhatta empire, Fort William, December 15, 1803. London, Debrett, 1804. 177p. **2676**

(ix) Rajputs

RAWLINSON, H.G. History of the 2/6th Rajputana rifles (Prince of Wales' own). London, Oxford University Press, 1936. x, 195p. illus. **2677**

TOD, JAMES. Annals and antiquities of Rajasthan; or the Central and Western Rajpoot States of India. London, Routledge, 1914. 2 vols. **2678**

(x) Sikhs

ARCHER, JOHN CLARK. The Sikhs. Princeton, the University Press, 1946. xii, 354p.   **2679**
"This distinguished work by the Hooker Professor of Comparative Religion at Yale University commands attention. It is both a history of the Sikhs and an analysis of their relations with Hindus, Moslems, Christians and Ahmadiyyas."

BANCROFT, N.W. From recruit to staff sergeant, with sketches of the four great actions of the Sutlej campaign. Calcutta, Smith, 1885. iii, 136, ixp.   **2680**

BELL, THOMAS EVANS. The annexation of the Punjab, and the Maharaja Duleep Singh. London, Trubner, 1882. 108p.   **2681**

BRUCE, GEORGE. Six battles for India : the Anglo-Sikh wars, 1845-6. 1848-9. Calcutta, Rupa, 1969. 336p.   **2682**

BUCKLE, E. Memoir of the services of the Bengal artillery; edited by J.W. Kaye, London, Allen, 1852. xvi, 592p.   **2683**

COURT, HENRY, *ed.* History of the Sikhs, translation of the *Sikhann de Raj di Vikhia*"; narratives of the ten gurus, history of the Sikhs from the rise of the Maharaja Ranjit Singh to the occupation of the Panjab by the English, a short resume of the customs, rites, songs and proverbs of the Sikhs, and twenty discourses regarding events in the life of Guru Nanak, taken from the Janam Sakhi; or Life of Nanak; with an appendix containing some useful technical words in Roman character. Calcutta, Susil Gupta, 1959. x, 273p.   **2684**

CUNNINGHAM, JOSEPH DAVEY. Anglo-Sikh relations; edited by Anil Chandra Banerjee. Calcutta, Mukherjee, 1949. lxxxiii, 192p. map.   **2685**

—— History of the Sikhs from the origin of the nation to the battles of the Sutlej, with a map. London, John Murray, 1849. xxxvi, 425p.   **2686**

Garrett, H.L.O. and Chopra, G.L., *eds.* Events at the court of Ranjit Singh, 1810-1817. Lahore, Punjab Government, 1935. 288p.   **2687**

GORDON, Sir JOHN J.H. Sikhs. Patiala. Language Department, Punjab, 1970. 236p. illus.   **2688**

900 History

Gough, Charles and Innes, A.D. Sikhs and the Sikh wars; the rise, conquest and annexation of the Punjab State. London, Innes, 1897. xiv, 304p. maps. **2689**

GREY, C. European adventures of Northern India, 1785-1849; edited by H.O. Garrett. Lahore, 1929. iii, 360, xlviii, xiip. illlus. **2690**

GRIFFIN, Sir LEPEL HENRY. The law of inheritance to chiefships as observed by the Sikhs previous to the annexation of the Panjab. Lahore, Punjab printing company, limited, 1869. 61. 109p. **2691**

——Ranjit Singh and Sikh barrier between our growing empire and central Asia; Oxford, Clarendon Press, 1898. 223p. front. fold map. (Half title page: Rulers of India. vol. xx). Reprinted by S. Chand & Co., Delhi in 1957. **2692**

HENTY, G.A. Through the Sikh war, a tale of the conquest of the Punjab. London, Blackie, n.d. 384p. illus. **2693**

HUGEL, BARON CHARLES. Travels in Kashmir and the Panjab, containing a particular account of the government and character of the Sikhs. London, John Petheram. 1845. xvi, 423p. **2694**

HUMBLEY, W.W.W. Journal of a cavalry officer: including the memorable Sikh campaign of 1845-46. London, Longmans, 1854. xii, 616p. maps. **2695**

KIERMAN, V.G. Metcalfe's mission to Lahore, 1808-1809. Lahore, Punjab Government, 1943. 89p. (Punjab Government mons.). **2696**

LAWRENCE, H.M.L. Adventures of an officer in the service of Runjeet Singh. London, Colburn, 1845. 2 vols. **2697**

LOGIN, Mrs. JOHN. Sir John Login and Dulcep Singh; with introduction by Col. G.B. Malleson. London, Allen, 1890. xx, 580p. **2698**

MACMUNN, Sir GEORGE. History of the Sikh pioneers, (23rd, 32nd, 34th). London, Samson Law, n.d. xvi, 560p. front. col. illus. **2699**

MGREGOR, W.L. History of the Sikhs; containing the lives of the gooroos; the history of the independent sirdars; or missuls and the life of the great founder of the Sikh monarchy, Maharaja Ranjeet Singh. London, Madden, 1846. 2 vols. illus. **2700**

OSBORNE, W.G. Court and camp of Runjeet Singh. London, Calburn, 1840. vi, 236p. illus. **2701**

────- Ranjit Singh: the lion of the Punjab. Calcutta, Susil Gupta, 1952. 90p. **2702**

PARRY, R.E. Sikhs of the Punjab. Patiala, Languages Deptt. Punjab, 1970. 128p. illus. **2703**

PAYNE, C.H. Short history of the Sikhs, London, Nelson, n.d. 248p. illus. map. **2704**

PRINSEP, HENRY THOBY. Origine et progres de la Puissance das Sikhs bars le Panjab et histoire du Maha-Radja Randjit Singh; tr. from French by Xavier Rayond. Paris, Bertrand, 1856. ix, 562p. maps. (F). **2705**

──── Origin of the Sikh power in the Punjab and political life of Muharaja Runjeet Singh with an account of the present condition of the Sikhs. Compiled by H.T.P...from a report by Captain W. Murray and from other sources. Calcutta, 1874. 187p. **2706**

Reprinted by Language Department Punjab, Patiala, in 1970.

SCOTT, G.B. Religion and short history of the Sikhs, 1469-1930. London, Mitre Press, 1930. 96p. **2707**

SMYTH, G.C. History of the reigning family of Lahore with some account of the Jammoo rajas, the Sikh soldiers and their sirdars. Calcutta, Thacker, 1848. xxx, 763, xlp. illus. map. **2708**

STEINBACK, *Lt. Col.* Punjab; being a brief account of the country of the Sikhs; its extent, history, commerce, productions, Govt. manufactures, laws, religion etc. 2nd ed. London, Smith, 1846. vii, 183p. **2709**

(xi) Nationalism, rise of

ANDREWS, C.F. The renaissance in India; its missionary aspect. London, Church Missionary Society, 1912. xii, 310p. ports. **2710**

BESANT, Mrs. ANNIE. The birth of new India: writings and speeches on Indian affairs. Adyar, Theosophical Publishing House, 1917. x, 440p. **2711**

BESANT, Mrs. A. England and India: a lecture, delivered in 1902. Adyar. Theosophical Publishing House, 1921. **2712**

—— For India's uplift: speeches and writings. Madras, the author, 1917. 326p. **2713**

—— Future of Indian politics. Adyar, and Banas, Theosophical Publishing House, 1922. vi, 351p. **2714**

—— The future of young India. Adyar, Theosophical Publishing House, 1915. 20p. **2715**

—— India: a nation. 4th ed. Adyar. Theosophical Publishing House, 1930. 226p. **2716**

—— India, bond or free ? A world problem. London and New York, G.P. Putnam's Sons, 1926. 216p. **2717**

—— India's awakening: a lecture. Banaras and Adyar, Theosophical Publishing Society, 1906. 30p. **2718**

—— A nation's rights. Adyar, Theosophical Publishing House, 1918. 7p. (New India political pamphlets, no. 17). **2719**

—— Patriotism and co-operating with the new government. Madras, Besant Press, 1920. 3p. (National home rule pamphlet, no. 8). **2720**

BEVAN, EDWYN ROBERT. Indian nationalism : an independent estimate. London, Macmillan and Co., 1913, 141p. **2721**

BOELL, PAUL. L'Inde tet le proble me indien. 2nd ed. Paris, the author, 1901. 320p. (F). **2722**

BRAILSFORD, HENRY NOEL. Subject India. New York, The John Company, 1943. viii, 274p. illus. **2723**

BRAISTED, PAUL JUDSON. Indian nationalism and the Christian colleges. New York, Association Press, 1935. xii, 171p. **2724**
Thesis (Ph.D.)—Columbia University, 1935.

BRISTOW, Sir ROBERT CHARLES. Real India: a problem of world importance. Johannesburg, African Institute of International Affairs, 1945. 16p. **2725**

BRYANT, JOHN FORBES. Gandhi and the Indianisation of the empire. Cambridge, J. Hall and Son. London, Simpkin Marshall, Hamilton, Kent and Co., 1924; vi, 228p. **2726**

CHERSI, EMANUELE. India inquieta. Geneva, Sec. Fornari and Co., 1933. 319p. **2727**

CHIROL, Sir VALENTINE. India old and new. London, Macmillan & Co., ltd., x, 319p. **2728**

CHIROL, Sir VALENTINE. Indian unrest: a reprint, revised and enlarged from the *Times* with an introduction by Sir Alfred Lyall. London, Macmillan and Co., ltd., 1910. xvi, 371p. **2729**

CLOSE, UPTON. Revolt in Asia: the end of the White Man's world dominance. New York, G.P. Putnam's Series, 1927. xiv, 325p. **2730**

COTTON, HENRY JOHN STEDMAN. New India, or India in transition. London, Kegan Paul, Trench and Co., 1885. xii, 184p. **2731**

COUPLAND, Sir REGINALD. Britain and India, 1600-1945. Rev. ed. London, New York, 1946. 190p. (Longman's pamphlets on the British Commonwealth, no. 1). **2732**

———The Indian problem, 1883-1935. Report on the constitutional problems in India, submitted to the wardens and fellows of Nuffield College, Oxford. London, New York, etc. Oxford University Press, 1942. vol. double map. **2733**

COUSINS, MARGARET E. Awakening of Asian womanhood. Madras, Ganesh & Co., 1922. ix, 104p. **2734**

CRAWFORD, ARTHUR TRAVERS. England sympathises with the peoples of India, opinions of the English and Anglo-Indian press. 1894-1899. London, William Fraser, 1904. 86p. **2735**

———The unrest in India. Bombay, Bombay Gazette, 1908. 79p. **2736**

CRESSWELL, FRANCIS G. India and her aspirations. Bombay, the author, 1908. 53p. (For private circulation). **2737**

DIGBY, WILLIAM. India for the Indians and for England. London, Talbot Brothers, 1885. xxxvii, 261p. **2738**

———Indian problems for English consideration: a letter. Birmingham, the author, 1881. 67p. **2739**

DUFFETT, WALTER ELLIOTT, ETC., comps. L'Inde d'anjourd'hui. Preface de l'hon Hector Perrier, traduit de l'anglais per J'erome cugnet. Montreal Public pour l'Institut Canadian des affairs internationales par. B. Valiquette, 1944. 217p. (Serie de l'enquete de l' 1. P.R.). (F). **2740**

DUTCHER, GEORGE MATHEW. The political awakening of the East; studies of political progress in Egypt, India, China, Japan and Philippines. New York, Cincinnati, The Abingdon Press, 1925. 372p. **2741**

900 History

FISCHER, LOUIS. Empire. London, D. Dobson ltd., 1945. 70p. **2742**

FULOP-MILLER, RENE. Lenin and Gandhi; translated from the German by F.S. Flint and D.F. Tait. London, and New York, G.P. Putnam's Sons, 1927. xi, 343p. **2743**

GILCHRIST, ROBERT NIVEN. Indian nationality, with an introduction by Ramsay Muir. London, Longmans, Green & Co., 1920. xviii, 246p. **2744**

GOODALL, NORMAN. The Indian deadlock; an interpretation and an appeal. London, the Livington Press, 1942. 19p. **2745**

GREY, L.J.H. India of the future. London, Clowes and Sons, 1907. 52p. **2746**

GUNTHER, FRANCES. Revolution in India. New York, Island Press, 1944. 122p. **2747**

HAMILTON, Sir D.M. New India and how to get there. Waterlow, 1930. 133p. **2748**

HEATH, CARL. Gandhi. London, G. Allen and Unwin ltd., 1944. 30p. **2749**

HOLMES, WALTER HARBERT GREAME. Twofold Gandhi: Hindu monk and revolutionary politician. London, Mowbray, 1952. 144p. **2750**

HOUGHTON, BERNARD. Bureaucratic government: a study in Indian polity. Madras, G.A. Natesan, 1921. ii, 136p. **2751**

—— Realities of today. Madras, G.A. Natesan. 1923. 160p. **2752**

—— The revolt of the East. Madras, G.A. Natesan, 1921. 93p. **2753**

HOWSIN, H.M. Die bedutung des indischen nationalismus. Berlin, 1918. 78p. **2754**

—— The significance of Indian nationalism. Madras, Tagore and Co., 1922. xx, 111p. **2755**

HOYLAND, JOHN SOMERVELL. The cross moves East: a study in the significance of Gandhi's satyagraha. London, G. Allen and Unwin, 1931. 160p. **2756**

—— Indian crisis: the background. London, G. Allen and Unwin ltd., 1943. 195p. **2757**

JOHNSON, ABE, *pseud*. Another's harvest. Calcutta. The Bookman, 1947. ii, 159p. **2758**

JOHNSTON, JAMES. Can the Hindus rule India? London, P.S. King and Son Ltd., 1935. xv, 144p. **2759**

LONDON. *National Liberal Club.* A debate on the awakening of India opened by the Hon. C.K. Gokhale. London, the Club, 1905. 12p. **2760**

LOTHIAN, Sir ARTHUR CUNNINGHAM. Kingdoms of yesterday; with a foreword by Compton Mackenzie. London, J. Murray, 1951. 240p. illus. **2761**

MACKENZIE, DE W. The awakening of India. London, Hodder and Stoughton, 1917. 159p. **2762**

—— India's problem can be solved. Garden City, New York, Doubleday, Doran and Company, Inc., 1943. x, 265p. **2763**

MAURER, HERRYMON. Great soul; the growth of Gandhi. Garden City, Doubleday, 1948. 128p. **2764**

MCCULLY, BRUCE TIEBOUT. English education and the origins of Indian nationalism. New York, Columbia University Press, London, P.S. King and Son, 1940. 418p. **2765**

MODAK, CYRIL JENNER. What price freedom? Allahabad, Kitab Mahal, 1945. x, 199p. **2766**

MORLEY, J. Speeches on Indian affairs. Madras, Natesan and Co., 1908. 220p. **2767**

MORRISON, J. New ideas in India. London, Macmillan, 1907. 282p. **2768**

MULLER, SIEGHILD. Ausserindische Einflusse und Vorbilder und die indische Nationalbowegung; eine Untensuchung an Hand der Sepriften von Fuhrin der Bewegung, u.a. Gopal Krishna Gokhale, Bal Gangadhar Tilak, Subhas Chandra Bose, Jawaharlal Nehru and Mahatma Gandhi. Heidelburg, 1946. 124p. (G). **2769**

MURDOCH, J. An Indian patriot's duty to his country. London, Christian Literature Society, 1904. 336p. **2770**

NARIMAN, K.F. Whither Congress. Bombay, D.R. Dewoolkar, 1933. 160p. **2771**

NEVINSON, HENRY WOOD. The new spirit in India. London and New York, Harper Brothers, 1908. xv, 353p. **2772**

O'DONNELL, CHARLES JAMES. Why India is rebellious. London, 1930. 10p. **2773**

PARKING, GEORGE RELEIGH. India today: an introduction to

Indian politics. Toronto, Longmans, Green; New York, the John Day Co., 1946. x, 387p. **2774**

POLAK, H.S.L. Indians of South Africa; helots within the empire and how they are treated. Madras, Natesan, 1909. viii, 96, 47, 15p. **2775**

READ, Sir STANLEY. India: the new phase. London, P. Allen & Co., 1928. viii, 175p. **2776**

——— India's evolution: the triumph of British rule. Bristol, 1920. 15p. **2777**

RECTER, A., *pseud*. India; a reflection; suggestion and appeal. London, Southland, 1934. 21p. **2778**

REYNOLDS, REGINALD. A quest for Gandhi. Garden City, New York, Doubleday, 1952. 215p. **2779**

———Why India? Enfield Middlesex, the War Resisters' International, 1942. 27p. **2780**

———White Sahib in India. London, Socialist Book Centre, 1946. xv, 247p. **2781**

ROHDE, P.P. Indien og den indiske Frihedskamp. Verdenskrisen og Indien. Kbenhavn, 1932. 335p. **2782**

RUTHERFORD, V.H. Modern India, its problems and their solution. London, the Labour Publishing Co., 1927. xvi, 268p. **2783**

SMITH, SAMUEL. India and its problems; letters from India, 1904-5. London, W. Isbister, 1905. 48p. **2784**

SMITH, WILLIAM ROY. Nationalism and reforms in India. London and Oxford, Yale University, 1938. vi, 485p. **2785**

STOKES, SAMUEL EVANS. Essays: political and national. Madras, S. Ganesan, 1921. 153p. **2786**

——— National self-realization. Madras, S. Ganesan, 1921. 99p. **2787**

SUNDERLAND, JABEZ THOMAS. India in bondage, her right to freedom and a study and a place among great nations. New York, Lewis Copeland Company, 1920. xviii, 531p. pls. ports **2788**

THOMPSON, EDWARD JOHN. Enlist India for freedom. London, V. Gollancz ltd., 1920. 120p. (Victory Books, no. 5). **2789**

———Ethical ideals in India today, lectures delivered at Conway Hall. Red Lion Square, W.C.I. on March 22, 1942. London,

Watts and Co., 1942. 39p. **2790**

TOLSTOI, LEV NIKOLACVICH, *Grof.* Tolstoi and India; an exchange of views on the struggle for Indian freedom. New York, America and India Feature and News Service, 1950. 32p. ports. **2791**

TOWNSEND, MEREDITH WHITE. Asia and Europe: studies presenting the conclusions formed by the author in a long life devoted to the subject of the relations between Asia and Europe. London, A. Constable & Co., 1905. xxiv, 404p. **2792**

WALLBANK, THOMAS WALTER. India: a survey of the heritage and growth of Indian nationalism. New York, H. Holt, 1948. vii, 118p. (The Berkshire Studies in European History). **2793**

WATSON, B. Gandhi: voice of new revolution. Calcutta, 1922. 56p. **2794**

WELLOCK, WILFRED. India's awakening; its national and worldwide significance. London, The Labour Publishing Company, 1922. 69p. **2795**

WERY, ROBBERT FRANS. De ontiwikkeling van Indie binnen de Britische Commonwealth en de samenleving der volken. Leiden, 1948. (G). **2796**

WILLIAMS, LAURENCE FREDERIC RUSHBROOK. What about India. London, New York, etc. T. Nelson and Sons, ltd., 1938. x, 11, 176p. (Half-title: Discussion books. General Editor: Richard Wilson and A.J.J. Ratcliff, no. 4). **2797**

YOUNGHUSBAND, Sir FRANCIS EDWARD. Dawn in India: British purpose and Indian aspiration. London, J. Murray, 1930, xvi, 331p. **2798**

(xii) Struggle for Freedom

ALEXANDER, HORACE GUNDRY. Congress rule in India; a study in social reform. London, V. Gollancz ltd. and the New Fabin Research Bureau, 1938. 31p. (On cover: New Fabian Research Bureau Publication, no. 39). **2799**

—— India since Cripps. Harmondsworth, Penguin, 1944. 93p. **2800**

A sympathetic appraisal of the negotiations made during

1942-43 between the British Government and Mahatma Gandhi and his colleagues in connection with India's struggle for freedom.

ALEXANDER, HORACE GUNDRY. The Indian ferment; a travellers' tale. Introduction by C.F. Andrews. London, Williams and Norgate Ltd., 1929. 9-253p. **2801**

———Social and political ideas of Mahatma Gandhi. New Delhi. Council of World Affairs. Bombay, Oxford University Press, 1949. 84p. **2802**

AMERY, LEOPOLD CHARLES MAURICE STENNETT. India and freedom. London, New York, etc. Oxford University Press, 1942. 122p. **2803**

"Selected speeches by the Secretary of State for India... to explain British policy in India." p. 1.

ANDREWS, CHARLES FREER. India and Britain: a moral challenge. London, Student Christian Movement Press, 1935. 189p. **2804**

Written in the form of a dialogue between Indian and British students, this book gives a fair idea of the political conditions in India.

———India and the Simon Report. New York, Macmillan, 1930. 191p. **2805**

A sympathetic appraisal of India's struggle for freedom by an Englishman giving an account of the reaction of the Indian nationalist leaders towards the Simon Report during 1928-29.

———The Indian problem. 2nd ed. Madras, G.A, Natesan & Co., 1923. viii, 136p. **2806**

A collection of essays on subjects like: Indian independence, *Swadeshi* movements, non-cooperation, national education, etc.

ANDREWS, CHARLES F. AND G. MUKERJI. Rise and growth of the Congress in India. London, Allen & Unwin, 1938. 304p. **2807**

A friend of India along with a nationalist summarizes the origin and growth of the Indian National Congress. Also gives a lucid account of the social and cultural movements which were directly or indirectly responsible for the rise of the nationalistic ideas in India during the 19th century.

Sources of Indian Civilization

ARDENNE DE TIZAC, ANDREE FRANC. Carolin d' L'Inde contre les Anglais; preface de nu. Sylvain L' evi. Paris. Editions des portiques, 1930. 270p. **2808**
    Author's pseud; Andree Viollis, at the head of title.
ARDITI, LUIGI. L' India di Gandhi. Ricordi di viaggi Firenze, Instituto geografico militore, 1930. 353p. **2809**
BAILLIE, Sir ANDRIEN WILLIAM MAXWELL, 6th bart, AND OTHERS. India from a back bench. London, Methuen, 1934. vii, 78p. **2810**
BARNS, Mrs. MARGARITA. Indian : today and tomorrow. London, George Allen and Unwin, 1937. 304p. **2811**
    Describes contemporary Indian situation from ten years of close contact with Indian affairs.
———The Indian press; a history of the growth of public opinion in India. London, G. Allen and Unwin, 1940. xv, 491p. **2812**
BARTON, Sir WILLIAM PALL. India's fateful hour. London, J. Murray. 1942. 157p. **2813**
BEAUCHAMP, JOAN. British imperialism in India; prepared for the labour research department. London, Lawrence, 1934. 224p. **2814**
    A member of the British Labour Party criticises the British policy in India and supports the national movement.
BESANT, Mrs ANNIE (WOOD). India and the empire: a lecture and various papers on Indian grievances. London, Theosophical Publishing Society, 1914. 152p. **2815**
———The parting of the way. Madras, Besant Press, 1919. 8p. **2816**
———Shall India live or die ? Madras, National Home Rule League, 1925. 159p. **2817**
BEVAN, EDWYN ROBERT. Indian nationalism : an independent estimate. London, Macmillan & Co., 1913. vii, 141p. **2818**
———Thoughts on Indian discontent. London, G. Allen and Unwin, 1929. 7-178p. **2819**
BLAIR, H. India: the eleventh hour. London, Chawton Publishing Co., 1934. 135p. **2820**
BOLTEN, JOHN ROBERT CLORNEY. Peasant and prince. London, G. Routledge and Sons, 1937. xi, 295p. **2821**
———The tragedy of Gandhi. London, G. Allen and Unwin,

1934. 326p. **2822**

BRAILSFORD, HENRY NOEL. Rebel India. New York, New Republic Inc., 1931. xi-xii, 262p. **2823**

—— Subject India. New York, The John Day, 1943. vii, 274p. **2824**

A liberal view of India's struggle for freedom and related subjects.

BRAISTED, PAUL JUDSON. Indian nationalism and the Christian colleges. New York, Association Press, 1935. xii, 171p. **2825**

Thesis (Ph. D.)—Columbia University, N.Y., 1935. "Selected bibliography": p. 164-171.

An attempt to discuss and prove that Indian nationalism was mainly inspired by English education. Some of the conclusions of this study are controversial as they are based mostly on secondary pro-British sources.

BRISTOW, Sir ROBERT CHARLES. Real India : a human problem of world importance. Johannesburg, South African Institute of International Affairs, 1945. 16p. **2826**

BRITTAIN, VERA MARY. Search after sunrise. London, Macmillan, 1951. 270p. **2827**

BROCKWAY, ARCHIBALD FENNER, 1888—The Indian crisis. London, Victor Gollancz, 1930. 208p. **2828**

"A sympathetic interpretation of the contemporary political situation."

BROWN, D. MACKENZIE, *ed.* The nationalist movement: Indian political thought from Ranade to Bhave. Berkeley. University of California, 1961. 244p. **2829**

A collection of writings of nine prominent Indian nationalist leaders with his introductory notes.

BRYANT, JOHN FORBES. Gandhi and the Indianisation of the empire. Cambridge, J. Hall and Son, London, Simpkin, Marshall, Hamilton, Kent and Co., 1924. vi, 228p. **2830**

That Gandhi's part is the major one in arousing the spirit of nationalism in India is the main thesis of this study.

BUCH, M.A. Rise and growth of Indian nationalism; non-violent nationalism; Gandhi and his school. Baroda, Atmaram Printing Press, 1939. vi, 246p. **2831**

A history of the nationalistic movement in India after the

first political rising in 1857 against the British power. Comments on Gandhi's techniques of organizing the non-violent revolution to overthrow foreign rule.

BUCK, OSCAR MACMILLAN. India looks for her future. New York, Friendship Press, 1930. viii, 214p. **2832**

CHIROL, Sir VALENTINE. India; with an introduction by the Right Hon. H.A.L. Fisher. London, E. Benn Ltd., 1926. 352p. (Half-title : The modern world : a survey of historical forces, vol. v). **2833**

—— Indian unrest. London, Macmillan, 1910. xvi, 371p. **2834**
An analysis and appraisal of the nationalist movement in India from its origin in the 19th century to the early 20th century.

CHURCHILL, Sir WINSTON LEONARD SPENCER. India : speeches and an introduction. London, T. Butterworth, 1931. 140p. **2835**

COATMAN, JOHN. India in 1925-26; 1927-1928; and in 1928-1929. Calcutta, Government of India Central Publication Branch, 1926-1930. xviii, 463, xviii, 462 and viii, 416p. **2836**

—— India: the road to self-government. 2nd imp. London, G. Allen & Unwin, 1912. 152p. **2837**

—— The Indian riddle: a solution suggested. London, H. Toulmin, 1932. 72p. **2838**

—— Years of destiny : India, 1926-1932; with a foreword by Lard Irwin of Kirby. London, Cape, 1932. 384p. **2839**

COBB, CYRIL STEPHEN. Imperium et libertes. India and our responsibilities and duties as citizens of the empire...being the substance of an address, etc. London, William Heinemann, 1890. 27p. **2840**

COELHO, M.A.F. Question: whither India ? Bombay, Thacker and Co., 1946. 185p. **2841**

CORBETT, JAMES EDWARD. My India. London, New York, Oxford University Press, 1952. 190p. illus. **2842**

COTTON, HENRY JOHN STEDMAN. New India, or India in transition. Rev. and enl. ed. with a portrait. London, Kegan Paul, Trench, Trubner and Co., 1907. ix, 301p. **2843**

COUPLAND, Sir REGINALD. Britain and India, 1600-1941. London, New York, Longmans, Green and Co., ltd., 1941. 94p. (On cover : Longman's pamphlets on the British commonwealth no. 1). **2844**

COUPLAND, Sir REGINALD. The Cripps mission. London, New York, etc., Oxford University Press, 1942. 64p. illus. ports. **2845**

——India : a re-statement. London, New York, Oxford University Press, 1945. viii, 311p. illus. map. **2846**

——The Indian problem : report on the constitutional problem in India. New York, London, etc., Oxford University Press, 1944. maps. tabs. diagrs. **2847**

COUSINS, JAMES HENRY. Footsteps of freedom: essays. Madras, Ganesh & Co., 1919. vi, 181p. **2848**

CRADDOCK, Sir REGINALD HENRY. Dilemma in India. 2nd ed. London, Constable, 1929. xviii, 378p. **2849**

CROMBIC, T.L. Towards liberty; being a Britisher's view concerning India. Adyar, Theosophical Publishing Society, 1916. 60p. **2850**

CROZIR, FRANK PERCY. A word to Gandhi : the lesson of Ireland. London, Williams and Norgate ltd., 1931. 142p. **2851**

DANIELL, C.R. Rebellion and remedy in India. Dacca, 19 Panchbhais Ghat, the author, 1931. 325p. **2852**

DARA, G.S. India—the position today. London, G.S. Dara, 1926. 32p. **2853**

DARLING, Sir MALCOLM LYALL. At freedom's door. Toronto and London, Oxford University Press, 1949. xiv, 369p. **2854**

DELLBRIDGE, JOHN. Revolution in India? London, Morley and M. Kennerly Jr., 1930. 56p. **2855**

DIETTRICH, FRITZ. Die Gandhi-revolution. Dresden, 1930. 214p. **2856**

DUFFETT, WALTER ELLIOT, etc. *comps*. India today; the background of Indian nationalism. New York, The John Day Company, 1942. 173p. illus. **2857**

DUNCAN, ARTHUR. India in crisis. London and New York, Putnam, 1931. xi, 270p. **2858**

DUNDRAS, L.J.L. The heart of Aryavarta: a study of the psychology of Indian unrest. London, Constable, 1925. 262p. **2859**

——Steps towards Indian Home Rule. London, Hutchinson, 1935. 128p. **2860**

DURANT, WILLIAM JAMES. The case for India. New York, Simon and Schuster, 1930. xii, 232p. "Bibliographical notes" : p. 212-228. **2861**

    For every chapter explanatory notes are listed at the end of each part. The second chapter on Gandhi has 138 notes.

DUTCHER, GEORGE MATHEW. The political awakening of the East; studies of political progress in Egypt, India, China, Japan and the Philippines. New York, Cincinnati, The Abingdon Press, 1925. 372p. (Wesleyan University, George Slocum Bennett Foundation Lectures. 5th series; 1922-1923). **2862**

    A survey of awakening of nationalism in India.

EATON, JEANETTE. Gandhi, fighter without a sword. Illustrated by Ralph Ray. New York, Morrow, 1950. 253p. illus. (Morrow Junior Books). **2863**

ELLAM, J.E. Swaraj; the problem of India; with a foreword by Lord Brontford of Newick, P.C. London, Hutchinson & Co., 1930. xiii, 15-288p. **2864**

ELWIN, HARRY VERRIER HOLMAN. Mahatma Gandhi. London, Golden Vista Press, 1932. 28p. **2865**

——Truth about India : can we get it ? With seven appendices. Preface by Laurence Housman. London, G. Allen and Unwin, 1932. 105p. **2866**

FIELDED, LIONEL. Beggar my neighbour. London, Seeker and Warburg, Bombay, International Book House, 1944. 99p. **2867**

FISCHER LOUIS. The life of Mahatma Gandhi. London, Cape, 1951. 593p. **2868**

FISHER, FREDERICK JOHN. India's silent revolution. with the collaboration of Gertrude M. Williams. New York, The Macmillan Company, 1919. 6, 192p. pls. **2869**

FULLER, JOHN FREDERICK CHARLES. India in revolt. London, Eyre and Spottiswoode, 1931. 272p. **2870**

GARRATT, GEOFFREY THEODORE. An Indian commentary. London, Jonathan Cape, 1930. 2nd rev. ed. 336p. **2871**

    First published in 1928, it is an exposition of the political problem of the time.

GILCHRIST, ROBERT NIVEN. Indian nationality, with an introduction by Ramsay Muir. London, Longman, Green and Co., 1920. xviii, 246p. **2872**

    An attempt to prove that it was the contact with the West which brought to India the concept of nationalism.

GRAY, R.M. The present deadlock in India. London, Shident Christian Movement, 1932. 15p. **2873**

GREENWALL, HARRY JAMES. Storm over India. London, Hurst and Blackett Ltd., 1933. x, 287p. **2874**

GREGG, RICHARD BARTLETT. A disciple for non-violence. Indian edition. Ahmedabad, Navajivan Publishing House, 1941. 42p. **2875**

———The power of non-violence. 2nd ed, London, George Routledge & Sons, 1938. xi, 308p. **2876**

    First published in 1935 it explains non-violence in modern western concepts and ideology and "tests the idea of non-violence with the recent findings of psychology, military and political strategy, political theory, economics, physiology, biology, ethics, penology and education."

———Psychology and strategy of Gandhi's non-violent resistance. Madras, S. Ganesan, 1929. viii, 169p. **2877**

———Training for peace : a program for peace workers, supplement to The Power of Non-Violence, Philadelphia, J.B. Lippincott Co., 1937. iv, 40p. **2878**

HALIFOX, EDWARD FREDERICK LINDLEY WOOD. Indian problem speeches. London, G. Allen and Unwin Ltd., 1932. 376p. **2879**

HARCOURT, HENRY. Sidelights on the crisis in India, being the letters of an Indian civilian and some replies of an Indian friend: the letter by H. Harcourt, with a foreword by Cyril Norwood. London, New York, Longmans, Green and Co., 1924. xi, 117p. **2880**

Harrison, Agatha and Bailey Gerold. India, 1939-1942. London, National Peace Council, 1942. 30p. **2881**

HART, ERIC GEORGE. Gandhi and the Indian problem. London, Hutchinson and Co., 1931. 155p. **2882**

HARTOG, MABEL HELENE. Living India. London, Blackie & Son, 1935. xiii, 200p. **2883**

    "A sympathetic study of India and Indian problems."

HEATH CARL. Gandhi. 2nd enl. ed. London, G. Allen & Unwin, 1948. 43p. **2884**

HOGG, DOROTHY. India : a plea for understanding. London, Allahabad, Kitab Mahal, 1946. 142p. **2885**

—— Moral challenge of Gandhi. Allahabad, Kitab Mahal, 1945. 38p. **2886**

HOLLAND, WILLIAM EDWARD SLADES. The goal of India. London, United States Council for Missionary Education, 1917. 256p. illus. **2887**

HOLLAND, WILLIAM L. Asian nationalism and the West. New York, London, Macmillan, 1953. 449p. **2888**

 An international symposium on nationalist movements in Southern and Eastern Asia.

HOLMES, JOHN HAYNES. Gandhi before pilot : a sermon on Indian revolution. New York, Community Church, 1930. **2889**

HOLMES JOHN HAYNES, and others. Mahatma Gandhi; the world significance. By John Haynes Holmes, P.C. Bridge and P.E. James. Calcutta, the Research Home, n.d. viii, 239p. **2890**

 Appended with Mahatma Gandhi's jail experiences (both South African and India) and all about his fast, pp. 88-239.

HOUGHTON, BERNARD. The issue in India. Madras, Tagore and Co., 1922. 34p. **2891**

HOULSTON F.M. AND PYARELAL. India analysed. London, V. Gollancz, 1933. **2892**

HOYLAND, JOHN SOMMERVELL. The case for India. London, and Toronto, J.M. Dent and Sons, 1929. vii, 173p. **2893**

—— The cross moves East. London, George Allen & Unwin, 1931. 160p. **2894**

"A study in the significance of Gandhi's satyagraha." -*t.p.*

—— Indian crisis, the background. London, George Allen & Unwin, 1943. 195p. **2895**

 A sympathetic study of India and her struggle for freedom.

HULL, WILLIAM ISAAC. India's political crisis. Baltimore, The John Hopkins Press; London, Oxford University Press, 1930. xvii, 190p. (Half-title: John Hopkins University Studies in historical and political science; Extra vols. New series, no. 7). **2896**

HUNTINGDON, Lord. Commonsense about India. London, and Toronto, William Heinemann, 1942. 76p. **2897**

HUTCHINSON, LESTER. Conspiracy at Meerut. Preface by Harold J. Laski. London, George Allen & Unwin, 1935. 190p. **2898**

Personal reminiscences of the Meerut trial in 1930, in which the author was one of the leading figures.

HYNDMAN, HENRY MAYERS. The truth about India. Madras, 1921. 53p. **2899**

JENNINGS, IVOR. Commonwealth in Asia; being the Waynflete lectures delivered in the college of St. Mary Magdalan. Oxford, 1949. London, Oxford University Press, 1951. 124p. **2900**

JOHNSON, JULIA EMILY, comp. Independence for India ? New York, The H.W. Wilson Company, 1943. 292p. **2901**

JOHNSTON, JAMES. Can the Hindus rule India ? London, King, 1935. xv, 144p. **2902**

——Political future of India: an examination of some of the government proposals. London, King, 1933. 67p. **2903**

JONES, ELI STANLEY. The Christ of the Indian road. New York, Cincinnati, The Abingdon Press, 1925. 213p. **2904**

——Mahatma Gandhi; an interpretation. New York, Abingdon Cokasbury Press, 1948. 160p. **2905**

JONES, GEORGE E. Tumult in India. New York, Dodd, Mead & Co., 1948. x, 277p. **2906**

Portrays the underlying problems and the consequent outlook of India's people and leaders during 1946-47.

JONES, MARC EMUND. Gandhi lives. New cheaper edition. Drexel Hill, Pa., Bell Publishing Co., 1950. **2907**

JOSEPH P. What is wrong with India? Bombay, 1937. 272p. **2908**

KEIR, DAVID. Guide to the Indian problem. London, News Chronicle, 1935. 56p. **2909**

KENDALL, Mrs. PATRICIA. Come with me to India : a quest for truth among peoples and problems. New York, London, C. Scribner's Sons, 1931. x, 467p. **2910**

——India and the British: a quest for truth. London, C. Scribner's Sons, 1931. x, 467p. **2911**

KENWORTHY, J.M. India : a warning. London, Elkin Mathews and Marrot, 1931. vii, 117p. **2912**

KLOTZEL, CHESKEL ZWI. Indian in schmelztiegel. Leipzig, F.A. Brockhaus, 1930. 285p. **2913**

KRAUS, WOLFGANG. Die staats and volkerrechtliche stellung Britisch Indiens. Leipzig, R. Noske, 1930. viii, 226p. (G). **2914**

KROPOTKIN, P.A. Selected writings on anarchism and revolution, edited by Martin. A. Miller. Cambridge, M.I.P., 1970. viii, 374p. **2915**

LACEY, PATRICK. Fascist India. London, Nicholson and Watson, 1946. 150p. **2916**

LEX, *Pseud.* India at the cross roads. London, India Publications, 1930. 32p. **2917**

LILLY, WILLIAMS SAMUEL. India and its problems. London, The author, 1902. 324p. **2918**

LINLITHGO, *The Marquess of.* Speechs and statements of the Marquess of Linlithgo (1936-1943). New Delhi, Bureau of Public Information, 1945. xxiii, 467p. **2919**

LONDON, *London Indian Society.* Report of the Annual Conference of all India residents in the United Kingdom, Dec. 1898. London, the Society, 1899. 16p. **2920**

LONDON, *National Liberal Club.* A debate on the awakening of India opened by the Hon. G.K. Gokhale. London, the Club, 1905. 12p. **2921**

LOTHIAN, Sir ARTHUR CUNNINGHAM. Kingdoms of yesterday. With a foreword by Campton Mackenzie. London, Murray, 1951. 228p. **2922**

LOVETT, Sir HARRINGTON VERNEY. The importance of a clear understanding of Britain's work in India; an inaugural lecture delivered before the University of Oxford on November 4, 1920. Oxford, the Clarendon Press, 1920. 16p. **2923**

LUDLOW, JOAN MALCOLM FORBES. Thoughts on the policy of the Crown towards India. London, J. Ridgway, 1927. vii 330p. **2924**

MACDONALD, JAMES RAMSAY. The awakening of India. London, Hodder and Stoughton, n.d. 192p. **2925**

MAC MUNN, Sir GEORGE. Turmoil and tragedy in India; 1914 and after. London, Jarrolds, 1935. 294p. **2926**

MACNICOL, NICOL. The making of modern India. London, New York, Oxford University Press, 1924. viii, 235p. **2927**

900 History

MARRIOTT, JOHN ARTHUR RANSOME. The English in India : a problem politics. Oxford, Calrendon Press, 1932. x, 322p. **2928**

MARTIN, BRITON. New India, 1885 : British official policy and the emergence of the Indian National Congress. Bombay, Oxford University Press, 1970. xii, 365p. **2929**

MARX, KARL & ENGELS, FRIEDRICH. Marx and Engels on India. Edited with a preface by Mulk Raj Anand. Allahabad, Socialist Book Club, n.d. 154p. **2930**

MONTAGU, EDWIN SAMUEL. Indian diary; edited by Venetio Montagu. London, Heinemann, 1930. xv, 410p. illus. **2931**

MOON, PENDEREL. Strangers in India. London, Faber and Faber, 1943. 212p. **2932**

"In this book an attempt has been made to connect discussion of Indian problem with typical Indian incidents, illustrative of the way of life and the modes of thought and speech of the people."

MUELLER, SIEGHILD. Ausserindische Einflusse und Vorbilder und die indische Nationalbewegung; eine Untersuchung an Hand de Schriften Von Fuhrern der Bewegung U.A. Gopal Krishna Gokhale, Bal Gangadhar Tilak, Subhas Chandra Bose, Jawaharlal Nehru and Mahatma Gandhi. Heidelberg, 1946. 224, xii, xilp. **2933**

A study of the nationalistic ideas of Gopal Krishna Gokhale, Bal Gangadhar Tilak, Subhas Chandra Bose, Jawaharlal Nehru and Mahatma Gandhi.

MURRAY, K.M. Some facts about India. London, Southend, 1934. **2934**

NANDY, ALFRED. Indian unrest, 1919-20. Dehra Dun. Garhwali Press, 1921. vi, 274p. **2935**

NORTON, EARDLEY. Two memorable speeches of Eardley Norton, delivered at Madras giving an account of the work of Indian political agency and his English travels. Lucknow, G.P. Varma and Bros., 1889. 24p. **2936**

O'DONNELL, CHARLES JAMES. The causes of present discontent in India. London, T.F. Unwin, 1908. 119p. **2937**

OSBURN, ARTHUR CARR. Must England lose India? the nemesis of empire. London, and New York, A.A. Knof, 1930. vii, 280p. **2938**

PAGE, KIRBY. Is Mahatma Gandhi the greatest men of the age? New York, the author, 1922. ii, 64p. **2939**

PALMER, JULIAN. Sovereignty and Paramountcy in India. London, Stevens, 1930. 104p. **2940**

PHILIP, ANDRE. India: a foreign view. With an introduction by the Viscount Burnham. London, Sidgwick and Jackson, ltd., 1932. viiii, 260p. **2941**

PICKLES, HERBERT AND TINKER, T. India, world and empire. London, Oxford University Press, 1939. 416p. illus. **2942**

PIRIOU, ERNEST. L' Inde contemporaire et le mouvement national. Paris, F. Allen. 1905. 273p. (F). **2943**

POLAK, HENRY, S.L. Arrest and the events leading up to it. London, Indian Conciliation Group, 1932. 32p. **2944**

——Mr. Gandhi's arrest and the events leading upto it. London Friends Book Centre, 1932. 32p. **2945**

—— Mahatma Gandhi; an enlarged and uptodate edition of his life and teachings, with an account of his activities in South Africa and India down to his departure for London to attend the Second Round Table Conference. With appreciations by Rt. Hon. Sastri and others. 9th ed. Madras, G.A. Natesan and Co., 1931. xvi, 200p. **2946**

POLAK, MILLIE GRAHAM. Mr. Gandhi : the man. Foreword by C.F. Andrews. Bombay, Vora and Co., 1948. 146p. **2947**

POLE, DAVID GRAHAM. India in transition; with a foreword by Rt. Hon. Wedgwood Benn, London, L. and Virginia Woolf at the Hogarth Press, 1932. xii, 395p. **2948**

——I refer to India. London, British Committee on Indian affairs. 1929. 197p. **2949**

POPE, MARGARET. Imperialism in action; with a preface by C. Rajagopalachariar. Bombay, Hind Printing Works, Kandewadi Girgaon, 1944. 95p. **2950**

READ, MARGARET AND COCKIN, F.A. Some aspects of the Indian situation. London, Student Christian movement. 1920. 32p. **2951**

REED, Sir STANLEY and P.R. CADELL. India : the new phase. London, P. Allen & Co. ltd., 1928. viii, 175p. (The Westminster Library). **2952**

REISNER, I.M. and GOLDBERG, N.M. Tilak and the struggle for

Indian freedom. New Delhi, People's Publishing House, 1966. 682p. **2953**

ROBERTS, W.H. Review of the Gandhi movement in India. New York, Academy of Political Science, 1923. **2954**

RUTHERFORD, V.H. Modern India; its problems and their solution. London, Labour Publishing Company, 1927. xvi, 268p. **2955**

SANDERSON, GORHAM D. India and the British imperialism. New York, Bookman Association, 1951. 383p. **2956**

SANFORD, CHARLES. India, land of regards; foreword by Robert Bernays. Cambridge Shire England, Fenland Press, 1934. 301p. **2957**

SAUNDERS, KENNETH. Whither Asia : a study of three leaders. New York, The Macmillan Co., 1933. vi, 221p. **2958**
   Deals with the movements of Mahatma Gandhi, Hu Shih and Kagawa.

SCATCHERD, F.R. The friends of India, 'Wise and otherwise'. London, East India Association, 1920. 31p. **2959**

SCHAUB, EDWARD LERORY. Progressism; an essay in social philosophy. Calcutta, the University, n.d. 305p. **2960**
   A collection of Calcutta University Readership lectures, it deals with subjects like : Basic factors of Indian life; the problem of nationality; the meaning of Indian nationality; present tendencies towards development of nationality.

Schuster, Sir GEORGE ERNEST AND WINT, GUY. India and democracy. Toronto, Macmillan, 1941. xvi, 444p. **2961**

SHARP, HENRY. Good-bye India. London, Oxford University Press, 1946. viii, 244p. **2962**

SIMON, Sir JOHN ALLSEBROOK. Two broadcast talks on India. London, Faber and Faber, 1930. 35p. **2963**

SKRINE, FRANCIS HENRY BENNETT. India's hope. London, W. Thacker, 1929. 61p. **2964**

SMITH, WILLIAM ROY. Nationalism and reform in India. New Haven, Yale University Press. London, H. Milford, Oxford University Press, 1938. vi, 485p. **2965**
   A detailed study of the origin and growth of nationalism, social and constitutional reforms in India from 1600 to

1935. The author's conclusions are on the Government documents and the books written by Englishmen. Comments on Gandhi's ideas about *Swaraj,* boycott movement, Caliphate movement, Civil Disobedience movement, Round Table Conference and the Government of India Act, 1935.

SPEAR, THOMAS GEORGE PERCIVAL. National harmony. Bombay, New York, Oxford University Press, 1946. 31p. (Oxford Pamphlets on Indian affairs, no. 38). **2966**

SPENDER, JOHN ALFRED. Changing East. London, Cassell, 1935. 287p. **2967**

STANDERATH, FRANZISKA. Indiens freiheitskamf 1930; gefangnisbriefe des mahatma aus der zeit vom 31, juli bis 6, november, 1930, mit originalaufrahamen und faksimile von handschriftlinchen briefen des mahatma an die venfesserin. Graz, etc., Leuschner and Lubensky, 1931. 478p. pls, ports, facsims. (G). **2968**

STOKES, ROBERT HENRY CYRIL. The moral issue in India; with an introduction by the Right Hon. Lord Meston. London, J. Murray, 1931, xi, 40p. **2969**

STRABOLGI, JOSEPH MONTAGUE KENWORTHY, *baron.* India: a warning. London, E. Mathews and Marret,1931. vii, 117p. illus. **2970**

SUNDERLAND, J.T. India. America and world brotherhood. Madras, Ganesh & Co., 1924. xv, 295, viip. **2971**

 Consists of three parts : Pt. 1 is devoted to three eminent Americans; Pt. 2 deals with India's struggle for freedom and nationhood; Pt. 3 deals with 'World-wide brotherhood'.

SUNDERLAND, JABEZ THOMAS. India in bondage. New rev. ed. brought strictly up-to-date, including the momentous events of the last two years. New York, Lewis Copeland Company, 1932. vii, xxiii, 589p. **2972**

——Truth about India : the story of a great nation struggling to be free, told in a series of selection from (the author's) timely and powerful book: India in Bondage. New York, Copeland, 1930. 63p. **2973**

SUTHERLAND, W.A. The British Government, the Hindus, the

Mohammedans and Swaraj in India. Madras, Graves and Co., 1907. 59p. **2974**

SWINSON, ARTHUR. Six minutes to sunset; the story of General Dyer and the Amritsar affairs. London, Davies, 1964. vii, 215p.

TEGART, Sir C.A. Terrorism in India. London, Royal Empire Society, 1932. 19p. **2975**

TESKE, HANS. Das heutige Indien und seine freiheitsbewegung. Plaven, 1930. 8p. **2976**

THOMAS, F.W. Indianism and its expansion. Calcutta, the University, 1942. vii, 107p. **2977**
    A collection of the Calcutta University readership lectures.

THOMPSON, EDWARD JOHN. Enlist India for freedom. London, V. Gollancz, 1940. 120p. **2978**

———Ethical ideals in India today. London, 1942. 39p. **2979**

THOMPSON, EDWARD JOHN. A farewell to India. New York, E.P. Dutton & Co., 1931. 292p. **2980**

———Reconstructing India. New York, L. Mac Veagl, The Dial Press; Toronto, Longmans, Green and Co., 1930. xii, 404p. **2981**

THOMPSON EDWARD AND G.T. GARRATT. Rise and fulfilment of British rule in India. Allahabad, Central Book Depot, 1958 xii, 690p. maps. **2982**
    First published in 1934, this is a sympathetic appraisal of India's struggle for freedom and criticises the British repressive policies.

TRCUB, MARIE WILLEM FREDERIK. Het gist in Indie. Een analyse der hedendaagsche inlandsche beweiging. Haarlem, 1927. 87p. **2983**

TREVASKIS, HUGH KENNEDY. Indian Babel. London, F. Muller, 1935. 212p. **2984**

TUKER, Sir FRANCIS VAN SIMMS. While memory serves; the story of the last two years of British rule in India. London, Cassell, 1950. xiv, 668p. **2985**

TYSON, G. Danger in India. London. Murray, 1932. 133p. **2986**

VAN TYNE, CLAUDE HALSTEAD. India in ferment. New York, London, D. Appleton and Company, 1923, xi, 252p. **2987**

VIATOR, A.K. Deutschlands Anteil an Indiens Schicksal. Leipzig, 1918. 94p. **2988**

Sources of Indian Civilization

WALLBANK, THOMAS WALTER. India : a survey of the heritage and growth of Indian nationalism. New York, H. Holt, 1948. vii, 118p. maps. (The Berkshire studies in European history).
2989

WATSON, BLANCHE. Gandhi and non-violent resistance, the non-co-operation movement of India. Madras, Ganesh & Co., 1923. xxiv, 549p.
2990

    A collection of gleanings from the American Press.

——Gandhi-voice of the new revolution: a study of non-violent resistance in India. With a foreword by John Hejnes Holmes. Calcutta, Saraswati Library, 1922. 56p.
2991

WENZ, H. Das indische reich. Leipzig, 1939. 182p. (G). **2992**

WERY, ROBBERT FRANS. De on wikkeling van India binnen de Britsche Commonwealth en de Samenleving der volken. Amsterdam, Keizerskroon, 1948. 263, ivp.
2993

WHATELY, M. Condition of India; report of the delegation sent to India by the India League in 1932. London, India League, 1934. 534p.
2994

WHEELER, POST. India against the storm. New York, Books Inco., distributed by E.P. Dutton and Company Inc., 1944. 350p.
2995

WHYTE, FREDERICK. India: a bird's eye view. London, Royal Institute of International Affairs, 1944.
2996

WILLIAMS, G. The Indian student and the present discontent. London, Hodder and Stoughton, 1910. 45p.
2997

WILLIAMS, LAURENCE FREDERIC RUSHBROOK. India. Oxford, The Clarendon Press, 1941. 32p. (Oxford pamphlets on world affairs, no. 32).
2998

——Indigenous rule in India. Manchester, John Rylands, 1930. 21p.
2999

——What about India? New York and Toronto, Nelson, 1938. 176p.
3000

WILSON, E.W. The India chaos. London, Eyre and Spotiswoode, 1932. 285p.
3001

——Some Indian problems; being some essays addressed to patriots with the "Congress Mentality". With a foreword by Jawaharlal Nehru. Allahabad, Ram Narain Lal, 1929. xii, 108p.
3002

900 History

WILSON, FREDERICK WILLIAM. Some Indian problems; being some essays addressed to patriots with the "Congress Mentality". With a foreword by Jawaharlal Nehru. Allahabad, Lala Rammohan Lal, 1929. xii, 108p. **3003**

    Impressions of an Englishman on the rise and growth of the nationalistic movement in India under Gandhi's leadership.

WINSLOW, JACK COPLAY AND ELWIN, VERRIER. Gandhi: the dawn of Indian freedom. Foreword by Archbishop of York. London, George Allen & Unwin. 1932. 224p. **3004**

    A biographical study of Mahatma Gandhi, with special reference to his attitude towards the role of the Christian church in Free India.

WODACOTT, JOHN EVANS. India on trial: a study of present conditions. London, Macmillan, 1929. xv, 257p. **3005**

——India: the truth. London, P. Allen, 1930. 93p. **3006**

WOFFORD, CLARE (LINDGREN). India afire. New York, J. Day Co., 1951. 343p. **3007**

WOLPERT, STANLEY A. Tilak and Gokhale: Revolution and reform in the making of Modern India. Berkeley. University of California Press, 1962. **3008**

    A comparative biographical study of two great leaders of Maharashtra and the role they played in India's struggle for freedom.

WOOD, F.F.L. *Viscount Halifax*. Indian problems: speeches. London, G. Allen and Unwin, 1932. 376p. **3009**

——Some aspects of the Indian problem. London, Oxford University Press, 1932. 31p. **3010**

WYLLIE, JOHN ALFRED. India at the parting of the ways, monarchy, diarchy, or anarchy; English version, revised and amplified of "La India en la bifurcacion de sus vias; monarquia, diarquia o anarquia". With a foreword by Sir Michael F. O'Dwyer. London, Lincoln Williams Ltd., 1934. xv, 243p. ports. **3011**

    Bibliography: p. 240-243.

    An annotated bibliography. Literature for and against Gandhi is separately listed.

YEATS-BROWN, F. Pageant of India. Philadelphia, Macrae-

Smith Company, 1943. xii, 304p. **3012**

YOUNGHUSBAND, FRANCIS EDWARD. Dawn in India: British purpose and Indian aspiration. London, John Murray, 1931. xvi, 331p. **3013**

    First published in 1939 it traces the historical and spiritual background of India's struggle for freedom and shows the enduring foundation upon which it rested.

ZACHARIAS, H.C.E. Renascent India, from Rammohan Roy to Mohandas Gandhi. London, G. Allen and Unwin, ltd., 1933. 304p. **3014**

ZETLAND, LAWRENCE JOHN LUMBY DUNDAS, *2nd Marquis of*— The heart of Aryavarta: a study of the psychology of Indian unrest. London, Constable & Co., 1925. xvii, 262p. **3015**

——, *2nd Marquis of India*. Retrospect and prospect. Nottingham, England, 37-4890, University College, 1936. 20p. (Gist Foundation lecture, 1935). **3016**

(xiii) India—Partition of

BIRDWOOD, C.B. *2nd Baron*. Continent decides: introducing two new members (India and Pakistan) of...Commonwealth. London, Hale, 1953. 315p. **3017**

BOUNKE-WHITE, MARGARET. Half-way to freedom. New York, Simon & Schuster, 1949. xi, 3-245p. **3018**

    "A report on the New India in the words and photographs of 'Life' correspondent."

BRECHER, MICHAEL. Succession in India: a study in decision making. London, Oxford University Press, 1966. xii, 269p. **3019**

CAMPBELL-JOHNSON, ALAN. Mission with Mountbatten. New York, Dutton, 1953. 383p. **3020**

    The Viceroy's press attache describes in details the account of the negotiations that preceded the transfer of power and partition.

HODSON, H.V. Great divide: British, India, Pakistan, London, Hutchinson, 1969. xii, 563p. front. **3021**

JONES, GEORGE E. Tumult in India. New York, Dodd, Mead,

1948. vii, 277p. **3022**

George E. Jones was a correspondent of the *New York Times*. In this book he reviews the political events in India during the years 1946-47.

LAMB, BEATRICE PITNEY. India: A world in transition. Rev. ed. New York, Praeger, 1966. 382p. **3023**

LUMBY, ESMOND, W.R. The transfer of power in India, 1945-47. New York, Praeger, 1954. 274p. illus. **3024**

An account of the events relating to the transfer of sovereignty from Britain to India and Pakistan.

MANSERGH, NICHOLAS & LUMBY, E.W.R., *eds*. Transfer of power, 1942-47. London, H.M.S.O., 1970-71. 3 vols. (Constitutional relations between Britain and India). **3025**

Contents :

V. 1: Cripps mission, Jan-April, 1942.

V. 2: Quit India, April-Sept. 1942.

V. 3: Reassertion of authority, Gandhi's fast and the succession to the Viceroyalty, 21st September 1942-12th June, 1943.

MELLOR, ANDREW. India since partition. London, Turnstile Press, 1951. viii, 156p. **3026**

MOON, PENDREL. Divide and Quit. Berkeley, University of California Press, 1962. 302p. **3027**

An analysis of the political and social issues which led to the partition of India in 1947.

MORELAND, WILLIAM H. AND A.C. CHATTERJEE. A short history of India. London, Longmans, Green, 1957. 4th ed. xiii, 552p. maps. **3028**

The present edition includes the story of the various forces which eventually led to the division of the continent of India into two new countries.

MOUNTBATTEN, *Lord*. Time only to look forward. London, N. Kaye, 1949. vii, 267p. illus. **3029**

A collection of Lord Mountbatten's important speeches which he made during 1947-48.

MURPHY, GARDNER. In the minds of men: the study of human behaviour and social tension in India. New York, Basic Books Inc., 1953. xiv, 306p. **3030**

"Based on the UNESCO studies by social scientists conducted at the request of the Government of India." -*t.p.*

PHILIPS, CYRIL H., ed. The evolution of India and Pakistan, 1857-1947. London, Oxford University Press, 1962. **3031**

> Contains materials on the economic, social and political matters which led to the partition of India. This is volume IV of a proposed four-volume series entitled: 'Select Documents on the History of India and Pakistan'.

PHILIPS, C.H. AND WAINWRIGHT, MARY D. Partition of India; policies and perspectives, 1935-1947. London, Allen & Unwin, 1970. 607p. **3032**

SMITH, R.A. Divided India. New York, McGraw-Hill, 1947. vi, 259p. **3033**

SPRATT, PHILIP. An approach to Indian constitutional problem. Calcutta, Renaissance Publishers, 1946. 20p. **3034**

TUKER, Sir FRANCIS. While memory serves. London and Toronto, 1950. xiv, 668p. illus. **3035**

> This is an illustrated and documentary tale of the partition of India, told by one who watched events from the Headquarters of the Eastern Command. The 39th chapter, "Why did we quit?" is particularly worth reading.

WALLBANK, THOMAS WALTER. India in the new era; a study of the origin and development of the Indian Union and Pakistan, new nations in a changing Asia. Chicago, Scott, Foresman, 1951. 204p. illus. **3036**

> A descriptive and illustrated account of the partition of India and an examination of the reasons which are responsible for the foundation of Pakistan.

(xiv) Kashmir issue

BIRDWOOD, *Lord*. Two nations and Kashmir. London, Robert Hale, 1956. **3037**

> An appraisal of the Kashmir problem.

BRECHER, MICHAEL. The struggle for Kashmir. New York, Oxford University Press, 1953. **3038**

> An appraisal of the events from 1947 to 1953 concerning

the Kashmir conflict.

STEIN, M.A., *tr*. Rajatarangini: Kalhana's Rajatarangini. Translated with an introduction, commentary and appendices by M. A. Stein. Westminster, Archibald Constable & Co., 1900. 4 vols. **3039**
    A chronicle of the Kings of Kashmir.

YOUNGHUSBAND, Sir FRANCIS EDWARD. Kashmir, described by Sir Francis Younghusband, K.C.I.E. Painted by Major E. Molyneux, D.S.O. London, A. & C. Black, 1909. xv, 283p. 70 col. pl. (incl. front.) fold map. **3040**

(xv) Independence and After (1947)

AUSTIN, GRANVILLE. Indian constitution: corner stone of a nation. Oxford, Clarendon Press, 1966. xvii, 390p. **3041**

BALABUSHEVICH, V.V. AND DYAKOV, A.M. Contemporary history of India. New Delhi, Peoples' Publishing House, 1968. viii, 585p. **3042**

BAXTER, CRAIG. Jan Sangh: a biography of an Indian political party. Bombay, Oxford University Press, 1971. x, 352p. **3043**

BETTELHEIM, CHARLES. India independent. London, Macgibbon & Kee, 1968. xv, 410p. **3044**

BOWELS, CHESTER. Ambassador's report. New York, Harper, 1954. 415p. **3045**
    An intensely readable report on his work by an American Ambassador who, in his own daughter's phrase, felt "at home in India."

—— A view from New Delhi; selected speeches and writings, 1963-1969. Bombay, Allied Publishers, 1969. 276p. **3046**

BOWLES, CYNTHIA: At home in India. New York, Harcourt, Brace, 1956. 178p. **3047**
    Few books by Americans about India have been so popular in both countries at this unassuming but perceptive story of her own experiences by the daughter of former Ambassador Bowles.

BRECHER, MICHAEL. Succession in India: a study in decision

making. London, Oxford University Press, 1966, xii, 269p. **3048**

BROWN, WILLIAM NORMAN. The United States and India and Pakistan. Cambridge (Mass). Harvard, (1953), 1955. 308p. **3049** Co-winner of the Watumull Prize awarded by the American Historical Association for the best book on the history of India. The author spent much of his childhood in this country, studied Sanskrit with a pandit in Varanasi, and later became Professor of English at a college in Jammu.

CATLIN, *Mrs.* GEORGE EDWARD GORDON. Search after sunrise. London, Macmillan & Co., 1951. 271p. **3050** "Describes the search of India and Pakistan for a new future."

DEAN, VERA (MICHALES). New patterns of democracy in India Cambridge, Mass. Harvard University Press, 1959. 226p. illus. **3051**

FINEGAN, JACK. India today. Bethany Press, 1955. 208p. **3052** Dr. Finegan spent a year in India on Fulbright award for research in archaeology and religion. A popular version of India.

FISHER, MARGARET WELPLEY. Indian approaches to a socialist society, by Margaret W. Fisher and Joan V. Bondurant. Berkeley, Institute of International Studies, University of California, 1956, 105, xiiip. (Indian Press Digest. Monograph series, no. 2). **3053**

FRIEDMAN, HARRY J. Consolidation of India since independence; a comparison and analysis of four territorial problems—the Portuguese possessions, the French possessions, Hyderabad, and Kashmir. Ann Arbor, University Microfilms, 1957. (University Microfilms, Ann Arbor, Michigan Publication no. 18, 280.) **3054**

GALBRAITH, JOHN KENNETH. Ambassador's journal; a personal account of the Kennedy years. Houghton, 1969. 656p. **3055**

GLEDHILL, ALAN. The republic of India. London, Stevens and Sons. 1954. 2nd ed. xii, 309p. **3056** A historical account of the development under British rule of formal governmental institutions, including central and provincial legislatures and the administrative and legal system.

GRIFFITHS, PERCIVAL J. Modern India. London, Benn, 1962. 3rd rev. ed. 255p. illus. (Nations of the modern world). **3057**
A valuable introductory survey of economic and political conditions in India since independence presented with historical background for the general reader.

HAHN, EMILY. The first book of India. Watts, 1955. 63p. **3058**
A delightful introduction to modern India written for young children.

HARRISON, SELIG S. India: the most dangerous decade. Princeton, Princeton University Press, 1960. **3059**
An American analysis of some political events which took place in India after 1947.

HARTEG, LADY. India: new pattern. London, George, Allen & Unwin, 1955. 158p. **3060**

JACKSON, COLIN. The new India. London, Fabian International Bureau, 1957. 33p. illus. (Fabian tract 306). **3061**

JUNCKERSTORFF, HENRY KURT. Reconciliation in South Africa and the states of the Indians in international law. Calcutta, Bookland, 1952. 82p. **3062**

LAMB, BEATRICE, P. India: a world in transition. New York. F. A. Praeger, 1966. 382p. 1st ed. published in 1963. **3063**
An account of India's political, social, and economic conditions, immediately after she won her independence in 1947.

LANZA DEL VASTO, JOSEPH J. Gandhi to Vinoba: the new pilgrimage. London, Rider, 1956. **3064**
An account of Vinoba Bhave, who founded the Bhoodan movement in India for the upliftment of poor and landless people of India, his life and teachings.

LEVI, WERNER. Free India in Asia. University of Minnesota, (1952), 1954. 161p. **3065**
This carefully documented study surveys India's position in the whole of Asia and her relations with each of the countries in the area, with emphasis on development since 1947.

LEWIS, MARTIN DEMING, ed. British in India; imperialism or trusteeship ? Boston, Heath, 1966. xiii, 114p. (Problems in

European civilization). **3066**

Low, D.A. *ed.* Soundings in modern South Asian history. University of California, 1968. 391p. **3067**

Lumby, E. W. R. Transfer of power in India, 1945-47. London, Allen & Unwin, 1954. 274p. maps. **3068**

Lyon, Jean. Just half a world away. Crowell, 1954. 373p. **3069**
Because she was born and reared in China, Miss Lyon came to India with more background for understanding an Asian country than many Westerners. She has lived in Indian villages; toured with Nehru in his private plane; walked for days on end with Vinoba Bhave. Her "search for the new India" ended in Almora, where she wrote her book.

Mellor, Andrew. India since partition. New York, F.A. Praeger. 1951. **3070**
An account of social, political and economic conditions in India after 1947.

Michener, James A. The voice of Asia. New York, Random. 1951. 338p. **3071**
An acknowledged authority examines and evaluates in human terms the changed outlook of the Asian world toward the West. The author recently revisited India.

Miller, J.D.D., *ed.* India, Japan, Australia partners in Asia. Canberra, Australian National University Press, 1968. xvii, 214p. **3072**

O'Connor, Edward Robert. India and democracy; an analysis of the 1951-1952 elections and their political impact. Ann Arbor, University Microfilms, 1955. (University Microfilms, Ann Arbor, Michigan. Publication no, 10, 782). **3073**

Parry, Clive. Commonwealth citizenship with special reference to India. Prepared for the Commonwealth Relations Conference, 1954. Lahore, New Delhi, Indian Council of World Affairs 1954. 25p. **3074**

Philips, C.H. and others. Evolution of India and Pakistan, 1858 to 1947; selected documents. London, Oxford University Press, 1963. xxi. 786p. **3075**

Rawlinson, H.G. India. New York. London, Macmillan. 1955. 90p. **3076**

A brief introduction to the new Republic of India, written for the "Lands and Peoples" series.

RENOU, MARIE-SIMORE. India I love. New York, Tudor, 1968. 138p. **3077**

ROOSEVELT, ELEANOR. India and the awakening East. New York, Harper and Row, 1953. 237p. **3078**
A pen picture of the impressions of authoress's visit to free India.

ROSENKJAER, JENS. Indien. Kobenhavn, Udenrigapolitiske selskab, 1958. 65p. (Udenrigspolitiske, ser. 3, no. 1). **3079**

SCHMID, PETER. India : miracle and reality. London, George G. Harrap, 1961. 256p. **3080**
A vivid account of the author's impressions of India's political and social problems.

Seminar on Leadership and Polical Institutions in India. University of California. Berkeley. 1956. **3081**
Leadership and political institutions in India, edited by Richard L. Park and Irene Tinker. Princeton. N.J. Princeton University Press, 1959. x, 486p.

SHEPHARD, G. Where the lion trod. London, Macmillan, 1960. 177p. **3082**
An account of the political, social and economic condition of the post-independent India.

SMITH, BRADFORD. Portrait of India. London, Robert Hale, 1962. 188p. **3083**
An objective version of India's social, political and economic problems.

SMITH, DONALD EUGENE. India as a secular state. Princeton, Princeton University Press, 1963.
A study of the efforts made by the Government of India in making India a secular state. **3084**

SPATE, O.H.K. India and Pakistan. New York, Dutton, 1954. 827p. **3085**
A detailed general and regional geography which also takes into account social facts and trends.

TALBOT PHILLIPS, *ed.* South Asia in the world today. Chicago, University of Chicago, 1950. 254p. **3086**
Fifteen lectures by experts on the social, economic, and

political forces emerging in South Asia.

TINKER, HUGH. Experiment with freedom: India and Pakistan, 1947. London, Oxford University Press, 1967. x, 165p. **3087**

——India and Pakistan: a political analysis. New York, F.A. Praeger, 1962. **3088**

> A controversial version of the forces which played a major role in the formation of Pakistan.

TRUMBULL, R. As I see India. London, Cassell, 1957. 256p. **3089**

> An account of a journalist's impression of India's social, political and economic problems of the post-independent period.

——As I see India. New York, Sloane, 1956. **3090**

> Mr. Trumbull came to India in 1947 as a correspondent for the *New York Times*, and stayed for seven and a half years. He saw India in the most dramatic period of her history, and writes about his experiences in direct, stimulating journalist's prose.

TUKER, FRANCIS, I.S. While memory serves. London, Cassell, 1950. xiv, 668p. **3091**

> An account of the partition of India, by the British General in charge of maintaining law and order during the partition days.

USEEM, JOHN. The Western-educated man in India; a study of his social roles and influence by John Useem and Ruth Hill Useem. New York, Dryden Press, 1955. xxii, 237p. **3092**

WALLBANK, T. WALTER. India in the new era. New York, Scott, Foresman. 1951. 204p. **3093**

> A study of the origin and development of the Indian Union and Pakistan, new nations in changing Asia, The author is a professor at the University of Southern California, and visited India in 1956 to work on a new book.

WARD, BARBARA. India and the West. Delhi, Publication Division, 1961. 247p. **3094**

WARD, DOROTHY JANE. India for the Indians. London, Arthur Barker, 1949. 239p. **3095**

> An account of India after Independence.

WOLSELEY, RONALD E. Face to face with India. New York, Friendship Press, 1954. 176p. **3096**

An account of the author's observations of India's religious political and social problems. The book has been written hurriedly and is meant for a casual reader.

WOYTINSKY, W.S. India, the awakening giant. New York, Harper, 1957. 201p. **3097**

The book deals with India's plans for industrialization, politics and social conditions of her people.

ZINKIN, MAURICE AND ZINKIN TAYA. Britain and India: requiem for empire. London, Chatto & Windus, 1964. 191p. **3098**

ZINKIN, TAYA. Report India. London, Chatto & Windus, 1962. 223p. **3099**

(xvi) Geography, Description & Travel

ADAMS, ANDREWLEITH. Wanderings of naturalist in India, the Western Himalayas, and Cashmere. Edinburgh, Edmonston and Douglas, 1867. xi, 338p. **3100**

ALBERUNI. Alberuni's India. English edition with notes and indices by Edward C. Sachau. London, Kegan Paul, Trubner & Co., 1910. 2 vols. **3101**

"An account of the religion, philosophy, literature, geography, chronology, astronomy, customs, laws and astrology of India, A.D. 1030." -*t.p.*

ALBRIGHT, M. CATHARINE. Letters from India. Birmingham, Cornish Bros., 1902. 120p. **3102**

ALEXANDER, Sir JAMES EDWARD. Travels from India to England: comprehending a visit to a Burman empire, and a journey through Persian Asia Minor, European Turkey. London, Prabury, Allen & Co., 1827. xv, (i) 301p. (part) plates, 2 maps. **3103**

ALLARDYCE, ALEXANDER. City of sun shine. London, W. Blackwood & Sons, 1877. 3 vols. **3104**

ALSDORF, LUDWING. Vorderindien: Bharat, Pakistan, Ceylon; eine Landesund Kulturkunde. Braunschweig, G. Westermann, 1955. 336. illus. **3105**

ANDREWS, C.F. True India: a plea for understanding. London, Allen & Unwin, 1939. 251p. **3106**

An account of the author's tour through India.

ARCHBOLD, WILLIAM ARTHUR JOBSON. Bengal Haggis: the lighter side of Indian life. London, Scholartis Press, 1928. 127p. **3107**

ARNOLD, Sir EDWIN. India revisited. Boston, Robert Brothers, 1890. 5p. 1, 324p. illus. **3108**

ARNOTT, PETER. More impertinence. Illustrated by Ivan Waller. London, Herbert Jenkins, 1948. 222p. **3109**

"Personal narrative based on the author's experience as an army officer in India."

ASHBY, LILLIAN LUKER AND WHATELY, ROGER. My India. London, Michael Joseph, 1938. 352p. **3110**

An account of the author's personal impressions of India covering the period from 1874 to 1936.

BARR, F. The imperial city: the story of Delhi and her royal rulers. Simla, Times Press, 1902. vi, 196p. **3111**

BEAL, SAMUEL, *tr*. Travels of Fah-Hian and Sung Yun. London. Trubner, 1869. **3112**

Fah Hian and Sung Yun, visited India in fifth and sixth centuries respectively. Translated from the Chinese it describes the conditions prevailing in the Buddhist India in those days.

BEATTLE, MALCOLM HAMILTON. On the Hoogly. London, Philip Allen, 1935. 307p. **3113**

Incidents and impressions during the author's employment in the Bengal pilot service.

BECHTOLD, FRITZ. Nanga Parbat adventure: a Himalayan expedition. Translated from the German by H. E. G. Tyndale. London, John Murray, 1935. xv, 93p. **3114**

BELL, THOMAS EVANS. The English in India: letters from Nagpore written in 1857-58. London, John Chapman, 1859. 202p. **3115**

—— The Oxus and the Indus (with map). London, Trubner & Co., 1869. 88p. **3116**

BERNIER, FRANCOIS. Travels in the Mughal empire. London, Oxford University Press, 1934. **3117**

Translated by A. Constable, and edited by V.A. Smith, it is an account of the author's stay at Aurangzeb's court for twelve years. Bernier was a French physician, arrived in India in 1658 and obtained first-hand knowledge of the life at the court of Aurangzeb.

BERNIER, FRANCOIS, *ed.* Travels in Hindustan or the History of the latest revolution of the dominions of the Great Mogol, from 1655 to 1661 as translated by Henry Ouldinburgh in 1684. Edited from the original with an elaborate index, glossary and appendices. Calcutta, Bangabasi Press, 1904. xx, 448, lxilip. **3118**

BERNOULLI, JEAN *ed.* and *tr.* Description historique et geographique de l' Inde, qui presente en trois volumes, enrichis de 64, cartes et antres planches : 1. La geographie de l' Indoustan, ecrite en latin; dan le pais meme, par le pere Joseph Tieffenthaler. 2. Des recherches historiques and chronologioues sur l' Inde and la description due cours du. 3. La carte general del' Inde, celles due cours, du Brahmapoutre and de la navigation in terienre du Bengale, avec des memoires relatifs or ces cartes, publies en angolois M. Jacques Rennell. Berlin, Impr. de C.S. Spener, 1786-89. 5 pt. in 3 vols and atlas (3 vols) of pls, maps. plans, fold tab. (F). **3119**

BLACKHAM, ROBERT JAMES. Incomparable India: tradition, superstition, truth. Forword by William Birdwood. London, Sampson Low, Marston & Co., 1923. xviii, 302p. **3120**

BONN, GISELA. Neues Licht aus Indien. Weisbaden, F.A. Brockhaus, 1958. 259p. illus. **3121**

BONSELS, WALDEMAR. Viaje a la India. Traduccion directa del abman por Gaby Maurer de laSerna y Consuelo Berges. Nota preliminer de F.S.R. Madrid, Aguilar, 1945. 536p. (S). **3122**

BOULNOIS, HELEN MARY. Mystic India. London, Methuen & Co., 1935. xi, 225p. **3123**

BOURKE-WHITE, MARGARET. Half way to freedom. New York, Simon & Schuster, 1949. xi, 3-245p. photos. **3124**

"A report on the new India in the words and photographs of *Life* correspondent."

BOWER, URSULA G. The hidden land. New York, Morrow, 1953. 260p. **3125**

A vivid and true description of a journey to the remote regions of Assam.

——Naga path. London, John Murray, 1950. x, 260p. pls, maps. **3126**

An account of journey into Ukhrul area, Manipur state, North Cachar and adjoining areas.

BROWNING, OSCAR. Impression of Indian travel. London, Hodder & Stoughton, 1903. xvi, 236p. **3127**

BRUNTON, PAUL. A hermit in the Himalayas: the journey of a lonely exile. London, Rider & Co., 1937. 190p. **3128**

BURGESS, JAMES. Geography of India. London, T. Nelson & Co., 1871. 68p. **3129**

——A handbook for travellers in India, Burma & Ceylon, 1901. **3130**

BURNELL, JOHN. Bombay in the days of Queen Anne. London, Hakluyt Society, 1933. **3131**

A vivid pen picture of Bombay and his people in the early 18th century.

BUSTEED, HENRY ELMSLEY. Echoes from old Calcutta, being chiefly reminiscences of the days of Warren Hastings, Francis and Impey. London. W. Thacker & Co., 1908. xviii, 431p. **3132**

First published in 1882.

BUTTERWORTH, ALAN. The Southland of Siva: some reminiscences of life in South India. London, John Lane, 1923. xvii, 258p. **3133**

CAMPBELL, Sir GEORGE. The capital of India with some particulars of the geography and climate of the country. Calcutta, Englishman Press, 1865. 67p. **3134**

CAMPBELL, Sir JAMES MACNABB. Gazetteer of the Bombay presidency. Bombay, Presidency of Misc publi., 1896, 1877-1904. 55p. **3135**

CANDLER, EDMUND. On the edge of the world. London, Cassell & Co., 1919. x, 218. **3136**

"An account of journey to Amarnath, Nanga Parbat, the Khyber and the Pir Pinjal."

CHAPMAN, FREDERICK SPENCER. Helvellyn to Himalaya. Foreword by the Marquis of Zetland. London, Chatto & Windus, 1940. xv, 284p. **3137**

"Including an account of the first ascent of Chamolhari." -t.p.

CHERKASOV, NIKOLAI KONSTANTINOVICH. In Indien; Reisenotizen. Ubers von Rolf Ulbrich, Leipzig, Bibliographisches Insti-

900 History

tut, 1955. 136p. **3138**

CHOOKOLINGO, FRANK C. India; the inside story, past, present and future; a comprehensive appraisal. Foreword by Paul A. Beeder. New York, Exposition Press, 1958. 195p. **3139**

CLUNE, FRANK. Song of India. Bombay, Thacker & Co., 1947. vi, 405p. **3140**

    First published in Australia in 1946, it is an account of the author's travel in India.

COLLIER, PRICE. The West in the East, from an American point of view. London, Duckworth & Co., 1911. xvii, 534p. **3141**

CORBETT, JAMES EDWARD. Jungle lore. London. Oxford University Press, 1953. 9, 168p. **3142**

────Man eaters of Kumaon. 2nd ed. Madras, Geoffrey Cumberlege, Oxford University Press, 1947. xvi, 218p. **3143**

    First published in 1944 it is a collection of stories of hunting in Indian jungles.

COTTON, HARRY EVAN AUGUSTE. Calcutta: old and new. Calcutta, W. Newman & Co., 1907. xvi, 1011, xviiip. **3144**

CRAIK, HENRY. Impressions of India. London, Macmillan & Co., 1908. viii, 251p. **3145**

    Travelogue on India, appeared partly in *Scotsman*.

CRANE, WALTER. India impressions: with some notes on Ceylon during a winter tour, 1906-7. London, Methuen Co., 1907. xvi, 325p. **3146**

CRAWFURD, JOHN. A descriptive dictionary of the Indian islands and adjacent countries. London, Evans, 1856. 459p. **3147**

CROOKE, WILLIAM. Things Indian : being discursive notes on various subjects connected with India. New York, C. Scribner's Sons, 1966. xi, 546p. **3148**

CUNNINGHAM, Sir ALEXANDER. The ancient geography of India. Edited by S.N. Majumdar. Calcutta, Chuckervorty, 1924. 2nd ed. **3149**

    First published in 1871, it is a valuable source book based on the accounts of Alexander's campaign, and the records left by Hsuan-fsan.

CURTIS, WILLIAM ELEROY. Modern India. Chicago, Fleming H. Revell Co., 1905. 513p. **3150**

    "Originally published as a series of letters in *The Chicago*

Record-Herald. 1903-04, it is a descriptive account of India."

DANIEL, WILLIAM. A picturesque voyage to India; by the way of China. London, Longman Hurts Rees, 1810. **3151**

DAVIES, CUTHBERT COLLIN. An historical atlas of the Indian peninsula. Reprinted (with corrections). Madras, New York, Indian Branch, Oxford University Press, 1953. 94p. 47maps. **3152**

DESORBAY, MICHEL. Visage del'Inde. Paris, R. Julliard, 1955. 180p. illus. (F). **3153**

DIGBY, WILLIAM. Indian problems for English consideration. England National Liberal Federation, 1881. 67p. **3154**

DOUGLAS, WILLIAM O. Beyond the high Himalayas. New York, Doubleday, 1954. 352p. **3155**

Justice Douglas trekked from Manali to Leh, and covered much more of the mountain area on foot during a trip through Central Asia. He writes with sincerity and warmth, and concludes that "understanding of Asia by the West will be the greatest reward which any Himalayan trek can offer".

DREW, FREDERIC. The Northern barrier of India. A popular account of the Jammu and Kashmir territories etc. London, 1877. **3156**

DUPUIS, DOBRILLO. Sotto il segno della charka; aventure reali nell' India misteriosa : usi, costumi, miserie, esperanza. Coperta-e-illustrazioni di R. Squillantini. Fireze, Marzocco, 1956. 162p. illus. **3157**

EAST, WILLIAM O. AND SHATE, O.H.K., *eds.* The changing map of Asia : a political geography. New York, E.P. Dutton. 1953. **3158**

EDIB, HALIDE. Inside India. London, George Allen & Unwin, 1937. 378p. **3159**

ELVIN, HAROLD. The ride to Chandigarh. New York, London, Macmillan, 1957. 328p. illus. **3160**

A lively description of the author's bicycle tour across India, from Satara to Chandigarh.

EMANUDLI, ENRICO. Giornale Indieno. Milano, Mondadori, 1955. 240p. (Grandi narratori italiani, v. 29). (I). **3161**

900 History

ESKELUND, KARL. Sa Korte vi til Indien. Kobenhavn, Gyldendal, 1952. 215p. **3162**

ETIENNE, GILBERT. India sacree, texte et photographies de Gilbert Etienne Neuchatel, Editions Ideas et Calendes, 1955. 19, 72p. (Collections des Ides Photographiques, 12). **3163**

EVEREST, Sir GEORGE. An account of the measurement of two sections of the meridional arc of India, bounded by the parallels of 18° 3′ 15″ 24° 7′ 11″ and 29° 30′ 48″. **3164**
  Conducted under the orders of the Honourable East India Company. By Lieut-Colonel Everest and his assistants. London, Printed by order of the Court of Directors of Hon. East India Company, by J. & H. Cox, 1847.

FIELD, CLAUD HERBERT ALWYN, ed. The charm of India : an anthology. London, Herbert and Daniel, 1912. xvi, 370p. **3165**
  "Compiled from writings of various people who knew India well."

FINEGAN, JACK. India today. St. Louis, Bethany Press, 1955. 208p. illus. **3166**

FISCHER WALTER of TYROL. Mit Frau und Motorroller durch Ceylons und Indiena. Wunderwelt, Bamberg, Bayerische Verlagsanstalt, 1957. 134p. (G). **3167**

FITZROY, YVONNE ALICE GERTRUDE. Court and camps in India: impressions of Viceregal tours, 1921-24. London, Methuen & Co., 1921 xi, 243p. **3168**

FODOR, E., ed. Fodor's guide to India. New York, Fodor's Modern Guide, 1970. **3169**
  A popular reference book specially meant for foreign visitors to India.

FORESTER, GEORGE. Extracts from Forester's travel, concerning the northern parts of Persia. (*In* Pinkorton, John, ed.) A general collection of the best and most interesting voyages and travels. **3170**
  Extracted from the author's "A Journey from Bengal to England, London, 1798."

——A journey from Bengal to England, through the northern part of India, Kashmir, Afghanistan and Persia, and into Russia, by the Caspian Sea. London, R. Faulder, 1798. 2 vols. front. (fold map). **3171**

FORREST, GEORGE WILLIAM. Selections from the travels and journals preserved in the Bombay Secretariat. Edited by George W. Forrest, ex-director of records, Government of India. Bombay, printed at the Govt. Central Press, 1906. 3 vols. 1, xxviii, 304, xxix p. maps. (1 fold). **3172**

FORREST, THOMAS. A voyage from Calcutta to Mergui Archipelago lying on the east side of the Bay of Bengal; describing a chain of islands, never before surveyed. Also an account of the island Jan Sylvan, Pulo Pinang, and the port of Queda; the present state of Atcheen; and directions for sailing thence to Fort Marlbro down to south west coast of Sumatra; to which are added, an account of the island Celebes; a treatise on the monsoons in India. 1792. 8p. lx, 140p. front. (port) pls. fold maps. **3173**

FORSYTH, JAMES. The high lands of central India; notes on their forests and wild tribes, natural history and sports. New ed. London, Chapman and Hall, ltd., 1919. xi, 387p. front. illus. pls. fold. maps. **3174**

FOSTER, WILLIAM, ed. Early travels in India. London, Oxford University Press, 1923. xiv, 351p. **3175**

"Contains the narratives of seven Englishmen who travelled in Northern and Western India during the reign of Akbar and Jahangir."

FRANCKLIN, WILLIAM. Observations made on a tour from Bengal to Persia, in the years 1786-7. With a short account of the remains of the celebrated palace of Penepolis, and other interesting events. "In Pinkerton, John, ed. A general collection of the best and most interesting voyages and travels." London, 1804-14. vol. 9, 1811p. **3176**

FRANKLIN, FREDRIK. Indien ser framat, Stockholm. Triengelforiaget, 1951. 168p. **3177**

FRERE, PAUL. La croisiere Minerva sur la route des Indes; Bruxalles. Bombay en automobile. Bruxalles, Editions JaRic, 1954. 133p. **3178**

GAMA, VASCO DA. Journal of the first voyage. Translated by E.G. Ravenstein. London, Hakluyt Society, 1898. **3179**

This anonymous journal of Vasco da Gama's historic voyage to India in 1497, contains information on Calicut, a port on the south-west coast of India.

GEARY, GRATTAN. Through Asiatic Turkey. Narrative of a journey from Bombay to the Bosphorus. London, S. Low, Marston, Searle & Rivington, 1878. 2 vols. fronts. pls. fold map. **3180**

GIBS, HERBERT A. The travels of Fa-Hsien. London, Routledge & Kegan Paul, 1956. xvi, 96p. **3181**

An account of Fa-Hsien's observations on fifth century India. He was a Chinese Buddhist pilgrim-scholar, residing in northern India from A.D. 405 to 411.

GODET, ROBERT J. A travers les sanctuaires de l' Inde de Khyber au Tibet. Paris, Amiot-Dumont, 1955. 188p. (F). **3182**

GRANT, WILLIAM JOHN. The spirit of India. London, B.T. Batsford, 1938. viii, 120p. **3183**

A descriptive account of India.

GUETTE, GEORGE. Un Gaulois chez les Hindous. Paris, Gallimard, 1956. 268p. **3184**

HAGEN, LOUIS EDMUND. Aux Index, cat autre monde. Traduit de l' englais per S. de La Baume. Paris, Hachette, 1948. 247p. **3185**

———Indian route march. London, the Pilot Press ltd., 1946. 192p. **3186**

HAHN, EMILY. The first book of India. Pictures by Howard Baer. New York, F. Watts, 1955. 62p. **3187**

HAKLUYT, RICHARD, *comp*. The principal navigations, voyages, traffiques and discoveries of the English nation. New York, Dutton, 1927-28. 10 vols. **3188**

First published in 16th century, it is a collection of several hundred original narratives by travellers to India.

HEARN, GORDON RISLEY. Seven cities of Delhi: a description. and history. 2nd ed. Calcutta & Simla, Thacker Spink Co., 1928. viii, 274p. **3189**

HEBER, REGINALD bp. OF CALCUTTA. Narrative of a journey through the upper provinces of India, from Calcutta to Bombay, 1824-1825. (with notes upon Ceylon) an account of a journey to Madras and the southern provinces, 1826, and letters written in India. 3d ed. London, J. Murray, 1828. 3 vols. pls. **3190**

HOLDICH, THOMAS HUNGERFORD. The gates of India. London, Macmillan & Co., 1910. xv, 555p. **3191**
    A historical narrative.

HOLLAND, WILLIAM EDWARD SLADEN. The Indian outlook : a study in the way of service. London, Edinburgh House Press, 1927. 256p. **3192**
    A book on India by a civil servant.

HOOKER, Sir JOSEPH DALTON. Himalayan journals; or Notes of a naturalist in Bengal, the Sikkim and Nepal Himalayas, the Khaisa Mountains and C. London, Murray, 1854. 2 col. front illus. col. p. 1 2 fold maps. **3193**

HSUAN, TSANG. Si-yu-ki. Buddhist records of the Western world. Chinese account of India. Translated from the Chinese of Hiuen Tsiang by Samuel Beal. New ed. Calcutta, Susil Gupta 1957. vols. **3194**

HUNTER, Sir WILLIAM WILSON. The imperial gazetteer of India. London, Trubner & Co., 1881. 9 vols. fold maps. **3195**

──── The Thackeroys in India and some Calcutta groves. London, H. Frowde, 1897. 191. (1) p. **3196**

IMPERIAL GAZETTEER OF INDIA; ed. by W.W. Hunter, Oxford, Clarendon Press, 1881. 9 vols. maps. **3197**
    Contents :
        V. 4. Hardwar-Jalalpur-Nahri. 1881.
        V. 5. Jalndhar-Kywon-Pyathat. 1881.
        V. 6. Labanakhya-Mysore. 1881.
        V. 7. Naaf to Rangmagiri. 1881.
        V. 8. Ranggon-Tappal. 1881.
        V. 9. Tapti-Zut-Thut and index. 1881.

────2nd ed. by W.W. Hunter. Oxford, Clarendon Press, 1885-1887. 14 vols. maps. **3198**
    Contents :
        V. 1. Abar to Balasinor. 1885.
        V. 2. Balasor to Biramganta. 1885.
        V. 3. Birbhum to Cocanada. 1885.
        V. 4. Cochin to Ganguria. 1885.
        V. 5. Ganjam to Indi. 1885.
        V. 6. Indian Empire. 1886.
        V. 7. Indore to Kardong. 1886.

900 History

V. 9. Madras Presidency to Muktai. 1886.
V. 10 Multan to Palhalli. 1886.
V. 12. Ratlam to Sirmur. 1887.
V. 13. Sirohi to Zumkha. 1887.
V. 14. Index. 1887.

IMPERIAL GAZETTEER OF INDIA; ed. by W.W. Hunter, New edition. Oxford, Clarendon Press, 1907-1909. 26 vols. maps. **3199**
First edition was published in nine volumes in 1881; Second edition augmented to fourteen volumes in 1885-87. Edited by W.W. Hunter.

New edition was published in 26 volumes by Government of India in 1907 after the death of W.W. Hunter;- Task of editorial supervision was shared between India and England. The editors in India were Sir Herbert Risley, W.S. Meyer & Burn and the editor in England was J.S. Cotton; Volumes 1-4 of new edition were published under the title "Imperial Gazetteers of India : Indian Empire".
Contents :

V. 1. Indian Empire: Descriptive. 1907.
V. 2. Indian Empire: Historical. 1908.
V. 3. Indian Empire: Economic. 1907.
V. 4. Indian Empire: Administrative. 1907.
V. 5. Abazai to Arcot. 1908.
V. 6. Argaon to Bardwan. 1908.
V. 7. Bareilly to Berasia. 1908.
V. 8. Berhampore to Bombay. 1908.
V. 9. Bomjur to Central India. 1908.
V. 10. Central Provinces to Coompta. 1908.
V. 11. Coondappor to Edwardesabad. 1908.
V. 12. Eeinme to Gwalior.
V. 13. Gyaraspur to Jais. 1908.
V. 14. Jaisalmer to Kara.
V. 15. Karachi to Kotaym.
V. 16. Kotchandpur to Mahavinyaka. 1908.
V. 17. Mahbubabad to Moradabad. 1908.
V. 18. Moram to Nayagarh. 1908.
V. 19. Nayakanhathi to Parbhani.
V. 20. Pardi to Pusad. 1908.

V. 21. Pushkar to Salween. 1908.
V. 22. Samadhiala to Singhana. 1908.
V. 23. Singh Bhum to Trashi-Chod-Zong. 1908.
V. 24. Travancore to Zira. 1908.
V. 25. Index. 1909.
V. 26. Atlas. 1909.

KEENE, HENRY GEORGE. A handbook for visitors to Agra. Rev. ed. Calcutta, 1874. 160p. **3200**

────Here and there : memoires Indian and other. London, Brown, Langham & Co., 1906. xvi, 215p. **3201**

────Keene's handbook for visitors to Delhi. Rewritten and brought up to date by E.A. Duncan. 6th ed. Calcutta, Thacker, Spink & Co., 1906. vii, 155p. **3202**

KENSEN, HANS. Indien; Pakistan, Indien, Burma, Thailand (Siam), Laos, Kambodscha, Vietnam. Einfuhrung und Bilderklarugen von Wolfgan Bretholz. Munchen, K. Desch, 1957. iv, 120p. **3203**

────South Asia; with an essay and notes by Michael Edwardes. New York, Praeger, 1958. 1 vol. (Books that matter). **3204**

KINGSBURY, ROBERT C. India. Prepared with the cooperation of the American Geographical Society. Garden City, N.Y.N. Doubleday, 1957. 63p. (Around the World program). **3205**

KISCH, HERMANN MICHAEL. A young Victorian in India; letters of H.M. Kisch of the Indian Civil Service, edited by his daughter Ethel A. Waley Cohen with an introduction by Philip Woodruff. London, Cape, 1957. 242p. **3206**

KOESTER, HANS, *German Consul*. Indien zwischen Gandhi und Nehru. Mannheim, Bibliographisches Institut, 1957. 146p. **3207**

KRUPARZ, HEINZ. Shisha Pargma; Reisebilder ans Indien, Nepal und Tibet. Geleitwort von Wilbelm Filchner. 95 Schwarzweisafotos, 8 Farbbilder und 2 Landkarten. Wien, Kremoyr and Scheriau, 1954. 190p. **3208**

LAWRENCE, WALTER ROPER. The India we served. London, Cassell & Co., 1928. xvi, 317p. **3209**

LAWSON, Sir CHARLES ALLEN. British and native Cochin. 2nd edition. London, Nissen & Parker, 1861. 176p. **3210**

LEAR, EDWARD. Indian journal; watercolours and extracts from the diary of Edward Lear, 1873-1875. Edited by Ray Murphy.

New York, Cow and Mc-Cann, 1955. 240p. **3211**
    Watercolours and extracts from Edward Lear's diary of his last journey, a two-year trip through India in 1873-75.

LEIFER, WALTER. Indien, Pakistan, Ceylon. Munchen. Verlag Volk und Heimat, 1956. 160p. **3212**

LEITNER, GOTTLIEB WILLIAM. Results of tour in "Dardistan, Kashmir, Little Tibet, Ladak, Zanskar & C". in four volumes. Vol. I. The languages and races of Dardistan. Pt 1(-III). Lahore, Indian Public Opinion Press; London, Trubner & Co. 1868—73. 3pt. in 1 vol. **3213**

LERBER, MARLIS VON. Indischer Hochsomner; Erlebtes und Erlanschtes. Bad Ragaz, Verlag Buchdr, Ragaz, 1956. 85p. **3214**

LIEWELLYN, BERNAND. From the back street of Bengal. London, Allen & Unwin, 1955. 286p. **3215**

LOCKE, JOHN C., *ed.* The first Englishmen in India. London, G. Routledge, 1930. **3216**
    An account of the adventures of Ralph Fitch, the first Englishman, who reached Akbar's court.

LOW, CHARLES RATHBONE, *ed.* Captain Cook's three voyages around the world; with a sketch of his life. London, G. Routledge & Sons, limited (1906 ?). 512p. incl. pls. 4 col. pl. (incl. front). **3217**

——— The land of the sun : sketches of travel, with memoranda, historical and geographical, of places of interest in the East, visited during many years' service in Indian waters. London, Hodder and Stonghton, 1870. xii, 356p. **3218**

LOW, SIDNEY. A vision of India as seen during the tour of the Prince and Princess of Wales. London, Smith, Elder & Co., 1906. xiv, 365p. **3219**
    An account of the anthor's impressions of India who accompanied as the special correspondent of *Standard*.

LUNDKVIST, ARTUR. India brand. Aus dem Schwedischen ubertragen von Otto Schwede. Leipzig, F.A. Brockhaus, 1954. 497p. **3220**

LYON, JEAN. Just half a world away; my search for the new India. London, Hutchinson, 1955. 385p. **3221**

MACCRINDLE, JOHN WATSON. Ancient India as described by

Ktesias. Being a translation of the abridgement of his 'Indika'. 1882. **3222**

MACCRINDLE. JOHN WATSON, *ed. & tr.* Ancient India as described by Megasthenes and Arrian. Calcutta, Chuckervertty, Chatterjee & Co., 1926. xiv, 227p. **3223**

    Reprinted from the *Indian Antiquary* (1876-77) it is a translation of the fragments of the *Indika* of Megasthenes collected by Dr. Schwanbeck and the first part of the *Indika* of Arrian.

——Ancient India as described in classical literature. Being a collection of Greek and Latin texts relating to India, extracted from Herodotus, Strabo and other works. Translated and copiously annotated by J.W. M'Crindle. With introduction and copious index. London, Archibald Constable & Co., 1901. xxi, 226p. **3224**

—— The invasion of India by Alexander the Great as described by Arrian, Q. Curtius, Diodoros, Plutarch and Justin. Being translation of such portions of the works of these and other classical authors as described Alexander's campaign in Afghanistan, the Panjab, Sindh, Gedrosia and Karmania. With an introduction containing a life of Alexander, copious notes, illustrations, maps and indices. Westminster, A. Constable & Co., 1893. xv, 432p. **3225**

MAJOR, RICHARD H., *ed.* India in the fifteenth century. London, Hakluyt Society, 1857. Series 1, vol. 22. **3226**

    A collection of writings of European travellers who visited India during 15th century.

MANNIN, ETHEL EDITH. Jungle journey. London, Jarrolds, 1950. 256p. **3227**

    An account of the author's travels in the jungles of India.

MANRIQUE, SEBASTIAN. The travels of Sebastian Manrique. Translated and edited by C.E. Luard & H. Hosten. London, Hakluyt Society Series, 1926-27. 2 vols. **3228**

    Manrique was a Portuguese missionary who travelled through North India in the early 17th century. His description is of the social life of the people of India as it prevailed in the 17th century.

MANUCCI, NICCOLO. Storia Do Mogor : or Mogul India. Trans-

lated by W. Irvine. London, John Murray, 1906-08. **3229**
A venetian, Niccolo Manucci, stayed in India from 1653 to 1703 and wrote a detailed account of the conditions prevailing in India during these days.

MARSHMAN, JOHN CLARK. Memoirs of Major-General Sir Henry Havelock K.C.B. London, Longman, Green, Longman, and Roberts, 1860. x, 462p. front. (port.) 2 fold. maps. plan. **3230**

MARTIN, ROBERT MONTGOMERY. The Indian empire : history, topography, geology, climate, population, chief cities and provinces; tributary and protected states; military power and resources; religion, education, crime, land tenures, staple products; government finance, and commerce. With a full account of the mutiny of the Bengal army, of the insurrection in Western India; and an exposition of the alleged causes. London, New York, The London Printing and Publishing Co. Ltd., (1858-61) 3 vols. front.pls. ports. 2 fold. maps. **3231**

MES MATEME INDIJA. J. Dovydaitis, al Vilnius, Volstybine grozines lieraturce leidyida, 1957. 262p. **3232**

METTIE, LOUIS. Wundersomes Indien. Bei den Waldmanscher des Dschungeis, Nomaden der Wuste, Bauern und Yogis der Himalayas, von herrlichen Wundern, Manschentigern, Kobras und Haien. Krenzlingen, Neptum Verlag, 1957. 526p. **3233**

MOHN, ALBERT HENRIK. Gjennom Pakastan og India. Oslo, Gyldandal, 1958. 191p. illus. **3234**

MOLONY, J.C. A book of South India. London, Methuen & Co., 1926. xii, 252p. front. pls. ports. **3235**

MONIER-WILLIAMS, Sir MONIER. Modern India and the Indians; being a series of impressions, notes, and essays. London, Trubner & Co., 1878. 2p. 1., 244p. **3236**

MORGAN, THOMAS B. Friends and fellow students. New York, Crowell, 1956. 175p. **3237**
In the summer of 1955 twelve adventurous students from the University of California at Los Angeles came to meet their counterparts in universities all over India. To the best of their ability, all twelve tried to understand India as well as to be understood by it. This was the fourth such group from California, and there have been others from other American colleges, as the thoughtful students'

Sources of Indian Civilization

horizon has steadily enlarged in the direction of Asia.
MUEHL, JOHN FREDERICK. Interview with India. New York, John Day Co., 1950. viii, 310p. **3238**
    An account of personal impressions of a tour in Kathiawar, Gujarat, Maharashtra, Kanara and Tamilnad.
MULLER, FRIEDRICH MAX. Auld lang syne. Second series: My Indian friends. New York, C. Scribner's Sons, 1899. xii, 303p. **3239**
MUNDY, PETER. The travels of Peter Mundy. London, Hakluyt Society, 1907-36. 5 vols. **3240**
    The author travelled in northern India from 1628 to 1634. These vols contain a description of his observations regarding social, economic and political conditions in India.
MURRAY, JOHN, *Publisher, London*. A handbook for travellers in India, Pakistan, Burma, and Ceylon. 17th ed. Edited by Sir A.C. Lothian. London, 1955. ii, 684p. **3241**
MURRAY, WILLIAM HUTCHINSON. The story of Everest. London, J.M. Dent & Sons, 1953. 193p. **3242**
NAWRATH, ALFRED. Eternal India; the land, the people, the masterpieces of architecture and sculpture of India, Pakistan, Burma, and Ceylon. Illustrated with 106 black-and-white and 12 full colour photos, taken by the author. New York, Crown Publishers, 1956. 148p. **3243**
—— Immortal India; 12 colour and 106 photographic reproductions of natural beauty spots, monuments of India's past glory, beautiful temples, magnificent tombs and mosques, scenic grandeur and picturesque cities, ancient and modern. Bombay, Taraporevala's Treasure House of Books, 1956. 148p. **3244**
—— Unsterbliches Indien; Landschaft, Volksbben, Meisterworke der Baukurst und Plastik ans Indien and Pakistan, Burma, und Ceylon. Wien, A. Schrol, 1956. 150p. **3245**
NERLICH, GUNTER. 20,000, i.e. Zwanzigtausend, Kilometer durch Indien. Leipzig, Brockhaus, 1957. xxx, 114p. **3246**
OATEN, EDWARD F. European travellers in India during the 15th, 16th and 17th centuries. London, Kegan Paul, Trench, Trubner, 1909. xiv, 274p. **3247**
    A useful source book on the social, economic and politi-

cal conditions of India during 15th to 17th centuries.

O' DWYER, MICHAEL FRANCIS. India as I knew it, 1885-1925. London, Constable & Co., 1925. xi, 464p. **3248**

OPPENHEJM, RALPH. En barber i Indien. Kebanhavn, C. Anderson, 1955. 182p. **3249**

PALMER, ROBERT. A little tour in India. London, Edward Arnold, 1913. xi. 224p. **3250**

PARTON, MARGARET. The leaf and the flame. New York, Knopf, 1959. 277p. **3251**

PELLENE, JEAN. Diamonds and dust : India through French eyes. Tr. by Stuart Gilbert. London, John Murray, 1936. x, 313p. **3252**

    An account of personal impressions about Rajputana and the adjoining provinces.

PETECH, LUCIANO. Northern India according to the Shui-Ching-Chu. Roma, M.E.O., 1950. viii, 89p. **3253**

PHILIP, ANDRE. India : a foreign view. London, Sidgwick and Jackson, 1932. x, 260p. **3254**

PIONEER, A. LADY. Indian Alps and how we crossed them. London, Longmans, 1876. xiii, 612p. illus. **3255**

PLAYNE, SOMERSET. Bengal and Assam, Behar and Orissa, their history, people, commerce, and industrial recourses. London, Foreign & Colonial Compiling and Publishing Co., 1917. 768p. **3256**

PRIOR, L.F. LOVEDAY. Punjab prelude. London, John Murray, 1952. xii, 218p. **3257**

    An account of North-West India and its people.

PYM, MICHAEL. The power of India. London, G.P. Putnam's Sons, 1930. 317p. **3258**

    "A record of some years of study and observation in India."

RAMBACH, PIERRE. Du Nil an Gange; a' la decouverte de l' Inde, par Pierre Rambach, Rasul Jahan et Francois Hebert-Stevena. Paris, Arthaund, 1955. 318p. **3259**

———Expedition Tortoise by Pierre Rambach, Raoul Jahon and Francois Hebert-Stevens. Translated by Elizabeth Cunningham. London, Thames and Hudson, 1957. 328p. **3260**

RAWLINSON, HUGH GEORGE. India. London, A. and C. Black,

1955. 90p. (The lands and peoples series). **3261**

RENNEL, JAMES. A Bengal atlas : containing maps of the theatre of war and commerce on that side of Hindoostan. Compiled from the original surveys; and published by order of the honourable the Court of directors for the affairs of the East India Co. London, 1781. 3p. 1., 21 double pl. (part fold). incl. 32 maps. illus. diag. **3262**

—— Memoir of a map of Hindoostan; or, The Mogul empire with an introduction, illustrative of the geography and present division of that country : and a map of the countries situated between the heads of the Indian rivers, and between the Caspian Sea : also, a supplementary map, containing the improved geography of the countries contiguous to the heads of the Indus. To which is added an appendix, containing an account of the Ganges and Burrampooter rivers. The 3rd ed. With a second supplementary map, containing the new geography of the Peninsula of India; and an explanatory memoir. London, Printed by W. Bulmer & Co., 2p. l-cxl, 428, viii, 51p. 5 maps. **3263**

RICE, BENJAMIN LEWIS. Epigraphia Carnatica. Published for government. By B. Lewis Rice, Director of the archaeological researches in Mysore. Mangalore, Basel mission press; v. in. pls. (part fold.) Photos. plans. **3264**

—— Mysore : a gazetteer compiled for government. Rev. ed. Westminster, A. Constable & Co., 1897. 2 vols. pls. fold maps. fold plan. **3265**

—— Mysore and Coorg. A gazetteer compiled for the Government of India. Bangalore, Mysore Government Press, 1876-78. 3 vols. pls. fold maps. **3266**

—— Mysore and Coorg from the inscriptions; published for government. London, A. Constable & Co., ltd., 1909. xx, 238p. 1 illus. pls. (part fold) fold map. facsim. **3267**

RICHARDSON, JANE. Tender hearts of India. Delhi, Vikas Publications, 1970. 255p. **3268**

A hurried pen picture of India and her people.

ROERICH, NICHOLAS. Himalayas : abode of light. London, David Marlowe, 1947. 180p. **3269**

A Russian artist describes the beauty of the Himalayas

900 History

and the customs and manners of the people who live around the highest mountains of the world.

ROMERO, HERNAN. India, enigma y presencia, Santago de Chila, Zig-Zag, 1956. 205p. (Collection Obres do actuaildad). **3270**

ROOSEVELT, ANNA ELEANOR. India and the awakening East. New York, Harper & Bros., 1953. xvi, 237p. **3271**
>An account of personal impressions during her visit to India in 1950.

ROSS, Sir EDWARD DENISON. Marco-polo and his book. In British Academy, London. Proceedings, 1934. London (1936). (v. 20). p. 181-205. **3272**

ROTT, RUDI. Durch Indien zum Himalaja; meine zweite Reise in die Welt der Achttausender. Reutlingen, Ensalin & Laiblir, 1957. 158p. **3273**

RUTTLEDGE, HUGH. Everest: the unfinished adventure. London, Hodder and Stoughton, 1937. xiv, 288p. **3274**

SEGOGNE, HENRY DE. Himalayan assault; the French Himalayan expedition, 1936. Introduction by C.G. Bruce. Translated by Nea E. Morin. London, Methuen & Co., 1938. xv, 203p. **3275**
>Contains 48 gravure plates and 3 maps. First published in France under the title: *L' Expedition Francaise a l' Himalaya.*

SEYMOUR, JOHN. Around India. New York, Day, 1954. 310p. **3276**
>The human side of India as seen by a traveller.

SEWELL, ROBERT. Eclipses of the moon in India. London, S. Sonnenschein & Co., ltd. 1898. 4p. 1., 13, 1x, p. incl. tables. **3277**
>"At head of title: Continuation of the 'Indian Calendar'."

SEYMOUR, JOHN. Round about India. London: Eyre and Spottiswoode, 1953. 255p. **3278**

SHERER, JOHN WALTER. At home and in India. A volume of miscellanies. London, W.H. Allen & Co., 1883. 330p. **3279**

SHERRING, *Rev.* MATHEW ATMORE. Handbook for visitors to Benares. With four plans of the city and neighbourhood. Calcutta, W. Newman & Co., 1875. vi, (2), 86p. plans (partly fold. incl. front). **3280**

SHIPTON, ERIC EARLE. Nanda Devi. Foreword by Hugh Rutt-

ledge. London, Hodder and Stoughton, 1936. xvi, 310p. **3281**
"An account of the expedition to the mount. Plates are accompanied by guard-sheet with descriptive letterpress."

SHIPTON, ERIC EARLE. Upon that mountain. Foreword by Geoffrey Winthrop Young. London, Hodder & Stoughton, 1948. 221p. **3282**
An account of expedition to the Himalayan peaks.

SHOEMAKER, MICHAEL MYERS. Indian pages and pictures; Rajputana, Sikkim, Punjab and Kashmir. London, G.P. Putnam, 1912. xxii, 475p. **3283**

SICHROVSKY, HARRY. Dschai Hind; Indien ohre-Schleier. Wien. Globus Verlag, 1954. 319p. **3284**

SINGER, ERIK. Das Antlitz Indiens. Deutsch von Stepenka Kampertova. Prag, Artis, 1954. **3285**

SLATER, ARTHUR R. Departed glory: the deserted cities of India. London, Epworth Press, 1937. 128p. **3286**
Describes some of the ancient cities now in ruins.

SLEEMAN, Sir WILLIAM HENRY. A journey through the Kingdom of Oudh, in 1849-1850. With private correspondence relative to the annexation of Oudh to British India, etc. London, R. Bentley, 1858. 2 vols. frons. (fold map) **3287**

SMITH, C. ROSS. A time in India. London. Macdonald, 1960. 282p. **3288**
A record of his impressions of his tour of India.

SMITH, GEORGE. The geography of British India, political and physical. London, J. Murray. 1882. xxvi, 556p. front. maps. (Murray's students' manuals) Half title page: The Student's manual of the geography of British India. At head of title: the student's geography of India. **3289**

SMYTHE, FRANCIS SYDNEY. Camp six: an account of the 1933 Mount Everest expedition. London, Hodder & Stoughton, 1937. xi, 307p. **3290**

——The Kangchenjunga adventure. London, Victor Gollancz, 1930. 464p. **3291**
"A personal account of the attempt made in 1930 to climb Kangchenjunga and the successful ascent of the Jonsong Peak, by a party of mountaineers from four nations, Germany, Austria, Switzerland and Gt. Britain."

SMYTHE, FRANK S. The valley of flowers. New York, Norton, 1949. 325p. **3292**
> A mountaineer, who stayed for four months in the Himalayas describes the natural beauty of the region.

SMYTHIES, OLIVE. Tiger lady: adventures in the Indian jungle. London, Heinemann, 1953. 230p. **3293**
> The wife of a forest officer in India describes her experiences of hunting and travel through jungles from 1911 to 1947.

SONNERAT, PIERRE. Voyage aux Indies Orientales et a la Chine, fait par ordre du roi, depuis 1774 jusqu'en 1781. Dans lequel on traite des moeurs, de la religion, des sciences and des arts des Indiens, des Chinois, des Pegouins and des Madegasses: Suivi d'observations sur le cap de Bonne-Esperance, les isle de France and de Bourbon, les Maldives, Ceylon, Malacca, les Philippines and les Moluques and de recherches sur l'histoire naturelle de ces pays. Paris, L' auteur, 1782. 2 vols. pls. (F). **3294**

SPATE, OSKAR HERMANN KRISTIAN. India and Pakistan; a general and regional geography, with a chapter on Ceylon by B.H. Farmer. 2nd ed. London, Methuen; New York, Dutton, 1957. xxxvi, 820p. illus. **3295**
> Includes detailed information regarding physical, economic and cultural geography.

SPENCER, JOSEPH E. Asia, east by south; a cultural geography. New York, Wiley. 1954. 453p. **3296**
> "If the geographic interpretation of man and nature in the Orient is going to be useful... it must range beyond matters of crop distribution, settlement forms, and the lines of transport." *Preface*. The author is Head of the Department of Geography at the University of California in Los Angeles.

SPENDER, JOHN ALFRED. The Indian scene. London, Methuen & Co., 1912. x, 232p. **3297**
> "A travelogue on India; partly appeared in the Westminster Gazette, 1911-12."

STACTON, DAVID. Ride on a tiger. London, Museum Press, 1954. 222p. **3298**

A pen picture of Victor Jacquemont's journey through India from 1828-31.

STERNBERGER, ADOLF. Indische Miniaturen; aus einem Reisetagebuch. Frankfurt am Main, Societate Verlag, 1957. 99p. **3299**

STOCQUELER, JOACHIM HEYWARD. Fifteen months pilgrimage through untrodden tracts of Khuzistan and Persia, in a journey from India to England through parts of Turkish Arabia, Persia, Armenia, Russia and Germany. Performed in the years 1831 and 1832. London, Saunders and Otley, 1832. 2 vols. col. fronts. fold map. **3300**

—— The old field officer; or, The military and sporting adventures of Major Warthington. *(pseud)* Edited by J.H. Stocqueler *(pseud.)* Edinburgh A. and C. Black, 1853. 2 vols. **3301**

—— The oriental interpreter and treasury of East India knowledge. A companion to "The Handbook of British India." London, C. Cox, 1848. 2 vols. 334p. **3302**

STRACHEY, Sir JOHN. India. New and rev. ed. London, K. Paul, Trench, Trubner and Co. ltd., 1894. xvi, 411p. front. (fold. map). **3303**

STRATTON, ARTHUR. One man's India. Illustrated with photos by the author. New York, Norton, 1955. 282p. **3304**

TALBOT, PHILLIPS, *ed.* South Asia in the world today by Henry Brodie and others. Chicago, University of Chicago Press, 1950. x, 253p. (Harris Foundation lectures, 1949). **3305**

TAVERNIER, JEAN B. Travels in India. London, Oxford University Press, 1925. xxxii, 506p. **3306**

Translated by V. Ball and edited by W. Crooke, it is a description of India ruled by Aurangzeb. Tavernier had an audience with the Emperor in 1665.

TAYLOR, MEADOWS. Confessions of a Thug. London, R. Bentley, 1839. 3 vols. **3307**

TEMPLE, Sir RICHARD, *1st hart.* A bird's eye view of picturesque India, etc. London, Chatto & Windus, 1898. xxviii, 210p. **3308**

—— Oriental experience: a selection of essays and addresses delivered on various occasions. With maps and illustrations. London, J. Murray, 1883. xx, 518p. illus. fold. pl. 5 fold maps. **3309**

900 History

TEMPLE, Sir RICHARD, *1st hart*. Progress of India, Japan and China in the century. London and Edinburgh, W. & R. Chambers, limited; Philadelphia, Detroit (etc.) The Bradley-Garretson Co. limited, 1903. xxxivp. II. 406p. 7 port (incl. front). **3310**

THOMSON, THOMAS. Western Himalaya and Tibet; a narrative of a journey through the mountains of northern India, during the years 1847-8. London, Reeve & Co., 1852. xii, 501p. col. front., illus. col. pl. 2 maps. (1 fold). **3311**

THORNTON, THOMAS HENRY. Lahore: a historical and descriptive note, written in 1860. 1924. **3312**

TIBBITS, Mrs. WALTER. Veiled mysteries of India. London, Eveleigh Nash & Grayson, 1929. x, 226p. **3313**

"A description of the author's visit to important places of India together with an account of the historical tales relating to them."

—— The voice of the orient. London, John Long, 1909. xiv, 244p. 2nd ed. **3314**

A travel account of India.

TICHY, HERBERT. Zum heiligsten Berg der Welt; anf Landstrassen und Pilgerpfaden in Afghanistan, Indien und Tibet. Gebitwort von Sven Hedin. Wein, Buchgemeinschaft Donauland, 1953. 199p. **3315**

TILMAN, HAROLD WILLIAM. Mount Everest, 1938. Cambridge, at the University Press, 1948. x, 159p. **3316**

"An account of the 1938 Mount Everest expedition."

TOD, JAMES. Travels in Western India, embracing a visit to sacred mounts of the Jains and the most celebrated shrines of Hindu faith between Rajputana and the Indus with an account of the ancient city of Nehrwalla. London, W.H. Allen & Co., 1839. lx, 518, (1) p. incl. front. illus. 8 pls. **3317**

TOUSSAINT, AUGUSTE. History of the Indian ocean. London, Routledge & Kegan, 1966. x, 292p. **3318**

TOYNBEE, A.J. Between Oxus and Jumuna. London, Oxford University Press, 1961. 211p. **3319**

A pen-picture of the author's journey in the region between the rivers Oxus and Jamuna.

TREASE, GEOFFREY. The young traveller in India and Pakistan; illustrated with photos, and map sketches by Rus Anderson.

Sources of Indian Civilization

Edited by Elsie E. Church. New York, Dutton, 1956. 191p.
3320

TUCCI, GIUSEPPE. Travels of Tibetan pilgrims in Swat Valley. Calcutta, Greater India Society, 1940. 103p. **3321**

TURNER, SAMUEL An account of an embassy to the court of the teshoo lama in Tibet; containing a narrative of a journey through Bootan, and part of Tibet. To which are added views taken on the spot by Lieutenant Sammuel Davis, and observations botanical, mineralogical, and medical, by Mr. Robert Saunders. 2nd ed. London, Sold by G. & W. Nichol, 1806. xxviii, 473p. 12pl. map. facsim. **3322**

VALLE, PIERTO DELLA. The travels of Pietro della Valle in India. Edited by E. Grey. London, Hakluyt Society, 1892. 2 vols.
3323

    An Italian by birth, the author visited India in 1623-24 and describes the Portuguese settlements in India.

VALVANNE BIRGITTE (GUIDAGAR). In love with India. London Allen and Unwin, 1957. 174p. **3324**

    Translated from Danish by Solvi Bateson, it is pen-picture of an Ambassador's wife about India.

——— Indien ver mit hjem. Bearb, at Otta Mikkelson, Kebanhavn, Jesperson or Pio, 1957. 217p. **3325**

VAN SINDEREN, ADRIEN. A passage to India. Photos by the author. New York, 1955. 158p. **3326**

VELTHEIM-OSTRAU, HANS HASSO VON. Tagebucher aus Asien. Koln, Greven Verlag, 1951-54. 2 vols. **3327**

VERTHEMA, LUDOVICODI. Travels. Translated by J.W. Jones. London, Hakluyt Society, 1863. **3328**

    Ludovico di Varthema, was an Italian traveller, who visited India from 1503 to 1508. This book is his travelogue and describes the conditions prevailing in South India in the early 16th century.

VINCENT, IRENE (VONGEHR). India, the many-storeyed house. Colour photos by John B. Vincent, monochrome photos, by John B. Vincent and the author. London, Faber and Faber, 1957. 255p. **3329**

    A pen picture of the author's travel through India.

VISSER, PHILIPS CHRISTIAON. Zo zag ik voor-India. Nijkerk,

G.F. Callenbach, 1954. 205p. **3330**

WADDELL, LURENCE AUSTINE. Among the Himalayas. With numerous illustrations by A.D. McCronick the author and others, and from photographs. New York, New Amsterdam Book Co, Westminster, A. Constable & Co., 1899. xvi, 452p. incl. front. illus. pls. ports. maps. fold. map. **3331**

WAKEFIELD, EDWARD. Past imperative; my life in India 1927-47. London, Chatto and Windus, 1966. xi, 226p. **3332**

    A description of the author's impressions and experiences during 1927 to 47.

WATTERS, T. On Hiuen Tsang's travels in India, A.D. 629-645. Edited by T.W. Rhyes-Davids and S.W. Bushell. Delhi, Munshi Ram, 1961. 357p. **3333**

    An account of Hiuen Tsang's travels through India between A.D. 629 and 645.

WELBY, THOMAS EARLE. One man's India. Introduction by Gerald Barry. London, Lovat Dickson, 1933. 208p. **3334**

    An account of the author's personal reminiscences of India.

WHEELER, JAMES TALBOYS. Adventure of tourist from Calcutta to Delhi. Printed for private circulation only. 1868. 2p. l., 88p **3335**

—— India and the frontier states of Afghanistan, Nepal and Burma. With a supplementary chapter of recent events by Edgar Saltus. With maps and tables. New York, Peter Fenelon Collier, 1899. 2 vols. fronts. illus. (maps) pls. port. **3336**

—— Madras in the olden time; being a history of the presidency from the first foundation. Comp. from official records. Madras, Printed for J. Higginbotham by Graves & Co., 1861-62. 3 vols. front. (facsim) fold map. (in pocket). **3337**

WHEELER, JAMES T. AND M. MACMILLAN. European travellers in India. Calcutta, Susil Gupta, 1956. **3338**

    A collection of the observations of twelve Europeans who travelled in India in 17th century.

WILSON, ANDREW. The abode of snow : observations on a journey from Chinese Tibet to the Indian Caucasus, through the upper valleys of the Himalayas, 2nd ed. Edinburgh and London, W. Blackwood & Sons, 1876. xxvii, 436p. col. front.

fold. map. **3339**

WILSON, ISABEL. Indian excursion. London, Heinemann, 1964. 202p. **3340**

  Impressions of a Canadian lady about India. The authoress is the wife of Canada's foremost geologist.

WILSON, MINDEN. History of Behar indigo factories; reminiscences of Behar, Tirboot, and its inhabitants of the past; history of Behar light house volunteers. Calcutta, Calcutta General Printing Co., 1908. viii, 334p. **3341**

WOODCOCK, GEORGE. Faces of India : a travel narrative. London, Faber and Faber, 1964. 280p. **3342**

  A description of India and her people with special reference to the travel facilities provided for a foreign visitor.

YEATS-BROWN, FRANCIS CHARLES CLAYPON. Bengal lancer. London, Victor Gollancz, 1930. 288p. **3343**

  An account of the author's personal narrative about India.

———Lancer at large. Victor Gollancz, 1936. 320p. **3344**

  An account of the author's impressions about India.

YOUNG, PETER. Himalayan holiday : a trans-Himalayan diary, 1939. Foreword by Bentley Beauman. London, Herbert Jenkins, 1945. 108p. **3345**

YOUNGHUSBAND, Sir FRANCIS EDWARD. The epic of Mount Everest. New York, Longamans, Green & Co.; London, F. Arnold & Co., 1926. 319p. front. illus. (maps). pls. ports. **3346**

———Everest : the challenge. London, New York (etc), T. Nelson & Sons, ltd., (1936). ix, 243p. front. illus. (maps) pls. **3347**

——— Geographical results of the Tibet mission. (*In* Smithsonian Institution. Annual Report. 1905. Washington, 1906. p. 265-277. iv pl. on 11). **3348**

———The heart of a continent, commemorating the fiftieth anniversary of his journey from Peking to India by way of the Gobi desert and Chinese Turkestan, and across the Himalaya by the Mustagh Pass. London, J. Murray (1937). 2p. 1., vii-xvi, 246p. front. illus. pls. port. map. **3349**

YOUNGHUSBAND, Sir FRANCIS EDWARD. Wonders of the Himalaya. London, J. Murray, 1924. vii, 210p. front. map. **3350**

ZETLAND, LAURENCE JOHN LUMBY DUNDAS, 2nd *Marquis*. India: a bird's eyeview. London, Constable & Co., 1924. xiii, 322p. **3351**

(xvii) Biography

ALEXANDER, MITHRAPURAM K. Indira Gandhi : an illustrated biography. New Delhi, New Light, 1968. 204p. illus. **3352**

ANDRESCO, VICTOR. Mohandas Karamchand Gandhi, el gran politico indio. Madrid, Casa Goni, 1948. 126p. **3353**

ANDREWS, CHARLES FREER. Mahatma Gandhi at work : his own story continued. London, George Allen & Unwin, 1931. vi, 7-407p. **3354**

—— Mahatma Gandhi : his own story. London, George Allen & Unwin, 1930. 350p. **3355**

—— Mahatma Gandhi's ideas, including selections from his writings, London, G. Allen & Unwin, ltd., 1929. 329p. **3356**

—— Sadhu Sunder Singh: a personal memoir. London, Hodner & Stroughton, 1934. 255p. **3357**

"The story of a soul's agonizing spiritual struggle and finding in Christ the fulfilment of its true desire."

—— Zaka Ullah of Delhi, Cambridge, Heffer and Sons, 1939. xvi, 159p. **3358**

Biographical study of Zaka Ullah of Delhi, a great figure of Urdu literature of early twentieth century.

ARBUTHNOT, Sir ALEXANDER JOHN. Memories of Rugby and India. London, Leipsic, T.F. Unwin, 1910. 2p. 1., vii-xvi, 336p. **3359**

ARDITI, LUIGI. L' India di Gandhi. Ricordi di viaggi. Florence, Instituto geografico, 1930. 353p. **3360**

ARONSON, ALEXANDER. Romain Rolland : the story of a conscience. Bombay, Padma Publications, 1944. 215p. **3361**

"Shows how the story of Rolland's life is the story of the conscience of Europe during the last sixty years."

BALE, THOMAS WILLIAM. The oriental biographical dictionary. Edited by the Asiatic Society of Bengal. Calcutta, Asiatic Society of Bengal, 1881. v, 291p. **3362**

BAROS, JAN. *ed.* Mahatma Gandhi; pictorial history of a great life. Collected, compiled, edited and published by Jan Baros. 2nd ed. Calcutta, Printed by Grossain and Co., 1949. 206p. ports. **3363**

BARR, F. MARY. Bapu : conversation and correspondence with Mahatma Gandhi. Bombay, International Book House, 1949. 214p. **3364**

BEAL, THOMAS WILLIAM. An oriental biographical dictionary. A new edition revised and enlarged by Henry George Keene. Ludhiana, Kalyani Publishers, 1972. vii, 431p. **3365**
   A useful reference book for biographies of prominent Indians of medieval and modern period.

BELL, THOMAS EVANS. The great parliamentary bore. (i.e. the case of Prince Azim Jah Bahadur). London, Trubner, 1869. 184p. **3366**

BERNAYS, ROBERT. 'Naked fakir'. London, Victor Gollancz, vi, 1931. 351p. **3367**
   A study of the contemporary Indian scene and the chief character upon its stage, specially Mahatma Gandhi.

BESANT, ANNIE (WOOD). Anni Besant : an autobiography. London, T. Fisher Unwin, 1908. 368p. **3368**
   First published in 1893.

BEUSEKOM, H.G. VAN. Gandhi en zijn beteckenis voor de tockonist van British-India. The Hague, Algem. Bockb, voor inw. en uitwzending, 1930. 96p. **3369**

BIDDULPH, JOHN. Stringer Lawrence, the father of the Indian army (with pl. port & map) London, John Murray, 1901. 133p. **3370**

BIGANDET, *Right Rev.* PAUL AMBROSE. The life or legend of Gautama, the Buddha. 1858. **3371**

——— In memoriam. Bassein, 1894. 75p. **3372**

BOLTON, GLORNEY. The tragedy of Gandhi. London, George Allen & Unwin, 1934. 326p. **3373**
   A hostile biographical study of Mahatma Gandhi and the problems he confronted and tried to solve.

BOODHUN, R.K. The spiritual triumph of Gandhi *maharaj*; being reflections on the spiritual and national significance of the life and doctrines of the Mahatma. Port Louis, Mauritius, the author, 1943. xiv, 114p. **3374**

BOOZER, LUZAME. Heritage of Buddha: the story of Siddartha Gautama. New York, Philosophical Library, 1953. x, 290p. **3375**

BORSA, GIORGIO. Gandhi e il risorgimento indiano. Milano, V. Bompiani, 1942. 310p. (I). **3376**
"Bibliography: p. 377-378."
Selected and annotated bibliography of books by and about Gandhi published up to 1930.

BOULGER, DEMETRIUS CHARLES. The life of Yakoob Beg. London, W.H. Allen & Co., 1878. xii, 344p. **3377**

——Lord William Bentinck. Oxford, Clarendon Press, 1892. 214p. **3378**

——Maharajah Devi Sinha and the Nashipur Raj. With 15 illus. London, the author, 1912. viii, 145p. **3379**

BRECHER, MICHAEL. Nehru: a political biography. London, Oxford University Press, 1959. xvi, 628p. **3380**
One of the best biographies of Jawaharlal Nehru.

——Nehru's mantle: the politics of succession in India. New York, Frederick A. Praeger, 1966. 269p. **3381**

BROWN, E.A., *ed.* Eminent Indians. Calcutta, Shanti Mitra, 1948. x, 120p. illus. **3382**

BRYANT, JOHN FORBES. Gandhi and the Indianization of the empire. Cambridge, J. Hall and Son; London, Simpkin, Marshall, Hamilton, Kent and Co., 1924. xi, 228p. **3383**

BUCHAN, JOHN. Lord Minto: a memoir. London, Thomas Nelson & Sons, 1925. viii, 352p. **3384**

BUCKLAND, CHARLES EDWARD. Dictionary of Indian biography. London, Sonnenschein, 1906. 494p. Reprint by Indological Book House, Varanasi, 1971. **3385**
Contains about 2600 concise biographies of persons—English, Indian or foreign—noteworthy in the history, service, literature, or science of India since 1750.

BULGAKOV, VALENTIN FEDOROVICH. Tolstoi, Lenin, Gandhi. I Ipara Tiskla Krihtiskarna P. Duska V. Ricanech, 1930. 50p. **3386**

BULL, H.M. & HAKSAR, K.N. Madhav Rao Scindia of Gwalior, 1876-1925. Gwalior, the authors, 1926. vii, 309p. **3387**

CAPRILE, EURICO. Gandhi. Rome, A.F. Formiggini, 1925. 62p.
3388

CARPENTER, MARRY. Last day in England of the Rajah Rammohan Roy. 1866. **3389**

CATLIN, GEORGE EDWARD GORDON. Auf Gandhis spuren Bercht, Ubertr. uis. u. Bearb V. Adf. Halfeld. Hamburg, A. Sprenger, 1949. 357p. **3390**

CATLIN, Mrs. GEORGE EDWARD GORDON. In the path of Mahatma Gandhi. London, Macdonald & Co., 1948. 332p.
3391

"The book is a piece of autobiography, a travel diary, a record of the question, 'By what rule should a man in these years best live his life', and seeks to find how far Mahatma gives an answer to it."

CIPOLLA, ARNALDO. In India con Gandhi: Torino, etc. G.B. Paravia and Co., 1933. 222p. **3392**

CLEATHER, ALICE LEIGHTON. H.P. Blavatsky as I knew her. Calcutta, Thacker Spink & Co., 1923. xi, 74p. **3393**

COLLET, SOPHIA DOBSON. Life and letters of Raja Rammohan Roy. Edited by Hem Chandra Sankar. Calcutta, A.C. Sarkar, 1913. lxxiv, 276p. **3394**

COUSINS, NORMAN. Profiles of Nehru. Foreword by Indira Gandhi. Delhi, India Book Company, 1968. **3395**

CROCKER, WALTER. Nehru: a contemporary's estimate. With a foreword by Arnold Toynbee. London, George Allen and Unwin, 1968. **3396**

CURRIE, ANNE ELIZABETH. Among the great Indians. Jullundur, University Publishers, n.d. 100p. illus. **3397**

DAVIDS, CAROLINE AUGUSTA (FOLLEY) RHYS. Gotama the man. London, Luzac & Co., 1928. 302p. **3398**

A biographical study of Buddha narrated in the first person.

DISERTORI, BEPPINO. Gandhi: pensiero ed azione. Torento, M. Disertori, 1930. 43p. **3399**

DOKE, JOSEPH J. M.K. Gandhi; an Indian patriot in South Africa. With an introduction by Lord Ampthill. London, the Indian Chronicle, 1909. vi, 97p. ports. **3400**

DREVET, CAMILLE. Mahatma Gandhi. Strasbourg LeRoux, 1951.

900 History

48p. **3401**

DRIEBERG, TREVOR. Indira Gandhi: a profile in courage. Delhi, Vikas, 1972. vi, 220p. illus. **3402**

DYER, HELEN S. Pandita Ramabai : her vision, her mission and triumph of faith. Glasgow, Pickering & Inglis. 173p. (A great life in Indian missions series). **3403**

EASTWICK, EDWARD BACKHOUSE. The Kaisarnmah-i-Hind, or Lay of the Empress. Vol. 1, 2. Printed for private circulation. London, 1877, 82. vol. 3 was apparently never published. **3404**

EATON, JEANETTE. Gandhi, fighter without a sword. New York, Morrow, 1950. 253p. **3405**

    A sincere and finely-written biography, designed to introduce older children to the great leader.

EDWARDS, MICHAEL. Nehru : pictorial biography. Bombay, Asia Publishing House, 1953. 143p. **3406**

ELENJIMITTAM, ANTHONY. Poet of Hindustan. Calcutta, Orient Book, 1948. 119p. **3407**

    A biographical study of Dr. Rabindranath Tagore and his literary achievements.

ELPHINSTONE, *Hon.* MOUNTSTUART. Selections from the minutes and other official writings of the Honourable Mountstuart Elphinstone. Governor of Bombay. With an introductory memoir. Ed. by George W. Forrest. London, R. Bentley and Son, 1884. x, 578p. **3408**

ELWIN, VERRIER. Gandhiji : Bapu of his people. Shillong, North East Frontier Agency, 1956. viii, 45p. **3409**

ESTBORN, SIGFRID. The religion of Tagore in the light of the gospel. Madras, the Christian Literature Society for India, 1949. vii, 182p. **3410**

EWART, Sir JOHN ALEXANDER. The story of a soldier's life; or peace, war and mutiny. London, Sampson Law & Co., 1881. 2 vols. **3411**

FIELDEN, LIONEL. Beggar my neighbour. London, Secker and Warburg, 1943. 128p. illus. **3412**

    Bibliography : p. 126-128.

FISCHER, LEOPOLD. Ochre Robe. London, Allen and Unwin, 1961. 294p. **3413**

Autobiography of Swami Bharati Agehananda whose original name was Leopold Fischer.

FISCHER, LOUIS. Das Leben des Mahatma Gandhi. Aus den Amerikanischen von George Goyert. Munchen, P. List, 1951. 537p. **3414**

———Gandhi and Stalin : two signs at the world's crossroads. New York, Harper 1947. 183p. **3415**

———Gandhi: his life and message for the world. New York, New American Library, 1954. 189p. (A signet key book, k. 300). **3416**

———The life of Mahatma Gandhi. New York, Harper, 1950. ix, 558p. ports. Published in London by Cape, 1951. **3417**

A vivid, rounded picture of Gandhi—the man, the statesman, and the saint.

——— Vie du Mahatma Gandhi. Traduit de l' americain par Eugene Bestaux. Paris, Calmann-Levy, 1952. 512p. **3418**

FISHER, FREDERICK BOHN. Gandhi och vi. Overs au Erik Thungvist. Stockholm, Natur Ockkultur, 1934. 232p. **3419**

———The strange little brown man Gandhi. With collaborative assistance of Grace Nies Fletcher. New York, R. Long and R. R. Smith Inco, 1932. viii, 239p. ports. **3420**

FOREST, Sir GEORGE WILLIAM. The life of Lord Clive. With six photogravaeure plates and other illustrations. London, New York (etc.), Cossell and Company, ltd., 1918. 2 vols. front. pls. port. fold map. 2 plans. **3421**

FOWERE, RENE. Krishnamurti the man and his teaching. Bombay, Chetana, 1952. xiii, 87p. **3422**

First French edition was published in 1950.

FRANCKLIN, WILLIAM, *comp*. Military memoirs of Mr. George Thomas; who by extraordinary talents and enterprise, rose from an obscure situation to the rank of a general, in the service of the native-powers in the North-West of India. Calcutta printed. London reprinted for J. Stockdole. 1805. 4p. 1. (17)-383p. front. (port) pl. fold. map. **3423**

FRANKLIN, FREDRICK. Den vapenlose fritheshjalten; Mahatma Gandhis liv och garning. Motala. The author, 1948. 139p. **3424**

FRASER, J. NELSON AND J.F. EDWARDS. The life and teaching

of Tukaram. Madras Christian Literature Society for India, 1922. xxiv, 323p. **3425**

FULOP-MILLER, RENE. Gandhi the holy man; London & New York, G.P. Putnam's Sons, 1931. 191p.

Translation of the second part of the author's *Lenin und Gandhi*. **3426**

—— Gandhi; storia di un unmo e di una lotta. Traduzione di B. Giachetti e.s. Casavecchia. Milano, Bompiani, 1930. 298p. **3427**

——Lenin and Gandhi. Mit 105 abbildungen. Zurich, etc. Amalthea-Verlag, 1927. 305p. illus. 58p. **3428**

"Literaturverzeichnis" : p. 289-293.

——Lenin and Gandhi; translated from the German by F.S. Flint and D.F. Tait. London, and New York, G.P. Putnam's Sons, 1927. xi, 343p. ports. **3429**

Bibliography: p. 321-329.

GABRIEL, WALTER. Gandhi, Christ und wir Christen Halle Buchhandlung des Waisenhauses, 1931. 61p. (G). **3430**

GEDDES, PATRICK. The life and work of Jagadish C. Bose. London, Longmans, Green & Co., 1920. xii, 259p. (An Indian pioneer of science series). **3431**

GRAY, R.M. AND PAREKH MANILAL C. Mahatma Gandhi. Bemynd, Overs. fran engelskan av Paul Sandergrer. Uppsala, Lindblad, 1926. 126p. **3432**

GRIFFIN, Sir LEPEL HENRY. The Punjab chiefs. Historical and biographical notices of the principal families in the Lahore and Rawalpindi divisions of the Punjab. New ed., bringing the histories down to date, by Charles Francis Massy. Lahore, "Civil and Military Gazette", Press, 1890. 2 vols. **3433**

GRIFFIN, Sir LEPEL. Ranjit Singh. Oxford, Clarendon Press, 1911. Reprinted in 1957 by S. Chand & Co., New Delhi. **3434**

A biography.

GUTHRIE, ANNE. Madama Ambassador: The life of Vijaya Lakshmi Pandit. Harcourt, 1962. 192p. **3435**

HAMPTON, H.V. Biographical studies in modern Indian education. Bombay, Oxford University Press, 1947. 256p. **3436**

A collection of biographies of eight eminent educationists who played prominent role in founding the educational system in India. Among the biographies included in this study are of Duff, Hare, Elphinstone, Munro, Gant and Thomson.

HANZA DEL VASTO, JOSEPH JEAN. Gandhi to Vinoba : the new pilgrimage; translated from the French by Philip Leon. New York, Rider, 1956. 231p. **3437**

HART, ERIC GEORGE. Gandhi and the Indian problem. London, Hutchinson and Co., ltd., 1931. 155p. **3438**

HEALTH, CARL. Gandhi. 2nd enl. ed. London, G. Allen and Unwin, 1948. 43p. **3439**

HEBER REGINALD, *bp.* of CALCUTTA. The life and writings of Bishop Heber : the great missionary to Calcutta, the scholar, the poet and the Christian, ed. by an American clergyman. Boston, A. Golby & Company, 1861. viii (9)-348p. front. **3440**

―――The life of Reginald Heber, by his widow. With selections from his correspondence, unpublished poems, and private papers; together with a journal of his tour in Norway, Sweden, Russia, Hungary, and Germany, and a history of the Cossacks. New York, Protestant Episcopal Press, 1830. 2 vols. front. (port). **3441**

HOGG, DOROTHY. The moral challenge of Gandhi. Allahabad, Kitab Mahal, 1946. 38p. **3442**

HOLMES, JOHN HAYNES. Gandhi before Pilate; a sermon on the Indian revolution. New York, The Community Church, 1930. 22p. **3443**

―――My Gandhi. New York, Harper & Bros., 1953. 186p. **3444**

――― What Gandhi is teaching the world. New York, the Community Church, 1942, 23p. **3445**

HOLMES, WALTER HERBERT CREAME. Twofold Gandhi : Hindu monk and revolutionary politician. London, Mowbray, 1952. 144p. **3446**

HOME, AMAL, *ed.* Rammohan Roy : the man and his work. Calcutta, Rammohan Centenary Committee, 1933. 162p. (Centenary Publicity booklet, 1). **3447**

A collection of articles on Rammohan by Rabindranath Tagore, Sivanath Sastri, Brajendra Nath Seal and Rama-nanda Chatterjee. Also includes a list of important publications of Rammohan Roy in chronological order.

HOYLAND, JOHN SOMERVELL. Gopal Krishna Gokhale : his life and speeches. Calcutta, Y.M.C.A. Publishing House, 1947. viii, 165p. **3448**

—— They saw Gandhi. New York, Fellowship Publications, 1947. 102p. **3449**

JACK, HOMER ALEXANDER, ed. The Gandhi reader : a source book of his life and writings. London, Dobson, 1958. xxiii, 532p. **3450**

JAMES, EDWARD HOLTON. Gandhi or Caesar ? Boston Citizens' Gandhi Committee, 1930. 320p. **3451**

——Gandhi, the internalist. Boston, Citizen's Gandhi Committee, 1930. 25p. **3452**

JONES, ELI STANLEY. Mahatma Gandhi: an interpretation. London, Hodder & Stoughton, 1950. 208p. **3453**

    First published in 1948 it contains chronology of Mahatma Gandhi's life at the beginning of the text.

—— Mahatma Gandhi. Een Vertolking vert. van. Joh E. Schipparkuiper. Amsterdam, H.J. Paries, 1950. 228p. **3454**

JONES, MARC EDMUND. Gandhi lives; with an afterword by Parmahansa Yogananda. Philadelphia, McKay, 1948. viii, 184p. illus. ports. facsims. **3455**

    General bibliography : p. 179-184. A list of books by and about Gandhi.

JONES, M.E. MONCKTON. Warren Hastings in Bengal, 1772-1774. Oxford, Clarendon Press, 1918. **3456**

    An evolution of Warren Hastings' life and work.

KAGAWA. Gandhi and Schweitzer. New York, Association Press, 1939. 156p. ports. **3457**

KAPLAN, ALEXANDRE. Gandhi et Tolstoi; les sources d' une filiation spirituelle. Nancy, Impr. L. Stoquesrt, 1949. 71p. ports. **3458**

    Bibliography : p. 65-69. Works by and about Gandhi.

KAYE, Sir JOHN WILLIAM. The life and correspondence of Henry St. George Tucker, late accountant general of Bengal and chairman of the East India Company. London, R. Bentlay, 1854. viii, 622p. **3459**

KAYE, Sir JOHN WILLIAM. Lives of Indian officers, illustrative of the history of the civil and military service of India. London. W.H. Allen & Co., 1883. 3 vols. **3460**
"Originally published in condensed form in 1865."

KEENE, HENRY GEORGE. A servant of 'John Company', being the recollections of an Indian official. Illustrated by W. Simpson. From original sketches by the author. London, W Thacker & Co.; (etc. etc). 1897. xviii, 337p. (1) p. front. (port.) pls. facsim. **3461**

KELLOCK, JAMES. Mahadev Govind Ranade : patriot and social servant. Calcutta, Association Press (Y.M.C.A.), 1926. x. 204p. (Builders of modern India series). **3462**

LAKE, EDWARD JOHN. Sir D. McLeod, a record of forty-two years service in India. London, Religious Tract Society (1874). **3463**

LAMBRICK, HUGH T. Sir Charles Napier and Sind. Oxford, Clarendon Press, 1952. **3464**
A biographical study of Sir Charles Napier, who conquered Sind in 1843.

LANCZKNOWSKI, GUNT. Gandhi und das moderne Indien. Der Mahatma als type Kassel-Sandershausen. Zahnwetzer, 1948. 31p. **3465**

LANDEAU, MARCEL. Gandhi tel que je l' ai connu. Paris, Landausons, 1938. 419p. ports. **3466**

LANGLEY, G.H. Sri Aurobindo Indian poet, philosopher, and mystic. Foreword by Marquess of Zetland. London, Royal India and Pakistan Society, n.d. 135p. **3467**
A biographical study of Sri Aurobindo.

LAWRENCE, ARNOLD WALTER. Captives of Tipu: survivors' narratives. London, Jonathan Cape, 1929. 243p. **3468**

LAWSON, Sir CHARLES ALLEN. The private life of Warren Hastings, first Governor-General of India. With 3 photogravure portraits and illustrations, etc. London, S. Sonnenschein & Co., 1895. viii, 254p. **3469**

LE PAGE, MARY. An apostle of monism. Calcutta. Ramakrishna Vedanta Math, 1947. xv, 314p. **3470**
"An authentic account of the activities of Swami Abhedananda in America." -t.p.

LESTER, MURIEL. Gandhi : world citizen. Allahabad, Kitab Mahal, 1945. 201p. **3471**

———My host the Hindu. London, Williams & Norgate, 1931. v, 9-158p. **3472**

———Weltburger Gandhi. Ubers V. Hildegard Meimberg. Meitingen, Kyrios-Verl, 1949. xv, 204p. **3473**

LETHBRIDGE, Sir ROPER. The golden book of India; a genealogical and biographical dictionary of the ruling princes, chiefs, nobles and other personages, titled or decorated, of the Indian empire, with an appendix for Ceylon. London, S. Low, Marston & Company ltd., 1900. xxp., 21., 366p. 11. **3474**

LEWIS, MARTIN DEMING *ed*. Gandhi, maker of modern India. Boston, Heath and Company, 1965. 113p. **3475**

LIGT BARTHELEMY DE. Gandhi our oorlog, Volkenbond en ontwapening. Utrech, Erven J. Bijlevold, 1930. 50p. **3476**

LYALL, Sir ALFRED COMYN. Warren Hastings. London, New York, Macmillan & Co., 1889. vi, 235p. **3477**

MACAULAY, THOMAS B. Essay on Lord Clive and Warren Hastings, New York, C.E. Merrill, 190. **3478**

A comparative study of the policies of Lord Clive and Warren Hastings and the role they played in establishing the British Empire in India.

MARTIN, G.C. The father of the nation. Madras, The National Publishing Co., 1957. vi, 98p. port. **3479**

MASS, WALTER. Mahatma Gandhi, sein Leben und Werk. Berlin, Comenius-Verlag, 1949. 96p. port. fold. map. (Comenius-Bucher, Bd. 102). **3480**

"Gandhi-Literature" : p. 95.

MENDE, TIBOR. Nehru; conversations on India and world affairs Bombay, Wilco, 1956. 144p. **3481**

These conversations took place in December 1955 and January 1956. They are completely spontaneous, and were directly recorded.

MENSCHING, GUST. Mahatma Gandhi. Kevelaer, Butzon and Bercker, 1949. 32p. **3482**

MERSEY, CLIVE B. Viceroys and Governor-Generals of India, 1757-1947. London, J. Murray, 1949. **3483**

A collection of thirty-three brief biographical sketches of

the British rulers of India.

Moraes, Francis Robert. Nehru sunlight and shadow. Bombay, Jaico, 1964. viii, 208p. **3484**

Morton, Eleanor, *pseud.* (i.e. Elizabeth Gertruade Stern). Women behind Mahatma Gandhi. Bombay, Jaico, 1961. 311p **3485**

Muhlmann, Wilhelm Emil. Mahatma Gandhi; der Mann. Seine wirkung. Eine untersuchuug zur religionssoziologie und politischen ethik. Tubingen, Mohr, 1950. 298p. **3486**

Muller, Friederich Max. Biographical essays. New York, C. Scribner's Sons, 1884. 3p. 1., 282p. **3487**

——The life and letters of the Right Hon'ble F. Max Muller; ed. by his wife. London, New York (etc.) Longmans, Green & Co., 1902. 2 vols. fronts. pls. ports. **3488**

——My autobiography: a fragment. New York, C. Scribner's Sons, 1901. xip. 21, 327p. 6 ports. **3489**

——Ramakrishna : life and sayings. Almora Advaita Ashram. 1951. ix, 200p. **3490**

   One of the best biographies of Ramakrishna, India's best well known mystic and saint.

Murray, Gertrude. A child's life of Gandhiji; illustrated by K.K. Hebbar. Bombay, Orient Longmans, 1949. 127p. **3491**

Muste, Abraham John. Non-violence in an aggressive world. New York, London, Harper and Brothers, 1940. 211p. **3492**

   "Selected Bibliography" : p. 204-205.

Page, Kirby. Is Mahatma Gandhi the greatest man of the age? New York, The author, 1922. ii, 64p. **3493**

Parker, Rebecca, J. Children of the light in India: biographies of noted Indian Christians. New York, Revell Co., 1929. 192p. **3494**

Pfare, Catherine Owens. Mahatma Gandhi; a biography for young people. New York, Holt, 1950. ports. 229p. **3495**

Peters, T., *ed.* Who's who in India. Poona, the Sun Publishing House, 1936. ii, 894, xvip. **3496**

Piddington, Albert Bathurst. Bapu Gandhi. London, Williams & Norgate, 1930. 54p. **3497**

Polak, Henry Salomon Leon. Mahatma Gandhi; an enlarged

and up-to-date edition of his life and teachings, with an account of his activities in South Africa and India, down to his departure for London to attend the Second Round Table Conference. With appreciation by the Rt. Hon. Sastri and others. 9th ed. Madras, G.A. Nateson & Co., 1931. xvi, 200p. **3498**

POLAK, H.S.L. Mahatma Gandhi, By H.S.L. Polak, Henry Navel Brailsford and Frederic William Pethick Lawrence. Bombay, Jaico, 1963. 368p. **3499**

—— Mahatma Gandhi: the man and his mission. 10th ed. Madras, G.A. Nelson & Co., 1943. xv, 144p. **3500**

—— Mahatma Gandhi; with a foreword and appreciation by Her Excellency Sarojini Naidu. London, Oldhams Press, 1949. 320p. **3501**

POLAK, Mrs. MILLIE GRAHAM. Mr. Gandhi: the man. Foreword by C.F. Andrews. London, George Allen, 1931. port. **3502**

PRINGLE, ARTHUR T., ed. The dairy and consultation book of the Agent Governor and Council of Fort St. George, 1682. Edited by A.T. Pringle, 1894. **3503**

PRIVAT, EDMOND THEOPHILE. Aux Indes avec Gandhi. Paris, V. Attinger, 1934. 282p. **3504**

—— In India con Gandhi. Trad. di Mariangelo Timbae. Milano, Garzanti, 1944. 269p. **3505**

—— Vie de Gandhi. Geneve, Labor et fides, 1949. 222p. port. **3506**

RAWLINSON, H.G. Great men of India. London, Nelson, (n.d.) v, 124p. **3507**

REYNOLDS, REGINALD (ARTHUR). Quest for Gandhi. New York, Doubleday, 1952. 215p. **3508**

—— The true book about Mahatma Gandhi; illustrated by N.G. Wilson. London, Muller, 1959. 144p. illus. **3509**

—— The true story of Gandhi, man of peace. Illustrations by Parviz Sadighian. Chicago, Children Press, 1964. 141p. **3510**

RHYS, ERNEST. Rabindranth Tagore: a biographical study. London, Macmillan & Co., 1915. xvii, 164p. **3511**

RICHARDS, NORAH. Sir Shanti Swarup Bhatnagar, F.R.S.: a biographical study of India's eminent scientist. Introduction by F.G. Donnon. New Delhi, New Book Society of India, 1948. 239p. **3512**

ROLAND, HOST-VAN DER SCHALK HENRIETTE. Gandhi. Amsterdam, Ploegsma, 1947. 210p. **3513**

ROLLAND, ROMAIN. The life of Ramakrishna. Almora, Advaita Ashrama, 1947. xiv, 326p. **3514**

    First published in 1930, as a part of 'prophets of the new India' it is a standard biography of Ramakrishna.

——The life of Vivekananda and the universal gospel. Almora, Advaita Ashrama, 1947. viii, 422p. **3515**

    First published in 1930, as a part of 'Prophets of the New India" it is a reliable biographical study of the life and work of Swami Vivekananda.

——Mahatma Gandhi. Ed. nouvelle revue, corrigee et augmentee. Paris, Delamain and Boutelleau, 1929. 208p. **3516**

——Mahatma Gandhi. Geautoriseerde vertaling von J.B. Meyer. 3rd ed. Amsterdam, Prometheces, 1931, 226p. **3517**

Mahatma Gandhi: the man who became one with the universal being. New York and London, Century Co., 1924. 250p. **3518**

—— Mahatma Gandhi. Mit einem nachwort: Gandhi seit seiner freilassung. Edenbach-Zurich und Leipzig, Rotapfelverlag, 1930. 165p. (G). **3519**

——Mahatma Gandhi; a study in Indian nationalism. Translated by L.V. Ramaswami Aiyar. Madras, S. Ganesan, 1925. vi, 140p. **3520**

—— Prophets of the new India. Translated by E.F. Malcolm-Smith. London, Cassell and Co., 1930. xxi, 548p. **3521**

    Scholarly written biographies of Ramakrishna and Vivekananda.

RONIGER, EMIL, *ed.* Gandhi in Sudafrika. Translated by E.F. Rimensberger. Erlanbach-Zurich, etc. Rotafelverlag, 1925. 248p. (G). **3522**

ROWE, J.G. Gandhi the Mahatma. London, Epsworth Press, 1931. 120p. **3523**

SAINT-HILAIRE, J. BARTHELEMY. The Buddha and his religion. London, Kegan Paul, Trench Trubner & Co., 1914. 384p. **3524**

SAMIOS, ELENI. La sainte vie de Mahatma. Prof. de Jean Herbert. 3rd ed. Gap. Ophrys, 1947. 212p. **3525**

SCHENKEL, GOTTHILF ADOLF. Mahatma, leben und werk. Stut-

tgart, Deutsch Verlags-Anstalt, 1949. 347p. **3526**
SETON, MARIE. Portrait of a director: Satyajit Ray. Indiana University, 1971. 350p. **3527**
SEVENSTER, J.N. Gandhi en het Christendom. Haarlem, De Erven F. Bohn, 1934. vii-x, 244p. **3528**
    Bibliography: p. vii-x.
SHARP, GENE. Gandhi wields the weapon of moral power: three case histories. Ahmedabad, Navajivan, 1960. xxiv, 316p. **3529**
SHEEAN, VINCENT. Le chemin vars la lumiere. Trad par claude Elson et Jacqueline Sellers. Paris, Plon, 1951. 260p. **3530**
———Lead, kindly light. New York, Random House, 1949. x, 374p. **3531**
    "An interpretation of Mahatma Gandhi's life and work based on personal observation."
———Leid Gij mij, Lieflijk Licht. Amsterdam, De Spieghal, 1952. 408p. **3532**
———Mahatma Gandhi, New York, Knopf, 1955. 204p. **3533**
    A brief study of Gandhi's life and work which skilfully selects the important facts.
———Mahatma Gandhi oder der weg zum frieden. Vienna, Zsoluay, 1951. 428p. **3534**
SKRINE, FRANCIS HENRY BENNETT. Life of Sir William Wilson Hunter, K.C.S.I., M.A., LL.D., a vice-president of the Royal Asiatic Society. London, New York, Longmans, Green & Co., 1901. xv, 496p. front. pl. port. **3535**
SMITH, GEORGE. Bishop, Heber, poet and chief missionary to the East, second lord bishop of Calcutta, 1783-1826; London, J. Murray, 1895. xix, 370p. front. illus. 2 pls. fold. map. **3536**
———Henry Martyn, saint and scholar, first modern missionary to the Mohammedans, 1781-1812. London, The Religious Tract Society, 1892. xii, 580p. incl. illus. pls. front (port). **3537**
——— The life of John Wilson for fifty years philanthropist and scholar in the East. 2nd ed. abridged. London, J. Murray, 1879. xiii, 378p. incl. front. (port.) illus. facsim. maps. **3538**
——— The life of William Carey, D.D.: shoemaker and missionary, professor of Sanskrit, Bengali, and Marathi in the college

of Fort William, Calcutta. With portrait and illustrations. London, J. Murray, 1885. xiii, (1), 463p; front. (port). illus. pls.　3539

SMITH, GEORGE. Twelve Indian statesmen. London, J. Murray, 1897. viii, p. 11., 324p. front (port).　3540

SMITH, *Rev.* THOMAS D.D. Alexander Duff. London, Hodder & Stoughton, 1883. 200p.　3541

SMITH, VINCENT ARTHUR. Asoka, the Buddhist emperor of India. Oxford, Clarendon Press, 1901. 204p. front. facsim. (Rulers of India series).　3542

SPRATT, PHILIP. Gandhism: an analysis. Madras, Huxley Press, 1939. xii, 516p.　3543

"Discusses Mahatma Gandhi's life and work from the point of view of 'qualified Marxism' and states what seems important about Mahatma Gandhi's achievements in the past."

STERN, ELIZABETH-GERTRUDE (LEVIN). Women in Gandhi's life, New York, Dodd, Mead, 1953. 304p.　3544

SUARES, CARLO. Krishnamurti, and the unity of man. Bombay, Chetna, 1953. viii, 212p.　3545

First published in French in 1950, it is biographical study of Krishnamurti and his philosophy.

SWAN, ROBERT O. Munshi Premchand of Lamhi village. Duke University, 1969. 149p.　3546

TAN YUN-SHAN. My dedication to Gurudeva Tagore. Chungking & Santiniketan, Sino-Indian Cultural Society, 1942. ii, 23p. (Sino-Indian Cultural Society Publications, pamphlet 7).　3547

TAYLOR, MEADOWS. Tippoo Sultan; a tale of the Mysore war. New ed. London, K. Paul, Trench & Co., 1883. 2p. 1459p. front.　3548

TEMPLE, Sir RICHARD, *1st hart.* Men and events of my time in India. London. J. Murray, 1882. xvii, (1) 526p.　3549

—— The story of my life. London, Paris and Melbourne, Cassell & Co., limited, 1896. 2 vols. fronts. (ports.)　3550

THACKERAY, Sir EDWARD TALBOT, *comp.* Biographical notices of officers of the Royal (Bengal) engineers, arranged and compiled by Col. Sir E.T. Thackeray. London, Smith, Elder &

Co., 1900. xp. 11, 276p. front. port. **3551**

THOMPSON, EDWARD J. Life of Charles Lord Metcalf. London, Faber and Faber, 1937. **3552**

Biography of Lord Metcalf who played a major role in consolidating the princely states under the British rule and acted Governor-General in 1835.

THOMPSON, EDWARD. Rabindranath Tagore; poet and dramatist. London, Oxford University Press, 1948. 2nd ed. xii, 330p. **3553**

A critical biographical study of Tagore's life and work.

THORNTON, THOMAS HENRY. Colonel Sir Robert Sandeman: his life and work on our Indian frontier. A memoir, with selections from his correspondence and official writings. With portrait, map. etc. London, J. Murray, 1895. xx, v, 392p. **3554**

TYSON, GEOFFREY WILLIAM. Nehru: the years of power. New York, Frederick A. Praeger, 1966. 206p. **3555**

ULLMAN, JAMES R. AND TENZING NORGAY. Tiger of the snows. New York, Putnam, 1955, 294p. **3556**

Tenzing, conqueror of Mount Everest, is as much a hero to Americans as he is in his own country. This is the authorized biography, written by Tenzing himself with the collaboration of James Ullman, an American novelist and mountaineer.

UNITED STATES INFORMATION SERVICE, *New Delhi*. Directory of Indians who have visited the United States from Chandigarh, Delhi, Haryana, Himachal Pradesh, Jammu and Kashmir, Madhya Pradesh, Punjab, Rajasthan, Uttar Pradesh. New Delhi, U.S.I.S., 1967. viii, 421p. **3557**

VULDA, LAURA. L' Inde sous Gandhi. Aix-en-Provence. Les. Editions du feu, 1931. 200p. **3558**

WALKER, ROY OLIVER. Sword of gold: a life of Mahatma Gandhi. London, Indian Independence Union, 1945. 200p. **3559**

WARNER, Sir WILLIAM LEE. The life of the Marquis of Dalhousie, K.T. London, Macmillan & Co., 1904. 2 vols. **3560**

WATSON, BLANCHE. Gandhi; voice of the new revolution: a study of non-violent resistance in India. Foreword by John Haynes Holmes. Calcutta, Saraswaty Library, 1922. 56p. **3561**

Sources of Indian Civilization

WATSON, FRANCIS (LESLIE). Talking of Gandhiji: four pogrammes for radio first broadcast by the British Broadcasting Corporation; script and narrative by Francis Watson; production by Maurice Brown. London, Longmans, Green, 1957. 141p. port. **3562**

WEBER, T.A. Gandhi. London, Pallas Publishing Co., 1939. 126p. **3563**

WEGMANN, HANS. Mahatma Gandhis leberswerk. 2nd ed. Zurich, Beer and Co., 1933. 43p. (G). **3564**

WILLIAMS, L.F.R., *ed.* Great men of India. Ceylon, Home Library Club, (n.d.). 5-640p. illus. **3565**

WINSLOW, J.C. Narayan Vaman Tilak: the Christian poet of Maharashtra. Calcutta, Association Press, (Y.M.C.A.), 1923. viii, 137p. (Builders of modern India series). **3566**

WINSLOW, JOHN COPLEY AND ELWIN VERRIER. Gandhi: the dawn of Indian freedom. New York, London etc. Fleming H. Reyell Co., 1931. 224p. **3567**

WOODRUFF, PHILIP. The men who ruled India. New York, St. Martin's Press, 1954. 2 vols. **3568**

A collection of biographies of those important British officials who played a decisive role in establishing the British empire in India between 1600 and 1947.

YAUKEY, Mrs. GRACE (SYDENSTRICKER). Nehru of India. New York, J. Day Co., 1948. v, 184p. illus. **3569**

YOUNGHUSBAND, Sir FRANCIS EDWARD. The light of experience; a review of some men and events of my time. London, Constable & Co., ltd., 1927. 4p. 1., ix-x, 305p. illus. **3570**

ZIMMERMANN, WERNER. Mahatma Gandhi, sein leben und sein werk, sein lehren fur uns alle. Munich, Vivas Voco-Verlag, 1958. 141p. **3571**

ZINKIN, TAYA (Mrs. MAURICE ZINKIN). The story of Gandhi; illustrations by Robert Hales. London, Methuen and Company, 1965. 190p. **3572**

INDEX

(References are to entry numbers)

Administration, 552-566
Agriculture, 1325-1388
Anthropology, 1325-1388
Applied Sciences, 1325-1388
Architecture, 1447-1502
Astronomy, 1325-1388

Biography, 3353-3573; see also, History
Botany, 1325-1388
Brahmanism, 243-279
British Period, (1858-1947), 2398-2637
Buddhism, 351-427

Christianity, 428-443
Classics and Epics, 1791-1852
Commerce and Industry, 567-574; see also, Economic Conditions; Social Conditions
Communications, 575; see also, History-Description and Travel
Communism, 576-580; see also, Economic Conditions; Social Conditions
Constitution and Constitutional History, 581-596; see also, Government and Politics
Culture and Civilization, 597-636; see also, Fine Arts (General); History (Ancient); Social Conditions
Cutoms and Manners, 637-665; see also, Culture and Civilization; Social Conditions

Dance, 1503-1509

Economic Conditions, 666-728; see also, Commerce and Industry
Education, 729-748
Encyclopaedias, 109-110
Essays and Letters, 1853-1860

Fiction (Drama, Novels, Plays etc.), 1861-1931
Fine Arts, 1389-1751
First Struggle for Freedom (1857), 2303-2397
Folklore, 749-752; see also, Literature
Foreign Relations, 753-790

Geography, Description & Travel,

Index

3100-3573
Geology, 1325-1388
Government and Politics, 791-826; see also, Administration; Constitution and Constitutional History
Grammar and Dictionaries, 1111-1324

Handicrafts, 1510-1543
Hinduism, 280-316
History—Ancient, 2080-2163
History—Muslim Period, 2164-2234

Iconography, 1544-1566
Independence and After (1947), 3041-3099
India—Partition of, 3017-3036
Islam, 444-457

Jainism, 337-350
Jews, 545-547
Journalism, 111-113

Kashmir Issue, 3037-3040

Labour and Labour Classes, 827-829; see also, Economic Conditions
Land and People, 830-912; see also, Biography, Culture and Civilization; Social Conditions
Land Reforms, 913-923; see also, Economic Conditions
Laws, 924-948; see also, Constitution and Constitutional History; Government and Politics; Peasants and Landlords; Labour and Labour Classes; Land Reforms
Linguistics, 1064-1324
Literature, 1752-1790

Marathas, 2660-2676
Museology, 1567-1576

Music, 1577-1596

Nationalism, rise of, 2710-2798
Numismatics, 1597-1625

Other Sects and Cults, 513-544

Painting, 1626-1679
Philosophical Systems, 317-336
Philosophy and Religion, 114-551
Photography, 1680-1684
Poetry, 1932-1965
Princes and their States, 2638-2659
Puranas, 317-336
Pure Sciences, 1325-1388

Rajputs, 2677-2678
Religion and Philosophy, 114-551

Sculpture, 1685-1740
Short Stories, 1966-2004
Sikhism, 458-469
Sikhs, 2679-2709
Social Conditions, 949-1048
Social Sciences, 552-1063
Struggle for Freedom, 2799-3016

Tantrism, 470-476
Theatre, 1741-1751
Theism, 529, 541
Theosophy, 477-488

Upanishads, 243-279

Vedanta, 489-501
Vedism, Brahmanism, Upanishads, 243-279
Women, their emancipation, 1049-1963; see also, Culture and Civilization; Social Conditions

Yoga. 283, 502-512

Zoology, 1325-1388
Zoroastrianism, 548-551